THE TRANSITION TO GUIDED DEMOCRACY:
INDONESIAN POLITICS, 1957-1959

Daniel S. Lev

THE TRANSITION TO GUIDED DEMOCRACY:
INDONESIAN POLITICS, 1957-1959

EQUINOX
PUBLISHING
JAKARTA KUALA LUMPUR

Equinox Publishing (Asia) Pte Ltd
No 3. Shenton Way
#10-05 Shenton House
Singapore 068805

www.EquinoxPublishing.com

The Transition to Guided Democracy:
Indonesian Politics, 1957-1959
by Daniel S. Lev

ISBN 978-602-8397-40-7

First Equinox Edition 2009

Printed in the United States

1 3 5 7 9 10 8 6 4 2

TABLE OF CONTENTS

PREFACE.. 7

FOREWORD... 9

INTRODUCTION 11

I.   THE END OF PARTY GOVERNMENT AND THE COURSE
     OF THE REGIONAL CRISIS.. 23
         The Fall of the Second All Cabinet and the Formation
             of the Kabinet Karya.. 25
         The National Council 37
         The PRRI Rebellion.. 43

II. GUIDED DEMOCRACY: SOEKARNO AND THE ARMY 61
         Soekarno and Guided Democracy.. 63
         The Army and Martial Law 77

III. INTER-PARTY CONFLICT - 1957 95
         The PKI and the United Front 95
         The Regional Elections: PKI Displacement of the PNI 104
         Regional PNI vs. PKI and the Posture of the National
             PNI.. 126
         Regional PNI-Masjumi-NU Cooperation............... 133
         The Failure of National PNI-Masjumi-NU Cooperation .. 136
         The Constituent Assembly 143

IV. THE REBELLION AND THE POLITICAL SYSTEM.................. 153
         The Parties After the Rebellion............................... 154
         The Cabinet Reshuffle of June................................ 166
         The PNI and the Re-emergence of Partindo........... 180

Postponement of the Elections 184

V.   THE DRIVE TO GUIDED DEMOCRACY (I) 193
     Djuanda 196
     The Army Initiative 202
     The National Council and Guided Democracy :
        First Phase... 219
     The National Council : Second Phase.................................... 238

VI. THE DRIVE TO GUIDED DEMOCRACY (II)............................ 253
     The Open Talks and the Decision to Return to 1945.......... 253
     The Constituent Assembly Debate and the Decree
        of July 5th.. 276
     The New Government and the Developing System 295

Appendix : THE CONSTITUTION OF 1945... 309

PREFACE

Periods of major political transition are generally so complex as to present the political analyst with one of his most difficult challenges. Indonesia between 1957 and 1959 was no exception. During these years a previously wide diffusion of political power was superseded by its increasing concentration in three major bases: President Soekarno, the Army and the Communist Party. This was also a period of crisis in the relationships of Djakarta and Java with the other major islands of the archipelago; and it was marked by ideological ferment and change, largely dominated by the views of President Soekarno. It was during these years that Guided Democracy was given its initial shape, with the stage being set for a power struggle which was to become increasingly intense. So dramatic were the political experiences of this period and so deeply etched in the minds of many Indonesians that their effect is still strongly felt and can be expected to influence the character of Indonesia's political development for many years to come.

Dr. Daniel S. Lev is particularly well qualified to examine the course of Indonesian political developments between 1957 and 1959. Arriving in Indonesia towards the end of this period, he remained there for three years engaged in an intensive study of its political life. His monograph constitutes by far the most searching analysis yet to appear of this critically important period. As well as providing a guide to these earlier formative years in the nation's political development, it will, I am sure, long remain relevant for all those seriously interested in understanding contemporary Indonesian political life.

Ithaca, New York   George McT. Kahin

August 10, 1966   Director

FOREWORD

The paper offered here is limited in scope. It deals narrowly with political developments during the years 1957 through mid-1959, the period that led up to the repromulgation of the 1945 Constitution. The study ends there not because the constitution was of major importance but only because it offered a convenient place to mark the end of the transition to Guided Democracy. Politically more significant events on which to end the study might have been the suspension of Parliament in March 1960, the conference of martial law administrators in September 1960, the convening of the Provisional People's Consultative Assembly in 1961, or even the start of a more forceful and determined West Irian policy in late 1961.

The study is also limited by its concern primarily with upper level politics in Djakarta, a fascinating and turbulent political system unto itself yet by no means fully representative of all of social and political Indonesia. Finally, for reasons of time, it has not been possible to add the new material which has recently become available on the events which I discuss. Nevertheless, this paper is humbly offered in the hope of adding some new material and perspectives on post-revolutionary politics in Indonesia. In time it will be revised as part of a broader study of the years 1957-1961.

In my acknowledgments, I will not try to name the many Indonesians who helped me in this research; but I am primarily indebted to them.

I want especially to thank George McT. Kahin for his guidance and friendship, and for his education of me. I owe him too much ever to be able to repay it.

Among those who read and criticized this paper, always too politely, and helped me in other ways with it, I am grateful to Ben Anderson, Fred Bunnell, John Echols, Herbert Feith, Claire Holt, John Legge,

James Mackie, Gerald Maryanov, Ruth McVey, and Audrey Richey. I want also to express my deep gratitude for years of knowing and being influenced by John R. W. Smail, to whom I apologize for the way this paper is written. I want to thank Susan Finch for her major contribution of editing the manuscript. Finally, for innumerable kinds of critical help and encouragement, I am grateful to Arlene Lev.

Berkeley, California   Daniel S. Lev
July, 1965

INTRODUCTION

The political history of Indonesia since the transfer of sovereignty from the Dutch on December 27, 1949, can be divided nicely into two periods. The first, from 1950 to 1957, has been admirably discussed by Herbert Feith in *The Decline of Constitutional Democracy in Indonesia*.[1] It was largely dominated, under the imperfectly operating parliamentary constitution of 1950, by the political parties which had existed before the war and been revived during the revolution or shortly afterwards. The main political event of that period was the inconclusive elections of 1955 for Parliament and the Constituent Assembly; from then onwards the parliamentary system came under increasing attack by extra-parliamentary forces. In the second period, defined for the sake of convenience as beginning in February 1957 with President Soekarno's *Konsepsi* (and as yet unended), the extra-parliamentary forces came into power. This period has been characterized by the decline of the parties and parliamentary institutions, the rise of the army, the growing power of the Communist Party, and the apparently dominant influence of President Soekarno. In contrast to the parliamentary democracy of the earlier period, the political system of the second period has been called by President Soekarno Guided Democracy.

There are certain obvious distinctions between the two periods. In the first, politics were freer and more open, there was a strong and active press, and political conflict had a recognized though inadequate institutional place. Guided Democracy, on the other hand, is explicitly authoritarian; political suppression has accelerated since 1957, with the government attempting to maintain a tight rein on an increasing number

---

1 Ithaca, N. Y.: Cornell University Press, 1962.

of activities. The divisive ideological conflict of the first period gave way in the second, on the surface, to more defined and exclusive ideological goals determined by Soekarno.

The development of Guided Democracy after 1957, however, was neither radical nor revolutionary. There was no rush of new people with essentially new ideas. A few new leaders entered the stage, mainly from the army, and a few left, mainly from the Islamic party Masjumi. There were major shifts of power and influence, consequent upon the resolution of important political issues, and these shifts gradually changed the style of national politics. But by and large the topmost leadership of the early 1960's is the same as it was in the early 1950'S, only older. To a limited extent, the period of Guided Democracy can be seen as an extension of the period of parliamentary democracy, in that the dominant elite simply gave up trying to maintain itself according to one set of rules and turned to another set that seemed to offer better protection. Thus if the leadership appears to be the same, the political institutions of the second period have become very different from those of the first.

Many of the institutions adopted in 1950 were unimaginative copies of those existing in Western Europe. They represented the power of Europe and a prestigeful European intellectual tradition. Increasingly that tradition came under attack after the revolution. It was never accepted unequivocally by more than a handful of highly educated men, and it was quickly undermined by the search for Indonesia's own traditions and by the fundamental struggle for political power. In the course of the development of Guided Democracy after 1957, the institutions of the earlier period were smashed and replaced by either impermanent new ones or variations of older ones. One of the few national structures of importance to remain intact through this second period was the *pamong pradja*, the centrally directed regional administration. The *pamong pradja* did not originate in the parliamentary system at all, but had been developed by the Dutch from its roots in the pre-Dutch kingdoms of Java. Indeed, the *pamong pradja* had been threatened with extinction during the parliamentary period. Similarly, the 1945 Constitution, to which the advocates of Guided Democracy turned in 1959, was more a copy of Netherlands-Indies than of European institutions. The bodies created after the repromulgation of this constitution stemmed from the authoritarian traditions of ancient Java, the colony, and, too, the Japanese occupation.

Those traditions knew little of institutionalized political control. Throughout Indonesia, traditional political concepts had assumed, if often without fulfillment, the moral responsibility of an ascriptive elite for the well-being of a popular clientele equipped with no regular means of enforcing that responsibility.[2] The matter of enforcement was usually left to supernatural intervention, however conceived. When the Provisional People's Consultative Assembly, one of the bodies provided for by the 1945 Constitution, was finally appointed in 1960, President Soekarno declared that he was responsible only to the Assembly, which formally gave him a full mandate, and to God. Under both the parliamentary system and Guided Democracy Indonesia continued to be ruled by a largely ascriptive elite — though this elite has been increasingly challenged by a more socially mobile youth, by the principle of merit, and by popular power. The difference in the second period has been that whatever institutional controls had earlier existed began to disintegrate. The moral responsibility of the elite, in both periods, rapidly deteriorated in the Hobbesian struggle for power, position, wealth, and prestige of post-revolutionary Indonesia.

Guided Democracy developed in the wake of several serious and interrelated conflicts which began to come to a head in 1956. These conflicts are basic to the post-revolutionary history of the country, but most of them are pre-revolutionary in origin and have been part of nearly all of Indonesian history. The great issues that concerned Indonesia after 1950 derived partly from the fact that the state, as presently constituted territorially, was the result of long years of Dutch domination over most of the islands. Once Indonesia became independent, the social and political issues which had been suppressed during the colonial period naturally reemerged. There were also new issues which appeared with the rise of relatively new social groups during the Japanese occupation and the revolution.

Three or four basic conflicts stand out. One, which culminated in open rebellion in 1958, was that between Java and the outer islands. The issues involved in this conflict cannot be described simply. The opposing economic interests of the over-populated importing areas of Java and the

---

2   See Soemarsaid Moertono, "State and Statecraft in Old Java" (unpublished manuscript).

under-populated exporting areas of the outer islands — particularly the oil, copra, rubber, and tin producing islands of Sumatra, Sulawesi, and, though much less significant, Kalimantan — was not nearly as important a factor as it was made out to be before the rebellion began. Nor was Communism, whose major stronghold was in East and Central Java; this issue was given exaggerated significance partly by American interest in the regional conflict. Rather, the Java-outer islands problem comprised a complicated combination of social and cultural, as well as political and economic, hostilities. These hostilities might be summed up as a test of Java's real and inevitable domination of the archipelago. Javanese dominance rested on superior numbers — the ethnic Javanese of East and Central Java constitute about 45% of the total population — a more elaborate culture, and the disunity of the other Indonesian ethnic groups. The Javanese elite saw in independence an opportunity, as it were, to fulfill the ambitions and promises of Javanese civilization in the new national state, while the smaller and more particularistic societies of the rest of Indonesia recoiled before the vision of their eventual subordination or assimilation in a Javanese-dominated nation.[3]

The process of assimilation — to use the term loosely — had already begun, a fact which may have lent more bitterness to the conflict. Except for the Sundanese of West Java, numbering seventeen million and enjoying many historical memories of their own, most of the outer island groups were not only small in numbers and mutually hostile but also culturally less self-assured than the Javanese. Their relationships with Java were and are ambivalent; the Javanese are seen as effete and elusive, but also as *halus* (refined and cultured) and as politically clever — a people to be disdained but also to be emulated. For their part, the Javanese never doubted their cultural superiority over other groups; nor did they doubt their right to the principal voice in independent Indonesia.

The possibility of open conflict between the *daerah* (regions) and the *pusat* (center, usually Djakarta but sometimes all of Java) was increased by the existence of a territorially organized army and a party system that

---

3 For a provocative comment on the Javanese view of the independent state, see Clifford Geertz's study of a Javanese village in G. William Skinner, ed., *Local, Ethnic and National Loyalties in Village Indonesia* (New Haven: Yale University Southeast Asia Studies Program, Cultural Reports Series, 1959).

divided to an extent along ethnic and religious lines. But it is important to emphasize that when the clash came neither side denied nationalist ideals. The battle took place in terms that recognized the continuing existence of a whole Indonesian state.

A second major conflict that helped to pave the way to Guided Democracy — that between the leaders of the army and the civilian governing elite — had its roots more strictly in the revolution. Basic to this conflict were the efforts of a large part of the officer corps to gain entrance to the political, social, and economic world controlled since the revolution by civilian politicians who allowed the army no extra-military role. More than any other immediate factor, it was the army which brought down parliamentary government — a system in which it had no stake and to which it had no commitment.

There is no easy way to describe the army as a political force. Indeed, to refer to "the army" is merely a convenience, for it has no common and compelling military or political tradition. The officer corps was and is divided, the origins of its members varied. A handful had pre-war Dutch military training. Many more started out in para-military organizations created by the Japanese. Still others began as members of the revolutionary armed student corps or of one or other of the politically aligned guerilla groups.[4] Consequently, some officers took as their military models the highly nationalistic and martial types who staffed the Japanese occupation force. Others shunned this in favor of a view that emphasized technical competence. Yet others leaned towards the notion of a people's army exercising an important measure of political leadership, as had been the case to some extent during the revolution.[5] The development of the army during the revolution differed from island to island; and the territorial organization maintained after 1950 — with each military district (at first roughly co-terminous with the provinces) having a division or smaller unit made up largely of native sons — militated against rapid and thorough unification. At first, top level staff and command training made

---

4 George McT. Kahin, *Nationalism and Revolution in Indonesia* (Ithaca, N. Y.: Cornell University Press, 1952), *passim*.
5 For a comment on these divergent views current within the officer corps, see Major Sajidiman, "Pertumbuhan Kepemim-pinan Militer di Indonesia" (The Development of Military Leadership in Indonesia), in *Pengantar Sedjarah Militer* (Introduction to Military History; Bandung: Military History Center, 1959), pp. 237-245.

little difference in the situation, and a national military academy was not founded until 1957.

During the early years of independence, the army was poorly organized, poorly disciplined, and poorly equipped. Yet there was no question of its isolating itself from national affairs and developing itself as a purely military organization once revolutionary hostilities had ceased. The revolution was too fresh in the minds of most officers; they saw themselves as having played too crucial a role in it to retire into the background immediately. Moreover, units of the army were constantly deployed after 1950 against various groups involved in violent internal disturbances: the fanatic Darul Islam in West and Central Java, Atjeh, and South Sulawesi; the Republic of the South Moluccas; the supposedly Communist-inspired rebels in the north-central hill areas of Central Java — the so-called Merapi-Merbabu Complex; and other groups creating disorders and minor rebellions. As a result, army officers remained impressed with their responsibility for saving the state, whose creation, some believed, was mainly the army's doing. Moreover, the ideological character of these rebellions kept them politically conscious. And, the officer corps not being a class apart, their political awareness was strengthened by their constant contact with civilian groups in the highly politicized atmosphere of post-revolutionary Indonesia.[6] Many officers maintained or developed connections with political parties, either on their own or through family and social connections. At the same time, some officers, from the vantage point of their novel military experience, felt justified in condemning the ineffectiveness of the civilian government, contrasting this with the accomplishments of the army, whose progress was impeded by few existing social-military traditions. Often simplistically and self-righteously, they deprecated the national disunity, ideological confusion, political bickering, inefficiency, bureaucratism, corruption, and lack of consensus so evident after the transfer of sovereignty; and they blamed the army's own deficiencies on the influence of the civilian

---

6   Gen. Nasution said in 1954 that, "it is often the case that a government which consists of various political parties emphasizes the desires of those parties. And in a state which is not yet well run, ambitious military men not infrequently use party channels to get the best chances. The Indonesian army has also given such bad examples" (*Tjatatan2 sekitar Politik Militer Indonesia* [Notes on Indonesian Military Policy; Djakarta: Pembimbing, 1955], p. 112).

order. These protests against civilian inadequacy also represented an incipient demand for recognition of the social and political aspirations of the officers themselves.

The challenge of the army to civilian government became clear during the early 1950's in a series of eruptions of military indiscipline. The first and most important of these "affairs," as they were called, occurred on October 17, 1952, when a group of officers led by Army Chief-of-Staff A. H. Nasution gambled for army control of the government by trying to force President Soekarno to assume a strong executive position to the detriment of Parliament. Constitutionally Soekarno was weak, but politically he was a major and growing power. He rejected the demands of the October 17 officers, however, asserting that he would not become a dictator.[7] This was the first of several occasions on which the President avoided making himself politically dependent on the army. The October 17th Affair indicated how badly the officer corps was divided, both on principle and on personal interest, and the division remained apparent for years afterwards. Nasution was relieved of his position soon after the incident, but he regained it in 1955 following another affair in which the officer corps, then led by Col. Zulkifli Lubis, embarrassed the Cabinet by rejecting its initial Chief-of-Staff appointee. By this time Nasution had reassessed the situation and decided to work with rather than against Soekarno. Indeed, he was too weak politically to do otherwise. Following his reappointment as Chief-of-Staff, Nasution set about unifying the top level of the officer corps under his own direction, aiming to accomplish this primarily through selection of the *panglimas*, the regional commanders of the several military districts. Before he could make any headway, however, the regional problem and the army problem came together in a new series of affairs in the second half of 1956. Encouraged and followed by regional civilian politicians, several outer island *panglimas* openly defied the authority of the central government, undertook their own external trade, and in some provinces of Sumatra and Sulawesi took over

---

7 On the complicated October 17th Affair, see Herbert Feith, *The Wilopo Cabinet, 1952-1953; A Turning Point in Post-Revolutionary Indonesia* (Ithaca, N. Y.: Cornell Modern Indonesia Project, Monograph Series, 1958), pp. 103 ff. For a general comment on the military "affairs," see Maj. Gen. T. B. Simatupang, *Pemerintah, Masjarakat, Ankatan Perang* (Government, Society, Armed Forces; Djakarta: Indira, 1961), pp. 90-94.

the regional governments by illegal proclamations of martial law.

Of the major skeletal structures of the state — the army, the political party system, and the bureaucracy (mainly the *pamong pradja*) — the army was the most important. The party system was itself divisive. Three of the four largest parties were based mainly in East and Central Java; only the Islamic party Masjumi, though predominantly an outer-island party, enjoyed an electoral distribution that divided about evenly between Java and the other major islands.[8] The *pamong pradja* was an enormously important instrument of central government control in Java, but elsewhere it was new and without traditional influence to lend it strength. Although national unity was buttressed by other non-institutional factors, institutionally it was primarily the army which held the state together; and if the army began to divide, the state threatened to divide with it. Consequently, when national seams appeared to be ripping apart in 1956 and 1957, the officer corps insisted that it must act to repair both the army and the state. In doing so, under martial law, army leaders stepped directly into the political affairs of the nation and became prime contenders for political authority.

The main opponents of the army were the political parties, whose survival was threatened by any serious challenge to parliamentary government. But the party system, representing another major source of post-revolutionary conflict, was paralyzed by internecine struggle. This, however, was a struggle of a different order from those previously mentioned, for in a sense inter-party hostility summed up much of the history of social, political, and economic conflict in Indonesia. The parties articulated long existing historical antagonisms; and even when the party system was decisively weakened after 1957, those antagonisms continued.

Inter-party conflict did not consist merely of the struggle for political power between the Nationalists (Partai Nasional Indonesia, PNI), Masjumi, the Moslem *Ulama* (Nahdatul Ulama, NU), the Communists (Partai Komunis Indonesia, PKI), and the several dozen minor parties of varying significance.[9]

---

8   On the 1955 elections, see Herbert Feith, *The Indonesian Elections of 1955* (Ithaca, N. Y.: Cornell Modern Indonesia Project, Interim Reports Series, 1957), and A. van Marie, "The First Indonesian Parliamentary Elections," *Indonesie*, IX, 3 (June 1956).

9   On the origins and orientations of Indonesia's many parties, see Kahin, *Nationalism and*

Among these parties there was little common ground of political and social consensus. The elite generally was small enough for its members to know one another well, but they were socially diverse and ideologically divided. Except for a few minor parties organized around Djakarta cliques, the party system was based primarily on pre-existing social divisions which were articulated, usually, in ideological terms. Of the major parties, the PNI, Masjumi, and NU particularly represented distinguishable *aliran* (literally "currents") of social-political origins and attitudes.

The PNI, formed in 1945 as the successor to the original PNI of the late 1920's — the first explicitly nationalist party, led by Soekarno — was and remains the party of the Javanese elite, the aristocrats who occupied the upper level of traditional Javanese society, the bureaucrats new and old, whose orientation was less ideological in fact than social. In the 1955 elections the PNI emerged as the strongest party partly because it controlled the regional bureaucracy, partly because it was identified with President Soekarno, and partly because it represented a middle ground between Islamic and Communist extremes. Even after the PNI began seriously to decline after 1957, this latter consideration remained one of its advantages. Moreover, no matter how weak the party seemed to become, its essential strength as the party of the Javanese elite, the quintessential in-group of Djakarta politics, remained. Several minor parties, some of them split off from the PNI, were largely of the same *aliran*. One common concern among them was their enmity towards the Islamic *aliran*.

Masjumi, NU, the Partai Sarekat Islam Indonesia (PSII) and four or five minor parties of mainly local significance represented Islam between them. It was a badly divided world. Masjumi was created originally during the Japanese occupation as an umbrella organization of disparate Islamic groups and was then organized again with the same name early in the revolution. The PSII split away from the party in 1947; and NU, which had been first organized in 1926, followed suit in 1952. The truncated Masjumi reflected the "modernist" trend in Islam, under strong Abduhist and purist influences, while NU represented a Javanese Islam of powerful conservative, traditionalist, and sufiist inclinations. Masjumi was the

---

Revolution, and Feith, *Decline of Constitutional Democracy*.

party of the outer islands and West Java, with adherents among small and middle-sized Islamic traders. NU was supported mainly by the landowning *ulamas* and *kiajis* of East Java and the Islamic bureaucracy (primarily Islamic courts and religious offices) of Central and East Java. Originally NU had been formed as a reaction against the modernist efforts of Muhammadijah, an educational and social foundation which became a major source of leadership for Masjumi. The differences between the two parties in orientation, interest, and character made Islamic unity almost impossible to achieve, even in the face of profound threats to the cause of political Islam.

The struggle between the proponents and opponents of ideological Islam is basic to post-revolutionary Indonesian history, but of much older origin. The Dutch had in effect imposed an uneasy truce on a centuries long struggle. It emerged again early in the nationalist movement and accelerated through the revolution and into independence. It appeared to be the main barrier to ideological consensus in the independent state, and sooner or later it had to be settled. The struggle was exacerbated by the election campaign of 1955, and thereafter was constantly articulated in the Constituent Assembly on the basic (but nevertheless somewhat spurious) issue of whether the state should be secular or based on Islamic tenets. Inevitably, because of the distribution of Islamic strength through the archipelago, the resolution of the struggle became entangled with the fate of the regional conflict. Divided, and in any case historically weak in the Central and East Javanese heartland, political Islam fell in the period of Guided Democracy. Masjumi was finally abolished, and NU quickly adjusted to the new situation, reducing the national role of the Islamic aliran.

In opposing the claims of Islam, the PNI and other nationalist parties were joined by the PKI, which in 1955 was the fourth largest party in the country and by 1957 had become the largest. The role of the PKI in the period of Guided Democracy was, however, quite different from that of the other parties. For while most parties grew continually weaker, the PKI was able to grow stronger and to bring increasing pressure to bear on the government, from which it was in large measure excluded.

One important reason for the differing fates of the parties was the PKI's ability to transcend *aliran* politics. A major source of Communist support, it is true, came from the *abangan* majority of Central and East

Java — the pre- and essentially non- but still nominally Islamic Javanese peasant class. The PNI and the PKI shared the *abangan* vote, but while the PNI approached the peasant through the traditional channels of the aristocratic and bureaucratic *prijaji* (gentry) elite, the PKI appealed directly to his interests. In general the PNI took the peasantry (and the urban lower classes) for granted; the PKI did not. The difference was indicated by the way in which leaders of the various parties conceived their political role. After the 1957 regional elections, in which the PKI greatly increased its electoral strength, the PNI accused the PKI of stealing PNI voters while pretending to be the PNI's friend. This accusation betrayed an assumption common in the party world except among the PKI that parties were mainly a means of selecting leaders, who would then exercise their leadership undisturbed by popular demands. Many party leaders felt that they had a well defined clientele, requiring only a certain minimum of attention, and that this entitled them to participate in the government without challenge. The antipathy of non-Communist party leaders to the PKI was due as much to that party's violation of the traditional rules as it was to the more sophisticated reasons sometimes offered. The fact was that the PKI came closer than the other parties to playing the parliamentary game as it should be played.

Unlike the PNI, the PKI was truly an ideological party; and, unlike Masjumi and the NU, its ideology was unquestionably modern. In this, and in its obvious concern for popular social and economic interests, the PKI was able to extend its appeal beyond a simple *aliran* context. The PKI therefore threatened not only the other parties but the entire traditional elite. It has been mentioned that this elite is an ascriptive one, a main threat to whose position would appear to be the growth of a forceful egalitarianism. In fact, however, the elite escaped this threat partly by adopting egalitarian ideological symbols. Thus there developed the contradiction that while Indonesian ideology often appears to be radical, the social reality of Indonesia — the very elite which articulates the radical ideology — is decidedly conservative. Assuming the garb of the opposition was not enough, however, and the traditional elite quickly recognized the danger of the PKI's more genuine radicalism. The development of Guided Democracy was also in part a reply to this challenge.

.

CHAPTER ONE

THE END OF PARTY GOVERNMENT AND THE COURSE OF THE REGIONAL CRISIS

The fall of the second Ali Sastroamidjojo Cabinet in March 1957 marked the end of parliamentary government in Indonesia. Like every Cabinet before it since the revolution, the second Ali Cabinet was based on a coalition, this time of the PNI (the party of the premier), Masjumi, NU, and a few minor parties. The coalitions had always been led by either Masjumi or the PNI, and of the larger parties only the PKI had been excluded from all post-revolutionary cabinets. In the six years since the transfer of sovereignty, the system of party government had come under increasingly strong attack; and when the 1955 elections failed to produce a more decisive national leadership the attacks intensified. Condemnation of the parties stemmed partly from Utopian attitudes about politics and from memories of a supposed golden age of national unity during the revolution; but still it was true that party government had not lived up to national hopes. The national press frequently charged that there were too many parties, about forty of which had survived the elections. No single party had a sufficient majority to govern; and the result was instability, with cabinets falling before they could hope to undertake — if they were so inclined — effective programs of economic development. The parties were accused of putting cabinets together on the basis of petty political bargaining, something which enabled the small parties to play disproportionately important roles. It was also claimed that it was the second echelon notables who were being chosen as cabinet ministers, while the top party leaders were taking the role of powers-behind-the-throne, making the Government always dependent upon their judgments. The parties were also accused, with some justice, of having become leadership cliques, with little representative character.

Only the Communists enjoyed the reputation of having a respectable party organization and good discipline. The other parties were plagued by corruption, and government offices under their influence fell prey to party and personal financial needs.

Under the pressure of national crisis, the Ali Cabinet received the full impact not only of these accusations but in addition of an assault upon parliamentary government by President Soekarno, who for the first time stepped actively and openly into the position of leader of the anti-parliamentary forces of independent Indonesia. When the Government finally resigned, Soekarno played the major role in creating a new Government. This new Government, formed in April, was a transitional cabinet, something between the old party type cabinet and the presidential cabinet that was to be introduced later.

The parties continued to be represented in it, informally, but their influence on policy was minimal, and Parliament's authority began to decline more rapidly. Shortly after the new cabinet took office, it created under Soekarno's leadership the National Council (Dewan Nasional) — an extraordinary constitutional innovation, which became the institutional focus of Guided Democracy for nearly the next five years, before it too declined in importance.

The formation of the new cabinet and the National Council were made possible by martial law, proclaimed on March 14, 1957, the day after Prime Minister Ali resigned. In retrospect, it is clear that martial law was the death blow to the parliamentary system. Not only did it place heavy restraints on normal political activity, but it also provided a legal basis for the anti-party activities of Soekarno and the army. In particular it brought the officer corps legitimately into politics.

The immediate cause of these events was the regional crisis, which dominated Indonesian politics from 1956 through early 1958, when the conflict broke out into open rebellion. The resolution of the regional crisis was to help consolidate the new political order of Guided Democracy.

This chapter will discuss very briefly the fall of the Ali Cabinet, the formation of the new *Kabinet Karya* (Work Cabinet), the establishment of the National Council, and the development of the regional conflict. Martial law will be left for the next chapter. Neither chapter I nor chapter II is intended to cover its subject fully, but only to sketch in major developments during 1957 and early 1958.

The Fall of the Second Ali Cabinet and the Formation of the Kabinet Karya

As it drew to its end, the Ali Cabinet had to contend with the combined effects of regional disobedience, army restlessness, and national impatience with the imperfect workings of parliamentary government. The Government had been trying for several months to control the illegal smuggling and barter activities that were being carried out under the aegis of military commanders in Sulawesi and Sumatra.[1] A series of army-centered crises began in October with the attempted arrest of Foreign Minister Roeslan Abdulgani by the West Java commandant, Col. Kawilarang, a highly respected officer from Sulawesi. In November a handful of West Javanese troops, led by Col. Zulkifli Lubis, a young political activist from Sumatra, tried to march on Djakarta. This attempt was foiled, but Lubis refused to appear before his military superiors and went into hiding; from there he later became involved in the rebellious activities of the outer island commanders. By the end of December bloodless coups had led to the establishment of dissident regional councils in Central, North, and South Sumatra. In North Sumatra, however, a successful counter-coup forced the *panglima*, Col. Simbolon, to flee to Central Sumatra (under the command of Lt. Col. Husein); his subordinate, Lt. Col. Djamin Gintings, took over the command of North Sumatra with Djakarta's help.

Already very high, national tension was increased by the resignation of Vice President Hatta, in December 1956. A Sumatran, Hatta was regarded by outer island groups as their own representative and a counterpoise to the Javanese Soekarno (for reasons of political attitude and approach as well as ethnic origin). But Soekarno and Hatta — the symbolically crucial *Dwitunggal* (duumvirate) of Indonesian national politics since the Japanese occupation — had found it increasingly difficult to get along with one another both personally and politically. When Hatta finally resigned, only partly because he disagreed with the Government's handling of the regional crisis, outer island leaders took the situation as another major

---

1 See Herbert Feith, *The Decline of Constitutional Democracy in Indonesia* (Ithaca, N. Y.: Cornell University Press, 1962), pp. 487 ff.

affront to the position of all non-Javanese. Thereafter Hatta became the symbol not of unity but of dissension.

At the same time, during the final months of 1956, the political party system was coming daily under more vehement attack — by Soekarno, by Hatta himself, by army leaders, and by the independent press. Elements within the party system itself even joined the attack, in particular the minor party Murba (Proletarian), whose leaders and sympathizers were developing a close political association with Soekarno.

In these critical months of early 1957, the major parties differed fundamentally in their response to the regional conflict and to the prospect of a new cabinet. Masjumi justified the regional movement as a proper demand for the redressing of the balance between the outer islands and Java. Masjumi therefore sought a new cabinet capable of working out a solution of the regional crisis which would be favorable to the regions. The party's future in fact depended upon such a solution. Thus Masjumi, and several allied parties, called for a new "business" (non-party) cabinet headed by Hatta to be established for an indeterminate period during which it could restore confidence in the government.[2] It was calculated that a Hatta cabinet would be the best means of both restraining Soekarno and countering his dealings with the Communists.

The PNI and NU were more inclined to take the Javanese view, that the regional challenge was a threat to national unity; both were distinctly reluctant to give up the existing cabinet. The PKI, supporting the cabinet but not represented in it, had good reason to encourage a firm stand against the regions. For not only were the outer islands strongly anti-Communist, but in addition the dissident regional councils were led by army officers; and to the extent that the officer corps was generally anti-Communist, the PKI had much to gain from a split among the officers and much to lose from their reuniting. Therefore, concerned lest a new cabinet favor Masjumi's position or bring the anti-Communist Hatta back into authority, the PKI gave as much support as the PNI and NU to the Ali Cabinet's attempt to continue.

---

2   Hatta had led two "Presidential" cabinets — formally responsible to the President — during the revolution; the last one had accepted the transfer of sovereignty from the Dutch. This kind of non-party business cabinet, as in the Netherlands, was regarded as the best means of handling a politically divisive crisis. Hatta himself wanted to become Prime Minister rather than to return to the vice-presidency, which he considered an ineffective position.

The burden of so many pressures, however, was too great for the cabinet to hold together. In December, IPKI, a minor party composed largely of former army members, withdrew its Minister of Veteran's Affairs from the Government, a move which probably reflected the army's interest in bringing the cabinet down.[3] On January 9, 1957, despite the opposition of several Masjumi leaders, all five Masjumi cabinet ministers resigned. A week later, the minor Islamic party Perti also left the cabinet. Following Masjumi's resignation, the truncated coalition of the PNI and NU decided to reshuffle the cabinet and continue with parliamentary support from the PKI. But President Soekarno, on being informed of Prime Minister Ali's intentions, said he was convinced that not even a complete renovation of the cabinet would enable it to achieve stability; nothing less than a new system of government was needed.[4] The cabinet lasted one more month.

Clearly much more was involved now than the mere demise of another Government. Five cabinets had fallen since 1950, but never with any question that parliamentary government would survive. Parliamentary debates in December and January touched on this issue again and again. Members of the PNI, NU, and the PKI argued that for the cabinet to resign because of the regional crisis would prove the incapacity of Indonesian government to cope with the most critical national problems. Supporters of the Government asked whether, "if we do not all defend this Cabinet, the result of general elections, should the parties now existing in Indonesia continue to have the right to exist?"[5] one MP asserted that what was important for his party was not the cabinet itself, but the question of the life or death of the parliamentary system of government.[6]

On March 2nd, Lt. Col. Sumual, commander of the seventh military district (Sulawesi and the rest of East Indonesia), followed the lead of his

---

3 IPKI (Ikatan Pendukung Kemerdekaan Indonesia, League of Supporters of Indonesian Independence) had been organized in 1954-1955 by a group of former army officers, including Gen. Nasution before his return to the position of Chief-of-Staff. It was more of an army pressure group than a party. Once back in command of the army, Nasution gradually pulled away from IPKI, though he maintained some influence over it. But IPKI continued to represent an army point of view and increased in significance during the next few years as the army itself became politically more active.

4 See Soekarno's speech of February 21, 1957, in Ministry of Information, Kronik Dokumentasi, *Demokrasi Terpimpin* (Guided Democracy), pp. 4-5.

5 Ajip Muchamad Dzukhri (of NU), in *Ichtisar Parlemen* (IP, Summaries of Parliamentary Debates) 1957, p. 50, session of Jan. 29, 1957.

6 Soepardi (Pembangunan, associated with the PKI) in IP/1957, p. 56, session of Jan. 30, 1957.

Sumatran colleagues by proclaiming a state of siege in his territory and announcing the creation of a "Total Struggle" movement (Perdjuangan Semesta, or Permesta) to assume governmental responsibility for the area.[7] The cabinet could not face this new challenge. Amidst conflicting but equally vociferous demands for the restoration of the Soekarno-Hatta Dwitunggal on the one hand and the implementation of Soekarno's Konsepsi on the other, Ali went to the President on March 14th to return the cabinet's mandate. Throughout the preceding weeks, Maj. Gen. Nasution and Deputy Chief-of-Staff Gatot Soebroto had been pressing their view that martial law should be declared throughout the state to counteract the effect of the regional proclamations of martial law and to enable military leaders to deal with the ominous split in the army. Soekarno agreed, and just before he resigned Ali signed a decree — the validity of which was much disputed because of the demissionary status of the cabinet — proclaiming a national state of siege.[8]

Martial law catapulted military commanders everywhere in the country into positions of formidable authority, such as they had known only during the revolution. In each region the civil administration was subordinated to army headquarters. At the national level in Djakarta, however, though the General Staff headed the martial law administration, it was not Gen. Nasution but Soekarno who became the chief martial law authority.[9] This did not follow from the law, however, for according to that the President's position as Commander-in-Chief of the armed forces was symbolic. But both Ali and the General Staff agreed that Soekarno should assume the role, and if the theory of this was never worked out it meant in practice that Soekarno's real political authority was unquestionable and that army leaders remained loyal to him. This fact did not reduce —

---

7   Feith, *Decline of Constitutional Democracy*, pp. 544-546.

8   The State of Siege was based on a Netherlands East Indies statute, the Regeling op den Staat van Oorlog en van Beleg (Regulation on the State of War and of Siege) of 1939, usually shortened to SOB. A State of Siege is the most drastic of the two levels of martial law; art. 37 of the law provided that "The military authority is empowered, in deviation from provisions of general regulations, to take measures of any kind whatsoever...when it considers them necessary in view of the immediate emergency situation." Since the beginning of the revolution, various parts of the country had been under either a State of War or a State of Siege, so that it was not altogether a new experience; indeed, martial law had been protested for years in several regions.

9   In formal terms, however, it was Djuanda, as Minister of Defense, who was ultimately responsible for all acts under the State of Siege.

although it did limit politically — the immense legal authority given to army leaders under martial law. Nasution was himself being challenged by the regionalist officers, and he did not then possess the political strength which he acquired subsequently. Between him and Soekarno a mutual political dependence arose which was to be of profound significance for the next two years.

Meanwhile Soekarno announced his "Konsepsi" on February 21st, after weeks of rumour about his intentions. In October 1956, on his return from a trip to China, the U.S.S.R., and Eastern Europe, he had attacked the parliamentary system and proposed, before the opening session of the Constituent Assembly, that political parties be "buried." He was later to say that he meant this to shock the parties into reform. Whether seeing the progress mainland China had made moved him to demand immediate change in Indonesia is not entirely clear, though that may have influenced him. It is likely, however, that the greater influence on him in late 1956 was the regional crisis and the apparent groundswell of opinion that had already developed against the parties. Moreover there was a possibility that the army might do something if he did not. In any event, the ideas he advanced then were old ones in his thinking. Following the Constituent Assembly speech, Soekarno declared his belief that Indonesia should develop a new political system, one more closely related to the country's traditions, a democracy with leadership that would give the nation a just and prosperous society. Near the end of 1956 he announced that he had an idea — a Konsepsi — whose implementation would save the country from impending disaster.

The Konsepsi contained two basic proposals. The first was that a new cabinet should be formed of all four major parties, thus ending the post-revolutionary ostracization of the PKI. Comparing the three-party cabinet to a horse with only three legs, Soekarno pointed out that the Communists represented a quarter of the nation and therefore should not be excluded from the government. The new four-party cabinet would be a *gotong-rojong* (mutual help) cabinet, one in which all the parties would somehow be made to work together for the national interest. Part two of the Konsepsi was that a National Council (Dewan Nasional) made up of representatives of functional groups — labor, peasants, youth, women, etc. — should be established under Soekarno's leadership. Its function would be "to give advice to the Cabinet, whether this advice is requested

or not. And because this National Council will consist of representatives...
of groups that are functional in society, therefore...it will be a reflection
of society, just as the Cabinet is a reflection of Parliament."[10] A major
purpose of the National Council would be to buttress the authority of a
new Government.

The first part of the proposal set off an explosive reaction. There
were several reasons why Soekarno sought to bring the PKI into the
Government, though it is impossible to determine now what his final
objectives were in relation to the party. The exclusion of the PKI was
an element in the national disunity which Soekarno wanted to end by
forcing all the parties to stand together. Moreover the PKI was by far
the best organized and most vigorous party in the country; its labor
federation, SOBSI (Sentral Organisasi Buruh Seluruh Indonesia, All
Indonesia Central Labor Organization), and peasant organization, BTI
(Barisan Tani Indonesia, Indonesian Peasant Front), were the largest
and most active of all such organizations.[11] To Soekarno it may have
seemed that Communist vitality and dedication — and their increasing
popular support — would be useful in stimulating the government to
more progressive policies. There may be some doubt about the relative
importance of these points in Soekarno's mind, but there were others of
unquestioned importance. Being feared by the other parties and disliked
by army leaders, the PKI was a useful ally to Soekarno, who possessed no
organized political following of his own. The PKI had already decided, a
few years earlier, to give the President its support — just as it made every
effort to cooperate with the PNI, the bourgeois nationalist middle group
— against the right wing, represented mainly by Masjumi and the small
but intellectually influential Socialist Party (Partai Sosialis Indonesia, PSI).
These tactics enabled the PKI to recover gradually from the decline it had
suffered after its rebellion against the revolutionary republic at Madiun
in 1948. In exchange for its backing, the PKI expected and increasingly
needed Soekarno's protection against the army. Through the operation
of inbuilt political hostilities, Soekarno was able to develop an intricate

---

10 See Kronik Dokumentasi, *Demokrasi Terpimpin*, pp. 4 ff, for the text of the speech; see also
   Ministry of Information, *Dewan Nasional* (National Council), 1957, *passim*.
11 All the major parties and a few of the minor ones had both labor and peasant organizations
   associated with them, but none were as effective as the PKI's.

system of tacit alliances: with the army against the party system on the one hand; and with the PKI (and to a lesser extent the other parties) against the army on the other.

Soekarno did not fear, as many others did, that the PKI would somehow take over the country. Not only were the Communists restricted by the army, but in addition Soekarno was convinced that they were as much nationalist as Communist and that the party could be divorced from its foreign allegiances.[12] It was also significant that the PKI alone among the parties remained untainted by responsibility for the political and economic decline of the post-revolutionary years; and from this fact the Communists drew strength. Soekarno's attempt to bring the PKI into the Government was partly aimed at giving it a share of responsibility, thus making it harder for the Communists to avoid some blame for whatever went wrong. For its part, the PKI wanted to enter the Government both for the protection this would offer it and for the step this might be on the road to power.

Opposition to the idea of a *gotong-rojong* cabinet was too great, however. Army leaders made their misgivings clear to Soekarno. Masjumi, the NU, PSI, Christian parties, and a host of others — not to mention regionalist leaders — who regarded Soekarno's support of the PKI as disastrous, attacked the four-legged cabinet notion vehemently. Under Soekarno's influence, the PNI might reluctantly have accepted PKI membership in the cabinet; but the PNI alone was not enough, and Soekarno was compelled to retreat. Opposition to a *gotong-rojong* cabinet was the first major strategic error of the parties in their attempt to defend the parliamentary system. By rejecting PKI inclusion in the Government, the anti-Communist parties also sacrificed party control of the Government.[13]

---

12 See Ruth T. McVey, "Indonesian Communism and the Transition to Guided Democracy," in A. Doak Barnett, ed., *Communist Strategies in Asia* (New York, London: Praeger, 1963), and Donald Hindley, "President Soekarno and the Communists: the Politics of Domestication," *APSR*, LVI (Dec. 1962), 915-927.

13 In 1958, Roeslan Abdulgani, vice-chairman of the National Council, said, "It should be borne in mind that his [Soekarno's] idea of a 'gotong-rojong' cabinet, if implemented, would have tended to divest the President himself of some de facto power. This. of course, the President well knew. His own position of political strength is, in the present instability, based to some extent on the fact that he, and the presidency, are stable factors. A 'gotong-rojong' cabinet would have been stable, resting on the elected Parliament, and sharing in whatever stability that Parliament maintained.

Ignoring Masjumi's claims to the right to form a new Government, and avoiding demands for either a Hatta cabinet or one led by himself, Soekarno on March 15, 1957, appointed the national chairman of the PNI, Suwirjo, as formateur of a party cabinet. Suwirjo failed, but on March 25th Soekarno reappointed him to form a business cabinet of experts, a cabinet "which will take…firm steps [to deal with the political crisis] and will establish a National Council in accord with the President's Konsepsi." Again Suwirjo failed, returning his mandate on April 2nd.

The inability of the PNI, NU, and Masjumi to come to terms ended the parties' opportunity to create a new Government, for Soekarno then took matters into his own hands. On April 14th he convened a meeting at the palace of sixty-nine leaders from various parties and half as many military officers and others. The President told the assembled group that he intended to appoint himself formateur of an extra-parliamentary emergency business cabinet. Much to their surprise, the politicians were then handed slips of paper on which they were asked to indicate whether they would be willing to serve in this new cabinet. A majority said they would; most Masjumi leaders present said they would not. The procedure betokened a graduation from old political forms. Masjumi and its allies accused Soekarno of a gross illegality, for he had no substantive constitutional authority; but the charge was no more effective than the earlier one that Ali Sastroamidjojo's signing of the proclamation of martial law had been invalid.[14]

Soekarno proceeded to form a new Government, which he called the Kabinet Karya. As Prime Minister he appointed Ir. Djuanda Kartawidjaja, an independent who had served in nearly every cabinet since 1945. Djuanda, who had earlier headed the National Planning Bureau, was

---

Thus, relatively speaking the President's de facto power would have been lessened." Roeslan Abdulgani, "The First Year of the National Council," *Far Eastern Survey*, XXVII, no. 7 (July 1958), 97-104.

It is questionable whether such a cabinet would in fact have been more stable, but the point is that the parties would at least have been in control of the cabinet. However, this proposition is qualified by some doubt about how army leaders would have reacted to a four-party cabinet.

14 Both "deviations" were justified by the chairman of the Supreme Court, Wirjono Prodjodikoro, on the grounds that an emergency situation — which undoubtedly existed — permitted a government to override some procedures. For Ali's defense of his counter-signature of the State of Siege decree, see *Pedoman*, April 9, 1957.

widely respected as a technically capable and moderate man with no political debts. But his appointment was politically important in that he was Sundanese (West Java); he thus represented the second most powerful ethnic group in the country, one whose enmity towards the Javanese had found expression in the regional crisis, and whose importance is enhanced by the fact that the capital is located in West Java.

Masjumi and the Catholic Party formally refused seats in the new cabinet, but Soekarno undercut their opposition somewhat by detaching individual members from Masjumi and by otherwise representing the Catholic community. The Protestant Party (Partai Keristen Indonesia, Parkindo) also refused initially to support the Kabinet Karya but reversed its stand soon afterwards. In the list of cabinet members that follows, party affiliations are given in parentheses because the Kabinet Karya was explicitly non-party:

Prime Minister	Ir.[15] H. Djuanda (non-party)	
First Vice-Prime Minister	Mr. Hardi	(PNI)
Second Vice-Prime Minister	K. H. Idham Chalid	(NU)
Third Vice-Prime Minister	Dr. J. Leimena	(Parkindo)
Defense	Ir. H. Djuanda	(non-party)
Foreign Affairs	Dr. Subandrio	(non-party)
Internal Affairs	Sanusi Hardjadinata	(PNI)
Justice	Maengkom	(non-party, a Catholic)
Information	Sudibjo	(PSII)
Finance	Mr. Sutikno Slamet	(PNI)
Industries	Ir. F. J. Inkiriwang	(non-party, a Protestant)

---

15 Ir. is an abbreviation of the Dutch title Engineer; Mr. is Meester in de Rechten, master of laws, or lawyer. H. before a name usually signifies Hadji, one who has made the pilgrimage to Mecca. K. H. is Kiaji Hadji, Kiaji being an honorific title for a venerated Islamic leader or teacher. Drs. (Doctorandus) is a Dutch academic degree higher than a master's but lower than a doctorate.

Trade	Prof. Drs. Sunardjo	(NU)
Agriculture	Mr. Sadjarwo	(BTI)
Communications	Mr. Sukardan	(non-party)
Navigation	Col. (Navy) Nazir	(non-party) (Masjumi)[16]
Public Works	Ir. Pangeran Moh. Noor	
Agrarian Affairs	Mr. Sunarjo	(NU)
Labor	Mr. Samjono	(non-party)
Education and Culture	Prof. Dr. Prijono	(Murba)
Health	Dr. Col. Aziz Saleh	(IPKI)
Social Affairs	Muljadi Djojomartono	(Masjumi)[16]
Religion	K. H. Iljas	(NU)
Veterans Affairs	Chaerul Saleh	(non-party)
Mobilization of People's Energies for Development	A. M. Hanafi	(non-party)
Interregional Relations	Dr. F. L. Tobing	(SKI)[17]

The cabinet program, determined by Soekarno, consisted of five points: 1) to establish the National Council; 2) to normalize the situation of the Republic; 3) to continue with the abrogation of the Round Table Conference agreements;[18] 4) to continue the struggle for West Irian; and

16 Noor and Muljadi Djojomartono were expelled from Masjumi for accepting posts in the new cabinet.
17 SKI — Serikat Kerakjatan Indonesia, Indonesia People's Association, a quite minor nationalist party.
18 The Round Table Conference agreements were concluded in The Hague before the transfer of sovereignty at the end of 1949. Among other things, they created a Netherlands-Indonesia Union, saddled Indonesia with a considerable debt, and offered protection to Dutch commercial enterprises in Indonesia. The Union was unilaterally abrogated by the Burhanuddin Harahap (Masjumi) Cabinet in 1955 (see Feith, *Decline of Constitutional Democracy*, pp. 450-456) and further abrogation of the agreements was in the programs of both the succeeding Ali

5) to undertake rapid development.[19]

The Kabinet Karya came immediately under attack from anti-Communists who mistakenly regarded several new ministers — including Hanafi, Sadjarwo, Prijono, and Chaerul Saleh — as either Communists or sympathetic to the PKI. Hanafi was the most suspect of these ministers because of informal connections he apparently had with PKI leaders. Sadjarwo had formerly been a member of the BTI but had left it and was not closely associated with the PKI thereafter; in 1958 he joined the PNI. Prijono, recipient of a Stalin Peace Prize, was a member of the Murba party, and Chaerul Saleh was merely sympathetic with Murba's views. Although Murba and the PKI had on occasion been close to one another, their relationship was in the main one of open and bitter hostility. Sometimes called a national communist group, though its views were hardly that clearly defined, Murba was of minor significance as a party organization. But its leaders had been the young radicals of the revolution; they had been followers of Tan Malaka, the longtime revolutionary thinker and leader who was killed during the revolution, and they remained devoted to his memory. In August 1945, several of these men — including Chaerul Saleh, who did not become a member of Murba, however — had kidnapped Soekarno and Hatta and forced them on to proclaiming independence. From this endeavor they apparently enjoyed a psychological influence over Soekarno, who was also sympathetic to the radical nationalist way of thinking they still represented. Soekarno chose Chaerul Saleh for special grooming. Chaerul and several Murba leaders were closely connected with the vaguely articulated "Generation of 1945," which, as a symbol of revolutionary radicalism, also received increasing attention from Soekarno.

Apart from the Communist issue, Masjumi attacked the Kabinet Karya as unconstitutional. More to the point for Masjumi was the fact that this Government seemed unlikely to favor the regional cause, to whose fate Masjumi's own position was closely related. There were others who rejected the cabinet, but most groups, having already concluded

---

Sastroamidjojo Cabinet and the Kabinet Karya. The demand for abrogation was party connected with Indonesia's attempt to force the Dutch Government to negotiate the status of West Irian. The RTC agreements were in fact finally swept away completely in late 1957.

19 See Djuanda's first report to Parliament in IP/1957, pp. 242 ff, session of May 17, 1957.

that something new must be tried, found it at least acceptable.[20]

Despite his calling this a non-party business cabinet, it is obvious that in forming it Soekarno paid careful attention to the parties. Implicitly the Kabinet Karya was a PNI-NU coalition, and it was to remain that for the next several years. Furthermore, both Soekarno and Prime Minister Djuanda emphasized the cabinet's continuing responsibility to Parliament; and Djuanda promised to report to it regularly. Several months after the new Government was inaugurated, Djuanda said that although there had been no motion or resolution of any kind in Parliament on whether the Kabinet Karya should be accepted, yet he felt it should be pointed out that in fact only Masjumi, the Catholic party, and the Indonesian People's Party (Partai Rakjat Indonesia, PRI, a very minor party, led by Sutomo — Bung Tomo — an East Javanese revolutionary hero) had rejected the cabinet.[21] The Kabinet Karya thus enjoyed a parliamentary majority and was therefore legitimate in constitutional terms. This was but one of the anomalies of the Kabinet Karya system, in which the formal structure of the government was adjusted to the realities of political power.

No one doubted, however, that Parliament had suffered a precipitous decline. Regardless of Djuanda's assurances, Parliament could no longer exercise full control over the Government. This was only partly because the cabinet could not be forced to resign — a guarantee of stability. More important was the fact that the cabinet itself, whatever pressure Parliament might bring to bear on it, no longer in fact exercised full governmental powers. Political authority in the new system was more diffuse than ever. Soekarno's power was great and could not be touched. Moreover, martial law reduced the powers of civil government generally, and it also justified an extraordinary use of executive emergency laws and decrees, over which Parliament could exercise very little control. Parliament's own legislative powers were not formally restricted, but in practice they were shared with the President and with the military commanders, and neither of these forces was in any way accountable to Parliament. Summing up the changing distribution of authority, Kahin said in 1958 that, "the inauguration of this cabinet has diminished the role of both Parliament

20 See press reports in Kronik Dokumentasi, *Demokrasi Terpimpin*, pp. 99 ff.
21 Ministry of Information, Djuanda's second report to Parliament, p. 19.

and the political parties in approximate proportion to the considerably increased role of the President and the army."[22]

The National Council

The Kabinet Karya established the National Council by emergency law in May 1957.[23] This major innovation was not intended simply as an aid to the cabinet. As a "reflection of society," in Soekarno's view, it must be of a higher order than the cabinet, which was only a "reflection of Parliament."

The National Council served several purposes. First, it did reinforce the authority of the cabinet by giving Soekarno a channel to it and by associating him with it. From now on, the public perceived the Kabinet Karya, Soekarno, and the National Council as collectively constituting the Government, formalities notwithstanding. Soekarno's tremendous prestige enabled the Government to govern, most importantly by making it acceptable to the officer corps.

Second, the National Council gave Soekarno an institutional forum and means of obtaining advice and support in dealing with other political forces. Previously he had required no regular assistance, for he had only occasionally made purposeful excursions to the center of political activity. From now on Soekarno was to be continually and critically involved, an arrangement for which the 1950 Constitution made no provision. A precedent for the National Council existed in the first constitution of the Republic, that of 1945. In this instrument the President had possessed extremely broad executive powers. For reasons that will be discussed later, however, in 1957 Soekarno did not wish to resume the formal authority given him by the 1945 Constitution.

Third, the National Council, based as it was on functional groups, was intended as a counterpoise to the ideological party system. This was an

---

22 George McT. Kahin, "Indonesia," in Kahin, ed., *Major Governments of Asia* (Ithaca, N. Y.: Cornell University Press, 1st ed., 1958), p. 568.
23 For the law, see Ministry of Information, *Dewan Nasional*, pp. 8-13. Use of the emergency law evoked strong criticism from Parliament by groups opposed to Soekarno and by others (in NU, for example) who feared that the National Council would push Parliament from the scene. See IP/1957, p. 341, session of June 3, 1957, and Djuanda's defense of the Council, IP/1957, p. 352, session of June 7, 1957.

important issue in the development of Guided Democracy, for Soekarno and many others regarded the ideological divisions of the party world as largely to blame for national disunity. The functional group concept, which Soekarno had had in mind already in the 1930's, was an alternative basis for organizing the nation. Functional groups — although they never acquired true organizational form — also offered a source of new political leadership, which the aging parties (excepting the PKI) had ceased to produce. And they were, moreover, a source of political support for Soekarno, insurance against the time when the parties might disappear altogether. From the beginning, party leaders recognized the threat of the functional group idea, and by the second half of 1957 they were warily trying to shunt it aside. Mr. Utrecht, a legal scholar and an active member of the PNI, had this to say of the National Council in 1959:

> What has been achieved by the National Council since its creation in 1957? It is necessary to point out first that although the National Council was not intended to replace Parliament as the highest legislative body, yet it did have a special objective...: the political parties — which control Parliament — were presented with a counterbalance in the form of functional groups, which in the National Council were given an opportunity...to participate in policy making. The National Council was meant to reduce the influence on the Government of Parliament, which suffered the instability of the party system...It was intended that there would be a shift of political power from Parliament — i.e., from the political parties — to the Government via the National Council! In practice, these objectives in forming the National Council have to some extent been realized. Since its establishment, as the "politbureau" of the President, the National Council has become an executive policy making body whose influence is greater than that of Parliament. Most measures taken by the executive during these last two years have been the result of the work of the National Council. Thanks to the National Council...we have a more stable Government.[24]

---

24 E. Utrecht, *Pengantar dalam Hukum Indonesia* (Introduction to Indonesian Law; Djakarta: Ichtiar,

Groups openly opposed to Soekarno also opposed the National Council as an unconstitutional creation; but from its inception it was an essential part of the government. In 1957 and 1958 it played a key role in dealing with the regional crisis, in formulating new domestic and foreign policy, and, following the outbreak of rebellion in early 1958, in further developing Guided Democracy. Although the cabinet was not formally bound by the National Council's advice, Djuanda and his Ministers rarely risked disregarding it. But an important reason for this was that until mid-1958 the National Council undertook little that directly threatened other interests.[25] When in 1958 it began to deal with revision of the party system, a major conflict developed between it and the cabinet. By that time, moreover, Djuanda had become a more confident and independent Prime Minister, inclined to try to pick his own course between opposing forces.

The procedure of the National Council was determined by Soekarno, who was its chairman; but organization and day to day leadership was in the hands of the vice-chairman, Roeslan Abdulgani, a member of the PNI, formerly Minister of Information and Minister of Foreign Affairs, and an intelligent and trusted associate of the President. Issues were not supposed to be put to a vote, but rather to be discussed in committee and plenum until some identifiable consensus had been reached. This was the *musjawarah* (discussion)-*mufakat* (agreement) deliberative process that Soekarno, seeking to revive Indonesia's own traditions, had urged on the entire government.

But neither in the National Council nor elsewhere — with the possible exception of village Indonesia, where issues are less complicated — did the practice of *musjawarah-mufakat* live up to the theory. Usually, in any group, it merely gave an added advantage to the recognized group leader, whose responsibility it was to determine what the sense of the discussion was; to his judgment everyone would normally submit. But where vital

---

1959), p. 442.

25 For a list of topics discussed by the National Council in 1957 and 1958, see Ministry of Information, *Mendjelang Dua Tahun Kabinet Karya* (Towards Two Years of the Kabinet Karya; 1959), pp. 748-752. Among the problems dealt with in 1957 were the establishment of a New Life Movement, the National Conference and National Conference on Development, security and national preparedness, problems of finance and the economy, decentralization, cultural problems, and foreign affairs.

interests were at stake, the procedure either did not work at all or it worked only on the surface, any decision being ignored once everyone had played his part by giving public assent. Thus in the National Council too, the *musjawarah-mufakat* approach seemed to work until, in late 1958, the members divided on an issue crucial to the existence of political parties. Then a vote had to be taken.

The National Council was inaugurated on July 12, 1957. Forty-two members were originally appointed to the body and a few were added by Soekarno in the course of the next year. Several men refused membership, in some cases because they disapproved of Government policy towards the regions. Besides functional groups, there were two other categories of representation. The first was regional representation, the hope being that the Council would serve as an effective channel for regional demands. It was often proposed — usually by those who feared the other aims of the National Council — that it might eventually become a kind of senate.[26] The second category was ex-officio representation; under this heading were included the vice-premiers — thus facilitating coordination with the cabinet — and the armed forces (also police) chiefs-of-staff. Providing a forum for the military greatly increased the significance of the National Council. It also constituted recognition of the fact that the army could not be denied a place in the inner circles of government.

The original members of the National Council were as follows:

Soekarno	Chairman
Roeslan Abdulgani	Vice-Chairman
Vice-Prime Ministers Hardi, Idham, and Leimena	Ex-officio
Army Chief-of-Staff Nasution	Ex-officio
Navy Chief-of-Staff Subijakto	Ex-officio
Air Force Chief-of-Staff Suryadarma	Ex-officio
Chief Public Prosecutor Soeprapto	Ex-officio
Chief of State Police Soekanto	Ex-officio
Munir	Labor

---

26 Djuanda suggested this as late as October 1958; see *Pos Indonesia*, Oct. 28, 1958.

Ahem Erningpradja	Labor
S. Sardjono	Peasantry
Sastrodikoro	Peasantry
Sujono Atmo	Youth
Dahlan Ranumihardjo	Youth
Achmadi	Ex-armed revolutionaries
Notohamiprodjo	National businessmen
Henk Ngantung	Artists
Armunanto	Journalists
B. M. Diah	Journalists
S. K. Trimurti	Women
Rangkajo Rasuna Said	Women
Sukarni	Generation of 1945
Sidik Kertapati	Generation of 1945
Achmad Chatib	Islamic religious leaders
K. Fatah Jasin	Islamic religious leaders
Ds. W. J. Rumambi	Protestants
Ds. W. J. Rumabi	Protestants[27]
Sugriwa	Balinese Hindu religion
Prof. Tjan Tjoe Som	Citizens of Foreign Extraction
E. F. Wens	Citizens of Foreign Extraction
Ir. Indra Tjaja	Sumatra
Abdullah	Sumatra
Nja' Diwan	Sumatra
Mr. Iwa Kusumasumantri	Java
Katjasungkana	Java
Lt. Col. Hasan Basri	Kalimantan
Tjilik Riwut	Kalimantan

---

27 It is not clear why a member was not appointed at this time to represent the catholics. One may have been chosen later on. Possibly the Catholic Party decided against accepting a seat in 1957; it is also possible that soekarno chose to ignore the catholics in order to make his displeasure with their party leadership clear.

Andi Mappanjuti	Sulawesi
Prof. Ir. H. Johannes	Nusatenggara (Lesser Sundas)
Muhammad Djambek	Nusatenggara
Prof. Dr. Siwabessy	Maluku
Muhamad Padang	Maluku
Rumagesang	West Irian
N. L. Suwages	West Irian

This formal breakdown is misleading in several respects. For example, the functional group representatives also represented regions, so that more than forty percent of the Council membership was Javanese — approximately in proportion to actual population distribution. Also, despite the lack of a distinct category of political representation — which was added in 1959 — only Masjumi was not in fact represented on the Council. Thus the PNI and the PKI largely shared the labor, peasantry, youth, and journalists categories. Ahem Erningpradja, for example, was a member of the PNI, and B. M. Diah was close to the party; Munir was a leader of the Communist labor front, SOBSI, while Sujono Atmo and Henk Ngantung were in varying degrees sympathetic to the PKI. NU monopolized the Islamic religious representation. Six or seven of these Council members with political party connections would, when necessary, firmly defend the interests of their parties against the encroachments of Guided Democracy.

The political and institutional changes of 1957 were only half-way measures. Martial law gave the army a legitimate part in the governance of the country, but this was explicitly a temporary arrangement supposedly dependent on Parliament for any temporal extension of the state of siege. The political parties and Parliament were greatly weakened, yet they continued to exist and to play a significant role in the politics of 1957-1958. Soekarno's political role assumed a somewhat more realistic institutional character, but he refused to make the jump to the formal position of a strong and responsible executive. He often reminded his public that the 1950 Constitution remained in effect, and this gave him no such position.

Soekarno also frequently said during this period that Guided

Democracy had not yet begun. The National Council and the Kabinet Karya, he insisted, were only the "antennae" of Guided Democracy. To those who assumed that the National Council was created mainly to deal with the regional crisis, he replied that that was not the case, that it was the forerunner of a new political system.[28] But he did not indicate what would be the shape of the new system; he probably did not know himself. In 1957 and early 1958 the further development of Guided Democracy was postponed while the regional crisis held everyone's attention.

The PRRI Rebellion

To call the regional crisis a simple confrontation between Java and the outer islands is to do Indonesia an injustice, for few political conflicts in that country have had the benefit of simplicity. There were numerous subsidiary issues of political interest that made the regional problem extremely complex. No attempt will be made here to analyze them all, for other writers have already dealt with the crisis, though its history has yet to be written in full.[29] The development of the rebellion will be discussed only briefly in this section to call attention to a few matters important for the rest of the study.

Djakarta's response to the regionalist movements was complicated by various tendencies and counter-tendencies. For example, to the extent that the PNI and NU represented Javanese views they were hostile to the regionalists' claims, while Masjumi was increasingly isolated by its identification with the other side. But PNI-NU attitudes were checked slightly by the views of their outer island branches. And the great increase in electoral support shown by the PKI in the 1957 local elections (cf. Chapter III) provided an impetus for the other major parties to move together, regardless of the regional issue. Those elections, however, also

---

28 See Soekarno's speech of July 3, 1957, on the occasion of the 30th anniversary of the PNI, in Ministry of Information, *Dewan Nasional*, p. 111; Roeslan Abdulgani's article in *Far Eastern Survey*, cited *supra*, note 13.

29 See especially Feith, *Decline of Constitutional Democracy*; Kahin, in *Major Governments* (2nd ed.); Justus M. van der Kroef, "Disunited Indonesia," *Far Eastern Survey*, XXVII, nos. 4 and 5 (April and May, 1958); B. H. M. Vlekke, *Indonesia's Struggle* (The Hague: Netherlands Institute of International Affairs, 1959). A forthcoming study by J. A. C. Mackie should be definitive on the politics of 1957.

had the effect of making regionalist objections to the PKI and to its Javanese stronghold more extreme.

Within the leadership of the army, the cabinet, and the National Council a strong inclination to be sympathetic to outer island demands was balanced by anger at the indiscipline of the regionalist councils, which threatened the unity of the state. Among Javanese leaders, both civilian and military, there was a conviction that the central government should not go too far in compromising with regional interests. Thus despite the strong desire of most army officers to heal the breach within their corps, at the National Conference of September 1957 Col. Suharto, *panglima* of Central Java, made it clear that he regarded appeasement of the dissidents in Sumatra and Sulawesi as perverse partiality. He pointed out that the 54 million people of Java would feel unjustly treated should the Government relax its development efforts there in order to permit the obstreperous regions to catch up.[30] Furthermore, both Soekarno and Nasution (a Sumatran) were personally under challenge by the regionalists. Distrusting Soekarno's dealings with the PKI, the regionalists wanted the President to give Hatta a greater role in government; and they opposed Nasution for his apparent attachment to Soekarno and for having forsaken both the regions and the regional officers.

In mid-1957, the National Council and army leaders in Djakarta set about trying to deal with grievances common to Java and the outer islands. The martial law administration undertook a massive anti-corruption campaign, which, as it turned out, claimed as victims several PNI and NU leaders, among others. In August, Soekarno inaugurated a New Life Movement (Gerakan Hidup Baru) proposed by the National Council — but with a precedent of the same name, interestingly, during the Japanese occupation — to promote austerity, to restore national morale, and generally to revitalize the state. It was completely unsuccessful and soon became the butt of elite jokes in the capital.[31] At the same time, the Djuanda Cabinet attempted to deal directly with the regionalist councils. Central government delegations were sent to the outer islands to talk with regional leaders and to deliver funds; the term "regional development"

---

30 "Diktat Musjawarah Nasional" (Minutes of the National Conference; mimeographed), p. 17.
31 On the New Life Movement, see Justus M. van der Kroef, "Indonesia's 'New Life Movement,'" *Eastern World*, Nov. 1957, pp. 16-19.

was much bandied about. Along with the new decentralization law, approved in late 1956, additional financial and administrative measures were drafted which it was hoped would cool regional tempers. A limited attempt was made to satisfy the demands of the regions for more of the foreign exchange earned by their exports.

The Government was restricted in these efforts, however, by general economic conditions — e.g., inflation, which became more rapid with the huge increase in deficit financing — and by its own depleted foreign exchange reserves. By May 1957 there was in fact a deficit in foreign exchange holdings amounting to 12 million rupiah, approximately $1,000,000 at the then legal rate of Rp. 11.40 to the dollar. Finance Minister Sutikno Slamet told Parliament in September that the state had been approaching bankruptcy earlier in the year.[32] To encourage exports the cabinet established a new export certificate system in June which permitted exporters to sell certificates (Bukti Expor, B.E.) representing their total exchange earnings to importers at the going free market rate. A tax of 20 percent on these sales was paid by the exporters.[33] This helped to improve the foreign exchange situation somewhat, but it did not eliminate completely the favorable exchange differential for importers against which the exporting areas were protesting; and it did not halt the large scale regional barter activities which had contributed to the serious exchange problems of the Government in the first place. Nor did it stop inflation; on the contrary, it seemed to encourage it. By August and September there were regional demands that the B.E. system be abolished, most generally on the grounds that it had caused higher prices. The market rate of the B.E. certificates, which became a current economic indicator, soared so high that in early 1958 Djuanda was compelled to freeze the rate.

In mid-August 1957 the National Council took up the question of "normalizing the situation of the Republic." Despairing of finding a solution through normal government channels, the Council proposed that all regional and military problems should be discussed in a great National Conference (Musjawarah Nasional) of leaders from all the major

---

32 IP/1957, pp. 709-710, session of Sept. 18, 1957.
33 See Douglas Paauw, "The High Cost of Political Instability in Indonesia," in Vlekke, *Indonesia's Struggle*. For further comment on the economic background, see Bank Indonesia, *Report*, 1957-1958.

islands. Djuanda organized the conference, which was held on September 10th-14th. It was followed in November by a National Conference on Development (Musjawarah Nasional Pembangunan) devoted to discussions of the economic development of all areas of the country; this second meeting was of much less significance than the first.[34]

The National Conference of September covered a broad range of difficult issues: restoration of the Soekarno-Hatta Dwitunggal, military disunity, the distribution of political and economic power throughout the country, economic development, and national morale. For a brief period the conference seemed to achieve a sense of unity. Lt. Col. Husein, leader of the dissident Buffalo Council (Dewan Banteng) in Central Sumatra, invited the delegates to make a pilgrimage en masse to the grave of the first commander of the national army, Gen. Sudirman, in Jogjakarta, capital of the revolutionary republic. At the end of the conference, Soekarno and Hatta signed a joint statement in praise of the national revolution and the *Pantjasila* — Soekarno's five-point statement of national ideology.[35]

It soon became apparent, however, that very little had actually been accomplished. The conference had appointed a committee to work out a practicable new relationship between Soekarno and Hatta, whose joint declaration, mentioned above, had been a general one, avoiding anything of substantive importance. Parliament also took one of its few initiatives in forming a Committee of Nine to help restore the Dwitunggal, but this did not add much to the effort. Neither Soekarno nor Hatta was prepared to come to the other's terms. If he could avoid it, Soekarno was not going

---

34 The November conference produced massive proposals and comments on national development. See *Risalah Musjawarah Nasional Pembangunan* (Proceedings of the National Conference on Development; four vols., mimeographed). On the National Conference of September, see also Djuanda's report to Parliament, IP/1957, pp. 715 ff, session of Sept. 20, 1957.

35 Soekarno delivered the Pantjasila speech, which will be mentioned often, in an address to the Preparatory Committee for Indonesian Independence in mid-1945. See Soekarno, *Lahirnja Pantjasila* (The Birth of the Pantjasila; Djakarta: Ministry of Information), the original speech. It consists of these five principles: Belief in God, Nationalism, Internationalism (or humanitarianism), Sovereignty of the People, and Social Justice. These translations do not do justice to the original Indonesian terms, by which Soekarno, and others, meant — especially in the cases of the third and fourth items — something rather different from the ideas Americans or Europeans might ascribe to them. It is unnecessary, however, to discuss that matter fully here. During the revolution and after, the Pantjasila became the symbol of parties and groups opposed to the ideas of ideological Islam.

to give Hatta a determining say in the Government; and Hatta had already decided, as he often said, to "let Soekarno try to run things his way." Soon after the National Conference ended Hatta made a trip to China, and not long after he returned Soekarno also went abroad, so that there was little opportunity to bring them together. Only when the rebellion finally broke out did the two leaders hold talks, but they had no apparent result.

The National Conference established another and more important committee — the Committee of Seven — to deal with the army's problems. More successful than the Soekarno-Hatta committee, the Committee of Seven was able to produce a set of proposals that, had they been implemented, might have contributed to settlement of several outstanding problems of military organization and army politics. In November the committee agreed on a formula under which the officers who had been involved in the various "affairs" since 1956 would be given an amnesty; those officers who had broken discipline would be asked to choose between army life and discipline on the one hand and civilian politics on the other. On the problem of dissatisfaction with the existing army leadership, a Military Council was to be created to which several regionalist officers would be appointed; this council would also discuss further settlement of difficulties besetting the army.[36] Although this solution was bound to be met with some discontent on all sides, it was in many ways a good compromise. But from the beginning the Committee of Seven suffered from a basic disability in the eyes of regionalist officers: though it included the Sultan of Jogjakarta — a national figure of immense prestige and a former Minister of Defense (at the time of the October 17th Affair) whom regionalist army leaders found sympathetic — it also included Nasution, whose removal from office was for outer island dissident officers an essential part of any solution to army disunity.[37] For his part, Nasution, who might have been seriously disadvantaged if the

---

36 See Nasution's lecture of Feb. 22, 1958, to army officers in Djakarta, on the events leading up to the rebellion, in *Madjalah Angkatan Darat* (Army Journal), VIII, no. 1 (Jan. 1958), 6-9; *Pesat* (PNI-leaning weekly), XIV, no. 9 (March, 1958), 16. For further comments on the Committee of Seven, see *Yudhagama* (Armed Forces journal), VIII, no. 77 (Dec. 1957), 3232-3234; *Siasat* (PSI-leaning weekly), Sept. 25, 1957, where it was pointed out that Soekarno's and Hatta's absence would made the Committee of Seven's progress difficult.

37 The members of the Committee of Seven were Soekarno, Hatta, Djuanda, Leimena, the Sultan of Jogjakarta, Azis Saleh, and Nasution.

committee's proposals had been carried out, took the first opportunity to declare them worthless.

The opportunity came soon, for whatever the National Conference had accomplished was swept aside by a wave of radicalism in late November and early December that gave Djakarta the political initiative. On November 30th, while Soekarno was visiting his children's school, a small team of assassins, apparently acting under the banner of Islam, threw several grenades at him. A number of adults and children were killed or injured, but Soekarno escaped this the first major attempt on his life. Col. Zulkifli Lubis was accused of having masterminded the "Tjikini Affair," though he denied it from his place of hiding, and some of the blame rubbed off on to the Sumatran regionalist officers with whom he had become associated.[38] One immediate result was that the Committee of Seven was brushed aside. Nasution said a month later that after Tjikini he had decided there could be no coming to terms with assassins.[39]

The pace of events quickened after the Tjikini Affair. Within a few days there came another major event in Indonesian political and economic history, this time in the context of the campaign to wrest West Irian from the grip of the Dutch, who had retained this one last vestige of their former eastern empire after the transfer of sovereignty. The West Irian campaign was peculiarly Soekarno's; he had always regarded it as a unifying nationalist cause, and in times of stress, as in 1957, he tended to put increasing emphasis upon it. In late 1957 the Irian question was once again before the United Nations. Soekarno warned that should the General Assembly vote go against Indonesia, "other means" would be used to force the Netherlands to give up the territory. But on November 29th the motion to support Indonesia's request that the Dutch negotiate the dispute failed to win a two-thirds majority in the Assembly. On December 3rd, three days after the Tjikini Affair, PNI and PKI labor unions — the PNI federation (KBKI) took the lead — began to take over the plants and offices of every significant Dutch company in the country. Two days

---

38 On the Tjikini Affair, see the book compiled from the trial of those involved and from other materials by the daily newspaper *Pemuda*, entitled *Peristiwa Tjikini* (The Tjikini Affair; Djakarta: Usaha Penerbit Pemuda, 1958).
39 *Madjalah Angkatan Darat* (Jan. 1958), p. 7.

later the Ministry of Justice issued an order expelling some 46,000 Dutch nationals.

The take-overs were begun with Soekarno's encouragement, and a few leaders of the recently established Youth-Military Cooperation Body (of which further mention will be made later) were involved in the action.[40] But if the take-overs were not entirely spontaneous, nor were they fully planned. Neither Djuanda, who did not agree with the take-overs, nor Nasution was entirely aware of what was happening, and policy during the tense days of early December was largely ad hoc, with the presidential palace, the cabinet, labor unions, and youth groups all working more or less at cross purposes. Djuanda and other members of the cabinet warned against ruinous "excesses," and the confusion was brought under control only with difficulty. With Djuanda's assent, Nasution and the army stepped in to take charge of the Dutch firms.[41] Thereafter the unions were ordered to desist from their operations. The army remained in control of the enterprises until late 1958. They were not nationalized until a year after the take-overs. Initially the Government was uncertain what action it should take in this connection, but there was no intention of restoring the firms to their original owners; Dutch control over the Indonesian economy was finally broken, however traumatically. Funds for compensation were later set aside in London pending settlement of the West Irian dispute, but they were consumed in a financial crisis before the Dutch agreed, in 1962, to surrender the territory.

From any point of view the immediate effects of the take-overs were troublesome. The economy, already strained, suffered from the sudden departure of Dutch personnel and the lack of any adequate replacement for them. Political tension increased. Masjumi, the PSI, the Christian parties, and allied groups attacked the take-overs as nonsensical and uselessly destructive radicalism. Hatta publicly disagreed with the Government's policy, forcing Djuanda — who respected Hatta — into an angry defense

---

40 Some time afterwards, Soekarno told Louis Fischer that he had ordered the seizure of the Dutch firms. Fischer, *The Story of Indonesia* (New York: Harper, 1959), p. 300. See also Feith, *Decline of Constitutional Democracy*, pp. 583-585.

41 For documents relating to the take-overs and the role played by Nasution's headquarters, see the appendices to Djuanda's statement to Parliament on extension of martial law in late 1958, *Risalah Perundingan Dewan Perwakilan Rakjat* (Parliamentary Debates), pp. 5145-5151, session of Dec. 8, 1958.

of the position into which the cabinet had been pushed. Soekarno, the PKI, and the PNI defended the action as necessary to Indonesia's existence as an independent nation in control of its own economy. It was also justified as a blow against the memory of Dutch colonial oppression, and most of the politically aware public probably appreciated it in that light. Djakarta became exceedingly tense as a result of this issue and the regional crisis in December. Masjumi leaders who opposed the take-overs — particularly Mohammad Natsir, general chairman of the party, and Sjafruddin Prawiranegara, head of the (circulation) Bank Indonesia — found themselves subjected to personal harassment by roaming youth groups who regarded themselves as acting for Soekarno. Natsir, Sjafruddin, and Burhanuddin Harahap, a former Prime Minister, finally left Djakarta for Padang, capital of the regionalist movement in Sumatra; there they soon joined the rebellion against Djakarta.

The events of December drove regionalist leaders even further from the central government. In part this was because the KPM, the Dutch inter-island shipping and sea transport line, had been among the enterprises seized in Djakarta. KPM succeeded in keeping its ships away from Indonesian waters in December, leaving the archipelago without effective sea communications. Regionalist leaders were encouraged to believe that Djakarta would consequently be even less capable of exerting its authority in the outer islands.

At the same time, United States sympathy for the regionalist cause was being expressed more openly, and American aid had already begun to flow into West Sumatra. There is evidence that several U.S. intelligence agents were present in Sumatra by the beginning of 1958.[42] As a result of American interest and encouragement — and in the hope, no doubt, that more assistance would be forthcoming — the anti — Communist aspect of the regionalist movement became much more prominent in late 1957 and early 1958. Fuel was added to the regionalist fire at the end of 1957 when rumors spread that a $100 million loan negotiated between

---

42 See the account of the rebellion by James Mossman, *Rebels in Paradise: Indonesia's Civil War* (London: Jonathan Cape, 1961). Several American journalists in Sumatra during early 1958 were aware of the presence of U.S. military agents, but — according to their own admissions in private conversations — were reluctant, partly for patriotic reasons, to report this to their newspapers. In 1961, after the rebels finally surrendered, it was indicated to me by one rebel military leader that American military advisors had been in Padang for some time before the rebellion broke out.

Djakarta and Moscow would be used to purchase arms. Washington had already made it clear — partly because of Dutch anxiety over West Irian — that it would not supply arms to Djakarta.

As tension mounted in late 1957, Soekarno was scheduled to go abroad on December 25th for an Asian trip. Opposition to his leaving during the crisis induced him to postpone his departure for a short while. But he left nevertheless on January 6th, not to return until February 16th, the day after Padang's ultimatum to Djakarta expired.

Regionialist leaders had themselves been moving away from a peaceful solution of the crisis since early September, even before the National Conference. They had become accustomed to opposing Djakarta. Their ultimate objectives with respect to the central government were never perfectly clear, and soon the more negative aspects of their opposition became as compelling as their original — and often vaguely formulated — demands for a fairer political and economic balance between Java and the outer islands, for more attention to regional needs, for better and more honest government, and so on. Thus the longer barter trade with Singapore, Hongkong, and elsewhere continued, the more it whetted the appetites of the regionalists for both capital and luxury goods, and the more reluctant they were to submit to any restrictions on their trade. Moreover, and more important, by mid-1957 those military commanders who had committed themselves to the regional cause — Simbolon, Husein, Sumual, and Lubis, among others — could not expect their positions to improve if the regionalist movement came to nothing. They would probably not be allowed to achieve again the power they enjoyed while the regions were running their own affairs; in all likelihood they would be transferred to uninfluential staff posts. Col. Simbolon had already lost his command in North Sumatra and could not hope to rise again in the central government's army. Among the civilians in the regionalist movement, Prof. Sumitro Djojohadikusumo — a PSI leader and a former Minister of Finance — had fled Djakarta under charges of corruption; he too had little to gain from a reasonable compromise with the central government. Finally, the hopes regionalist leaders had of forcing Djakarta into complete surrender to all their demands were encouraged by American hostility to Soekarno's willingness to cooperate with the PKI.

On September 7th and 8th, Lt. Cols. Husein, Sumual, Barlian — *panglimas* of Central Sumatra, North Sulawesi, and South Sumatra respectively — Simbolon, Lubis, and several others met in Palembang, provincial capital of South Sumatra, to discuss the position of the regionalist movement. Skeptical that the National Conference would achieve anything, they agreed on six demands: 1) the Soekarno-Hatta Dwitunggal must be restored; 2) the existing leadership of the army must be replaced; 3) the regions must be given extensive autonomy; 4) a senate must be formed; 5) there must be a general rejuvenation of the government and of the nation; 6) "internationally oriented Communism" must be forbidden. Following the National Conference, these demands were reduced to three essential points: 1) the Dwitunggal must be restored in such a way that Soekarno's "pro-Communist" activities would be restricted (i.e., by making Hatta Prime Minister); 2) Nasution and his staff must be replaced; and 3) Communism must be outlawed. The Sumatran officers also agreed at this time to set up a common Sumatran command, with headquarters in Padang, and to establish closer political and economic relations with the Permesta (Sulawesi) area in order to strengthen the regionalist movement as a whole. All this was set down in a signed document, the Palembang Charter.[43]

The regionalist officers felt that Soekarno had evaded their demands at the National Conference, though they had apparently expected as much from the beginning. Hatta's trip to China made them doubt that a real effort would be made to restore the Dwitunggal. Further, the National Conference had not discussed the possibility of a senate. Nor had anything been done about the Communist issue. And the regional officers were also frustrated by Nasution's membership of the Committee of Seven.

On October 5th the officers met again in Sumatra to draw up another document emphasizing the failure of the National Conference to satisfy regional demands.[44] They decided upon a new policy, one major element of which was that the Dwitunggal "mythos" should be dropped — that the

---

43 The documentary material here is taken from a publication by the Ministry of Information, *Peristiwa Sumatera Barat* (The West Sumatra Affair), Vol. I, 1960; see pp. 52, 58. The documents, according to official sources, fell into army hands in a raid on regionalist headquarters in 1958. They check with other sources, particularly pieces written abroad by Sumitro Djojohadikusumo.

44 There was an earlier meeting in Padang on September 21 and 22 between Husein, Barlian, and others to review the National Conference results. Soon afterwards Husein and Barlian flew to Makassar to meet with Sumual, who agreed with their assessments.

regionalists should no longer depend upon restoration of the Dwitunggal to cure all the country's ills. It was agreed, however — indicating how powerful the "mythos" was — that this decision should not be made public, in part to avoid the possibility that Djakarta leaders might use it against the regionalists. The regional officers also agreed that henceforth they would work for a general election to choose a new President of Indonesia. Nor was this made public, however, presumably because the power of Soekarno as a symbol of national unity was too great to risk an attack on him until the time was ripe. The officers gave increased emphasis to other symbols of national unity: the Pantjasila, the Proclamation of Independence, and the revolution itself, which formed a special bond for all army officers.[45]

The October 5th document also voiced the intention of regionalist officers to form a counter-government:

> As long as the PKI continues to exist in the Center (Java) [sic], the central government cannot be recognized as the central government of the Republic of Indonesia...From now on efforts must be made in the direction of forming an Emergency Central Government of the Republic of Indonesia, situated outside of Java.[46]

The Sumatran common command was eventually to be expanded into an inter-regional command. Propaganda was to be intensified, and Communism made the basic issue in order to attract the attention of all Indonesians (and, it must be added, of numerous Americans).

Rumors were current in December and January that the dissident Sumatrans were about to establish an independent state. In mid-January news reached Djakarta of an important gathering of regionalist leaders in Sungai Dareh, a small town east of Padang in the Djambi area. The meeting was attended by Husein, Simbolon, Lubis, Dahlan Djambek — a respected Sumatran officer — and the civilian leaders Natsir, Sjafruddin,

---

45 *Peristiwa Sumatera Barat*, pp. 55-58.
46 *Ibid.*, p. 61. On January 6, 1958, a raid in Djakarta resulted in the capture of a document alleged to have been written by Zulkifli Lubis for the benefit of his anti-Djakarta associates. Dated June 9, 1957, it proposed the establishment of an independent countergovernment. See Djuanda's statement to Parliament, in IP/1958, p. 83, session of Feb. 3, 1958.

and Sumitro Djojohadikusumo. They discussed the necessity of issuing a final challenge to Djakarta.[47]

Politicians in the capital actively sought to avoid the disaster that threatened. Masjumi leaders who had not gone to Padang and who were horrified at the thought of open rebellion went to Sumatra in an attempt to dissuade the regionalists. A PSI mission did the same, but with no more success. The cabinet also made numerous efforts, as did those close to the Government with family or other connections in Sumatra and Sulawesi. Nasution, in the meantime, took steps to try and prevent rebellion or, if it broke out, to localize it. On January 23rd he flew to Sumatra, where he spent three days sounding out the military commanders of Tapanuli (North Sumatra), East Sumatra, Atjeh, and Riau. He was assured of their loyalty — or at least their neutrality.[48] He had visited Sulawesi earlier on the same mission.

Following several days of public meetings and demonstrations in Padang, the regionalist leaders on February 10th issued their ultimatum to Djakarta. Five demands were made: 1) that within five days the Djuanda Cabinet resign; 2) that Hatta and Hamengku Buwono (the Sultan of Jogjakarta) be appointed formateurs of a new cabinet; 3) that Hatta and Hamengku Buwono accept this charge; 4) that Parliament permit Hatta and Hamengku Buwono to form a national business cabinet with a mandate to work until the next general elections; and 5) that Soekarno resume a "constitutional position" and give full opportunity and his assistance to the new national business cabinet.[49] The cabinet rejected the ultimatum a day after it was received. Husein, Lubis, Djambek, and Simbolon were dishonorably discharged from the army, and on February 12th Nasution ordered their arrest for "attempting to assassinate the President and attempting to change the state and government by violence."[50] When

---

47 See the comments by Nasution on Feb. 22, 1958, in *Pesat*, XIV, no. 10 (March 8, 1958), 6.

48 *Ibid*. See also Djuanda's statement to Parliament on Feb. 3, IP/1958, p. 83.

49 *Peristiwa Sumatera Barat*, pp. 41-46. The ultimatum has been preceded on January 29 by a radio message containing nearly the same demands which the Radio Republik Indonesia was requested to give to Acting President Sartono and to Djuanda. The message was sent by the Badan Aksi Rakjat Sumatera Tengah (BARST, Central Sumatran People's Action Body) a front for the regionalist officers in Padang. See Djuanda's statement to Parliament on Feb. 3, IP/1958, p. 84.

50 Of all the officers who joined the rebellion, only one was not dishonorably discharged: Col. Alex Kawilarang, who joined the rebellion in Sulawesi in May, travelling there from Washington, where he had been military attache. Army leaders may have hoped Kawilarang — a highly respected

the ultimatum expired on the 15th, the Padang group announced the formation of a Revolutionary Government of the Republic of Indonesia (Pemerintah Revolusioner Republik Indonesia, PRRI). Sjafruddin was appointed Prime Minister and fifteen ministries were established.[51] On February 17th, Lt. Col. Somba in Sulawesi declared for the PRRI and severed all relations with Djakarta. The rebellion had begun.

Soekarno returned to Djakarta from his trip abroad on February 16th, and the next week was taken up in deliberations. Several groups outside the Government were opposed to using military force against Sumatra and Sulawesi; Masjumi, and PSI, the Christian parties, and Hatta deprecated Padang's action but nevertheless wanted compromise and no bloodshed. Possibly a few members of the cabinet took the same view. On the other side were those — including Soekarno, Nasution, and Djuanda, many in the PNI, and certainly the PKI — who insisted that the line must be drawn at rebellion. They argued that the Government could not permit rebellion to go unpunished without admitting its own failure as a government and Indonesia's failure as a state. The ultimate issue of civil war having been raised — and compounded by the apparent threat of possible intervention by the United States — there was really no choice but to meet it squarely.

A further effort at conciliation was made nevertheless, partly, it seems, because of Soekarno's own uncertainty. On February 19th he went to see Hatta at the latter's home, and the two men met again on March 3rd, but without result. It is unlikely that they could have found much to agree upon at that stage. On February 21st, Soekarno resumed his office from acting President Sartono (Speaker of Parliament) and praised the cabinet's action thus far against the PRRI. Djuanda added that Government measures against the rebels would be confined mainly to an economic blockade, though perhaps shooting could not be avoided

---

officer who appears not to have been in full agreement with the aims of the PRRI — could be induced to stop fighting and bring the rebellion in Sulawesi to an end.

51 Those included in the cabinet were Sjafruddin, Simbolon, Djambek, Burhanuddin, Moh. Sjafei, Warouw, Said, Saladin Sarumpaet, Muchtar Lintang, Saleh Lahade, A. Hani Usman, and Sumitro Djojohadikusumo. The last, it might be mentioned, was the first of the civilian leaders to flee Djakarta, in May 1957, where corruption charges were being brought against him. Mr. Assaat had been president of the Republic of Indonesia for a short time before the United (Federal) States of Indonesia — of which Soekarno was president — became the unitary state in 1950. He was later appointed vice-premier of the PRRI. See *Peristiwa Sumatera Barat*, p. 50.

altogether. Yet that same day and the following day — possibly without Djuanda's knowledge or concurrence — the air force bombed a bridge in West Sumatra and rebel-controlled radio stations in Padang, Bukittinggi (PRRI headquarters), and Menado (North Sulawesi).

The major military campaigns in Sumatra were over within two months. Nasution had laid his military plans early. On March 12th, the army quickly occupied Pakanbaru, a strategic area both because the Caltex oil fields were located there and because it offered a position from which to control Medan. Major Nainggolan took over Medan for the PRRI for one day, on March 16th, but government forces bombed the city radio station and on the 17th Mainggolan and his troops fled to Tapanuli and Atjeh, where they were able to take refuge among a few friendly groups. In mid-April, Padang itself was taken with virtually no resistance from the PRRI defenses.[52] Thereafter the Government army turned its primary attention to Sulawesi, which was considered a much tougher military nut to crack. In mid-May, Gorontalo was brought under control; and Menado fell in late June. The rebellion was by no means over, but the major rebel cities had been captured; the PRRI retired to the jungles to carry on as guerillas.

So rapid were the government's military successes, particularly in Sumatra, that it is difficult to understand why rebel leaders decided on open revolt when they were obviously unprepared to carry it through. There are probably several contributory explanations. One is that other regions were expected to join the rebellion immediately. But the PRRI lost its most important ally when Lt. Col. Barlian failed to bring South Sumatra into the rebel camp; pressure from many primarily Javanese groups — particularly organized oil workers — resident in his area and the fear of a major attack from nearby Java apparently persuaded Barlian to take no risk. Most of North Sumatra, South Sulawesi, and Kalimantan (except for pockets) also held fast with the Government, partly because of the effect of internal rivalries and partly because of their unwillingness to act without prior assurance of success. Atjehnese neutrality followed from the same reasons and in addition the fear of a renewed outbreak of violence between fanatic Moslems and traditional aristocratic groups; but

52 See Mossman's account of the invasion of Padang in *Rebels in Paradise*.

there was some sympathy there for the rebellion against the government, and within two years violent hostilities did resume in Atjeh when the Darul Islam accepted arms from the PRRI in exchange for an alliance. But by 1958 the rebellion was effectively contained within the relatively manageable areas of Central Sumatra, South Tapanuli, and Djambi in Sumatra, and Central and North Sulawesi.

Rebel leaders had also hoped to cripple Djakarta financially by cutting off its foreign exchange. They tried to stop the foreign oil concerns in South Sumatra from making payments to the Government, but without success; Djakarta assured Caltex, Stanvac, and Shell of protection and the opportunity to keep their wells flowing. Djafruddin attempted to induce the United States Government to freeze Indonesian accounts, but this effort also failed. PRRI leaders continued to believe nevertheless that Djakarta would eventually be strangled by the economic consequences of the rebellion. In this too they were wrong.

The PRRI had also expected substantial assistance from the United States and SEATO. American arms and radio equipment had been dropped near Padang and other areas before Padang fell, and afterwards some aid came in from Taiwan to Sumatra and Sulawesi. American-flown airplanes based at Clark Field supplied Sulawesi and bombed government targets in the east. In May a B-26 piloted by an American, Allan Pope, was shot down in the vicinity of Ambon, seriously but only temporarily hindering efforts then being made to improve Indonesian-American relations; Pope was captured and brought to Djakarta for eventual trial. Britain also aided the rebels, and South Korea, Taiwan, the Philippines, and Malaya expressed sympathy for the rebel cause and hostility to the central government, usually on anti-Communist grounds. Relations were particularly strained between Djakarta and Malaya and Singapore, whence the rebels smuggled arms, found contacts, and enjoyed enough sympathy to allow them to travel freely.

During the early months of the rebellion, the foreign intervention issue was the most volatile one in Indonesia, and anti-American sentiment in Djakarta was at fever pitch. The decision to occupy Pakanbaru was made in part out of fear that the United States would send marines to the area to protect American oil company personnel — a proposal actually made by Washington and rejected immediately by Djakarta. For weeks before the invasion of Padang it was unclear what Washington would do; the fact that several ships of the Seventh Fleet, including a carrier, were in the area caused Djakarta great anxiety, though the ships were not finally used to intervene. It appears that after the fall of Padang the State Department decided the PRRI could not succeed and Washington should therefore quickly attempt to restore amity with Djakarta. A new ambassador, Howard Jones, had been appointed earlier to replace Ambassador Allison — who had been reassigned in 1957 following a serious disagreement with the State Department's policy towards Indonesia — and Jones began his attempt in late April and May of 1958 to improve relations between the two states. At that time Soekarno, Djuanda, and Nasution were also anxious to ease the strain with Washington and to eliminate the threat of intervention, so that Jones' effort met with some success. On May 20th, Secretary of State Dulles made a statement condemning intervention of any sort in behalf of the rebels, and an agreement was later concluded to sell American small arms to Djakarta.[53] Soekarno and Jones had lunch together to symbolize the rapprochement. But Indonesian suspicions of U.S. intentions never ceased.

The PRRI rebellion continued until mid-1961. It caused considerable economic strain for the country, and though it never threatened to become unmanageable yet it constantly tied down several battalions from each of the three Javanese divisions.[54] Although casualties were higher than sometimes supposed, there was little wanton destruction in areas from which the rebels originated and took sustenance. Officers on both sides knew and often respected one another, and they were not entirely out of sympathy with one another's ideas. Negotiations between the rebels and army leaders began several times during the next two and a half years. But until 1961 they were unsuccessful, despite the desire of Nasution and other loyal officers to bring their former colleagues out of the woods, for the rebellion was also a significant issue in Djakarta politics. The PKI particularly opposed any hint of a compromise, and so did Soekarno, for

---

53 See Djuanda's statement to Parliament on July 4, 1958, IP/1958, pp. 728-741, in which considerable space is devoted to the foreign intervention threat earlier in the year.

54 Most of the fighting in rebel areas was done by the Javanese divisions, because they were better trained and equipped, because their loyalty was certain, and because this would prevent intra-island ethnic rivalries from flaring up. Siliwangi division (West Java) troops were sent to North Sumatra, Diponegoro (Central Java) troops to West Sumatra, and Brawidjaja (East Java) troops to Sulawesi.

fear that it might greatly strengthen the leadership of the army and favor the demands of the regionalists.

As for the PRRI, at the end of 1959 it changed itself into the RPI — Republik Persatuan Indonesia, United Republic of Indonesia, a "federal" arrangement — signifying among other things its alliance with Darul Islam. Rebel leaders themselves, however, soon began to divide into ideological, religious, ethnic, and personal factions — not to mention a civil vs. military split — indicating that the PRRI suffered from the same splintering tendencies as the rest of the Indonesian elite.[55]

For as long as it continued, the rebellion influenced the course of national politics. Its immediate consequences for the political structure and the balance of political forces in Indonesia were crucial to the development of Guided Democracy. These consequences will be discussed in a later chapter.

---

[55] See Herbert Feith and Daniel S. Lev, "The End of the Indonesian Rebellion," *Pacific Affairs*, XXXVI, no. 1 (Spring 1963).

GUIDED DEMOCRACY:
SOEKARNO AND THE ARMY

The extent of Guided Democracy's challenge to the parliamentary order was not clear at first, for the central issues of 1957 did not concern the political system *per se*. The *crise de régime* of that difficult year revolved around the question of who should exercise power in whatever government existed. In the bewildering maze of mutually reinforcing conflicts between Java and the outer islands, between the PNI-PKI and Masjumi, between Soekarno and Hatta, and between Nasution and the dissident colonels, the form of government was a secondary issue. Had it been primary, the battle lines would have formed mainly around Soekarno and army leaders on the one hand and the political parties on the other — which is approximately what happened after the rebellion had decisively settled the other major questions posed in 1957. But before the rebellion the two camps consisted of Soekarno, the PNI, the PKI, and NU — though the last much preferred the middle of the road — against Masjumi, the PSI, the Christian parties, and allied groups, with the army uncertainly divided between the two.

Inevitably there were major contradictions between the anti-party, regional, and inter-party conflict themes in 1957. The development of Guided Democracy, initially held in abeyance, obviously acquired some of its flavor from the other ongoing struggles. Thus the opposition of Masjumi and its allies to Guided Democracy must be seen at first primarily in terms of their hostility to Soekarno and his supporters. It has already been suggested that had Masjumi and the NU accepted a *gotong-rojong* cabinet in early 1957, this *might* have left the parties in a better position to defend the party system than they were after a cabinet had been appointed by Soekarno. D. N. Aidit, chairman of the PKI, later claimed that his party did all it could to ensure a party-based cabinet, indicating his awareness of the issues involved.[1] But the implacable opposition of Masjumi and NU to the PKI blinded them to the necessity of defending party control of the Government. For them — and also for a growing number of PNI followers — the PKI itself became the central issue of politics. From another point of view, the support which the PNI, the PKI, and, to a lesser degree, NU initially gave to Guided Democracy — once Soekarno had dropped the proposal that parties be abolished — was ambiguous. Such public support actually represented approval of Djakarta's side in the regional crisis and, to some extent, of the Kabinet Karya and Soekarno himself, but certainly not of the anti-parliamentarism inherent in the ideas of Guided Democracy. In 1958, the PNI, the PKI, and NU were to be without any defense against the charge of hypocrisy when the National Council began to fill in the details of Guided Democracy, for then they had no choice but to oppose it. Similarly, the PKI approved the proclamation of martial law in 1957, despite the anti-Communist sentiments of the officer corps, because this was regarded as a Djakarta initiative against the regional councils — whose destruction had top priority with the PKI — and because it would bring the two main opponents of the PKI, the army and Masjumi, into conflict.[2]

The saga of Guided Democracy thus embraced several distinct but related battles; its development must be seen in the light of kaleidoscopically changing conflict situations, in which assessments of political interest necessarily influence relative positions on other battle fronts — particularly in the confrontation between the parties and anti-party forces. The latter, Soekarno and the officer corps, also suffered increasingly divisive tensions which were only partly submerged in 1957 by their common cause against the regional challenge.

This is not to say that there were no differences in the commitments of men to democratic or authoritarian institutions, though the differences were not so great as they are sometimes portrayed as being. The question was much less one of commitment, however, than of political interest — admitting that the distinction between political interest and political

---

1   *Harian Rakjat* (PKI daily), April 8, 1957.
2   *Harian Rakjat*, March 15, 1957.

commitment is not always easily drawn. Whether or not the PNI, the PKI, and NU were dedicated to democratic institutions — and there is little evidence that they were — they unquestionably had an interest in maintaining parliamentary institutions. As parties, they had nothing to gain from a party-less state, nor from one in which parties enjoyed no authority. Beyond the basic issues of conflict in 1957, therefore, most political parties — except those, like Murba, which had fully allied themselves with Soekarno — responded alike to threats against the party system. But they were unable to respond together.

Inter-party conflict will be discussed in the next chapter. This chapter is concerned with the anti-party allies and their role in developing Guided Democracy during 1957 and 1958. The discussion will touch, though in no great detail, on the appeals of Guided Democracy which Soekarno articulated and on the growing political role of the army.

Soekarno and Guided Democracy

The political changes begun in 1957 were made possible by the power of the army; but it was Soekarno who provided the symbols which made Guided Democracy seem a reasonable and necessary alternative to the parliamentary system. He was himself a major national symbol, particularly for the Javanese, towards whom men would look to identify the state — or if not the state, the political community. He possessed two great advantages over his opponents — his effective political personality and his well known oratorical ability. To these, the presidency added the authority not only of office but also of the palace (*istana*), previously occupied by the colonial governor-general and itself a source, like the older Javanese kingly *kratons* (palaces), of enormous, even mystical, power; Soekarno used the traditional symbols and attributes of this authority very effectively. The president had played a sporadic part in politics since the revolution; but in the development of Guided Democracy he became a political pivot, never possessing an effective organization of his own but depending on the manipulability of natural political balances to enhance his power as an extremely active buffer.

A shrewd, charming, and energetic man — admired for those qualities by friends and enemies alike — Soekarno appears to be the archetype of the pure politician, far more interested in power and leadership than in particular policy goals and broad objectives. (This is a frequent enough phenomenon that one is tempted to call it culturally Javanese, deriving from a conception of leadership in which it is sufficient to symbolize the community without further organizing or changing it. It is also true, however, that the peculiar diffuseness of political power in Indonesia — as in many of the ancient Javanese kingdoms as well — leaves the government without adequate strength to pursue predetermined goals, so that the practice of politics as a vocation alone is both less demanding and more necessary for survival than the attempt to use political power for policy purposes.) It is often very difficult to assess Soekarno's motives, for despite his outgoing character he plays a cautious and solitary political game; he has no permanent and intimate political friends or confidants.

Soekarno is familiar with ideas from innumerable sources, both European and Asian, which he has always been fond of quoting at length — as, for instance, in "Indonesia Accuses," his defense before the colonial court in 1930. Yet one cannot easily pinpoint the intellectual influences on him. Frequently he speaks the language of the early Marxists and insists that Marxism is a basic element in his thinking, as is the case with most Indonesian intellectuals who participated in the pre-war nationalist movements. But a careful reading of his many speeches brings to light little evidence to show that he has in fact been deeply affected by Marxist analysis, even though he may rely on its terminology.[3] Since the 1920's and 1930's, the ideas which he has emphasized have been remarkably

---

3   For Soekarno's early views, see especially his defense in 1930, *Indonesia Menggugat*, and *Mentjapai Indonesia Merdeka* (Towards a Free Indonesia) written in jail in 1933 and often reprinted by the Ministry of Information in recent years.
Soekarno seems most inclined to use Marxian analysis with respect to the development of colonialism. But in dealing with post-colonial Indonesia, he leaves Marxism behind in favor of a mixture of modern and traditional ideas, frequently of powerful symbolic significance. For a good example of his use of Marxism, see Soekarno's speech for the 30th anniversary of the PNI on July 3, 1957, translated by Claire Holt, *Marhaen and Proletarian* (Ithaca, N. Y.: Cornell Modern Indonesia Project, Translation Series, 1960). This speech contains ample indication that Marxism is not the controlling strain in Soekarno's thought.
For further comment on Soekarno, see George McT. Kahin, "Indonesia" in Kahin, ed., *Major Governments of Asia* (Ithaca, N. Y.: Cornell University Press, 2nd ed., 1963), pp. 601-604; also, Leslie H. Palmier, "Sukarno, The Nationalist," *Pacific Affairs*, XXX, no. 2 (June, 1957), 101-120; John Koe, "Sukarno: An Examination of a Charismatic Leader in a Non-Western Society," *The Indian Journal of Political Science*, XXIV, no. 1 (Jan.-March, 1963), 33-50; J. M. van der Kroef, "Sukarno and Hatta: The Great Debate in Indonesia," *The Political Quarterly*, XXIX, no. 3 (July-Sept. 1958), 238-251.

consistent: the themes of anti-imperialism, anti-colonialism, national unity, mass organization, and reliance on Indonesian traditions appear again and again, though without further development over the years. Never having studied abroad in his youth — he took his engineering degree in Bandung — he seems much less influenced by Europe than many of his contemporaries who did go to Holland. Like most of the Javanese elite, he is culturally proud; and though he often demands social, political, and economic change — to which the whole twentieth century nationalist struggle was explicitly dedicated — perhaps he is not truly convinced that much in Java ought to be different.

Although practical and skillful in daily politics, Soekarno is romantic, almost Utopian, in his ideas. He is capable of tremendous abstract anger against historical wrongs, as he sees them — colonialism is one obvious and understandable example, "liberalism" another — an anger which is maintained both out of personal feeling and for its usefulness as a national rallying point. As Feith has emphasized, Soekarno has always been politically concerned mainly with national unity, consensus, and solidarity, and he takes seriously the need to produce a constant flow of unifying symbols. By temperament he is radical and adventurous, virtues which he often proclaims and which he insists Indonesia as a nation must substitute for the submissive psychology he believes was left over from the colonial period.

Soekarno is profoundly ideologically inclined, but without a fully developed and effective ideology. The five-point Pantjasila, which Soekarno delivered in 1945, was at once an effort towards unity and political compromise (with Islamic groups) and a statement of attractive ideals attesting to his own humanistic sentiments and ability to synthesize; but it was not a social analysis or a plan of political, social, and economic organization and action. He has always sought to lead the whole people. Long associated with the PNI, where his oldest political friends were, he pulled away from that party in the mid-1950's because it was insufficiently radical, popular, and mass-based. Soekarno wanted to lead the "revolutionary" forces of Indonesia — forces of momentous change in the abstract — a movement without precise aim. Thus, at its initiation Guided Democracy was less an idea than a protest. Soekarno's ideas had got no further than a desire for a political transformation, which he should direct, and an inclination towards a more "Indonesian" political system, whose details could be left to future negotiation.

In his attack on the existing political system beginning in 1956, Soekarno assumed the role of spokesman for every strand of dissatisfaction with national conditions. He dissociated himself from the entire post-war history of political parties and challenged the very basis of parliamentary government. In the debate that developed in 1957 his antagonists were primarily Hatta, Masjumi, the PSI, Christian parties, and independent moderates; the PNI and PKI remained silent so long as no concrete measures were threatened against the political parties. The arguments in defense of democracy will not be discussed here; they were mainly traditional arguments — the need for a legal opposition, freedom, liberty, pluralism, and the iniquity of dictatorship.[4] Soekarno expatiated on quite different themes; but as well as his ideas his sense of timing was important, for his words exactly matched the heart of Indonesia's mood after half a decade of independence. He had said many of the same things before, but in the mid-1950's Indonesia was more receptive; and Soekarno began to drive his points home.

The national temper to which Soekarno addressed himself was one of deep malaise, a dissatisfaction with the results of independence but with no particular direction and no obvious resolution. Adam Ulam has analyzed the appeals of Communism to societies in transition from agrarianism to industrialism partly in terms of the anarchist protest that arises in the incipient transformation.[5] Indonesia was not yet in transition to industrialism, but it suffered similar symptoms, and in many ways the mood of the country had become anarchic. Whatever stability, security, and social certainty had existed in the past was disappearing after the revolution, but the promises of a new post-revolutionary society were as

---

4   See, for example, the article by Masjumi general chairman, Moh. Natsir, in *Abadi*, March 1 and 4, 1957. Having clearly restated democratic principles, Natsir turned abruptly and called for obliteration of the PKI.

5   Adam Ulam, *The Unfinished Revolution* (New York: Random House, 1960): "Marxism inherited the most rigid expression of early liberal materialism, but supplanted it with a Hegelian methodology that weakened the earlier bias toward individualism and, paradoxically, with an anarchist protest against materialism and industrialism. Hence Marxism has been able to appeal to both the grievances and the aspirations of a society in the process of transition, whereas liberalism appeals to the society that has forgotten both nostalgia for the past and excessively Utopian visions of the industrial future" (pp. 288-299).

yet unfulfilled.[6] Instead the revolution was followed by a pervasive struggle for power, felt at nearly every level of society. Competing and confusing political symbols invaded the villages and urban *kampongs*. Thrown together in the new state, without any foreign power to act as a buffer between them, hostile ethnic groups came into often violent conflict. At the same time, economic processes began to show signs of break-down. Corruption seemed appallingly widespread, and bureaucratic unconcern was oppressive. Social tensions found expression, as always, in anti-Chinese activities. New religious sects mushroomed.[7] And tough and lawless youth groups roamed the cities; in Djakarta some of these who had fought in the revolution rallied to Soekarno in 1956-1957, devoting themselves to harrassing his opposition. Political parties, most of them closed cliques at the top, offered little leadership; Parliament seemed to spend its time in eternally hopeless bickering. Groups to whom the revolution had given hope of active participation now resented their being shunted aside in the independent state.

Possibly the PKI's rise after 1952, as an out-group sharing no responsibility for the situation, was partly attributable to its riding the wave of these tensions among the poor peasantry and urban labor. But Soekarno was riding precisely the same wave after 1956. With a cultural depth which the Communists were hard put to match, he spoke to the grievances of a traditionally-inclined people by glorifying tradition — even as he attacked some of its social characteristics, such as "feudalism" — and portraying its restoration in a future Utopia.

Soekarno attacked, for example, the alien ways which Indonesia had adopted, thereby giving direction to the general discontent by focussing it on the political system and on ideas taken over from the imperialist West,

---

6 Curiously, the colonial period is often referred to in lower class Indonesia as *djaman normal* — the normal period. The origins of the phrase are unclear, but it expresses a consciousness that security and calm (*tenang*) times have disappeared, giving way to times that are decidedly not calm. In a more abstract sense, *djaman normal* sometimes expresses the hope for a Utopian future. That the symptoms of social transition may exist without industrialization is an obvious point. Urbanization proceeds apace without factories to attract people from the villages; rather, it is population growth that forces people from the land. General economic decline brings with it social misery. Politics enters the villages and urban *kampongs* via political party competition, adding to the new tensions.

7 Herbert Feith, *The Decline of Constitutional Democracy in Indonesia* (Ithaca, N. Y.: Cornell University Press, 1962), p. 509; Justus M. van der Kroef, "New Religious Sects in Java," *Far Eastern Survey*, XXX, no. 2 (Feb. 1961).

the very source of Indonesia's anguish. Attacking liberalism, conceived largely in nineteenth century terms, as the Western import to blame for both the party system and an individualistic economy — which Hatta also condemned — Soekarno stressed two themes in particular that had deep meaning for many to whom he spoke. One was the constant political, economic, social, and psychological strife which, though in fact endemic, liberal democracy was damned as having introduced. The continual tensions between Parliament and Cabinet had always brought down Governments before they could accomplish anything; the idea that a loyal opposition was necessary had led to simple obstructionism. At another level, the nation as a whole was divided into a thousand selfish factions. From any point of view this fissility was discomfiting and debilitating. Possibly it was even more so for most Indonesians, particularly Javanese, for whom conflict, though recognized as inevitable, is not perceived as productive; it is upsetting in a world-view that prefers unity, harmony, and esthetic balance in the relationships of all things. Soekarno insisted that conflict and contradiction must be eliminated from the government and from society. Unity, he demanded, must be restored and maintained, "dualisms" of various kinds weeded out, opposition replaced with a harmonious search for consensus.

The second, and related, theme was the return to Indonesia's own identity. The existing political system, according to Soekarno, was nothing more than a copy of something that might work in Europe — though even this he occasionally doubted in his attack on liberalism — but not in Indonesia, which must create its own system. *Gotong-rojong, musjawarah,* and *mufakat* were the traditional ways of Indonesia, he argued, not the rule of the 50% plus one majority.[8] Ignoring these traditions, said Soekarno, had contributed to Indonesia's adversity; in his Konsepsi speech he appealed to the nation to return to them: "Ah, what is freedom, my friends. I've always

---

8   In March 1956, Soekarno had appealed to the first session of Parliament after the 1955 elections not to rely on 50 per cent plus 1 democracy. See Feith, *Decline of Constitutional Democracy,* p. 515. Hatta objected, in his last speech before resigning the vice-presidency, that decisions by *mufakat* (consensus) were not possible in Parliament: "Here, like it or not, we must accept the Western system of democracy — i.e., making decisions by majority rule"; speech of Nov. 27, 1956, at Gadjah Mada University, *Lampau dan Datang* (Djakarta: Penerbit Djambatan, 1957), p. 45. This speech has been translated as *Past and Future* (Ithaca, N. Y.: Cornell Modern Indonesia Project, Translation Series, 1960).

said that freedom means to return to one's individual character. Let us return to our own character; who cares if foreigners say this or that. Who cares if foreigners say 'this system is wrong.' Let them. But the system is right (*tjotjok*) for the Indonesian soul."[9]

With this appeal, Soekarno touched a very tender spot. The political elite was uncomfortably sensitive to the judgment of the world — particularly the Western world, whose social and political standards it sometimes imitated indiscriminately. This sensitivity was a basic element in the much talked about inferiority complex of Indonesian leaders, the result partly of Dutch tutelage and numerous other cultural and historical factors. What Soekarno demanded, in effect, was that Indonesians be proud of their own heritage and to hell with the rest of the world, a notion which for some was truly liberating. In order to become a great nation, Indonesia must become confident, courageous, and assertive; Soekarno appealed to the *ksatria* strain in Java, insisting that to look up to others who were outside the circle was shameful. He also condemned the imports of foreign culture (rock and roll dancing, for one) and pointed accusingly at how Indonesia's youth had been led astray from their own rich culture.[10] If he did not make much impression on the younger generation of the urban elite in this respect, he did among the older people, whose sensitivities were offended by the inevitable relaxation in social standards and morals that accompanied the post-revolutionary plunge into the fast-moving world of the 1950's.

While calling for a purely Indonesian political system, however, Soekarno also offered the elite an alternative source of international approval. If Western Europe favored parliamentary systems, the great nations of Soviet Russia and the People's Republic of China successfully used another system — and this had nothing to do with the ideology involved. Soekarno tried to overcome the implicit anti-Eastern bias of highly educated leaders whose uneasy orientation was to Western Europe; at the same time, he made less educated nationalists aware of clear alternatives to the existing political order.

---

9 Speech of Feb. 21, 1957, in Ministry of Information, *Dewan Nasional*, p. 35.

10 See his Independence Day address, Aug. 17, 1957, in the collection of Soekarno's August 17th speeches from 1945 through 1961, *Dari Proklamasi sampai Resopim* (Ministry of Information), p. 324.

Another theme that Soekarno played upon was that of revolution, which became his own symbol in contrast with the staid conservatism of Hatta. The advantage which Soekarno had in the political temper of the time is evident. The revolution was modern Indonesia's hour of glory — a time too of anarchic moods, as are all revolutions. It was a reference point for many, close enough in time for everyone to remember exictedly and for all to want to share in the prestige of having participated. Those whose roles in it had been important forever reminded their public of the fact; those who had played insignificant parts invented new and more spectacular versions of them. When compared with the years of independence, the revolution seemed more glorious stilly and it was recalled in increasingly romantic terms for its expression of great ideals, sacrifice, and national unity. The "Spirit of the Proclamation of 45" became a popular symbol for these feelings.[11] Exciting the fascination of men with the revolution, Soekarno demanded its resuscitation and continuation in terms well suited to a period of political dissatisfaction. Everything, he declared time and time again, must be torn down and rebuilt; a revolution was *umwertung aller werte*.[12]

In recalling the revolution, Soekarno also tacitly recalled the political differences and tensions of those years: for example, the division, usually oversimplified, between those who had been willing at times to negotiate

---

11 In early 1958, the National Council undertook to interpret the Independence Proclamation of August 1945. Soekarno reported the result in his August 17th address of 1958: "1) The Proclamation of 17 August 1945 is the summit of the Indonesian people's centuries long struggle, with sacrifice of property, blood, and life, to build their unity and to seize their national independence from the hands of the colonialists. 2) The Proclamation of 17 August 1945 is the lighthouse that illuminates and points out the path of history, the giver of inspiration and of eternal strength in the struggle of the Indonesian people and nation in all fields and in every situation. 3) The Proclamation of 17 August 1945 is a treasury of mental virtues and the best ideals collected by Indonesian authors, leaders, and people, who in carrying out the revolution continually equipped themselves with new national virtue, thus giving shape to the Indonesian identity which determined the emergence of the State" (*Dari Proklamasi sampai Resopim*, p. 359). The actual text of the Proclamation of Independence is singularly brief, unromantic, and businesslike.

12 Speech of June 9, 1957, to military and civilian officials in Serang, West Java, entitled "Revolusi — Umwertung aller Werte," in *Dewan Nasional*, pp. 37-56. Hatta used the same phrase to describe revolution, but said that because of it revolutions must end quickly. "Those who say that our national revolution is not yet finished [as Soekarno constantly did] are making a big mistake. A revolution is a sudden explosion of society, which carries out an 'umwertung aller Werte.' Revolutions shake the floor and the foundation...For that reason a time of revolution cannot go on too long, not more than several weeks or months. After that they must be restrained; the time comes for consolidation, to realize the fruits of the revolution" (Speech of Nov. 27, 1956, Djambatan edition, p. 55).

with the Dutch and those who had wanted to fight on for unconditional victory.[13] Soekarno, whose role late in the revolution had been in many ways less prominent than Hatta's, retrospectively identified with the uncompromising diehard group. His encouragement of Chaerul Saleh — who had organized a "bamboo spear" group in West Java during the revolution to oppose a soft Republican policy towards the Dutch — and the Murba leaders after 1956 was in a sense a measure of his own return to the revolution.[14] Those who were supposed to have taken the "moderate" stand during the revolution (and included among those, often quite incorrectly, were some leaders of Masjumi and the PSI) stood condemned by the radical view. Incomparably more delicate was the position of those men who, for one reason or another, had crossed over the lines to work for the Dutch-sponsored federal states.

The renewed call to revolution evoked an enthusiastic response from army officers. In fact, the army was a primary impetus behind the idea of the ongoing revolution, and this made it even more necessary for Soekarno to establish his own claims to revolutionary symbols. For the army was born in the war of independence, which many officers remembered as the time of their greatest glory. To revive the revolution was to restore the army to its heritage. Numerous officers, including Nasution himself, had felt cheated of the opportunity to drive the Dutch out by force of arms, and they remained angry at what they regarded as civilian perfidy.[15] It was they who insisted most fiercely that all who had cooperated with the Dutch must be ejected from the government. And in general it was also

---

13 On politics late in the revolution, see George McT. Kahin, *Nationalism and Revolution in Indonesia* (Ithaca, N.Y.: Cornell University Press, 1952), *passim*.

14 It has been mentioned that men associated with Murba considered themselves followers of the ex-Communist and revolutionary thinker, Tan Malaka, whose fascinating life ended during the revolution. Tan Malaka had once challenged Soekarno's leadership of the revolution; yet he represented an orientation to which Soekarno was sympathetic. One might speculate that Soekarno's turn to the Murba group — for its psychology rather than its power — also symbolized an effort to merge in himself the spirit of two great revolutionary leaders, Soekarno and Tan Malaka.

15 On the reluctance of army officers to give up the fight in favor of a negotiated settlement, see Maj. Gen. T. B. Simatupang, *Laporan dari Benaran* (Report from Benaran; Djakarta: Pembangunan, 1960), p. 139. Simatupang, a Sumatran intellectual usually associated with the PSI, was Chief-of-Staff of the armed forces in the early years of independence until the position was abolished in late 1953, partly as an after-effect of the October 17th affair. Thereafter, he continued to write on problems of military development. See also on the army and the revolution, *The History of the Armed Forces of the Republic of Indonesia* (Ministry of Information, 1960?).

the leadership of the army who first sought in the revolution answers to the perplexing questions of independence. Revolutionary symbols provided the army elite with the ideological satisfaction which it lacked as a non-ideological group; as the army became politically more involved, from 1957 onwards, those symbols became more important to it.[16]

One significant, and rather negative, symbol from the revolution was used by Soekarno with considerable effect as a double barrelled attack on the political parties and Hatta.[17]

The President asserted that he had had nothing to do with creating political parties:

> On the matter of parties…I am not responsible. I wash my hands of all wrong, because it wasn't I who ordered the existence of parties. Not I. In November 1945, a decree was issued to establish parties. Thank God, it wasn't Soekarno who signed that decree.[18]

---

16 The essentially non-ideological character of the army was reflected in the early attempts of army leaders to create specific sets of principles — for example, the seven point statement of duties and purposes of the army — the *Saptamarga* — which would serve to unify and identify the army. See *The Identity of the T.N.I.* (Tentara Nasional Indonesia, Indonesian National Army) published by the army information service in 1960(?). In national ideological terms, however, the army was dedicated to the Pantjasila.

17 It should be emphasized that Soekarno and Hatta, who seem to have had at least a rhetorical influence on one another during their debate — a bitter one without names — were both saying much the same thing about the political system after mid-1956. Both spoke in glowing terms of the Indonesian heritage, collectivism, the social conscience and social justice of the Pantjasila, which ideals the parties had raped, siring the bastards of particularism and individualism. See especially Hatta's Nov. 27, 1956, speech. Thereafter they diverged, the jacobin Soekarno advising devastation of the political system and its replacement, the conservative Hatta calling for preservation of parliamentary government and its improvement. But both demanded reform, one in more extreme terms than the other, both equally idealistic in the heat of the argument. Their debate was influenced as well by mutual dislike, distrust, and fear — shared by their respective supporters — and by concern for the eventual shape of the political system. Lashing out at one another's ideas, they were also striking at one another personally. Soekarno, for example, was accused of wanting a dictatorship by the opponents of Guided Democracy, a charge which he denied vehemently. In June, Hatta gave a speech before the alumni of the University of Indonesia in which he said that dictatorships were at times useful in history to encourage the growth of new forces to lead transitional traditional societies responsibly. But such dictatorships, he said, "can only be run well and safely by a man with high moral standards, with courage to act and to accept responsibility, and with extraordinary ability to organize and administer — an organizer." He went on to say that such men are rare and therefore dictatorships must always give way quickly to democracies. The qualities he demanded of a dictator, however, were precisely those which many Indonesian leaders believed Soekarno lacked and Hatta possessed. See *Tanggung Djawab Moril Kaum Intelligensia* (The Moral Responsibility of the Intellectual Elite; Djakarta: Penerbit Fasco, n.d.), speech of June 11, 1957, pp. 18-20.

18 Speech of June 9, 1957, in Serang, *Dewan Nasional*, P. 44.

Hatta had signed it.[19] Every attack thereafter on the parties and on the Decree of November 3rd, 1945, implied an attack on Hatta.

Soekarno also drew upon the struggle for independence to indict the political parties for deviating from the true ideals of Indonesian nationalism. At the PNI anniversary celebration in July 1957, he pointedly asked the party members to compare themselves with the young and dedicated nationalists they had been in 1927, when the original PNI was founded under his leadership. He reminded them of their early agreement that mass action was the key to the nationalist movements.[20] How far those ideals had been left behind was obvious; except for the PKI, all the parties remained — as they had originated — as essentially elite groups enjoying little contact with the millions whom they were supposed to represent. The revolution, said Soekarno elsewhere, indeed the entire nationalist movement, was "for the people"; but the parties did not represent the people, not did Parliament, and therefore nor did the cabinet.

It was to serve the function of representing the people that the National Council was formed. The reasoning behind this claim was indicative of some basic tendencies in Guided Democracy. Because the first general elections had failed to satisfy national aspirations, Soekarno — and many others — denied the validity of those elections as a source of popular legitimacy. But Soekarno's own appeal, unlike that of the parties, was unquestioned; even his enemies paid it their respect. This popular appeal was itself legitimate, and it lent legitimacy to the Government behind which Soekarno stood. In the later development of Guided Democracy this was a central consideration. For beneath the surface appeals to such notions as *gotong-rojong* and *musjawarah-mufakat*, which had very little real significance for the style of national politics, there was also a more subtle and implicit appeal to traditional sources of legitimate authority, which the political system fell back on as soon as the novel forms — elections — began to collapse.

---

19 For the Decree of Nov. 3, 1945, see Koesnodiprodjo, *Himpunan Undang2, Peraturan2, Penetapan2, Pemerintah Republik Indonesia* (Compilation of the Laws, Regulations, and Decrees of the Government of the Republic of Indonesia), vol. for 1945, p. 76. The decree proposed the rapid establishment of political parties before the beginning of 1946. For the background of the November 3rd decree, see Kahin, *Nationalism and Revolution*, pp. 147 ff.
20 Marhaen and Proletarian, passim.

When Soekarno turned from the failures of the old system to the expectations of the new one, the picture became much more cloudy. Having addressed himself to such problems as the lack of singleness of purpose, national disunity, social upset bordering on anarchy, cultural disintegration, and the declining authority of political leadership, Soekarno outlined the restorative powers of Guided Democracy in terms that indicated a great deal of political work would be needed to flesh out the future system. The National Council, he explained, was only a beginning, necessary to bridge the gap between the people and the Government. Conflict would eventually be eliminated; there would be no institutional opposition. Strong and unified leadership would stimulate and direct national economic progress. The main objective of Guided Democracy, according to Soekarno, was a just and prosperous society, to be achieved through planning — a Guided Economy, as it came to be called.

But what would be the structure of Guided Democracy? The demands of Soekarno's opponents for a clearer view of the government he wished to create were never satisfied, because Soekarno himself was uncertain and, also, because his aims were severely limited by what he believed to be practicably attainable.

As well as introducing functional groups, Soekarno indicated in 1957 that he would prefer a single mass party to lead the state. This was a longtime predilection. In August 1945, the Preparatory Committee for Indonesian Independence, under Soekarno's leadership, had agreed to establish a single Partai Nasional Indonesia, but the idea never got beyond the paper stage and was succeeded shortly by the introduction of the multi-party system, encouraged, for a number of reasons, by the revolutionary Government.[21] Soekarno's interest in single party systems was apparently stimulated again during his trip in 1956 to the Soviet Union and China. In June 1957 he described his view of Soviet practice to a group of military and civilian officials in Madiun:

> ...the decree to establish parties, thank God, did not come from me. But — well — what can you do? It's too late...Now there are

---

21 See Kahin, *Nationalism and Revolution*, pp. 147 ff; Benedict R. O'G. Anderson, *Some Aspects of Indonesian Politics Under the Japanese Occupation; 1944-1945* (Ithaca, N.Y.: Cornell Modern Indonesia Project, Interim Report Series, 1961), pp. 109-112.

many big parties and small parties. In other countries the situation is different. There it is easy to bring about [social and economic] change. In the Soviet Union for example...there is only one party! Change is easy there. [Soekarno then describes the Soviet government.]

Thus the ministers in the Soviet Union are a "distillation," — the people are distilled to form the Supreme Soviet, the Supreme Soviet is distilled to form the Presidium, the Presidium is distilled to form the Government. So there is always a straight line between the government and the people. Consequently all development there runs smoothly...What the ministers determine is in fact distilled from the people, and what is ordered by the ministers penetrates to the common people.

But not here, my friends, or in parliamentary democracy as in the Western world; no, no, the system is different...all the more so what is called constitutional parliamentary democracy.[22]

Soekarno also dwelt on the advantages of Nehru's Congress and U Nu's AFPFL. But in 1957 he did not propose to create a new single state party. Nor did he insist, as he had in 1956, that all political parties ought to be abolished; on the contrary, he said later that it would be difficult to eliminate the parties.[23] The gap between what Soekarno may have desired and what it was politically possible to achieve was too great. In 1957 the situation was not ripe for replacing the parties; and it never became so. Political conditions were too much in flux to risk the additional upheaval which an attempt to get rid of the parties would cause. If the army undertook the job, it would inevitably take control of the entire country,

---

22 Speech in Madium on June 19, 1957, *Dewan Nasional*, pp. 72-73.
23 On occasions Soekarno said that he had intended the abolition proposal in 1956 only as shock therapy for the parties. At other times, he said that this was the first in a series of moves intended to reform the political system. The second move was the Konsepsi, with the *gotong-rojong* cabinet proposal. This having failed to gain acceptance by the anti-Communist parties, he retreated yet another step and established the Kabinet Karya and the National Council. See speech by Roeslan Abdulgani at the Pantjasila Seminar in February 1959, *Seminar Pantjasila ke-I* (Jogjakarta: Seminar Committee, 1959), pp. 149-150.

a possibility against which Soekarno was on constant guard. Moreover, there was as yet no real alternative to the parties; no organization existed, amenable to the President's control, that could assume the role of a national mass organization. When such a body was established — the National Front for the Liberation of West Irian — it was led by the army and therefore hardly useful to Soekarno.

Having no organization of his own through which to exert political control, Soekarno therefore wanted institutional change to proceed at a moderate and controllable pace. In spite of his surface radicalism, he continually insisted that Indonesia's new political system would be created by constitutional means; and he appealed to the Constituent Assembly to draft a constitution incorporating the ideas of Guided Democracy.[24] Soekarno justified the National Council partly as an experiment for the Constituent Assembly to take into consideration. In view of his prolonged assault on the party system, the specific proposals he made in 1957 for its modification were quite moderate; one, for example, was to adopt a law, similar to West German practice, eliminating parties which failed to win the support of at least five per cent of the electorate.

The National Council spent little time in 1957 discussing Guided Democracy — primarily because of the pressing regional situation. One highlight, however, was a lecture to the Council in October by Professor Djokosoetono, the highly respected Dean of the University of Indonesia Faculty of Law. Djokosoetono offered a political analysis suggesting that real authority had shifted from the parties to President Soekarno, in whose hands therefore now rested the ability to determine policy and to bring about further change in the political system. He also presented a learned discourse on the theory, origins, and practice of functional representation elsewhere in the world. But Professor Djokosoetono made no proposals that the Council took up at this time, and his talk appears to have received scant attention.

The Army and Martial Law

Though it was not always evident, because of the dominating figure of

---

24 See his August 17th address, *Dari Proklamasi sampai Resopim*, pp. 332-333.

Soekarno, the main driving force behind Guided Democracy was the army. Its officers were contemptuous of the old political system and most of its civilian leaders. They were angry at the confusion of political parties, the corruption, the ideological strife, the political instability, all of which they believed, in simplistic fashion, was to blame for the lack of progress in the country and for the divisions within the army and the nation. Nasution and many other officers sought a highly disciplined social order, a government undisturbed by parliamentary politics, and a reorganization of political activity down to a minimum of nationally unified and consolidated groups under the tight control and direction of a powerful governmental executive. These at least were a few elements in the thinking of politically conscious army leaders.[25]

But much more was involved in the army's quest for a new political system. The development of Guided Democracy also turned on a direct conflict of interest between the officer corps and the political parties: the army was trying to gain admission to the center of the political arena, while the parties were trying to save themselves from being removed from exactly that spot.

Martial law legalized the entry of the officer corps into the political life of the nation. The power of regional army authorities was greater than that of the national military administration, which in Djakarta

---

25 No attempt will be made here to undertake a full discussion of the development of the army, in either its military or its political aspects. A body of material is beginning to build up on the Indonesian army and on armies in the new states generally. For background, see Kahin, *Nationalism and Revolution*, and in *Major Governments of Asia*; Feith, *Decline of Constitutional Democracy*, and "Dynamics of Guided Democracy" in Ruth T. McVey, ed., *Indonesia* (New Haven: HRAF, 1963); Guy Pauker, "The Role of the Military in Indonesia," in J. J. Johnson, ed., *The Role of the Military in Underdeveloped Countries* (Princeton: Princeton University Press, 1963) and "The Role of Political Organizations in Indonesia," *Far Eastern Survey*, XXVII (Sept. 1958); Daniel S. Lev, "The Political Role of the Army in Indonesia," *Pacific Affairs*, XXXVI, no. 4 (Winter 1963-64). In Indonesian, see A. H. Nasution, *Tjatatan2 sekitar Politik Militer* (Djakarta: Pembimbing, 1955), an extremely important introduction to the army and to Indonesian politics since the revolution, and T. N. I. (Tentara Nasional Indonesia; Djakarta: Jajasan Pustaka Militer, 1956) on the revolutionary history of the army; T. B. Simatupang, *Pelopor dalam Perang, Pelopor dalam Damai* (Pioneer in War, Pioneer in Peace; Djakarta: Jajasan Pustaka Militer, 1954), *Soal-Soal Politik Militer di Indonesia* (Problems of Military Policy in Indonesia; Djakarta: Gaja Raja, 1956), and *Pemerintah, Masjarakat, Angkatan Perang* (Djakarta: Indira, 1961); see also *The History of the Armed Forces in Indonesia* (Ministry of Information, 1961). General works on the military role in the new states include S. Huntington, *Changing Patterns of Military Politics* (Glencoe: The Free Press, 1962); S. Andrzejewski, *Military Organization and Society* (London: Routledge, 1954); H. Daalder, *The Role of the Military in the Emerging Countries* ('s-Gravenhage: Mouton, 1962).

was subject to more restraining influences, but the army everywhere set out haphazardly to exercise maximum authority after March 1957. The emphasis of the General Staff was mainly political: Nasution called several conferences of martial law administrators in the first half of 1957 to deal not only with regional problems but also with army disunity, restoration of the Dwitunggal, and the establishment of the National Council.[26] In the regions, army commanders initially stressed economic development, promising the people of their territories that the army would now put things right.

The powers given to the army under the state of siege were extensive; even so they were often exceeded, for there was no authoritative civilian supervision. Nearly every civil office was subject to military control or the possibility of it. But although the administration of the country was therefore overcapped by a new authority, the army did not actually attempt to assume responsibility for running the state. Rather, army headquarters in the several provinces and in Djakarta intruded into parts of the administration, then stayed or withdrew as circumstances dictated. Offices of particular importance — those in charge of economic affairs in the provinces, for example — quickly came directly under army control. But the martial law administration was enabled to intervene anywhere and at any time it chose.

The result was a growing number of dysfunctions in the governance of the country. For the relationship between the new martial law administration and civil government was unclear, and there was little effective coordination of the two. In his capacity as Minister of Defense, Djuanda was formally responsible for the activities of the armed forces under martial law; but, although his relations with Nasution were good, his actual authority over the General Staff was limited and over the regional army almost non-existent. Military authorities were not reluctant to promulgate regulations — often in contradiction to existing laws — on every conceivable subject, from gambling to taxation.[27] Legal forms were

---

26 See *Madjalah Angkatan Darat* (Journal of the Army), VII, no. 4 (April 1957), 34-35, and 37; and no. 5 (May 1957), 36-40.
27 See, for example, *Himpunan Peraturan, Penetapan, Instruksi, Pengumuman dan Surat Keputusan* (Compilation of Regulations, Decrees, Instructions, Announcements, and Decisions) of the West Javanese martial law administration for the first six months of 1958. See also G. Kanahele, "The Role of the Military in Indonesia: 1957-1960" (unpublished paper, Cornell Modern Indonesia

not the army administration's strong point. Within weeks of the March proclamation, the army came under attack for causing confusion in the law, in the government, in economic affairs, and in numerous concerns of private citizens. Some groups expressed the suspicion that army leaders wanted to rule the country alone, which Nasution took pains to deny, and there was considerable misgiving in Parliament (and in the Cabinet) over the baffling lines of authority which arose when the martial law administration was superimposed on the civilian governmental structure.

Martial law was everywhere in evidence; and everywhere the novel oppressiveness of military control — albeit not always intentionally, consistently, or efficiently oppressive — contributed to the growing unpopularity of the army. But the state of siege did not affect all regions equally. The differences were related to the position of the army in each territory prior to March 1957 and to the character of the local civil administration. Where the army had been continually active in suppressing local rebellions or dacoity, regional commands were much stronger and more assertive under martial law than elsewhere. Thus in West Java, home of the Darul Islam, the army assumed greater authority than in Central or East Java.[28]

In the latter area, which had never suffered serious security problems, civil-military relations under martial law were the best in the country; the regional command, under Col. Sarbini, supported the widely respected governor of the province, Semadikoen, and was the source of more assistance than interference in local industry. Throughout Java, the army initially worked with and through the *pamong pradja*, which remained the effective administration over the island. In part this reflected not only the prestige of *pamong pradja* officials, but also a concurrence of

---

Project, 1962) and Daniel S. Lev, "State of Siege in Indonesia" (unpublished paper, Cornell Modern Indonesia Project, 1957).

28 The Siliwangi division of West Java was by far the best trained and equipped in the army, and as the first division formed during the revolution its *esprit de corps* was second to none. One of its commanders in the revolution was Nasution, who maintained a close personal relationship with it thereafter. Siliwangi was of prime political importance because its jurisdiction included the capital city until 1960, when a separate garrison and command was created in Djakarta primarily in order to reduce Siliwangi's control. Siliwangi officers had always been more politically minded than officers of the other divisions, because of their higher education, their revolutionary experience, and their continual operations against the ideological rebellion of the Darul Islam.

interest between the *pamong pradja* and the army, neither of which was sympathetic to the political parties or had any profound commitment to a parliamentary order.[29] Within two years, however, local army commands began to make their presence felt in the villages, a traditional sphere of influence of the *pamong pradja*, and the latter soon began to turn back to the parties for help.

In the outer islands, the army commands assumed authority in nearly every phase of civil administration far beyond anything known in Java. One obvious reason for this was that army leaders there were either at the helm of regional opposition to Djakarta — and indeed, had themselves proclaimed martial law in their areas — or else, in some non-dissident areas, were in a good position to take advantage of the critical situation (e.g., through smuggling activities). In addition, however, no administrative structure existed in the outer islands of comparable strength, organization, and authority to the *pamong pradja* in Java. In the outer islands the *pamong pradja* was an import from Java with few local roots, while the pre-war traditional political and social organization was shattered at the top levels. A potential vacuum of authority existed into which the army was rapidly drawn as soon as a crisis developed.[30]

The powers exercised by the regional army under martial law operated in a significant way to restructure the state. Already identified with their provinces, army commands hyper-actively and over-optimistically undertook to fulfill local demands for the economic development which civilian government had been unable to accomplish. Soon local officials and groups began to look to the powerful military to assist them or to serve as a shield against Djakarta policies considered damaging to local interests. Regional military headquarters gradually took it upon

29 There was a high degree of political compatibility between the *pamong pradja* and the army elite. The strength and sustenance of neither derived basically from the parliamentary system. Since the Japanese occupation, the *pamong pradja* had been in decline and was eventually to be eliminated altogether under the new decentralization law. *Pamong pradja* officials looked to the army for help to avoid abolition of their corps, and army leaders saw in the *pamong pradja* the unifying national administration they believed Indonesia must have. An alliance thus evolved. Before long Nasution began (in early 1958) to demand a reconsideration of the decentralization law (Law 1/1957) approved by Parliament in late 1956. The *pamong pradja* was in fact rescued and its position greatly strengthened by new regional administration laws in 1959, which served also to weaken the parties' hold on local government.

30 See Feith's stimulating discussion in "Dynamics of Guided Democracy," pp. 332-334.

themselves to decide which government regulations to apply, which to put aside, and which to alter in the application. Neither the Cabinet nor, for that matter, the General Staff was able to exercise full control over the regional martial law administrations. The result was that through the structure and authority of the army under martial law, a kind of *de facto* federal arrangement evolved. A true federal system, which outer island-based parties had demanded in the Constituent Assembly, was an emotional negative symbol for most national leaders, partly because the Dutch had sponsored a federal constitution during the revolution and because federalism was regarded as a threat to national unity. The irony of this aspect of martial law was that it worked to satisfy regional demands for local autonomy even as the regional crisis, one of the explicit bases of which was over-centralization, was coming to a head.

Apart from the structural consequences of martial law, its influence on the character of politics generally was profound. Civil liberties suffered enormously. Although it had not been unusual before, particularly in areas where local martial law had existed, arrests and long detentions without accusation or trial now became frequent. In most areas, military headquarters had no compunctions about taking men into custody on grounds of being a threat to security. Too often there was insufficient evidence to bring charges; sometimes those arrested were simply forgotten. Parliamentary protests did little to mitigate this problem. Along with other abuses of martial law powers, the constant possibility of arbitrary arrest laid a pall of fear over political activity that was to become worse as time went on.

A serious political blow was also struck at labor unions, the most important of which was the Communist-controlled SOBSI. Soon after martial law was proclaimed, regional army commands began to restrict union activity; strikes were forbidden in certain "vital industries," and in some areas the martial law administration assumed the function of labor arbitration. Unions were compelled to request permission of army authorities before undertaking labor actions of any sort. The PKI was the most hurt by these restrictions and openly protested them. In August 1957 a national military regulation forbidding strikes in all "vital industries" — which were to be designated by army headquarters — evoked an angry attack by the PKI that martial law was being used against working class interests.[31] The anti-Communist press, however, had praised earlier measures of similar import and called for further restrictions on SOBSI and the PKI.[32] Indeed, the non-Communist parties took increasing interest in the army as an anti-PKI weapon. But it was a weapon over which they had no control, and frequently it turned against them as well.

Press restrictions called forth protests from all sides. Army leaders in general regarded the press as provocative, divisive, sensationalist, and politically motivated.[33] No sooner had the state of siege begun than the martial law administration clamped down first on news reports concerning army affairs and then, increasingly, on nearly all other kinds of political reporting. Before long the daily press was suffering temporary closures, bans, and the arrest of journalists and editors. The Indonesian press had always been lively and vital, and journalists put up a continual and vigorous battle against all restrictions, but to no avail. Limitations on daily newspapers varied from region to region, but everywhere martial law damaged press freedom and morale. During the first two years of martial law, the press gradually became more silent on major political issues; editors resorted increasingly to the art of oblique statement in the effort to say something significant without being held criminally responsible.[34]

The direct challenge of martial law to the political parties became obvious almost before the ink was dry on the March proclamation. Both in Djakarta and in the provinces, the parties faced formidable restrictions on their activities. Political meetings were controlled, demonstrations curtailed, and organizational efforts blocked by military headquarters. Members of Parliament and of the regional legislative assemblies were arrested on various grounds. Parliament was permitted to convene, though some MPs had feared that it might not be, but in the regions military authorities sometimes ordered the legislative assemblies

---

31 *Persbiro Indonesia* (PIA), Aug. 28, 1957.

32 *Pedoman*, March 25, 1957.

33 For one comment on the press, see M. Istijarso, "Pers didalam Negara SOB" (The Press under Martial Law) in *Madjalah Angkatan Darat*, VII, no. 5 (May 1957), 4-6.

34 On press restrictions, see *Kronik Pers*, published by the Lembaga Pers dan Pendapat Umum (Press and Public Opinion Institute) in Jogjakarta, 1957 and 1958. See also Lev, "State of Siege in Indonesia."

to refrain from discussing "political" topics, and in a few instances the assemblies were forbidden to meet at all. At the same time, in an effort to "clean up" the country soon after martial law began, Nasution ordered a large-scale anti-corruption campaign that badly damaged the leadership circles of several parties. Personal bank accounts were made liable to examination in order to determine the origins of sizable holdings. In addition, many sources of party funds were co-opted by military headquarters as they established control over key government offices, especially in the regions. Only the Communists did not suffer from this diversion of funds and from the anti-corruption campaign, for the PKI did not depend on the government for funds and harbored few corruptors. But all the parties found themselves increasingly hemmed in by the hostile army.

Army leaders were more than negatively active in politics, however. The organizational efforts which they pursued beginning in June 1957 indicated that Nasution and several of his staff officers were aware of the political potential of martial law. In that month, the first Youth-Military Cooperation Body (Badan Kerdja Sama Pemuda Militer, BKS-PM) was established under the leadership of Lt. Col. Pamurahardjo, who later played a leading role in the take-over of Dutch firms. Following formation of the BKS-PM, several other civil-military cooperation bodies were formed during the next two years among labor and peasant organizations, women's groups, religious leaders, and others.[35] The cooperation bodies consisted of youth organizations most of which had political party ties, including the Pemuda Demokrat (PNI), GPII (Masjumi), Ansor (NU), Pemuda Rakjat (PKI), and more than two dozen other youth and student organizations belonging to various federations.[36]

Nasution's purpose in creating the cooperation bodies was to loosen the parties' grip on these "functional groupings" and to bring them instead under the army's wing. All the activities of the constituent organizations were to be channelled through the cooperation bodies,

---

35 For background on the several civil-military cooperation bodies, see *Karya Kerdja Sama Sipil-Militer: 25 Djuni 1958-6 Djuli 1959* (The Results of Civil-Military Cooperation: June 25, 1958-July 6, 1959) published in 1959 by the State Ministry for Civil-Military Cooperation Affairs, established in mid-1958.

36 See *Program Kerdja Sama Pemuda Militer* (Program of the Youth-Military Cooperation), published in 1958 by the BKS-PM.

which would exercise extensive control over them. The theoretical basis of the effort was the concept of territorial warfare, the basic doctrine of defense strategy to which Nasution had committed the army. Possibly originating in Japanese occupation ideas and undoubtedly influenced by revolutionary experience, territorial warfare, as Nasution explained it, was essentially a guerilla strategy in which each area of the country would be prepared to defend itself, independent of central direction, against outside attack. This would require not only proper logistics and tactics but also considerable social, economic, and political preparation, in which the army would necessarily assume the leading organizational role.[37] The political implications of the doctrine are obvious and, after 1957, tended to take precedence over its military significance. As for the civil-military cooperation bodies, they were justified as an attempt to unify the multifarious organizations then divided among the political parties in order to prevent further splintering of the nation.[38]

The effort was not successful. Most parties had willingly allowed their subsidiary organizations to join the cooperation bodies at first, but they quickly became aware of the danger of doing so. After a year's experience, the PKI declared that it would avoid further involvement in the cooperation bodies, and other parties were similarly inclined. Army leaders were never able to establish complete control over the various groups — partly because the officers designated to work with them were often politically incompetent — and the parties retained their hold on the constituent organizations. But the cooperation bodies remained a civil arm of the military, which never ceased its attempt to infiltrate the civilian polity. The one group over which the army was able to establish control was that of the veterans, due to the special relationship involved. Veterans of the revolutionary war had been organized under the political parties for several years. In 1957 and 1958 Nasution successfully undertook to dissolve all previously existing veterans' groups, which were then reorganized into a single Veterans' Legion supervised by the army. The protests of the parties — especially the PKI, which had a powerful veterans' organization — were ignored.

---

37 On territorial warfare, see Nasution, *Tjatatan2*, especially pp. 199-200, and *Perang Gerilja* (Guerrilla Warfare; Djakarta: Pembimbing, 1953), *passim*.
38 See *Karya Kerdja Sama Sipil-Militer*, p. 83.

Nasution's next step, after the initial formation of the cooperation bodies, was to attempt to create a larger and more comprehensive national organization under the army's aegis. Both Soekarno and army leaders were interested in establishing an all-inclusive national front which would eventually replace the political parties. But the problem was who should lead it and what should be its political orientation. Following the take-overs of late 1957, Nasution took the initiative in setting up a new organization that would assume responsibility for all further actions in connection with the West Irian campaign. Soekarno attempted to have this organization based on the People's Congress (Kongres Rakjat), an ephemeral body that had first met in 1955 and was considered to be distinctly on the political left, the PKI having played an important part in it after both the PNI and Masjumi (along with the PSI and Christian parties) had refused to participate.[39] Nasution side-stepped Soekarno's proposal, however, and in January 1958 succeeded in forming a National Front for the Liberation of West Irian (Front Nasional Pembebasan Irian Barat, FNPIB) based upon the civil-military cooperation bodies.[40] Thereafter Nasution tried to expand the FNPIB into a multi-branched national structure which would be able to compete with the parties for popular support. But its effectiveness was contained by the parties, which did everything possible to obstruct it, and by Soekarno, who gained influence in the FNPIB through several of its individual leaders. The FNPIB lasted until 1960, but as in the case of the cooperation bodies it never became an effective political organization; its leaders were politically inexperienced and, particularly in the regions, their occasional misuse of the body for the improper collection of funds quickly brought it into disrepute.

Meanwhile, by mid-1957 martial law, the formal basis of these army activities and the chief threat to the parliamentary system, became a prime target of the political parties. The army was under continual attack in the press from April onwards for its interference in political and economic affairs and for the numerous restraints imposed under martial law. The martial law statute itself was vulnerable because of its Netherlands East

---

39 On the Kongres Rakjat, see Feith, *Decline of Constitutional Democracy*, p. 408, n. 154. The Kongres Rakjat consisted of a core of the PKI, PSII, and Murba.

40 See *Karya Kerdja Sama Sipil-Militer*, pp. 110 ff, and Kanahele, "The Role of the Military in Indonesia," pp. 73-81, on the development of the FNPIB.

Indies origin; a frequent accusation was that the colonial law was being applied in free Indonesia much as it had been when the country was still a colony. A new statute had been under consideration since the early 1950'S, for the "state of war" then existing in several provinces, including all of Java since 1952, had provoked widespread agitation. But it was only in 1957, when civilian leaders were thoroughly shaken by the use to which the state of siege regulation was put by the now politically aggressive army leadership, that both the Government and Parliament considered it imperative to pass a new law. The Government introduced the new bill in June, and the debates, lasting intermittently until December, were among the hottest in Parliament's history, ranging over the entire question of the army's place in independent Indonesia. But the regional crisis gave army leaders the advantage in pressing the Government both for an extension of martial law and for a new statute which would provide the military with powers no less drastic than before.

Initially the Cabinet had requested a statute with four progressive levels of martial law. This the parties opposed vehemently, fearing that four stages would enable the Government to declare martial law on the least provocation and that it would be all too easy for the military to maintain it in force for a prolonged period merely by dropping down one level as a concession. Djuanda then offered a three-level statute, but this too was unacceptable to Parliament, which insisted upon a two-level progression, one giving the military extensive powers and the other maintaining the civilian government's authority. Under this scheme, once a serious crisis had passed, administrative authority would be transferred from the military to civilians; parliamentary control would be restored to some extent, even though the Government would still possess extraordinary powers under the less drastic stage of martial law. The Cabinet accepted the views of Parliament after informal talks in late 1957, and the new law passed in December incorporated only two martial law levels: a *keadaan darurat* (state of emergency) in which civil authority obtained, and a *keadaan perang* (state of war) in which the military held dominant authority.[41] Little was accomplished in the new law in the way

---

41 On the legislative history of the new martial law statute from the early 1950's onwards, see Jusmar Usman, "Sedjarah Perkembangan Pembentukan Undang2 Keadaan Bahaja 1957" (History of the Development of the State of Danger Law of 1957) mimeographed in 1958 by the University of

of clarifying military-civil relations under the *keadaan perang*, though a few articles were included whose purpose was to establish some control over the army's powers.

In practice the 1957 law gave the parties no relief. For the old state of siege now became the new style state of war, and the limitations on military authority put into the statute had almost no effect in restraining army officers; for example, regional martial law administrators were enjoined by the new law to establish collegial bodies, including some civilian officials, but these councils never became strong and in some areas they were never even created. Moreover, under its new name martial law was extended for a further full year until December 17, 1958. Thereafter the law of December 1957 became more a focus of interpretive attention than had ever been the case with the 1950 Constitution, which it largely supplanted.[42]

The army's rapidly increasing involvement in political affairs was accompanied by a plunge, from the diving board of martial law, into the warm waters of the economy. Officers became accustomed not only to the exercise of legitimate authority but also to its perquisites. Control of key administrative offices opened new vistas of wealth in the form of bribes and contacts with private (often Chinese) businessmen. This became a matter of concern for civilian opponents of martial law and for some army leaders themselves. The main event in the army's economic evolution was the seizure of Dutch firms in December 1957. Soon after the army took charge of the firms, a stream of surplus officers was fed into them. Those appointed to management positions within the companies were not the best officers; most were either ready for pension with nothing else to do or were men for whom the army did not have good use. Even the cream of the officer corps, however, would not have been well suited to manage

---

Indonesia Institute for Social Research; also, Djody Gondokusumo, foreword in Koesnodiprodjo, *Undang2 Keadaan Bahaja dengan Peraturan Pelaksanaannja* (The State of Danger Law and its Implementing Regulations- Djakarta: S. K. Seno, 1957), pp. 1-8.

42 See, for example, Erman, *Ichtisar Undang-Undang Keadaan Bahaja 1957* (Survey of the State of Danger Statute of 1957; Djakarta: Tantular, 1957); Koesnodiprodjo, *Peraturan Dasar S. O. B. dengan Peraturan Pelaksanaannja* (Basic Regulation on the State of War and Siege and Implementing Regulations; Djakarta, S. K. Seno, 1957) with supplement; Basarudin Nasution, *S. O. B.* (Djakarta: Fasco, 1957); Goenawan and Soedarto, *Undang-Undang Keadaan Bahaja 1957* (State of Danger Statute of 1957; Semarang: Kreshna, 1958). Numerous publications on martial law appeared from the Ministry of Information and the martial law administration itself.

the complicated affairs of the companies, whose decline may be attributed partly to the army's role in them.

Aside from this problem, however, the important point to be made here is that the officer corps had acquired an institutional foothold in the economy that it would not willingly relinquish. In late 1958 the large diversified firms (as well as the smaller ones) were nationalized and broken up into their component parts for distribution among several appropriate ministries. But before this could be accomplished, Nasution insisted that the companies remain a source of jobs for older army personnel about to be displaced by younger officers. At the same time, on August 30, 1958, he issued an order placing a large number of officers attached to the central martial law administration on the management boards of the former Dutch firms.[43] Only after the Government had agreed to these conditions were the companies allowed to pass from full army control. For a time army personnel in the companies remained under military discipline and sanctions, making it very difficult for civilian managers to supervise them. Eventually, however, growing pressure brought them under the same criminal and civil code provisions as other employees; but their connections with the army continued to be distinctly advantageous, both for those officers in the firms and for those outside.

It should be mentioned that, once ensconced in the economy, the array elite lined up with other groups that favored a thoroughgoing state economy. An element in the development of the Indonesian economy after 1957 is evident here, for only those groups and parties — like Masjumi and the NU — which represented some private commercial interests made any plea at all for the Dutch firms to be turned over to private hands. Apart from a strong ideological predilection for socialism inherent in the nationalist movement since the 1920's, there was also a natural impulse for groups grounded in the government to favor state ownership. And this meant not only the bureaucracy itself and those parties, like the PNI, closely related to the bureaucracy, but also the officer corps, which possessed no legitimate basis for individual commercial activity and had no appreciation of the private economy.

---

43 See the appendices to Djuanda's report to Parliament on the operation of martial law in December 1958, *Risalah Perundingan D. P. R.* (Parliamentary Debates), Dec. 1958, pp. 5145-5151.

Some of the points mentioned in the preceding pages are relevant to a discussion of the army's evolution as a political force. A comparison with other countries in Southeast Asia and elsewhere shows the Indonesian army to be peculiar as armies go in the new states. The most obvious distinction is that at no time did it seriously attempt to take over the state, though within a year or two the army's political involvement came to be called, by puzzled journalists, a "creeping coup d'état."

One reason for this was that most army leaders in fact had limited ambitions. They did not see themselves as permanently running the state and assuming full responsibility for its concerns. Politically they were not overly confident. Nasution himself had been burned in 1952 by his first confrontation with Soekarno and apparently feared a repeat performance.[44] But the likelihood of a coup did not depend on Nasution's views alone; it was influenced by the character of the officer corps as a whole. In many respects, Nasution was no more than *primus inter pares* within the top leadership of the army, and though he was highly regarded and often admired there were nevertheless serious restrictions on his ability to maneuver. He needed the support not only of the General Staff but also of the regional *panglimas*, whom Nasution tried constantly to cultivate. Far from being politically unified, however, the officer corps was badly divided on several crucial issues.

With admitted over-simplification, the officers might be classified as radicals and moderates. Despite their common sentiment that the army must play a significant role in the state, that civilian politicians must be restricted, and that the PKI ought to be eliminated, the officer corps enjoyed no consensus on two primary issues: the character of the army's role and the place of Soekarno. The "moderates," particularly the Javanese officers, were as loyal to Soekarno as most Javanese. Many outer island officers, on the other hand — including those who finally joined the PRRI — recognized Soekarno as a symbol of national unity but did not feel an emotional commitment to the man. Similarly, officers in the Javanese divisions believed that the army should serve as a driving force behind the civil administration rather than attempt to assume full responsibility

---

44 For indications of Nasution's high regard for Soekarno's strength as a popular leader and as a skilled politician, see *Tjatatan2, passim.* See also Feith's comments on Nasution's resumption of his position in 1955; *Decline of Constitutional Democracy*, pp. 440-444.

for administration and policy making; often they doubted their own ability to deal with difficult problems of policy in which they had no experience. In the outer islands, however, army leaders were much less impressed with the civilian regime, and this attitude was not balanced by a respect for the social superiority of the civilian elite, as was the case in Java. In part the reasons operative here were the same as those for the differing character of martial law in Java and the other islands. Yet it must be emphasized that there were vast differences between the outer island regions themselves in these respects, and moreover other — frequently personal — factors entered into the considerations of officers who did or did not incline to a coup. Thus, not even all of those who joined the PRRI believed that the army should try to rule the country by itself.

General Jani, one of the officers in charge of Sumatran operations against the PRRI in 1958 and a future Chief-of-Staff of the army, described the division of the officer corps before the rebellion as follows:

> One group of officers wanted a very quick change in the government [in 1956-1957], one that if necessary would go ahead without the President. This group ended up in the rebellion. The second group was more moderate, and it…is now the leadership of the army. This second group realized that there could be no very rapid change — i.e.; no military coup — and certainly not one that left out the President. These officers realized that the President was essential, that there was no other political leader with the influence of the president over the masses and over other political groups in the country.

> Also, this moderate group took the view that if the President were pushed aside, unity in the army would be endangered. Above all, the most important factor is army unity; it is essential to the nation and to the welfare of the army as a participant in the life of the nation.

> There was no unity in the army between these two major groups, and the moderates realized that a military coup would prevent unity from being achieved, since the differences between the two groups would then be thrown into stark relief.

The moderate group also feared…government by coup. Because there was no unity in the army, the first coup would eventually set off another coup by an opposing group and so on ad infinitum. This the moderate group wanted to prevent at all costs.[45]

Jani's analysis ignored the regional conflict itself, important generational differences in the army elite, and many other complicating factors in military politics, but it does indicate part of the range of army thinking on these issues. It also offers significant clues to the style of army participation in national politics after the rebellion.

The rebellion served to bring about greater unity within the officer corps by eliminating many of its "radicals." The moderates left in control were determined to have more of a say in the government, but with some important exceptions during the following years they were opposed to a coup. Furthermore, the rebellion also militated against renewed radicalism on the part of officers in the regions; it was in effect a "lesson." But the unity achieved as a consequence of the rebellion did not extend equally to all political issues. Army leaders were never able to forge the true consensus in the officer corps that would make it an effective political organization with well defined and articulated goals. It was partly for this reason that the FNPIB and the civil-military cooperation bodies were unsuccessful as political instruments of the army. And so long as differences continued to exist within the officer corps, it was more convenient to recognize the authority of President Soekarno than to risk exacerbating internal disunity by assuming more political responsibility.

There were other important factors at work reducing the likelihood of a coup. It was of crucial significance that the officer corps was not excluded from the political arena. Had they been on the outside, as in Burma and Pakistan, for example, a coup — other conditions remaining constant — would probably have occurred. But martial law gave the officer corps legal power, and the power satisfied, corrupted, and moderated. The economic engagement of the army elite was clearly important in this regard. Utrecht, with typical trenchancy and some bias, had this to say

---

45 Interview of Oct. 18, 1961.

about the army's role in the take-overs and subsequent disposition of the Dutch firms:

> In 1958 the contest for political authority between the political parties and…the army, as a new force which rose to the throne of power on 14 March 1957 under martial law…entered its second phase. Beginning on 3 December 1957 Dutch property was taken over from private Dutch businessmen by the Indonesian government. This take-over was accomplished under the direction of the Armed Forces, particularly the Army. Subsequently the State Firms — the new form of the old Dutch companies — became a new field of endeavor for a certain group of officers of the Army. As a result, the Army also participated in the Indonesian economy, becoming a force with economic interests. These officers who entered the economic arena became a new social group with a special place in the economic life of Indonesia. Consequently — and this is often forgotten by those involved — the Army shares the responsibility for [economic conditions] in our country;

> Using part of the state apparatus, this new social group, continually strengthening its position as a new 'ruling class,' has made every effort to transfer the entire significant part of the economy into the hands of the State Firms which it controls. It has also tried to push aside the national private firms, only *some* of which are controlled by political party leaders [or] adventurers…connected with the parties.[46]

Utrecht went on to point out that the corrupt activities of the parties were not necessarily eliminated when the "new social group" took over the firms.

To sum up some of these points, the army elite under martial law was rapidly absorbed into the national political elite. Political and economic power brought not only such material perquisites as homes, cars, trips

---

46 E. Utrecht, *Pengantar dalam Hukum Indonesia* (Introduction to Indonesian Law; Djakarta: Ichtiar, 1959), pp. 450-451.

abroad, and imported luxuries; in addition, the social position of officers naturally improved, and it might be that research would indicate a rising ratio of marriages between daughters of the social elite and army officers after 1957. Officers as a group did not want to give up these benefits which had been denied them for so long. One of the few open channels of upward social mobility, the army offered a way up that its officers finally managed to use.[47]

This too militated against military radicalism; and it also reduced the potential of the army as an instrument of social and political change. Like the civilian elite which it was to some extent succeeding, the officer corps became a political group with visible interests to defend. The antagonism between the army elite and the PKI must be understood partly in these terms. For the existing hostility of officers towards the Communists — on nationalist, religious, and historical (the Madiun rebellion) grounds — was intensified by the threat that the PKI's true radicalism offered to the interests of what Utrecht called "the new social group."

The development of the army as a political participant caused noticeable strains within the officer corps that also help to explain why there was no coup. Burdened by something of a split personality, the army suffered constantly from uncertainty about its proper role. Nasution and other politically conscious officers tried to formulate flexible conceptions of the military function which would admit a place for the army in government. Their concern was to find a legitimate basis for military participation in the state, independent of martial law, and it was in pursuing this goal that the army leadership played a key part in the development of Guided Democracy. On the other hand, there were numerous field officers, with primarily martial conceptions of the military function, who resented the idea that the army must perform non-military tasks. The fact that their colleagues were becoming engaged in all manner of political and economic pursuits — and becoming spattered with the grime of corruption — increasingly irritated professional soldiers who understood the army as a technical organization with highly specialized functions. This cleavage in

---

47 For a comment on armies as counter elites — and in general for a profound analysis of elites in the new states — see Harry J. Benda, "Non-Western Intelligentsias as Political Elites," reprinted in John H. Kautsky, *Political Change in Underdeveloped Countries* (New York, London: John Wiley and Sons, 1962), pp. 235-251.

the officer corps between the narrower and broader views — conventional and unconventional conceptions, as Nasution labelled them — of the army's relationship to the state never disappeared. It served as another limitation on the freedom of action of the political leaders of the army.

CHAPTER THREE
INTER-PARTY CONFLICT — 1957

The threat which Guided Democracy posed to the entire party system did nothing to bring the parties nearer one another in a common defense of parliamentary democracy. In 1957, in fact, partly as a result of the regional elections, party conflict grew more intense, and the ability of the party system to maintain itself against the attacks of the anti-party forces became more open to question. The major issue within the party world from 1956 onwards was the rapidly increasing strength of the PKI, which was illustrated dramatically by the regional elections. It is an essential point of this analysis that Communist successes in the parliamentary system contributed to the eventual replacement of that system by Guided Democracy.

This chapter will deal with the position of the PKI, the attempts in 1957 to forge an anti-Communist alliance, and the reasons why such efforts failed. The discussion will also examine the inadequacy of the party system for its own defense.

The PKI and the United Front

Long before February 1957 it was evident that the PKI had become a major political force. Its recovery since the Madiun rebellion of 1948 was completed under the youthful, dynamic, and intelligent leadership of D. N. Aidit, whose policies had worked convincingly well since 1952. The heart of those policies was the national united front approach to the PKI's domestic political position and (as defined in 1956) acceptance of parliamentary methods as a means to power.

In Aidit's terms, the elections of 1955 had indicated that Indonesian political forces divided into three major groups of roughly equal strength:

the progressive, the middle, and the reactionary "pig-heads."[1] The first included the urban proletariat and the peasantry, led by the PKI; the second was the petit bourgeoisie and the national bourgeoisie, represented by NU, the PNI, and a few of the smaller parties; the third was "the feudal and comprador class working hand in hand with foreign imperialism,"[2] led chiefly by Masjumi and the PSI. Aidit's national united front policy required an alliance between the progressive and middle groups against the pig-heads.

This united front from above was based on sound political considerations.[3] Being weak and vulnerable when the transitional Alimin leadership gave way to Aidit and other young men in the party, the PKI needed protection in order to survive. Its chief antagonists were Masjumi and the intellectual-led PSI, either of which would have been pleased at any time to see the PKI crushed. And that such a danger indeed existed was brought home to the Communist leadership in August 1951, when the Masjumi Prime Minister, Sukiman, undertook to suppress a series of Communist-led strikes and to arrest some regional and national Communist leaders on charges of conspiracy against the republic.[4] In order to defend itself from similar anti-Communist actions and to win time to organize an effective mass proletariat and peasant base, the PKI had to seek protective cover. It turned to the PNI, which also saw its most powerful competitor for power in the Masjumi.

A tacit arrangement with the PKI was useful to the PNI in that it offered parliamentary support for which little positive repayment was necessary; the PNI need only permit the PKI freedom to develop. PNI leaders

---

1 "Bersatulah untuk menjelesaikan tuntutan2 Revolusi Agustus 1945," report to the fourth pleno session of the PKI Central Committee in July 1956, in D. N. Aidit, *Pilihan Tulisan* (Selected Writings; Djakarta: Jajasan "Pembaruan," 1959-1960), II, 44-45. Also on the national unity front policy see, inter alia, Aidit, "Menempuh Djalan Rakjat" (1952), *ibid.*, I, 41-64, "Front Persatuan Nasional dan Sedjarahnja" (1952), *ibid.*, I, 66-75, and the Department of Agitation and Propaganda of the PKI Central Committee, *Mengapa Front Nasional* (Why the National Front; Djakarta, 1957).

2 *Mengapa Front Nasional*, p. 5.

3 For an excellent discussion of the development of the national unity front, see Ruth McVey, "Indonesian Communism and the Transition to Guided Democracy," in A. Doak Barnett, *Communist Strategies in Asia* (New York, London: Praeger, 1963). See also Arnold Brackman, *Indonesian Communism* (New York: Praeger, 1963).

4 Herbert Feith, *The Decline of Constitutional Democracy in Indonesia* (Ithaca, N.Y.: Cornell University Press, 1962), pp. 187-192.

were not complacent about the PKI's potential, but many of them were less concerned with this threat than with the immediate danger posed by Masjumi. It is important to emphasize what an ominous challenge those in East and Central Java who genuinely feared the possibility of a militantly Islamic state perceived in Masjumi. With moral support and encouragement from President Soekarno, who was also much less worried about the PKI than Masjumi, the left wing radical nationalist PNI leadership of Sidik Djojosukarto and Sarmidi Mangunsarkoro induced their party to "cooperate" with the PKI. The most important manifestation of this cooperation appeared during the parliamentary election campaigns of 1955, when PNI opposition to the PKI was played down in favor of a common drive against Masjumi.

The PNI was not the only object of the PKI's united front attentions. There were also efforts directed to some extent at courting the NU, with two objectives in mind: to blur the anti-religious label with which Communism had been stamped, and to isolate Masjumi from its natural Islamic allies. Neither of these ends was of course fully attainable, but the second was frequently within sight. Differences of origin and character between NU and Masjumi leaders, which had been a contributory factor in the NU's withdrawal from Masjumi — made the Islamic bonds between the parties meaningful only on purely Islamic issues.

As much cooperation, or uneasy truce, as there was in this temporary camp which the PKI sought to create was limited territorially to East and Central Java. It was most necessary there, because these were the areas of major strength for the PNI, NU, and the PKI. And it was also most feasible there, so long as those three parties for one reason or another regarded Masjumi as their chief opposition. For — with many qualifications, however — it was easier for the Javanese parties to cooperate with each other than with the primarily non-Javanese-based Masjumi. McVey and Feith have both noted that the shared values of the *abangan*-related PKI and the *prijaji-abangan*-based PNI facilitated cooperation between those two parties.[5] Moreover the *santri kolot*

---

5 For a discussion of the *abangan*, *santri*, and *prijaji* variants of Javanese religious culture, see C. Geertz, *The Religion of Java* (Glencoe: Free Press, 1960). Briefly (and much too simply) the *abangan* are the majority of village and urban Javanese whose religion is nominally Islamic but primarily pre-Islamic in origin. The *santri* are the more devout Moslems, divided between

(conservative Islamic, as opposed to modern reform Islamic) outlook which NU represented had something in common with *abangan* and *prijaji* views. The NU *kiaji* (Islamic leader), the PNI *prijaji*, and the PKI peasant spoke the same language and shared the same stereotypes of the non-Javanese for whom Masjumi often spoke. Social communications between the three groups in Java flowed with more or less traditional ease — which is not to deny the occasional violence of santri-abangan relations — and this was not true of the relations between those groups and the majority of non-Javanese *santri* in Masjumi.[6]

Working on their common Javanese base and common opposition, in some form, to Masjumi, the PKI sought to maintain an alliance with the PNI and a friendly agreement to disagree with the NU. The effort was almost entirely the PKI's. Communist newspapers and party journals avoided attacking the two parties, frequently flattered them, and aimed their artillery at Masjumi and the PSI. PKI policy statements promised full support for the "progressive" parts of PNI-NU cabinet programs. Indeed, the only government which the PKI did not support was the Burhanuddin Harahap (Masjumi) Cabinet in 1955. To maintain its individuality, however, the PKI also insisted that it would criticize "the incorrect ideas and mistaken policies...of these parties"[7] with which it sought to cooperate.

In 1955, the general elections confirmed the success — for the PKI — of its united front policy and determined organizational efforts. At the fourth plenum of the central committee (CCPKI) in 1956 — following the twentieth party congress of the CPSU, which took the same view —

---

the modern reform oriented and the conservative (and more *sufi* influenced) groups. The NU represents a greater proportion of the second *santri* group; Masjumi is based on the first. The much smaller *prijaji* group consists of higher and lower Javanese officials, many of whose religious practices seem to be a more sophisticated form of *abangan* practices. However, among the *prijaji* are some who are more closely related to *santri* than non-*santri* views, and who were to be found in Masjumi rather than PNI.

6 In Masjumi's leadership there were some Javanese, among them Jusuf Wibisono, Sukiman Wirjosandjojo, Kasman Singodimedjo, Mohd. Roem, Prawoto Mangkusasmito, and others. When Masjumi began to divide in 1958 over what to do about its leaders who were in the PRRI, the Javanese leaders of the party split between those who wanted to condemn them and those who refused to do so. Within the Masjumi itself, apart from personal inclinations and predilections, tension existed between its Javanese and non-Javanese components. But on the whole the outer island and Sundanese (West Java) Islamic strength of Masjumi gave the party the character to which Javanese parties reacted.

7 Aidit, "Menempuh Djalan Rakjat," *Pilihan Tulisan*, I, 46.

Aidit reviewed the parliamentary efforts of the party and made it clear that they would continue:

> Indonesian Communists have long thought that the road to socialism which the Indonesian People must take need not be precisely the same as that taken by the Russian People, the Chinese People, or the Peoples of other countries which now constitute the socialist family. [On the 32nd anniversary of the PKI, May 23, 1952, the CCPKI said that] "every people will follow its own road to socialism, in accordance with the development of its own national, situation, political, economic, and cultural situation."...

> In the PKI program accepted by the fifth National PKI Congress in 1954, it was said inter-alia that "the PKI has participated and will continue to participate most actively in the parliamentary struggle. The PKI, fully conscious of its political responsibility, carries out its parliamentary work with full seriousness."

> The Communists consider the execution of the general elections of late 1955 as an important success of the People's struggle.[8]

By mid-1956, however, there were already threatening anti-parliamentary and anti-Communist clouds on the horizon. In the same CCPKI speech, Aidit averred that the Communists would always choose the peaceful, parliamentary path to socialism. "Now," he said, "the question arises whether other groups and parties will allow a peaceful, parliamentary, transition to a system of People's power."[9] He feared two possibilities, the first being that parliamentary institutions might be destroyed or the PKI's future endangered by rigged election laws which would make parliamentary successes meaningless. On this point he offered a caution:

> We need to be reminded of a simple matter, that is, if we want

8   "Bersatulah untuk Menjelesaikan Tuntutan2 Revolusi Agustus 1945," *Pilihan Tulisan*, II, 76-77. See also D. N. Aidit, *Selamatkan dan Konsolidasi Kemenangan Front Nasional* (Secure and Consolidate the Victory of the National Front; Djakarta: Pembaruan, 1955).
9   "Bersatulah," p. 79.

to have a transition to a better situation in a peaceful way, in a parliamentary way, then above all there must be a parliament...a transition via parliament isn't possible without a parliament. Therefore one of the important responsibilities of Communists, democrats, and patriots now is to oppose every force that wants to abolish parliament, to oppose efforts to make undemocratic election laws, and to fight for a more democratic election law than the one we have now.[10]

The second fear was that repressive steps might be taken against the PKI. As in 1951, the answer to this problem was that, "Arbitrary measures by the reactionaries against the People and the Communist Party can only be broken by a People's strength greater than the strength of the reactionaries and by firm leadership from the *Communist Party united with other democratic parties*."[11] The united front policy remained necessary to the PKI for the foreseeable future.

The very electoral successes the Communists had achieved in 1955, however, contained the seeds of destruction for the united front policy. In part this was because they bred over-confidence in lower echelon party leaders.[12] But more important, the PKI had been returned as the fourth largest party, with its greatest strength in the PNI-NU bastion of East and Central Java, and such an outcome might well cause all other parties serious second thoughts about the Communist danger. In an analysis of the parliamentary elections, Aidit was full of praise for the PKI, PNI, PSII, and NU victories. He compared NU with Masjumi — a comparison showing the former to be infinitely preferable.[13] The PSII and Perti, Aidit

---

10 *Ibid.*, pp. 79-80.
11 *Ibid.*, p. 79.
12 There had always been some opposition to the united front. Alimin, from whom Aidit had taken over the party leadership, attacked it in March 1956. The CCPKI replied critically in July. See *ibid.*, p. 90. Alimin was not so influential, however, as to cause great concern among party leaders.
13 Aidit, *Selamatkan dan Konsolidasi*, pp. 10-11. Aidit said of the NU, that:
There are people who think that the shift of the Islamic masses from Masjumi to NU proves that the Islamic masses are becoming more conservative. This is not true, because the policies of the NU in the Ali-Arifin Cabinet and the policies set forth by NU leaders in their campaign speeches were not all conservative, but rather indicated the willingness of the NU to cooperate with democratic parties, also with the PNI and PKI, with the condition of course that Islam not be damaged.
Thus in political problems...the NU is more democratic and more national than Masjumi-PSI...

guaranteed, would achieve important advances as Islamic parties if they retained their progressive and democratic policies. Of the PNI, he had this to say:

> The PNI is the oldest nationalist party...and according to its tradition the PNI is anti-colonialist. Experience shows that to achieve its anti-colonialist goals, the PNI considers it a must to cooperate with all parties which are struggling for national freedom, thus also with the PKI...

> In the Ali-Arifin Cabinet the PNI indicated the large and important differences between its policies and those of Masjumi-PSI. This is the most important factor among others which has made it possible for the PNI to appear as the largest party in these last elections.

> As long as the PNI is faithful to its democratic and anti-colonial tradition, and as long as the PNI holds firmly to its foreign policy formulated at the Asia-Africa Conference in Bandung, and all the more if the PNI successfully cleanses itself of corrupt elements, then the PNI will remain the most important nationalist party.[14]

Throughout 1956 the PKI avoided clashes with the PNI and NU, emphasizing its own support for the anti-imperialist, progressive ideas of Soekarno (until he suggested burial of political parties) and bidding the PNI and NU continue their joint struggle with the PKI against reaction, against Masjumi and the PSI, and against foreign monopoly capital.

But the concern about the PKI which its showing in the general elections had aroused among leaders of other parties was increased a hundredfold by Soekarno's demand for a four-party cabinet. This threw

---

The adjustment of Islam to the special character of Indonesia along with the anti-colonialism policy of the NU is more attractive to the Islamic masses than the "modernism" of Masjumi in religion and the agreement of that party's policies with the interests of foreign monopoly capital.

14 *Ibid.*, pp. 12-13. The PKI reserved to itself the right to accuse the PNI of harboring corrupt elements. Three paragraphs above this quote, Aidit stated that Masjumi-PSI accusations against PNI corruption and dealings in special licenses were only a cover-up for the Masjumi-PSI defense of foreign monopoly capital and of the terrorist Darul Islam.

an even brighter spotlight on the powerful position which the PKI had achieved in six years.

The advantages which the PKI enjoyed after 1956 were considerable. It was without competition as a well organized, unified, active, and spirited political party. The PNI, NU, and Masjumi, all of which had participated in the second Ali Cabinet, were under attack for their inability to govern, for the deterioration of their party organizations, for their corruption; their demoralization was progressive. Soekarno had favored the PKI with his trust, and the party stood with him against the dangers of regionalism, with which Masjumi was increasingly identified. But the PKI's problems were perplexing. In the first place, the fall of the Ali Cabinet imperiled the continued operation of parliamentary institutions, to which the PKI was committed. Even if the opposition of other parties to the PKI prevented it from joining a new cabinet, the Communists nevertheless preferred a party cabinet to one that was extra-parliamentary. The only condition for the PKI was that a new party cabinet would have to be one in which Masjumi played at most a peripheral role around a PNI-NU nucleus. The PKI supported Suwirjo's efforts as formateur, "so that the crisis could be overcome by the political parties."[15] When Suwirjo failed and Soekarno appointed himself formateur, the PKI had no choice but to give him full backing. The resulting Djuanda Cabinet, with its implicit PNI-NU core, was the second best development the PKI could hope for. Thereafter the PKI made every effort to shore up Parliament and to improve prospects for the return of the parties to a position of power.

The second great worry of the PKI was that the army, under martial law, was threatening both parliamentary government and, in a very direct way, the PKI. Other parties, worried by Communist successes, might encourage amenable army commanders to restrict the activities of the PKI and its subsidiary organizations; or they might demand an outright ban on the PKI. It was this thought that prompted Aidit in 1956 to ask whether other parties and groups would permit a parliamentary transition to socialism. To discourage army leaders from contemplating any action against the PKI, Aidit reminded them in a parliamentary speech in early 1957 that:

---

15 CCPKI statement on its attitude concerning Soekarno as formateur, *Harian Rakjat*, April 8, 1957.

It is a public secret that in the elections for both Parliament and the Constituent Assembly more than 80% of armed forces members voted for Democratic parties, and 30% of the armed forces vote was given to the PKI.[16]

Aidit was defending the PKI from an attack by a Masjumi MP on its responsibility for the Madiun rebellion and replying with an attack of his own on the Sumatran dissident councils. Later in the speech he expressed his conviction that no responsible person would want the Madiun tragedy to be repeated:

[We in the Indonesian Communist Party] want to, and we are convinced that we can achieve our political goals in a Parliamentary way. We will avoid every possibility of civil war so long as we are guaranteed political rights to fight for our ideals. But if bayonets are thrust at us and bullets whistle towards us as in the Madiun Affair,... we will not present our breasts to be punctured by the bayonets and pierced by the bullets of the counterrevolutionaries.[17]

Aidit and other party spokesmen repeated this threat several times, in 1957 and later, warning the army that the party might be forced to go underground.[18]

In facing these challenges, the PKI needed the united front in order to avoid the dangers of complete isolation. But the logic of the PKI's position made a deterioration of the united front almost inevitable. As Masjumi grew weaker, the threat of the PKI to the two center parties, the PNI and NU, appeared ever stronger.

---

16 "Konfrontasi Peristiwa Madiun (1948) — Peristiwa Sumatra (1956)" (Confrontation: The Madiun Affair [1948] — The Sumatra Affair [1956]), speech before Parliament, February 11, 1957, in *Pilihan Tulisan*, II, 127. The rest of the comment is as follows: "The PSI and the Masjumi got less than 20%, thus less than the votes given to either the PKI or PNI alone. The PSI, which has influence over a number of high echelon officers, was the fifth party in the armed forces, while the Masjumi, because of its pro-Darul Islam character, was the sixth party." The remark about the PSI was intended to indicate a division of political loyalties between military brass and ranks.

17 *Ibid.*, p. 132. The entire paragraph is italicized.

18 At a PKI meeting in Bandjermasin, Kalimantan, a member of the PKI provincial committee stated, using Aidit's words, that if the Communists were denied the use of parliamentary methods, they could not be blamed for "choosing another road." A Communist leader in Surakarta, Central Java, said the same thing; *Pedoman*, November 16, 1957.

In these circumstances, it was of the utmost necessity for the PKI to prevent Communism from becoming a central political issue. The united front policy was based on the assumption that there were grounds for cooperation with several non-Communist parties, and that by emphasizing those grounds the PKI could survive without sacrificing its program. From 1956 on, the tangle of difficult issues that emerged, running between and through most groups on the political scene, worked in the PKI's favor in this respect. Thus, if the NU was moving towards Masjumi on the Communist issue, it was moving away from it on regionalism. The same was true of the PNI — which was also amenable to pressure from Soekarno — and to some extent of the army, whose officers were divided over the issues of regionalism, army leadership, and army policy. Anti-Communist unity was unattainable so long as no agreement existed between the most important parties and groups on other pressing matters. The PKI had maintained that colonialism, imperialism, and continued Dutch control of the economy were the essential issues which the nation must face; in 1957 it added regional "separatism" to the list. These problems, said the PKI, deserved the undivided attention of all loyal parties. In taking this position the PKI could point to the similar views of Soekarno, making it awkward for national PNI leaders to disagree too fervently.

By mid-1957, however, it was becoming increasingly hard for the PKI either to take the spotlight off itself or to make the PNI and NU feel secure against an eventual Communist triumph. Regionalist charges against the Communists became more vituperative after Soekarno asked for their inclusion in the cabinet. In July, PKI and SOBSI headquarters in Djakarta were grenaded, increasing the political tension. And the regional elections which began in June delivered a further powerful blow to the united front, particularly to PKI-PNI "cooperation."

The Regional Elections; PKI Displacement of the PNI

Despite martial law, the regional elections scheduled for 1957 were held throughout Java, South Sumatra, Riouw, and, in 1958, Kalimantan.[19]

---

19 No thorough research has been done on the elections of 1957, and there will be no attempt here

Elsewhere political conditions resulting from the regionalist movement precluded them, but the mere fact that elections took place in some areas was significant, for it seemed to indicate that the parties would maintain their rightful place in the political system.

The elections were for representative councils in the provinces and second level districts (*kabupaten*), including municipalities. They marked a transformation of local government, the result of years of debate over the issue of centralization versus local autonomy.[20] Those advocating more local autonomy had triumphed in Parliament in 1956, and a larger measure of autonomy was incorporated in Law 1/1957.[21] In the second half of 1956 local legislative assemblies which had been in existence since the early 1950's had been replaced with transitional assemblies — to function until the elections of 1957 — constituted according to party strength in each area in the 1955 parliamentary elections. Law 1/1957 authorized three local government levels, corresponding to the province, regency, and village.[22] At the first two levels, popularly elected legislative councils (Dewan Perwakilan Rakjat Daerah, DPRD) were to select executive councils (Dewan Pemerintahan Daerah, DPD) according to distribution of party strength. The DPRD were also to select a chairman of the DPD to act as regional executive (*kepala daerah*), his appointment being subject to approval by the central government. Although certain central government supervisory powers were retained in Law 1/1957, in the main regional government was accorded vastly increased authority. For the political parties, regional autonomy portended a tremendous expansion of their influence, if they were capable of taking advantage of it.

---

to discuss them fully apart from their influence on political party relations. What material is available on the elections can be found in Indonesian newspapers and a few political journals. Legge has provided some statistical data on the elections and the make-up of the regional legislative councils, as well as more discussion than can be found anywhere else of the workings of post-election regional government; see J. Legge, *Central Authority and Regional Autonomy in Indonesia* (Ithaca, N.Y.: Cornell University Press, 1960).

20 See G. Maryanov, *Decentralization in Indonesia as a Political Problem* (Ithaca, N.Y.: Cornell Modern Indonesia Project, Interim Reports Series, 1958) and *Decentralization in Indonesia: Legislative Aspects* (same, 1957).

21 For a full discussion of Law 1/1957, see Legge, *Central Authority*.

22 They were called first, second, and third level autonomous districts. The third level was to consist of a unit comprising one or several villages. Its establishment was postponed, however, primarily because of the difficulty of deciding upon the optimum size and powers of the unit.

In spite of the importance of the regional elections, both to local government and as an indicator of national political trends, the campaigns of 1957 were lackadaisical and unexciting compared with those of 1955 for Parliament and the Constituent Assembly. With the exception of the PKI, the parties had lost their élan. Parliament's impuissance had become apparent, and the government parties of the last cabinet seemed to have lost control of everything.

Moreover, the issues of 1957 which were considered important had little to do with the elections. The regional conflict was of overriding importance, but no one thought that the regional elections would solve it. In the campaign, the PKI and Masjumi exchanged charges involving the regional problem, but most of the other parties did not bring it up. Guided Democracy, the second issue of the day, was not one that the parties cared to discuss either, insofar as it meant restriction of parliamentary government. Generally their activities were confined to praising their own ideologies, pointing out one another's ideological deficiencies, and promising a better life to the people of the villages and cities. These platitudes could not compete with broader national issues for public attention. Finally, the elections of 1957, unlike those of 1955, did not themselves offer hope of a great national reformation. Rather they seemed merely another event in an extremely eventful year.

Regional election campaigns suffered from what was called "the martial law atmosphere." Everywhere restrictions were imposed by military authorities on political activities. In East Java, for example, after an initial postponement of the elections, the martial law administration limited the campaign to five days, from July 21 to July 25.[23] Political rallies and demonstrations were watched closely. But election campaigning also suffered from a lack of interest within party headquarters themselves. According to one reporter who surveyed the pre-election mood in East Java, many parties simply did not consider it as urgent to campaign for the DPRD as for the national Parliament and the Constituent Assembly.[24] The rewards of local government did not increase quickly enough after the general elections to exert a counter-attraction. And because national

23 *Duta Masjarakat* (NU daily), July 15; *Keng Po*, July 5, 1957.
24 *Keng Po*, June 16, 1957. The non-party *Keng Po*'s was by far the best reporting on the elections, and for that matter on politics generally.

party organizations were not especially responsive either to lower echelons within the party or to local electorates, the sense of importance of very few regional politicians was satisfied.

Also, most parties' treasuries were depleted, as is illustrated by the fact that, in East Java for example, several parties were using campaign posters left over from the 1955 elections.[25] Small parties complained that their pocketbooks were empty. Only the PKI seemed to have enough money; its posters and party insignia, assiduously hung up everywhere possible, were new.[26]

Everywhere in the campaign, the PKI began first and expended the greatest energy.[27] Each of the other parties tended to campaign in the locale of its known strength, conceding areas where the 1955 elections had shown it to be weak. Masjumi worked hardest in Djakarta and West Java, the NU in East Java — where it confidently told other parties to stop worrying about the PKI[28] — the PNI somewhat haphazardly throughout Java. But following the elections of 1955, the PNI, NU, Masjumi, and other parties had permitted their organizations to atrophy.

Little attention was paid to local party workers, with the result that their interest flagged once the major campaigns for Parliament had ended. National leaders of these parties concentrated on Djakarta politics, while the PKI worked feverishly in villages and cities throughout the nation. It took nothing for granted.

In addition to its high morale, healthy financial position, and powerful organization, the PKI could also campaign on issues not available to other parties. Never having been in the Government, it abjured responsibility for all governmental failures since 1950. It could identify itself with Soekarno, and in the campaign used the slogan "To Carry Out the Konsepsi Choose

---

25 These posters were decorated primarily with the party insignia. In Indonesian elections a vote was cast by puncturing the symbol of the party. Among the many illiterate it was therefore of crucial importance that the parties make their symbols well known.

26 *Keng Po*, June 16, 1957. The source of PKI funds has always been a matter for speculation. Some came from contributions of party members. It was often claimed by the non-Communist parties that prime sources of Communist funds were sympathetic Chinese and the embassies of the Soviet Union and Communist China, but there is no real evidence of this. It should be mentioned that the PKI seems to have been much more efficient and careful in handling its funds than the other parties. Communist Party journals paid considerable attention to budget procedures, something that one would not expect to see in the publications of other parties.

27 See *Keng Po*, comment on the West Java campaign, July 19, 1957.

28 *Duta Masjarakat*, July 4, 1957, July 25, 1957.

the Hammer and Sickle!"[29] The PKI was also able unhypocritically to attack the corruption of the other major parties.[30] As if to prove the point, martial law authorities had begun to arrest prominent members of the PNI, Masjumi, and NU on usually well-founded charges of corruption; no PKI leaders were similarly accused. Other parties lamely explained that the Communists had had no opportunity to be corrupt.[31] There were also more substantive issues: for example, the PKI demanded land for the peasant, and in this the party was convincing, for the Communist-associated Barisan Tani Indonesia had proved its dedication to peasant interests.[32] Regional PNI, NU, and Masjumi leaders could not very well vigorously take up this cry of "land to the peasant," because in some cases it was their land or that of important financial supporters which was at stake. Communist charges of landlordism against the PNI and NU in several areas stung painfully.

The PKI also apparently enjoyed a campaign windfall from the state visit of USSR President Voroshilov (May 6 - May 11) shortly before the elections began. Soviet flags were flown all along Voroshilov's itinerary, adding by that many to the number of PKI election posters. Even without the flags, however, the visit of the Soviet leader would probably have benefitted the PKI cause.

Understandably, the Communists entered the elections optimistically; but they also had reason to be concerned, particularly with respect to the united front, for in Java the PKI and PNI necessarily competed. NU and Masjumi electoral support came primarily from groups unlikely to change their affiliations quickly — NU relying on *kiaji*-led villagers in East Java, Masjumi on the devout Moslems of West Java (as well as outer

---

29 See the campaign speech by M. Lukman, vice-chairman of the CCPKI, in *Harian Rakjat*, June 21, 1957.

30 An election slogan frequently used was "Anti-Subversion — Elect the PKI; Anti-Corruption — Elect the PKI; Anti-Bureaucratism — Elect the PKI"; *Harian Rakjat*, June 19, 1957.

31 See *Duta Masjarakat*, July 4, 1957; and for an analysis of the elections, combined with an attack on the PKI, by Darsono, see *Keng Po*, Sept. 9, 1957. Darsono pointed out that PKI accusations were made more effective by the failure of the PNI, Masjumi, and NU to condemn their corrupt members. Indeed, they usually felt obliged to defend them.

32 *Harian Rakjat*, June 20 and 21, 1957. The BTI's legal aid was constantly provided to peasants squatting on government land, and it was almost always available for help, advice, and leadership. For a comment which throws some light on the difference between the BTI and PETANI (Persatuan Tani Indonesia, Indonesian Peasant Union) of the PNI, see *Sikap* (PSI journal), March 20, 1957, p. 10.

island Moslems). Except for the Protestant and Catholic vote, the PNI and PKI divided most of the rest of the Java vote between them. By 1957 it was obvious that while the PKI had expanded its support among both the urban and the rural electorate, the PNI had lost ground since the 1955 elections.

There were several reasons for the PNI's decline, one of which was the fact that it was truly a center party, stranded between the ideological poles of Communism and Islam at a time when those poles were increasing their force of attraction. For those who wanted a middle ground ideology, the vague *Marhaenism* (Indonesian Proletarianism) had once provided satisfaction, but it could do so less and less as the demand for answers to political, economic, and social problems became more insistent. Much of the politically conscious electorate, including younger people within the PNI itself, was angered by the corruption in the party and by the inadequacy of its leadership.[33] Frustration with the PNI was exacerbated by its failure to win greater electoral support in 1955, the inability of the second Ali Cabinet to settle the crises besetting the nation at the end of 1956, and the failure of Suwirjo to form a new cabinet. The result was that many who had voted for the PNI in 1955 lost their faith in the party. When they sought another, the Islamic parties were automatically excluded on ideological grounds. Of the major parties, the PKI remained; and it had much to offer.

Although the PKI concentrated most of its fire on Masjumi and the PSI, it did not avoid battle with the PNI during the campaign. Communist attacks were directed at PNI corruption. The PKI also accused the PNI of being a "half-way group," unwilling to choose between the right and the left;[34] it tried constantly to convince the PNI that its proper place was on the left. At the same time, Aidit and the Central Committee were especially solicitous of the PNI outside the campaign itself.[35] But once the

---

33 See *Keng Po*, June 16, 1957, for an analysis of the pre-election situation in East Java. The *Keng Po* correspondent correctly predicted that PNI would fall to third place after NU and the PKI in East Java.

34 *Harian Rakjat*, July 4, 1957; in the daily corner squib, one character (Njoto) asks the other (Aidit) who Soekarno would vote for, since he was the founder of the PNI but called himself a Marxist. The answer was that Soekarno would choose the party which was not "half-way." See also *Suara Marhaenis* (PNI party journal), March 31, 1957, p. 29, in which the PNI replied to attacks by the PKI and NU.

35 Aidit continually spoke of the united front and national unity during the campaign. He and

election returns began to appear there was no stopping the groundswell reaction within the PNI at the local level.

The first election held was in the special district of Greater Djakarta, on June 22, 1957. Forty-two parties participated, some twenty more than in 1955. There were fewer voters than in 1955, possibly because it was raining that day, a flu epidemic was just ending, some voters did not receive their registration cards, and interest was flagging. But approximately 70 per cent of registered voters turned out, compared with about 75 per cent in the 1955 elections.[36]

When the results were tabulated, the PKI was seen to have taken a great leap forward. The total votes in Djakarta of the ten largest parties, compared with figures from the 1955 elections, were as follows:[37]

Sakirman, a top member of the CCPKI, attended the 30th anniversary celebration of the PNI in Bandung on July 5, 1957, while someone else read Aidit's speech to the fifth CCPKI plenary session in Djakarta; *Harian Rakjat*, July 4-5, 1957. In an editorial on the PNI birthday, *Harian Rakjat*, July 5, noted that unlike Europe, where socialist parties traditionally existed alongside Communist parties, in Asia the socialists were replaced by nationalists. Asian nationalist parties, said the editorial, were progressive and anti-colonialist — while in Indonesia the PSI was not. In its anti-colonialism, the PNI meets with the PKI and NU; more than that, they work shoulder to shoulder. Of course there were differences between the three parties, but they were secondary, even tertiary differences compared with the great principle of anti-colonialism which binds together the national unity front. The editorial concluded that PKI experience in its cooperation with the PNI was very good, though at times not smooth.

36 See *Keng Po*, June 23, 1957. The total Djakarta vote in the parliamentary elections was 766,764; in the Constituent Assembly elections, 738,890; and in the 1957 council elections, 698,575. Despite what has been said above about this being a lackadaisical campaign, and despite the interpretation of *Keng Po* and a few other newspapers that the people were not as interested in elections in 1957 as they had been in 1955, it is important to point out that a sizeable proportion of the electorate did turn out. If more were known about the voting behavior of the Indonesian electorate, some tentative conclusions might be drawn from this fact about the popular evaluation of the parliamentary system; for if one assumes that parliamentary democracy had lost its legitimacy in the eyes of the people, then the question must be answered: why did so many people cast their votes in the 1957 elections? But even if the legitimacy problem were a clear one — which it is not — it remains to be asked whether elections and the parliamentary system were obviously related in the public mind. They probably were not, in which case the size of the vote in 1957 cannot be taken as a popular judgment in favor of the parliamentary system. It was certainly not considered to be such a judgment.

37 These figures are from Herbert Feith, *The Indonesian Elections of 1955* (Ithaca, N.Y.: Cornell Modern Indonesia Project, Interim Reports Series, 1958) and *Keng Po*, July 9, 1957.

	Parliament	Constituent Assembly	Regional Council
Masjumi	200,460	180,488	153,709
PNI	152,031	173,580	124,955
NU	120,667	124,923	104,892
PKI	96,363	89,612	137,305
PSII	23,245	19,971	22,717
PSI	34,949	27,136	20,089
Parkindo (Protestants)	17,456	17,667	14,583
Baperki[38]	26,944	23,384	26,642
IPKI	14,586	12,313	9,818
Katolik	7,570	7,052	7,234

Masjumi and the PNI had dropped approximately four and two percentage points respectively from their parliamentary vote; NU had lost less than one point, and the PKI had gained six percentage points.[39] Masjumi remained in first place, but the PKI moved from fourth to second, the PNI from second to third, and NU from third to fourth. Most other parties remained more or less the same, though both the PSI and IPKI suffered heavy losses.[40]

Newspapers immediately pointed out the shift to the left. *Harian Rakjat* headlines claimed the PKI victory was at Masjumi's expense, but the polls spoke for themselves; the PNI had slipped, and the PKI was victorious.[41] The results of the Djakarta election indicated what the trend was going to be in Central Java, East Java, West Java, and the special

---

38 Badan Permusjawaratan Kewarganegaraan Indonesia (Consultative Body for Indonesian Citizenship), an organization of Chinese, representing mainly anti-assimilationist views.

39 In the parliamentary elections, Masjumi won 26% of the vote in Djakarta, the PNI 19.6%, NU 15.7%, the PKI 12%. In 1957, Masjumi received 22%, PNI 17.9%, NU 15%, and PKI 19.6%. It should be pointed out that Djakarta's population, despite major influxes of Central Javanese after the revolution, is mainly (and naturally) from West Java. The West Javanese and indigenous Djakartans are strongly Islamic and, as is clear from the above figures, Masjumi-oriented.

40 Only three parties which had also run in 1955 increased their vote in Djakarta in 1957: the PKI, Gerpis (Gerakan Pilihan Sunda, Sundanese Election Movement), and Banteng Republik Indonesia (RI Buffalo), the latter two being West Javanese-based parties. In 1957, the four major parties received 74.5% of the total vote in Djakarta; in the parliamentary elections they had 73.4%. Thus even with the addition of 20 more parties in 1957, the major party vote remained about the same, the tiny newcomers having gained their support almost exclusively at the expense of the small parties among the old-timers.

41 See *Harian Rakjat*, June 24, 1957.

district of Jogjakarta. Political leaders wondered how strong the PKI would prove to be in those areas, whether the PNI would suffer most, and if so, whether it would do anything about it.

Central Java was the key region of the PNI-PKI conflict of 1957. It was an area of strength for both parties, the PNI having won over 33 per cent of the vote there in 1955 and the Communists something more than 25 per cent. The large PKI vote in 1955 had caused local PNI leaders (in East as well as Central Java) much consternation. When the transitional second level legislative assemblies were constituted in 1956 on the basis of party strength in the parliamentary elections, the PKI assumed majority control of seven areas, including the regional capital of Semarang.[42] Consequently tensions between the two parties were very great. Although Semarang had a PKI majority in 1955, the mayor of the city was Hadisubeno, the influential chairman of the Central Java PNI and a member of the national party council. Between Hadisubeno and the PKI relations were constantly strained.[43]

The election in Central Java was held on July 17. Apparently some PNI leaders were not pessimistic. On election day, Hadisubeno told the press that the Central Java PNI would not suffer the decline of the PNI in Djakarta; if it did, he promised to resign his party chairmanship.[44] When he was asked, however, about rumors of future cooperation between the PNI, Masjumi, and NU — against the PKI, and in conflict with national PNI policy — Hadisubeno replied "That's not impossible."[45]

Over eight million voters, about 85 percent of those registered, cast

---

42 The PKI had an absolute majority of council seats in the municipalities of Semarang, Surakarta, and Salatiga and in the *kabupatens* of Bojolali, Klaten, Semarang, and Sukohardjo. The PNI had majorities in the *kabupatens* of Banjumas, Pekalongan, Purworedjo, and Sragen. In Bandjarnegara, Pemalang, and Purbolinggo, the PNI had exactly half the seats. (Legge, *Central Authority*, appendix A.)

43 As mayor, Hadisubeno was able to exercise considerable control over the city executive council (DPD), a majority of whose members were Communists. PKI policy innovations consequently were often frustrated. But in mid-1957, the DPD reduced taxes in the major marketplace of Semarang while Hadisubeno was on a trip to Bandung. He angrily accused the PKI of using the city government for its own political benefit, but to rescind the DPD act was politically awkward. For their part, PKI leaders in Semarang believed that the PNI had been behind the razing of squatters' houses in the area, an action that would be attributed to the PKI city government. See *Keng Po*, July 17, 1957.

44 *Ibid.*

45 In early July, Suwirjo denied that any meetings had taken place between Masjumi, NU, and PNI leaders to discuss cooperation. *Keng Po*, July 11, 1957.

their ballots in the province. Although it was several weeks before the final tabulations were made, the electoral pattern was clear within a day or two.[46] Hadisubeno and other PNI leaders, one may surmise, were stunned by the outcome. The total votes for each of the major parties in Central Java in 1955 and 1957 were as follows:[47]

	Parliament	Assembly Constituent	Council Provincial	All Central Java 1957 (including special district of Jogjakarta)
PNI	3,019,568	3,171,588	2,235,714	2,400,282
Masjumi	902,387	892,556	714,722	833,707
NU	1,772,306	1,822,902	1,771,556	1,865,568
PKI	2,326,108	2,305,041	2,706,893	3,005,150

Here there was no question about where the PKI's gains had come from; the electoral positions of the PNI and PKI in 1955 were reversed in 1957. In 30 out of the 34 second level districts of Central Java, the PKI increased its vote proportionally more than any other major party, assuming majority control of three cities and six *kabupatens*.[48] The PNI retained majority control of only one *kabupaten*, Purworedjo. There was a violent reaction against the PKI in regional PNI circles. In vain the PKI attempted to treat the election results in Central Java as it had those in Djakarta; *Harian Rakjat* proclaimed the rise of the PKI and the decline of Masjumi, which no one considered to be important in Central Java. A day after the Central Javanese elections began, Aidit reminded party

---

46 Central Java was divided into two zones for the elections, which were held a few days apart. Reports of provisional figures for the two zones can be found in *PIA*, July 22, 30, Aug. 3, 7.

47 Compiled from Feith, *Indonesian Elections*, p. 66, Legge, *Central Authority*, p. 150, and the official report of the Jogjakarta elections from the national committee on elections. The figures for Parliament and the Constituent Assembly above include the special district of Jogjakarta. In the parliamentary elections, Jogjakarta gave the four major parties approximately the following support: PNI 207,000 votes, Masjumi 134,000, NU 99,000, and PKI 237,000. See Feith, *Indonesian Elections*, p. 85. The Jogjakarta election in 1957 was held several weeks after the rest of Central Java. The results gave the PNI 164,568 votes, Masjumi 118,985, NU 94,012, and the PKI 298,257.

48 In addition to those which it controlled since 1956, the PKI added Grobogan and Tjilatjap. See Legge, *Central Authority*, appendix A, for a complete list of Javanese second level districts and a comparison of the composition of their DPRD's in 1956 and 1957.

workers in East Java that their task was to win without damaging the united front.[49]

East Java was no happier an experience for the PNI than Central Java. The PNI was weaker in East than Central Java, having come in third behind the NU and PKI in the parliamentary elections, though second (displacing the PKI) in the Constituent Assembly elections. Since 1955, the PNI organization in East Java had deteriorated seriously, there being dissension within its leadership and considerable dissatisfaction among younger members of the party. Although the real contest in this province was between the PKI and NU, most attention was focussed on the position of the PNI; should it suffer a bad defeat, many expected an anti-Communist alliance to be that much closer. For its part, NU was to some extent worried about the PKI challenge but was generally confident of its hold on East Javanese villages.

In fact, all fears of Communist strength were well founded. Alone of the major parties the PKI increased its vote — and by the considerable amount of 400,000. The statistics for the major parties follow:[50]

	Parliament	Constituent Assembly	Provincial Council
PNI	2,251,069	2,329,991	1,899,782
Masjumi	1,109,742	1,119,595	977,443
NU	3,370,554	3,260,392	2,999,785
PKI	2,299,602	2,266,801	2,704,523

The NU remained in first place, but the PKI had moved within striking distance.[51] The PNI was firmly displaced by the PKI, and again it seemed likely that a large portion of the PKI's new support had formerly belonged to the PNI. It also appeared, however, that the PKI had begun to invade

---

49 *Harian Rakjat*, July 18, 1957.
50 See Feith, *Indonesian Elections*, p. 66, and Legge, *Central Authority*, p. 150. For provisional figures on other parties, see *PIA*, Aug. 7, 1957. In the parliamentary elections, the four major parties polled 9,030,967 votes; in 1957, 8,581,533 votes. A considerable number of smaller parties in both elections received over 25,000 votes. The election was held on July 26.
51 In fact, during the first several weeks of the election count it seemed that the PKI would win, *Keng Po* of Sept. 8, 1957, going so far as to predict that the PKI would get 23 seats to the NU's 20 on the provincial council.

NU territory in the villages. The PKI won majority control of seven second level districts, an increase of five; the NU maintained its control of eight but won no more.[52] In Surabaja, a major industrial city and the provincial capital, the PKI nearly won a majority, while the PNI vote fell drastically. The Surabaja PNI immediately protested irregularities and demanded a new election.[53] After considerable wrangling, Minister of Internal Affairs Sanusi (PNI) ordered a re-election which was held in 1958, when the PKI came close to an absolute majority.

West Java, where the election was held on August 10, confirmed the trend. In 1955, Masjumi had emerged as the largest party of the strongly Islamic area, its greatest support coming from villages and small cities. The PNI ran second and the PKI third, the latter showing strength in the major cities of Bandung and Tjirebon. West Javanese PNI leaders did not perceive in Islam the threat feared by PNI supporters in the ethnic Javanese areas of the island; indeed, in some cases they shared with Masjumi a common antipathy to Communism based on religious grounds. The coolness of PNI-PKI relations in West Java challenged the view of those who claimed that the PNI decline was due entirely to the party's cooperation with the PKI. More graphically than in Central or East Java, the West Javanese elections illustrated the seriousness of the PNI's plight. Masjumi remained the province's strongest party, with nearly the same strength as in 1955. NU lost 75,000 votes, but the PNI dropped by nearly half a million, and the PKI rose by three-fifths of that amount:

---

52 In 1956, the PKI had majority control of the cities of Blitar and Madiun, the latter being the capital of the area in which the Communist rebellion of 1948 started. In 1957, the PKI won absolute majorities also in the *kabupatens* of Blitar, Madiun, Magetan, Ngawi, and Ponorogo. NU retained control of the city of Pasuruan and the *kabupatens* of Pasuruan, Probolinggo, Panarukan, Bangkalan, Pamekasan, Sampang, and Sumenep, the latter four making up the entire island of Madura. See Legge, *Central Authority*, appendix A.
53 The irregularities had involved the failure of the local election committee in Surabaja, headed by a Communist, to send election summons to all registered voters. This had also occurred in Djakarta and Central Java, in areas where Communists did not head the election committees. See *PIA*, Aug. 28, *Duta Masjarakat*, Sept. 21 and Oct. 3, 1957. Election irregularities resulted in several re-elections in various parts of Java. It should be noted in passing that the elections were marked by a minimum of violence and untoward incidents.

	Parliament	Constituent Assembly	Provincial Council
PNI	1,541,927	1,586,507	1,055,801
Masjumi	1,844,442	1,761,406	1,841,030
NU	673,552	692,755	597,356
PKI	755,634	827,858	1,087,269

Communist strength increased in nearly all of the 23 second level districts of West Java. A plethora of smaller parties did about as well as they had in 1955.

By the time South Sumatra went to the polls in December, the PNI was in a state of boiling internal conflict, as a consequence of the election results in Java. The South Sumatra statistics are given here to point up the fact that the trend in favor of the PKI was not limited to Java:

	Parliament	Constituent Assembly	Provincial Council
PNI	213,766	257,528	187,042
Masjumi	628,386	594,662	553,276
NU	115,938	136,008	113,888
PKI	176,900	168,095	228,965

These elections had been preceded by considerable anti-Communist activity — in many cases by both civil and military authorities of the region. In September, a conference of Islamic leaders in Palembang, the regional capital of South Sumatra, had issued a strongly worded condemnation of Communism. During the month before the election began on December 1, anti-Communist pressure in South Sumatra seemed to take on campaign proportions and was reported as such in the anti-Communist press.[54] The PKI vote increased nevertheless, possibly because of intensive organizational activity among South Sumatran oil

---

54 See *Keng Po*, Nov. 25, Dec. 1, 1957. At the same time, anti-Communist activity in West Sumatra was intense and growing every day. The same was true of several areas in Sulawesi, where a number of Communist leaders were arrested late in 1957. As the regional crisis grew worse, anti-Communist pressure in the regions increased.

workers. Perhaps, too, the PKI had picked up more support among the numerous Javanese migrants in the area as a result of the regional conflict. Whatever the source of Communist support — and some of it probably came from former Masjumi voters — it had put the party in second place, behind Masjumi, moving the PNI to third.

The consequences of the Communist election victories were manifold. For one thing, they exacerbated the suspicions of the outer island dissidents, making a Djakarta-regions settlement more difficult. Second, it seems likely that the rapid rise of the PKI stiffened the determination of some army leaders to destroy the party system altogether. Third, the election results may have caused President Soekarno to have second thoughts about the PKI and how to deal with it. More immediately, however, the impact of the elections was felt within the party system itself.

The non-Communist parties offered various explanations for the PKI's success. Some ascribed it to the moral support given the party by Soekarno's demand for a *gotong-rojong* cabinet, to the visit of Voroshilov, or to apathy among voters.[55] Others, like Isa Anshary, the West Javanese Masjumi firebrand, stated bluntly that the PKI had worked harder, while the fighting spirit of the other parties had withered away.[56] Yet others argued that poor economic conditions and the unsatisfied demands of the people had given the Communists an advantage.[57] There was some serious soul-searching among regional party leaders following the elections. Natsir Lahay, of the East Java PNI, said that his party was weak because it was internally divided, based on cliques which eliminated good and upright men who did not belong to the right clique or enjoy the right family connections. He accused the PNI of overweening pride and laziness, its leaders, intoxicated by wealth, of neglecting their work among the peasants, forgetting about religion, and failing to train young cadres.[58] In South Sumatra, Djalil Abdullah, regional chairman of Masjumi, pointed out that his party might have done better had it spent

55 See, for example, the statement by Mawardi Noor (Masjumi) in *PIA*, Aug. 9, 1957; *Suara Marhaenis*, before the elections, May 15, 1957, p. 1; Hadji Moh. Soleh (NU) in East Java, *PIA*, Aug. 8, 1957.
56 *Keng Po*, July 11, 1957. Anshary was the leader of the Front Anti Komunis (FAK), a loosely organized but noisy group.
57 Darsono in *Keng Po*, Sept. 9, 1957.
58 *Trompet Masjarakat*, Aug. 13, 1957.

less time attacking the PKI and more time bettering the living conditions of the people.[59]

	% of Total Vote Parl. 1955 (total vote = 37,785,299)	% of Major Party Vote, Parl. 1955 (total major party vote = 29,470,594)	% of Major Party Vote, Parl. 1955, in Djak, West Java, Central Java, East Java, South Sumatra (total major party vote in those areas = 23,571,402)	% of Major Party Vote, 1957, in Djak, West Java, Central Java, East Java, South Sumatra (total major party vote in those areas = 22,195,906)
PNI	22.3	28.8	30.5	24.8
Masjumi	20.9	26.8	19.5	19.0
NU	18.4	23.5	25.7	25.1
PKI	16.4	20.9	24.0	30.9

1. These percentages are calculated from figures for the provincial council elections not for the second level council elections

2. Data from the districts of Jogjakarta, Riouw, and Kalimantan are not included.

3. The percentages are approximate.

59 *Pedoman*, Jan. 15, 1957.

The PKI offered additional explanations. Aidit noted after the Djakarta election that PKI voters did not seem to be apathetic, and without belittling the effect of Voroshilov's visit he insisted that because the PKI was based on the masses its campaign was original, creative, and inexpensive.[60] "But the campaign would not be very meaningful if it were not preceded by continual and concrete deeds of the PKI, if the PKI did not continually prove the worth of Communist programs and action, both in representative bodies and among the masses."[61] Arguing that the voting shift had been from Masjumi and its allies to the PKI, Aidit rejected the notion that Masjumi voters would turn to the NU or at the furthest to the PNI: "The People's Dynamic does not need a PNI-NU intermediary station to go from the Masjumi to the PKI." If the PNI and NU had lost votes, said Aidit, it was only because they had been insufficiently firm in traveling the road of unity and doing battle with the reactionaries.[62]

At the fifth and sixth sessions of the CCPKI (July 1957 and April 1958), M. H. Lukman, first vice chairman, dealt with the significance of the regional elections for the future of the PKI. Lukman told the July CCPKI session, a few days after the Djakarta balloting, that the regional elections would confirm the shift to the left indicated by the parliamentary elections of 1955. The new political balance would accelerate the implementation of the President's Konsepsi:

> Comrades, following this reasoning it becomes more comprehensible and we become more convinced that we can prosecute the parliamentary struggle, the struggle via elections for Parliament as well as the DPRD's, not simply as a means of propaganda, but also as a means of achieveing fundamental political goals.[63]

---

60 Aidit, "Rakjat Indonesia Sedang Bergeser Kekiri" (The Indonesian People are Shifting to the Left), statement of June 27, 1957, *Pilihan Tulisan*, II, 189. Of the Voroshilov visit, Aidit said that the PKI "never...slighted the meaning of election campaigning." Furthermore, the visit of the Soviet leader "was a great demonstration of the failure of the anti-Soviet and anti-Communist policies of foreign imperialists and domestic reactionaries."

61 *Ibid.*

62 *Ibid.*, pp. 190-191.

63 M. H. Lukman, "Tentang Pemilihan Untuk DPRD" (On the Elections for the DPRD's), statement to the CCPKI in July 1957, *Bintang Merah* (Red Star, Official PKI journal), XIII (March-April, 1957), 220.

It was no longer impossible for a Communist party to win an electoral majority, said Lukman. The international balance of power was favorable — i.e., the Soviet Union was capable of preventing intervention by the imperialists — and the political consciousness and radicalization of the masses in "certain countries" (e.g., Indonesia) had risen sufficiently for the Communist Party to defeat bourgeois parties in both local and national elections. These were objective factors and therefore irrevocable.[64]

With its greatly increased strength in the local legislative assemblies (DPRD) and its full control of eighteen second level DPRD's in Central and East Java, the PKI could now undertake activities designed to show the party's sincere dedication to the people's interests. Lukman paid careful attention to this aspect of the party struggle in his report to the sixth plenum of the CCPKI in April 1958.[65] He told the party that it must assure the implementation of Law 1/1957, insist on the formation of first, second, and third level autonomous districts, and obtain for local government the fullest measure of autonomy. Powers still exercised by the *pamong pradja* must be transferred to local authorities; local financial autonomy must be guaranteed.[66] Lukman urged party members to study the procedures of local government, to make those procedures more efficient, and to eliminate corruption.[67] Wherever the PKI was strong, he said, it must make every effort to improve the living conditions of the people. This would have the effect not only of keeping the party strong in

---

64 *Ibid.*, pp. 220-221.

65 Lukman, "Gunakan DPRD Untuk Membela Demokrasi dan Kepentingan Rakjat" (Use the DPRD's to Defend Democracy and the People's Interests), report to the sixth CCPKI plenary session, in *PKI dan Perwakilan* (PKI and Representation, Journal dealing with parliamentary affairs), III, no. 2 (2nd quarter, 1958), 70-76.

66 The PKI was the leading opponent of the *pamong pradja*, the traditional arm of the central government in the regions. Particularly in Java, the *pamong pradja* formed a conservative bulwark over which the PKI had little influence. This was an important factor in PKI-PNI disunity, for the PNI was by and large the party of the *pamong pradja*, upon which the party relied for much of its strength in rural Java. Through Law 1/1957, the PNI was committed to abolishing the *pamong pradja*, but its commitment was reluctant and was to be evaded. Hadisubeno, chairman of the Central Java PNI, was also chairman of the *pamong pradja* employees association in Central Java; he did not believe the *pamong pradja* should be done away with.

67 An indication of the importance accorded local government by the PKI is the translation, in *PKI dan Perwakilan*, III, no. 1 (1st quarter, 1958), 29-48, of Jacques Duclos' report of the 14th Congress of the French Communist Party in July 1956, concerning local government assemblies and the interests of the working class. Many other articles appeared in PKI journals on party work in local government.

those areas but also of inspiring other areas where the PKI was weak.[68]

In Lukman's otherwise glowing account of the PKI's electoral successes, the one sour note concerned the united front. Partly, he explained, the strain in the united front resulted from "excesses" during the election campaign — e.g., PKI attacks on the PNI and NU. But it was especially due, said Lukman, to the fact that the "middle force" (the PNI particularly) had suffered a decline. The difficulties which this placed in the way of strengthening the united front would have to be overcome.

In fact, however, this had become almost an impossibility by mid-1957. As the last table shows, the PKI emerged from the regional elections as Indonesia's largest party, at least in those major areas of the country where elections were held.[69] The PNI had slipped in less than two years from first place to third in the five districts considered.[70] Masjumi and the NU had declined, but retained their relative positions in the provinces. The ominous thing for these last two parties was less the fact that they had declined slightly than that the PKI had made such a startling advance. What was most disturbing was that the PKI was the only party to have increased its support since 1955. It was a growing party, while the others were apparently shrinking; and all the evidence pointed to the

---

68 Lukman, "Gunakan DPRD," pp. 74-75.

69 The 1958 election statistics for the major parties in South, East, and West Kalimantan follow, with 1955 parliamentary election figures in parentheses. It will be noticed that the upward trend of the PKI obtained in Kalimantan too.

	South Kalimantan	East Kalimantan	West Kalimantan
NU	282,691	18,235	31,703
	(380,874)	(20,795)	(37,945)
PKI	22,283	14,952	17,124
	(17,210)	(8,209)	(8,526)
Masjumi	188,606	29,245	139,741
	(252,296)	(44,347)	(155,173)
PNI	18,566	38,245	62,734
	(46,440)	(43,067)	(64,195)

In the newly created province of Central Kalimantan, NU received 23,186 votes, the PKI 16,717, Masjumi 26,470, and the PNI 18,810.

70 If the figures are based on the vote for second level DPRD's rather than first level (provincial) councils, including the districts of Jogjakarta and Riouw, the PNI came in second, less than 95,000 votes above the NU.

likelihood of the PKI continuing to grow and the others continuing to shrink. It seemed highly improbable that the non-Communist parties could reorganize and recover before the second national parliamentary elections scheduled for 1959. It was for this reason that these parties were later to be reluctant to hold the 1959 elections.

The conclusion of the regional elections, a parliamentary exercise, called forth a traditional parliamentary response. Menaced by the PKI, the PNI turned against it and made motions in the direction of an anti-Communist alliance, for which Masjumi and the NU were also eager. In a meaningful parliamentary situation this might have been immensely significant, producing a major party realignment as crucial as that which had occurred in the early 1950's when the PNI and PKI had moved together. Masjumi, increasingly isolated since the 1955 elections as a non (ethnic)-Javanese party, might have been able to link forces with NU and the PNI in a national coalition, in turn isolating the PKI on the left.

But in the second half of 1957 the situation was no longer meaningfully parliamentary. The parties were not in control of the country. Uncertain of their positions, they were unwilling to endanger their apparently precarious hold on the government. The PNI, NU, and the PKI were already beginning to adjust to the new circumstances in mid-1957. While Masjumi continued recalcitrantly to oppose Soekarno, Guided Democracy, the National Council, and the Kabinet Karya, the other major parties came uneasily to terms with them.

The drive towards an anti-Communist alliance following the regional elections was led mainly by younger party leaders. But the roots of their concern went deeper than hostility to the PKI, being fed by general discontent with the party system. Within the parties, the powerful dissatisfactions aroused in the lower echelons by the breakdown of parliamentary government often took the form of contemptuous indignation with the older party leaders who had proved to be such conspicuous failures. Only the PKI did not suffer this type of internal reaction. In the PNI, especially, younger members began openly to condemn their party's disorganization and dishonesty; in East Java, for example, PNI leaders suffered the shock of having their designs on the governorship (following the regional elections) revealed by an angry PNI youth group. Moreover, many young PNI and NU leaders were disturbed by their parties' reactions to Guided Democracy and the events of March-July 1957. To them it seemed that party leaders had given up without a fight, sacrificing on the altar of personal ambition and security the right of the parties to control a parliamentary government. To the argument that the parties had to go along with the President's ideas in order to weather the storm, a few younger men evinced skepticism and asked about the place of principle. In NU, Imron Rosjadi — an untypical member of the party council and chairman of the NU youth organization, ANSOR — challenged the party council's unconditional approval of the Djuanda Cabinet and the National Council, but was voted down.[71]

Older party leaders were on the defensive against their young challengers.[72] This was particularly true in the PNI and NU, though less so in the latter, where the challengers were fewer and the hold of the older leaders stronger. No movement actually formed in any of the parties to displace the existing leadership, but party leaders may have feared even that as a possibility. At the same time, both the PNI and NU were anxious to defend their stake in the government — parliamentary or not — which Soekarno and the army had the power to threaten. PNI and NU leaders thus faced something of a double hazard from within and outside their parties. To a considerable extent they depended upon Soekarno to help them with their internal difficulties. By giving him support, or at least not openly opposing him, they could hope to stay in the government; and they could also expect reciprocal assistance — which Soekarno, because of his great personal prestige and growing power, could give — in dealing with their own parties.

---

71 The NU party council had at first decided that it could join the cabinet and accept the National Council only if the latter were accompanied by a National Planning Council led by Hatta. Once in the cabinet and the National Council, however, NU leaders — including Idham Chalid, chairman of the party council, Wahab Chasbullah, protector (Rois Aam), and S. Zuhri, secretary-general — publicly supported both bodies. They were able to get majority support on the party council for their positions. See *Keng Po*, June 18, 30, July 11, 1957.

72 This classification of old and young leaders is useful but obviously imprecise. It is used here in a general sense to differentiate between men who were already mature and politically active in the 1920's and early 1930's and those whose major initial political experience came during the late 1930's or the Japanese occupation or the revolution. The categories are by no means exclusive; nor should it be assumed that all older leaders thought the same way and that all youngers were young Turks. Younger men often were quick to join the cause of older men, both out of loyalty in a society where age is considerably respected, and out of simple ambition. It should be repeated, by the way, that the political origins of most army officers were during the Japanese occupation or the revolution.

It is important to emphasize that Soekarno found it necessary to give this assistance. Despite his condemnation of the parties for their failure to encourage younger cadres, the fact remained that he wielded greater influence over the older leaders than the younger ones. He trusted his ability to control men of his own generation; of the younger generation, at least those men in the parties, he was much less certain.[73] This was a dilemma that Soekarno never really solved. He continued to attack the parties for growing old, yet he also continued to prefer their older leaders.

Soekarno's relationship with the PNI was especially important in the failure of the PNI, NU, and Masjumi to achieve a workable alliance. The older radical nationalist group in command of the PNI was quite close to Soekarno. It was this wing of the party, formerly led by Sidik Djojosukarto and Sarmidi Mangunsarkoro (who, however, did not always get along with the President) which had pushed the PNI towards the PKI in the interests of weakening Masjumi. Sidik died in 1955 and, as a compromise between the left wing of the party and a more moderate group led by former Prime Minister Wilopo, Suwirjo was chosen to replace him as party chairman in 1956. Sarmidi Mangunsarkoro, who had begun to regret the "alliance" with the PKI immediately after the 1955 elections, died in June 1957, leaving the left wing without a really effective spokesman.[74] On the question of the PNI's relations with the PKI after the regional elections, the older national leaders were as disturbed by the PNI's decline as were regional party leaders, but this influenced their reaction less than Soekarno did. Having been Soekarno's friends and colleagues since the 1920's, older party leaders could not imagine a PNI which was not close to him. His influence had been instrumental in moving the PNI towards the PKI in the early 1950's, and by mid-1957 all other reasons for the party's shift to the left were subordinated to the felt need to remain by Soekarno's side and to retain his favor.

The younger group in the PNI was partly inclined to Wilopo's views and partly not. It was not this that distinguished them from the older men.

---

73 The few younger men who were brought into the government by Soekarno — those like Chaerul Saleh, Achmadi, and men of similar inclination — came from outside the parties, or they were men over whom the President had a strong personal influence. They attached themselves to him partly because they did not have the strength of powerful parties behind them; hence also, in part, their opposition to the party system.

74 See *Suara Marhaenis*, June 30, 1957, p. 17, for Sarmidi's obituary.

They respected Soekarno, and they were convinced that both the party and the country needed him. But they were less inclined than older leaders to tie the PNI to Soekarno so completely. They did not have the same faith in the President's willingness to save the party whatever happened. Having had less experience in the pre-war nationalist movement and less contact with Soekarno, there was not the same emotional attachment existing between them and the President. This difference in view with respect to Soekarno showed strongly after the regional elections, producing what some called pro- and anti-Soekarno factions in the PNI.[75] There is an element of truth in this analysis, but few indeed in the PNI were willing to speak out against the President. There were those, however, who would not follow him, and this brought the party to grief in its friendship with Soekarno.

Soekarno was unalterably opposed to a PNI-Masjumi-NU alliance. He was also opposed to an open break between the PNI and the PKI, for that would divide his primary support among the parties, possibly forcing him to side with one or the other. To choose the PKI alone was impossible, though that party was in many ways his most useful ally. A break between the PNI and the PKI would also make the PNI less amenable to Soekarno's attempts to instill in it more consistently "progressive" attitudes. Moreover, for Soekarno, the original purpose of the PNI-PKI "cooperation" — to isolate Masjumi — was still valid, for Masjumi was still his worst enemy.

Soekarno had few intimate personal connections with NU leaders that would automatically induce the party to follow his lead. But he could depend on the older group within its leadership — led by Wahab Chasbullah, Idham Chalid, and Zainul Arifin — to act only at a minimum risk to their political security. In Djakarta, the NU's opportunism was taken for granted, so that most politicians, including Soekarno, considered the party a constant factor. For the most part, it was.

The fear which beset the non-Communist parties following the regional elections drove them a considerable, though obstacle-strewn, distance along the road to cooperation in 1957. For everyone, the PNI was the main center of interest with respect to an alliance. Many supposed that

---

75 See *Keng Po*, Aug. 25, 1957.

the PNI's "cooperation" with the PKI had helped the Communists in their rapid climb; it was also supposed that the PNI was in a position to change the whole political outlook of Indonesia by joining forces with the NU and Masjumi against the PKI. The NU would not risk being isolated on the right with Masjumi without the PNI. For a time it seemed that these three parties might erect the frame of a significant alliance — thereby causing the PKI and Soekarno, for different reasons, some anxiety. The issues that divided the PNI, NU, and Masjumi, however, were greater than the pressures for unity.

Regional PNI vs. PKI and the Posture of the National PNI

Even before all the Javanese elections had ended, Masjumi, NU, and the PNI were reacting vehemently against the PKI. Idham Chalid, chairman of the NU executive council, declared in mid-August that the PKI's victories would cast it into the abyss of its own destruction, for the PNI, Masjumi, and NU would unite against Communism.[76] Masjumi spokesmen called for immediate measures against the PKI. And, while PNI leaders in Djakarta were upset but non-committal, regional PNI leaders levelled a hurricane of abuse at the PKI, deprecating Communism as atheistic, internationalistic, and totalitarian. The past PNI-PKI association was regarded as a vicious trick, a ruse by which the PKI had hoped to lull the PNI into complacency before slitting its throat. With encouragement from the anti-Communist press, regional PNI members reasoned that, had their party recognized the threat from the beginning, the PKI would never have been permitted to accumulate such strength.[77]

Nowhere was the PNI regional reaction stronger than in Central Java, where Hadisubeno assumed the leadership of the growing party protest and immediately began to round up support for a total overhaul of party policy towards the PKI. In early August, twenty-three Central Javanese PNI branches urged the party executive council to review PNI-PKI relations.[78]

---

76 *Haluan*, Aug. 12, 1957. Idham accused the PKI of having won the elections by deception, but then unwittingly admitted Communist strength by saying that the PKI could not win in a general election against the combined forces of NU, the PNI, and Masjumi.
77 For a typical statement of this argument, see *Sikap*, Sept. 25, 1957, p. 7. *Keng Po*, July 27, 1957, found this view to be particularly prevalent among younger groups in the PNI.
78 *Keng Po*, Aug. 9, 1957.

Almost as the corollary to rejecting the PKI, PNI regional leaders turned to the possibility of an alliance with Masjumi and NU. Here regional PNI views differed. In East and West Java, the PNI stood to gain much from local anti-Communist alliances but was unconcerned or wary about a national alliance. In Central Java, on the other hand, local alliances had less meaning because of the number of second level districts which the PKI controlled absolutely. Furthermore, the psychological effects of defeat were greater in the Central Java PNI than elsewhere, for this had been the very heartland of PNI power. Hadisubeno was apparently convinced that the only real hope for salvation lay in a nationwide alliance that would eventually overwhelm the PKI.

National PNI leaders were caught on the horns of this dilemma. The party council was divided between those who agreed with the Hadisubeno view and those who refused to risk alienating Soekarno. Within this second group, moreover, there remained powerful feelings of hostility to Masjumi, which the latter's resignation from the Ali Cabinet had recently fanned.[79] Just after the West Java elections, I. B. P. Manuaba, PNI secretary-general, attacked Communist totalitarianism and said that the PNI was ready to cooperate with Masjumi and NU "to firm up democracy in Indonesia."[80] But one day later, Suwirjo asserted that even if the party council decided to break off with the PKI, that would not automatically imply that it was ready to cooperate with Masjumi.[81] He reiterated the traditional line that the PNI would cooperate with any party, including

---

79 In *Suara Marhaenis*, July 15-20, pp. 33-35, there is an interesting "open letter" entitled "Tindakan-Tindakan Masjumi Menguntungkan P.K.I." (Masjumi's Steps Profit the PKI), in which several sources of PNI resentment against Masjumi appear in the discussion. Ostensibly the point of the article was to show that Masjumi, by working against the PNI in the past, had helped to strengthen the PKI. But the policies of Masjumi Cabinets, the Darul Islam, and Masjumi accusations against Soekarno are all given emphasis.

80 *PIA*, Aug. 11, 1957. Manuaba accused the PKI of wanting a "dictatorial proletarian state," while the PNI upheld democratic rights and principles. The people, he remarked, must be made aware of the iniquities of the Communist system. Manuaba also belittled the significance of past cooperation between the PNI and PKI, arguing that the PNI had never asked for it (which was technically quite true, since the initiative was taken by the PKI in offering support to PNI Cabinets). In Parliament the cooperation was "mere coincidence." On cooperation with Masjumi and NU, Manuaba said it was now up to them whether they were prepared to cooperate.

Before the West Java elections began it was rumored that the PNI had made up its mind to turn against the PKI and that the "secret instruction of Sidik Djojosukarto to cooperate with the PKI had been revoked by the party council. *Keng Po*, Aug. 9, 1957.

81 *Keng Po*, Aug. 13, 1957.

the PKI, according to what practical political considerations and local circumstances demanded.[82] This was a flexible course, one which allowed the party to lean in any direction with a maximum of adjustability. But that the party was turning away from the PKI was clear. A week after the West Java elections, Suwirjo ordered the Jogjakarta branch of the PNI to withdraw from a vote pooling agreement it had made with the PKI, an action which caused a considerable stir in the party world.[83] Suwirjo and Sajuti Melik, a party leader with influence in Jogjakarta (and editor of the weekly *Pesat*), denied that annulment of the agreement meant *a priori* rejection of cooperation with the PKI; but Sajuti delivered a gratuitous attack on Communism, and the abrogation of the local PNI-PKI arrangement spoke for itself.[84]

By mid-August, the force of anti-Communist sentiment within the party forced Suwirjo to call an executive council meeting on September 6th to discuss future PNI relations with the PKI. In anticipation of this meeting, Hadisubeno convened a conference of the Central Java PNI in Semarang on September 1st. The first order of business here was for Hadisubeno to resign his chairmanship, as he had promised to do if the PNI lost in the elections, but his immediate re-election had been carefully pre-arranged. Hadisubeno's strength, despite the PNI's poor

---

82 *Ibid.* For a reasoned defense of this policy after the elections, see Sajuti Melik, "Anggaran Dasar jg. Menentukan, Bukan Opportunis!" (A Party Charter that is Firm, Not Opportunistic!) in *Suara Marhaenis*, Sept. 15, 1957, pp. 12, 34-35.
83 A vote pooling agreement was intended to pool all surplus votes remaining after the proportional representation division. Two minor parties had entered this agreement: Gerinda, with considerable strength in Jogjakarta, and Adari. The Jogjakarta PNI had long been badly split between its right and left wings. A battle between them led to the resignation of the party chairman, Dr. Suwito, leaving the party under the control of the left, led by Susilo. (*Hikmah*, Sept. 14, 1957, p. 8.) Susilo and his followers were quite close to the local PKI, a relationship, according to PNI sources, that went back to the revolution when members of the Susilo group were associated with the Communists in the left wing People's Democratic Front (FDR). See *Keng Po*, Sept. 5, 1957. The PNI mayor of Jogjakarta city, Soedarisman Poerwokoesoemo, was outspokenly anti-Communist.
Susilo defied the PNI party council, even after the elections, when he said that he would continue to cooperate with the PKI. See *Sin Po*, Jan. 14, 1958. In the Jogjakarta elections, the PNI lost votes, which the PKI blamed on the abrogation of the arrangement with the PKI (Njoto, in Bandung, *Harian Rakjat*, Nov. 15, 1957). After the elections, all the parties in the Jogjakarta DPRD agreed in any case to choose the independent Sultan of Jogjakarta as regional head, the only serious choice they had. This goes some way to explain the intricacies of party politics in Jogjakarta, for all parties were overshadowed by the extraordinary prestige and authority of the Sultan. See Selosoemardjan, *Social Change in Jogjakarta* (Ithaca, N.Y.: Cornell University Press, 1962).
84 *Antara* news bureau, Aug. 22; *PIA*, Aug. 27, 1957.

electoral showing, was due partly to his personal hold on the party but also reflected the strength of anti-PKI sentiment in the Central Java PNI.[85] The second order of business was nearly as pre-arranged: a strongly worded resolution was passed declaring that the Central Java PNI could no longer cooperate with the PKI "because such cooperation is ideologically damaging and in the past has been a bitter experience." A local PNI leader said later that the decision was absolute and that all PNI branches in the region would be instructed not to cooperate with the PKI in the DPRD's.[86] Hadisubeno declared that the two parties were irreconcilable.[87]

The Semarang conference gave hints, too, of further probes into other PNI tender spots. A few party members wanted to review the PNI's position in the cabinet, indicating that they might be thinking of a new three-party cabinet including Masjumi. The delicacy of this subject, however, led the conference to leave it and the possibility of a new alliance to the Djakarta meeting.[88] An even more difficult matter was that the rejection of the PKI, which the political public interpreted as a slap at Soekarno, raised the whole question of the PNI's relationship with the President. Disturbed by comments that the anti-PKI group was also anti-Soekarno, Hadisubeno reaffirmed his party's belief that Soekarno was needed as head of the Indonesian state.[89]

The anti-Communist camp was elated by these developments; every shred of evidence was adduced of an imminent three party alliance.[90]

---

85 *Keng Po*, Aug. 30, 1957. According to this report there were to be some conditions attached to Hadisubeno's re-election, but it is not clear what they were.

86 *Keng Po*, Sept. 2; *Kedaulatan Rakjat*, Sept. 4, 1957. *Suara Marhaenis*, Aug. 30, 1957, p. 5, announced the Central Java PNI rejection of the PKI before the conference began. This party organ stayed more or less neutral during the party battle, but published some anti-Communist items and cartoons.

87 *Trompet Masjarakat*, Sept. 3, 1957.

88 *Keng Po*, Sept. 2, 1957.

89 *Ibid.* Hadisubeno denied that the PNI was a docile follower of Soekarno, as common a stereotype of the PNI as opportunism was of NU. He went on to say, however, that for the PNI no other leader had Soekarno's influence over the people. Groups which wanted to eliminate Soekarno, he said, actually would bring the Indonesian state to disaster, for the people would divide without him. Hadisubeno also concurred in the PNI's defense of the National Council.

90 Actually, however, leaders of the three parties continued to treat one another with distrust. In late August, Ali Akbar, a prominent Masjumi MP, said in The Hague that the chief difficulty in bringing the three parties together was caused by personal differences between older generation leaders. He did not expect Suwirjo, Natsir, and K. Moh. Dahlan (NU) to be able to get together (*PIA*, Aug. 22, 1957). A *Keng Po* report of Aug. 12, 1957, observed that so far most of the pro-PNI-

Masjumi and NU urged the PNI to follow the lead of its regional branches. Yunan Nasution, a Masjumi party council member, replied enthusiastically to Manuaba's invitation to cooperate. Playing down past differences between the two parties, Yunan said that the recent elections had created a new situation in which all democratic parties faced a "totalitarian danger."[91] By the end of August it appeared that Masjumi and NU were waiting only for a firm commitment from the PNI. The PNI conference to be held in September 1957 was therefore regarded as being immensely important. Many assumed that if the PNI came out strongly against the PKI, it could fulfill the conditions for a three party alliance. This might set the stage for a revival of the party system by the parties' uniting to assert their leadership in resolving the regional crisis and to resist Soekarno's attack on parliamentary democracy. But most Djakarta politicians were skeptical that the PNI would come through, for they correctly judged that the party's leaders would not imperil their relations with the President by publicly rejecting the PKI. Indeed, Soekarno had already indicated his displeasure with the PNI's position at its anniversary in early July, when he challenged party members to compare themselves as they were now with the young and dedicated radicals they had been in 1927.[92] No doubt this greatly strengthened the position of those who argued that the PNI must do nothing further to irritate Soekarno.

The party executive council and PNI cabinet ministers met in Suwirjo's home on September 6th and 7th. Precisely what transpired is not clear, but the meeting's conclusions are a fascinating study in equivocation, reflecting the disparate pulls on the party. Although on the surface the older national PNI leaders had their way, the decisions were in fact more complicated than that.

With regard to the central issue of relations with the PKI, the conference resolution reaffirmed the policy of cooperation with all parties and groups "in matters not conflicting with the goals of the party." But the meeting also declared that "it understands the thoughts and feelings of [the

---

Masjumi-NU alliance activity had been via the press.

91 *Keng Po*, Aug. 12, 1957.

92 See "Shaping and Re-shaping Indonesia," in Ministry of Information, *Dewan Nasional* (National Council), 1957, pp. 82-118; in translation as *Marhaen and Proletarian* (Ithaca, N.Y.: Cornell Modern Indonesia Project, Translation Series, 1960).

regional PNI] towards the PKI, as for example those recently expressed by the regional council of the Central Java PNI."[93] Hadisubeno was not completely satisfied with this, and in late October he said that the party conference did not alter the Central Java PNI's absolute stand against cooperation with the PKI. At the same time, however, he remarked that there was only the appearance of differences between the regional and national PNI concerning the Communists, for really the spirit of regional demands was confirmed by the party council decision. The apparent difference, he explained, was due to the dissimilarity of decision making procedures between the regional branches and the national party council; in Djakarta the party council had to consider extra-party conditions and influences — which was perfectly true.[94]

It appears that PNI leaders chose a double-barreled approach to their multiple targets. They resolved the contradictory pressures working on the party by leaving all political doors open on the one hand, and on the other agreeing within party circles to wage war on the PKI. As a free agent, the PNI could pick and choose among the myriad political possibilities of 1957. The mood of Suwirjo and other national PNI leaders was to sit tight and wait for things to develop on most issues, particularly those, like Guided Democracy, in which the palace was intimately involved. But with respect to the PKI, regardless of the latter's attempts to prove that PNI doctrine still accepted Communist cooperation,[95] in the real world the PNI's main concern after the 1957 elections was to eliminate the threat which the PKI posed.[96] Thus the PNI would do all it could to damage

---

93 For the full resolution of the meeting see *Suara Marhaenis*, Sept. 15, 1957, pp. 4-5.

94 *Keng Po*, Oct. 31, 1957.

95 Aidit praised Suwirjo for sticking to the old policy, implying that so long as nationalist goals remained anti-colonialist and anti-imperialist, progressive groups would not be afraid that the PNI might prostitute itself (*Antara*, Oct. 31, 1957). In November, Njoto, the third man in the party hierarchy, said in Bandung that the PKI was aware that some PNI and NU leaders opposed cooperation with the PKI, but they were in a minority, and the official policies of the two parties remained "national and democratic" — i.e., they continued to accept cooperation with the PKI (*Harian Rakjat*, Nov. 15, 1957).

96 This interpretation of PNI policy after the September meeting is supported by an editorial in the daily *Merdeka*, an independent nationalist Djakarta newspaper. *Suara Marhaenis* reprinted the editorial, September 15, 1957, on the same page on which the conference decision was reported. *Merdeka* noted that there was no sharp switch in PNI policy, but quoted the resolution on regional party sentiments against the PKI as evidence that the PNI was aware of the problem. The newspaper, itself following a strong pro-Soekarno and anti-PKI course, implied that the PNI would soon overcome the PKI menace, even though the approach would not be in the form of a

the PKI, but there would be no official denunciation of the Communists; nor would there be a formal alliance with NU and Masjumi, the latter remaining out in the cold on all issues except Communism.

The trouble with this approach was that for all the other problems with which the PNI had to deal it was consistently neither here nor there. By choosing the middle of the road on most issues in 1957 the PNI put itself — perhaps unavoidably — in an awkward position, because it was not strong enough to play a leading role either in the government or among the parties. Abdicating any initiative itself, it left everyone uncertain of how it would react to other initiatives. It did not unite the party either, for some groups chose to emphasize the pro-Soekarno leanings of the strategy, others the anti-PKI. Wavering along this precarious route, the PNI ended up by alienating Soekarno, achieving little against the PKI, confusing the other parties, and finally giving up the last vestiges of what political initiative remained to it.

Uncertainty about PNI policy, following the September conference, did not diminish the excitement over a possible PNI-Masjumi-NU alliance. PKI leaders did not stop courting the PNI, though their tone became sharper after the elections. Aidit held the PNI to its profession of support for Soekarno and the Konsepsi, and he also warned that without the Communists the nationalists would be weak, without initiative, and devoured by the reactionaries — a remark that angered many in the PNI.[97] On the other hand, the PKI continued to interpret its electoral success in a modest light; local Communists were urged not to respond in kind to PNI attacks.

Masjumi, NU, and other anti-Communist parties continued to prod the PNI into clarifying its position.[98] The PNI's own activities seemed to encourage the hope that a meaningful alliance might yet materialize. Particularly in the elections of regional executive councils and regional executives, an effective collaboration appeared to be in the making.

"new look" in official party policy.

97 *Harian Rakjat*, Oct. 22-23; *Antara*, Oct. 31, 1957.

98 H. A. Achalen, an NU parliamentary leader, said in October that the sole condition for an alliance between the religious parties and the PNI was that the latter clearly revoke all its ties with the PKI. *Java Bode*, Oct. 28, 1957.

Regional PNI-Masjumi-NU Cooperation

PNI-Masjumi-NU cooperation was already apparent during the regional election campaigns in West Java and South Sumatra. Masjumi party workers in West Java were instructed to campaign not only for Masjumi but for all "democratic parties"; Masjumi and the PNI both used the slogan "If you don't want to see [another Madiun Affair] elect the PNI or Masjumi."[99] In South Sumatra, PNI-Masjumi collaboration, in the form of an agreement not to attack one another, was more uneasy than in West Java and more clearly the result of concern over election trends in Java.[100] It was during the post-election period, however, that regional cooperation between the non-Communist parties took on the greatest significance, fairly threatening to nullify the PKI's election victories. But there were two distinct purposes in this cooperation: to limit the PKI's benefit from the election, and to retain for the other parties influential positions in local government despite the outcome of the elections. These motives varied in intensity from district to district, reducing the effectiveness of the cooperation.

Several regional PNI, Masjumi, and NU branches throughout Java arrived at understandings to collaborate in electing DPRD chairmen, executive councils (DPD), and regional executives (*kepala daerah*).[101] In West Java, the three parties and the PSII signed a secret document, the Sukadjadi agreement, binding them to cooperate in preventing the PKI from getting the positions of DPRD chairman and *kepala daerah* in second level districts. Elsewhere provincial party leaders worked

---

99 This was reported by Muttaquien, chairman of the Masjumi youth organization, GPII; *Keng Po,* Aug. 13, 1957.

100 See *Pedoman,* Oct. 14-15, 1957. NU also apparently participated in the South Sumatran agreement, but it played an incidental role, and general interest was focussed on the PNI and Masjumi. The cooperation was favored in the PNI by only one faction, led by Nawawi Saleh, which took a strong regionalist stand against Djakarta. On the factional split in the South Sumatran PNI, see *Pedoman,* April 20, Aug. 13; *Suara Rakjat,* July 1; *Keng Po,* Aug. 15, 1957; *Pedoman,* Jan. 10, 1958. The other PNI faction inclined to neutrality in the regional crisis.

101 The DPRD's selected their own chairmen and other officers and nominated the *kepala daerah* by majority vote. The DPD was also elective, but its four or five seats were distributed according to party strength on the DPRD. Within the councils the parties bargained for positions. Only when a single party controlled a majority of the DPRD could it do as it pleased, but it would normally avoid difficulties for its administration, which a solid bloc of opposition could cause, for example, by boycotting sessions and preventing a quorum. See Legge, *Central Authority,* pp. 151 ff.

out their collusion less dramatically. The cooperation got off to a triumphant start in Djakarta, where PNI and Masjumi leaders agreed to support Mayor Soediro (PNI) for re-election and to choose a Masjumi candidate, Abdullah Salim, as chairman of the council. According to party strength in the DPRD, the PKI, with eight seats, might have expected the vice-chairmanship of the council, but it was given instead to Parkindo (Protestants), which had only one seat in the DPRD. In other areas of Java it seemed initially that the cooperation would work equally well.

The PKI's response was cautious and diplomatic. Its strategy was to divide either the PNI or NU from Masjumi by appealing to individual ambitions. Thus the PKI offered undeserved DPD seats to the PNI or NU, supported their candidates for *kepala daerah* or DPRD chairman, and often humbly withdrew its own candidacy in favor of one of those two parties. Local PNI leaders were the chief focus of these ministrations, but the NU served the purpose in a pinch. Legge has pointed out that in the elections of *kepala daerah* there was no obvious pattern of alliances.[102] There was one consistent factor, however: the PKI's search for weak links in the PNI-Masjumi-NU collaboration.[103] Its more than occasional success accounts in good part for the lack of uniformity in local party alliances. PNI and NU leaders at the provincial level were not always able to keep second level branches in line. Party chiefs in the *kabupaten* were often primarily concerned with purely local interests, and where this was the case an opening existed for a PKI wedge. In Tjirebon city, for example, the PKI undercut the anti-Communist cooperation by supporting the eager NU for the *kepala daerah* post.[104]

---

102 *Ibid.*, p. 152.
103 An example of an unsuccessful PKI effort was the *kepala daerah* election in Bandung *kabupaten*, where the PNI pledged its support to the Masjumi candidate. The PKI nominated a PNI member for the position, hoping to force the PNI to withdraw from its agreement with Masjumi. The PNI nominee obeyed his party, however, and would not stand. See *Keng Po*, Nov. 11, 1957. Thereafter the PKI shifted its support to the IPKI candidate, supported also by GERPIS, Murba, GPPS, PRIM, and other minor parties. But the Masjumi candidate, Oja Soemantri, was elected by the PNI, NU, PSII, PSI, and Masjumi. *Keng Po*, Feb. 2, 1958.
104 *Keng Po*, Feb. 4, 1957. The candidate of the NU (2 DPRD seats) was supported by the PKI (5), PRIM (1), and Baperki (1), the latter being an association of Indonesian Chinese which nearly everywhere voted with the PKI. The PNI (3) was supported by Masjumi (2) and P3RD (1). The P3RD represented police officials. In Tjirebon *kabupaten* the PNI-Masjumi-NU front held. See *Keng Po*, Nov. 11, 1957.

Where the PKI controlled a majority of DPRD seats, it was circumspect in pressing its rights. The Communists were later accused of abdicating responsibility in order to avoid the blame for inevitable deficiencies in local government, but Legge has shown this to be untrue. In 13 out of the 18 Javanese *kabupaten* which it controlled, the PKI did make one of its own men *kepala daerah*, thereby assuming full responsibility in those districts.[105] But in some cases the PKI majority offered the *kepala daerah* position to the PNI or to NU in the interests of keeping Masjumi isolated. The PNI-Masjumi-NU combination held successfully as often as not. There were instances of the three parties boycotting DPRD sessions completely, as in Semarang city where the PKI majority elected a PKI *kepala daerah*, or forcing the PKI to run the local government alone pending Djakarta decisions on demands for re-elections. But there were failures too. In several districts of Central Java — including Temanggung, Salatiga, Sukohardjo, and Sragen — local PKI and PNI branches concluded cooperation agreements; Hadisubeno tried, not always successfully, to order the PNI to withdraw from these arrangements.[106]

At the provincial level in Central Java, PNI, Masjumi, and NU leaders agreed to support Hadisubeno's own candidacy for *kepala daerah* (governor) and to divide the remaining positions among them.[107] The PKI would gladly have supported any PNI candidate but Hadisubeno for governor, but it had little choice in the matter and in early 1958 he was elected by acclamation. Iman Sofwan of the NU was elected chairman of the provincial DPRD, with a PNI vice-chairman. In the DPD election, the PKI disagreed with the voting procedure and left the session, which then proceeded to distribute the five DPD seats one each to the PNI, NU, Masjumi, Buruh (Labor), and PKI.[108] Thus the PKI, largest party of

---

105 See Legge, *Central Authority*, p. 151.

106 See *Harian Rakjat*, Nov. 11, 1957. Hadisubeno was at pains to deny that there was any PNI-PKI cooperation in Central Java. Of Sragen, where he was unable to control the local PNI leaders, he said that the PNI took positions away from the PKI — which supported the PNI candidates — and that it was therefore hardly cooperation (*Keng Po*, Oct. 31, 1957). For vivid accounts of instances of PNI-Masjumi-NU cooperation against the PKI, see *PKI dan Perwakilan*, III, no. 1 (1st quarter, 1958), 51-52, a report by Sukardi on Tulungagung, East Java; and Nungtjik A. R., "Dua Pengalaman dari Daerah" (Two Experiences from the Regions) in *ibid.*, III, no. 2 (2nd quarter, 1958), 77-83. PKI counter tactics are also clear from the articles.

107 See *Keng Po*, Oct. 2 and Nov. 5, 1957, for a detailed discussion of pre-DPD election politics in Central Java.

108 *PIA*, Jan. 4, 1958. The division of seats in the DPRD was as follows: PKI 24, PNI 20, NU 16,

Central Java, received next to nothing in the way of provincial leadership positions.

Although regional PNI-Masjumi-NU cooperation continued through the early months of 1958, it was limited mainly to local interests and did not overcome differences with respect to national issues. The three parties agreed consistently in their opposition to the PKI; anti-Communist statements became more vitriolic with practice. Some local NU branches branded Communism as *haram* (forbidden), and in November 1957 the East Java PNI followed Central Java's lead in vehemently rejecting all cooperation with the PKI.[109] But only in Central Java was the PNI interested in a national alliance. The West Java PNI, under the leadership of Osa Maliki, worked actively against such an alliance, with the encouragement of Suwirjo. In September and October, while PNI-Masjumi-NU local cooperation was in the making, West Javanese PNI leaders undertook to form a united center Peace Front against the PKI and Masjumi-PSI extremes. Those parties were to be excluded entirely because their conflicts "obstructed political harmony."[110] The effort was unsuccessful, as were others that followed, but it reflected the desire of most PNI (and NU) leaders for a comfortable center alliance — which existed inchoately in the Kabinet Karya — led by the PNI and NU and excluding the troublemakers, Masjumi and the PKI.

The Failure of National PNI-Masjumi-NU Cooperation

Those who anticipated a major shift to the right in 1957 were encouraged by the limited three-party collaboration in the regions. But there was in fact no national cooperation between the major non-Communist parties, for the PNI and NU were too uncertain of their positions and consequently unwilling to take risks.

After August, the regional crisis dominated the headlines, pushing political party issues into the background and displaying in stark relief the

---

Masjumi 8, Buruh 2, Catholics 2; PSII, Baperki, Permai, 1 each; and a few other minor parties and individual candidates combined, 1.

109   *Keng Po*, Nov. 5, 1957.

110   *Duta Masjarakat* (NU Djakarta daily), Sept. 30; *Sin Po*, Oct. 17; *Kedaulatan Rakjat*, Oct. 19, 1957.

weakness of parliamentary institutions. President Soekarno and the army assumed the extra-parliamentary initiative in dealing with the regions. The parties seemed to stand on the sidelines, occasionally trying to lend a hand. At one point in late 1957 a group of MPs proposed that Parliament mediate the dispute between the regions and Djakarta, as if that body were an objective neutral. Parliament's Committee of Nine, whose task it was to reconcile Soekarno and Hatta, did not have a fraction of the importance of, nor did it attract the same attention as, the Committee of Seven, appointed by the National Conference to work out the army's political problems. The reorientation of the parties within this new political framework was accomplished only with considerable strain.

For the PNI it was particularly trying. Among national PNI leaders there was a growing feeling of discomfort at Soekarno's disgust with the party for its conservative softness and vacillation. The September party council meeting did not clarify the party's strategy towards the PKI. Nothing approaching an official PNI attack on the Communists appeared until November, when Selamat Ginting, a PNI MP from North Sumatra, accused the PKI of complicity in a revolt of village guard units in North Sumatra in early October.[111] Ginting's vituperative fire swept the entire field of Communist activities. This speech caused some speculation among capital city politicans, for officially the PNI seemed still to accept the PKI as an ally. Ginting told the press that the PNI party council had not only approved his speech but assumed responsibility for it.[112]

Such assurances of PNI hostility to the PKI did not dispel the doubts of Masjumi and NU, however, and they did not bring an anti-Communist alliance any nearer fruition. For what was really demanded of the PNI was concrete evidence of its willingness to cooperate not only on the Communist problem but also, and perhaps more importantly, on other outstanding issues before the state. Masjumi, threatened with permanent isolation, sought agreement on the regional crisis above all and also on the issues posed by Guided Democracy. An understanding to gang up

---

111 *Ichtisar Parlemen*, session of Nov. 11, 1957, pp. 879-887.
112 *Keng Po*, Nov. 12, 1957. *Suara Marhaenis*, Nov. 30, 1957, pp. 10-12, published parts of the speech. Ahem Erningpradja, a PNI labor leader and MP who was also a member of the National Council, praised Ginting's attack on the PKI and said that it had the full support of the party. He also called attention to another anti-PKI volley by Doedi Soemawidjaja, a PNI MP from West Java. *Abadi* (Masjumi Djakarta daily), Nov. 13, 1957.

on the PKI would not solve these problems. NU leaders regarded the prospect of a three-party alliance in similar terms but from a different perspective: unless the PNI, Masjumi, and NU could agree on the other major issues, NU was not going to imperil its position within the government by supporting Masjumi. Just before the PNI meeting of September 6th-7th, Wahab Chasbullah, the NU's official elder statesman, declared that the purpose of any three party cooperation would be "on the one hand for very pressing state and national interests, and on the other to deal with the PKI." Among the "pressing interests," he mentioned the President's Konsepsi and the regional crisis, both of which he insisted must be settled first before cooperation between the three parties could get underway.[113] In effect, Wahab was saying that the parties must agree to face the challenge to party government unanimously; otherwise, NU would make its own peace with the new order, leaving Masjumi to suffer out of power.

Here the PNI gave only occasional encouragement to the other parties. On the regional crisis it moved away from the PKI in 1957, but primarily towards the middle-of-the-road. The PKI's interest in an uncompromising outlawing of the anti-Communist regionalists was as clear as was Masjumi's in a compromise favorable to its outer island strongholds. But although the dominant Javanese elements in both the PNI and NU felt threatened by outer island hostility, neither party had anything to gain from civil war; both inclined towards peaceful settlement, but without a firm commitment to correcting the Djakarta-outer islands political and economic imbalance. Both parties gave their full support to the National Conference and refused to join the PKI in hurling epithets at regional leaders.[114] The anti-Communist press contrasted the common sentiment of the PNI, NU, and Masjumi in favor of peaceful settlement with the PKI's tough policy.[115] A stand favoring reconciliation was not problematic for the PNI, however, because nearly everyone, including Soekarno, seemed to want a peaceful solution of the crisis.

---

113 *Abadi*, Sept. 5, 1957.
114 In August, the PNI secretary-general, Manuaba, in attacking the PKI, noted that the PNI had never condemned the regionalists as "separatists." He also said, however, that it was possible that separatist elements were taking advantage of the regional situation (*PIA*, Aug. 9, 1957).
115 See *Keng Po*, Aug. 12, 1957.

On another issue connected with the regional situation, that of Hatta's position, the PNI knew Soekarno's views and in following them moved away from Masjumi and (to a lesser extent) NU. Soekarno did not want Hatta back in the government, but if he had to make way for him it would be as Vice-President, or chairman of a planning council, or some other suitably symbolic position; he was not going to allow Hatta to be prime minister, as Masjumi and many others were demanding. Public discussion of Hatta's possible return to the government became lively again after he and Soekarno signed their noncommittal statement at the National Conference in September. In Central Java Hadisubeno openly favored Hatta as prime minister, assuming perhaps that Masjumi would be invited to join the cabinet along with the PNI and NU, while the PKI and even those left-wing ministers already in the Kabinet Karya would be excluded.[116] Other PNI support for a Hatta Cabinet came from several members of Parliament and a few party council members.[117] But Suwirjo was reluctant, fearing that PNI support of Hatta would further estrange Soekarno, and other party leaders agreed. In October Suwirjo attended a West Java PNI conference which issued a resolution declaring, with remarkable caution, that the regional branch was not opposed to Hatta's returning to the vice-presidency.[118] This wording was most likely for bargaining purposes with "pro-Hatta" PNI leaders when the party council took up the issue. On November 22nd the PNI executive council decided to support Hatta for vice-president, a short compromise away from the West Javanese PNI position. Suwirjo said later that the possibility of Hatta becoming prime minister was "not yet a problem for the PNI."[119]

---

116 See *Keng Po*, Oct. 12, 1957.
117 Soetojo Martodimoeljo, an MP and former secretary-general of the PNI, claimed that many in the PNI favored Hatta as Prime Minister, including himself and Ahem Erningpradja (*Keng Po*, Nov. 21, 1957). Those in the PNI who wanted a Hatta Cabinet carefully avoided casting aspersions on Djuanda — as nearly everyone did. The implication was always that a Hatta Cabinet would restore national unity, which the Djuanda Cabinet could not do, despite Djuanda's many other admirable qualities. But if a Hatta Government did not materialize, no one in the PNI, including Hadisubeno, wanted to jeopardize the party's position in the Kabinet Karya.
118 *Trompet Masjarakat*, Oct. 9, 1957. Kosasih, deputy chairman of the PNI in West Java, said afterwards that the difference of views between the West and Central Java PNI branches on the Hatta question would be settled by the national party council (*PIA*, Oct. 17, 1957). This makes it seem likely that PNI leaders in Djakarta encouraged the West Java branch to take this stand on Hatta in order to force the issue into the national party council, whose decision all regional party leaders would have to obey.
119 *Keng Po*, Nov. 26, 1957.

Again the attachment to Soekarno determined PNI policy, and again the party fell between two stools. For what it gained in its relations with Soekarno by opposing a Hatta premiership, it lost by working for a Hatta vice-presidency. The PNI combined with Masjumi, NU, and several minor parties in Parliament to form the Committee of Nine to help restore the Soekarno-Hatta Dwitunggal; its chairman was Ahem Erningpradja of the PNI. The PKI, on the other hand, stood consistently against Hatta, just as it stood consistently with Soekarno on nearly every other issue in 1957.[120] It is clear why Soekarno should have found the PKI a more trustworthy ally than the PNI, which he would otherwise have preferred.

It is also clear why Masjumi and NU could not trust the PNI. But non-Communist disunity was not only a matter of PNI vacillation. It was also a major fact of Islamic party life, which is why a Masjumi-NU alliance was impossible without the full involvement of the PNI.

The reaction which the regional elections aroused in NU hearts at first drove the party towards Masjumi, a natural anti-Communist ally. Rumors were current in mid-1957 that the Islamic parties would unite to defend the Faith against the threat of atheistic Communism. NU had joined with Masjumi, the PSII, and several secular parties in rejecting Soekarno's four-party cabinet proposal, and later it had refused Suwirjo's invitation to join a cabinet without Masjumi. NU leaders felt that Masjumi must be included in the Government if it was to deal effectively with the regional crisis.[121] In addition, however, it is likely that they also wanted a Masjumi buttress against the PKI, and perhaps against the influence of Soekarno. Despite Masjumi-NU hostility, many NU leaders had usually relied to some extent upon the guidance of the better educated and more broadly experienced Masjumi leaders, and they were reluctant to stand entirely alone in the Government without a Masjumi partnership.[122] The Kabinet

---

120 For a comment by Aidit on Hatta, see *Harian Rakjat*, Oct. 22, 1957. Aidit said that what was important was the policy not the man, a formula which he applied to Hatta but not to Soekarno. The policy, he said, should be implementation of the President's Konsepsi.

121 Deliar Noer, "Masjumi" (MA thesis, Cornell University, 1960), p. 392. Noer's comment is based on an interview with K. H. M. Dahlan of the NU.

122 The NU did enter the first Ali Sastroamidjojo Cabinet without Masjumi, though apparently there was some feeling then that it should not do so. See Feith, *Decline of Constitutional Democracy*, p. 338. I do not think this changed the discomfort of older NU leaders with governmental responsibilities, nor did it breed in them confidence that they could handle the political threats posed later by the PKI and, more generally, by Soekarno. Some Masjumi leaders continued

Karya cut this gordian knot, however, for not only did it exclude the PKI but it also permitted NU participation on an individual basis, thus relieving the party of responsibility for government policy. And once in the cabinet, NU leaders were extremely reluctant to risk being pushed out of it again; Masjumi's religious appeals could not easily overcome this.[123]

There was a long-standing desire in Islamic circles to unite the *ummat*, particularly among younger members of the Islamic parties who did not share the political grudges of their elders. But it had been political reasons that divided NU from Masjumi in 1952, however, and it was political differences that were likely to keep the parties apart, religious affinities notwithstanding. Both NU and Masjumi leaders stated in mid-1957 that a fusion of Islamic parties was not possible.[124] Some, like Wahib Wahab of the NU, gave religious doctrinal differences as the reason, but few believed this issue to be important.[125] Although leaders of the two parties were willing to speak of a federation of Islamic parties, this came to nothing because of NU-Masjumi competition for control of it. The Moslem League, a loose federation consisting basically of the NU, PSII, and Perti, had been in ineffectual existence for years, dating from NU's withdrawal from Masjumi. Dominated by the NU, it had little to offer Masjumi.

---

to exert an influence over various NU party council members, even after the Kabinet Karya was established, providing guidance in situations which NU leaders were not uniformly adept at assessing. The limited intellectual and political leadership resources of the NU was given something of a commentary by Idham Chalid during the election campaigns in mid-1957, when he pointed out with bravado that only the *kiaji* group in Indonesia had never been given an opportunity to lead the government (*Duta Masjarakat*, Aug. 6, 1957). The statement probably caused Djakarta intellectuals some mirth at this basic plight of the NU.

123 Masjumi also appealed to NU economic interests. In attacking the political and economic decline under the Kabinet Karya, the Masjumi leaning weekly, *Hikmah*, X, no. 32 (Sept. 7, 1957), 23, noted that generally the Indonesian Islamic community was not a civil servant group but a trading and entrepreneurial group. As a result of the Cabinet's economic policies, said *Hikmah*, these trading groups were suffering considerably. From this the argument led to the need for political unity among the Islamic parties in order to protect their interests, to defend the Faith, and to smash Communism.

124 See statement of Kasman Singodimedjo (Masjumi), *Duta Masjarakat*, July 23, 1957; Ahmad Siddiq (NU), *Duta Masjarakat*, July 11, 1957.

125 *Kedaulatan Rakjat*, July 15, 1957. There were doctrinal differences between the two parties that their members sometimes emphasized; Masjumi followed a modernist interpretation of the law which NU members found uncongenial, and of course the whole modernist Islamic approach was discomfitting for NU leaders. See *Hikmah*, X, no. 33 (Sept. 14, 1957), 23, for a Masjumi denial that doctrinal differences prevented fusion of the parties. These differences, said the article, were insignificant compared with the binding force of Islamic ideology, especially in the face of the Communist threat.

The essential difference of political interest between Masjumi and NU in 1957 was emphasized by the national Congress of *alim ulama* (Islamic religious leaders) held early in September in Palembang. Masjumi had taken the initiative in organizing this Congress, and it was clear beforehand that it would become a forum for both anti-Communist and anti-Djakarta views.[126] All Islamic organizations were invited in the hope that a solid Islamic front might be created, but mixing the goals of the Congress was politically disastrous. Knowing that it could not control the meeting, and unwilling to associate itself with Sumatran regionalist opinion, NU shied away. A. Zuhri, NU secretary-general, warned the Congress against playing with the destructive fire of political questions, and NU refused to send an official delegation.[127] As expected, the *alim ulama* meeting launched a vehement attack on Communism, declaring it *haram* for Moslems and demanding that the PKI be banned. But it also displayed a distinctly "opposition" flavor, many of its participants calling for a new cabinet and abolition of the National Council.[128] Masjumi afterwards stressed the significance of the Congress, but NU was compelled to side with the PKI in condemning it, albeit for different reasons.[129]

Soon after the Palembang meeting, the Masjumi and NU youth organizations, GPII and Ansor, led by Mattaquien and Imron Rosjadi respectively, took the initiative in trying to call a conference of all Islamic parties to promote unity.[130] Leaders of the several Islamic parties

---

126 A leading organizer of the Congress was the West Javanese Masjumi leader, Isa Anshary, one of Masjumi's most fervent supporters of the Islamic state. Moderate Masjumi leaders, such as Natsir, Roem, Prawoto, and Sukiman, were usually dismayed by Anshary, but they could not control him.

127 *Duta Masjarakat*, Sept. 6, 1957.

128 See *Muktamar Ulama se-Indonesia di Palembang*, the report of the Congress, in a special number of the monthly, *Daulah Islamyah* (edited by Isa Anshary), no date. The meetings lasted from September 8 to 11.

129 At the end of October, the Moslem League secretary, H. Sofjan Siradji, said that the League would vote to condemn the decisions of the *alim ulama* congress (*Harian Rakjat*, Oct. 31, 1957). M. Sjafei, a South Sumatran PSII leader, censured the *alim ulama* meeting and invited the PKI to exchange ideas on uniting the Indonesian people against colonialism. See *Sin Po*, Oct. 2, 1957. He was somewhat outside the normal course of PSII public thinking, but the party leadership generally was intent on making itself secure and avoiding contamination by Masjumi.

130 See *Kuang Po*, Sept. 9; *Pedoman*, Sept. 28, 1957. In early October the Islamic party PPTI (Partai Politik Tharikat Islam) in Central Sumatra sent an open letter to all Islamic parties, urging them to unite under one symbol in the next elections (*Harian Penerangan*, Oct. 5, 1957).

expressed pro-forma approval of the effort to unite Indonesian Islam, but there was in fact little non-Masjumi support for the move. NU leaders perceived it as another attempt to force their party into a closer political association with Masjumi. Arguing that such a conference would not profit Islam, Wahab Chasbullah made the amazing assertion that a display of unity among Moslem parties would only unite the enemies of Islam.[131] Without NU's support, the conference could not take place. In the months after September, the NU emphasized the Moslem League as the proper organization for unifying political Islam and directing Islamic efforts against Communism.[132] But here Masjumi was not interested, for the League would obviously not serve the rest of Masjumi's political demands.

The Constituent Assembly

Only in the Constituent Assembly did Masjumi and NU finally act together in 1957, for here all Islamic parties had to respond to the call of the Faith. In the process, the Konstituante stalled, the party system suffered another setback, and Masjumi remained politically isolated.

The issues involved in the Konstituante operated at several different levels of political and ideological conflict. Without exception the parties were anxious to resolve the ideological stalemate which stymied the Konstituante, whose failure would merely prove Soekarno's point that the parties were incapable of working out the nation's affairs and that the party system was deleterious. Moreover, unless the Konstituante succeeded, the parties would lose their opportunity to buttress the legitimacy of the parliamentary system by renewing it in a permanent constitution. But the division between secular and Islamic groups was insurmountable, secular parties having a voting edge of approximately 285 against 230 but lacking

---

131 *Pedoman*, Sept. 25, 1957. Wahab said that he would not mind a conference of all parties which acknowledged the existence of God, thus including the Christian parties and all others except the PKI. Obviously Wahab was determined to separate the PKI problem from all others on which the NU did not care to identify with Masjumi. In doing so he sometimes seemed to come very close to denying the Islamic struggle. For a reply to Wahab, see *Hikmah*, X, no. 40 (Nov. 2, 1957), 23.

132 *Duta Masjarakat*, Oct. 29, 1957.

the two-thirds majority required to approve constitutional articles.[133] Therefore a compromise was necessary, but an ideological compromise depended upon political pre-conditions.

Political strife unrelated to ideology naturally carried over into the Konstituante. Thus the second most important issue in the constitutional debates was that of federalism vs. unitarism. Masjumi's national position was reflected in its support of a federal state. It has been mentioned that the unitary state *per se* was a powerful nationalist symbol, especially appealing to the Javanese parties and to the army officer corps. However, the regional crisis had the effect of making several members of the NU particularly and also the PNI more amenable to arguments favoring some kind of federal arrangement, though even these men often insisted on retaining the term "unitarism."[134]

The possibility of an anti-Communist alliance bore directly on compromise efforts in the Constituent Assembly in 1957. Those who eagerly advocated a three-party coalition saw the Constituent Assembly as a last hope; an ideological rapprochement between the PNI and Masjumi would help to end the latter's isolation and perhaps make it possible for the two parties to come to terms on other issues that separated them. For its part, the PKI, though it desired a successful Konstituante, nevertheless was opposed to the compromise that might bring it about. Not only

---

133 The representations of the Major parties in the Konstituante were as follows: PNI 117, Masjumi 114, NU 90, PKI 59. The total membership of the Konstituante was approximately 500. A majority of the secular groups supported the Pantjasila as the state ideology. The Murba and Labor parties, however, proposed a "social-economy" state philosophy, partly as a compromise; but their nine votes had little influence. On the Konstituante's organization and the substantive materials considered by it, see Simorangkir and Mang Reng Say, *Konstitusi dan Konstituante Indonesia* (Djakarta: Soeroengan, 1958), vol. 1.

134 In mid-1957, Gen. Nasution spoke accusingly of a movement to change the unitary state into a federal state. He was referring primarily to regionalist tendencies, though he may have had the Konstituante in mind too. See *Abadi*, July 24, 1957. Even army officers who later joined the PRRI were not unanimously agreed upon federalism, for many of them shared the sensitivity of the officer corps generally to the disunity and indiscipline which federalism represented, as well as to its negative symbolism. However, many officers were convinced that a political structure falling just short of federalism was necessary to satisfy the regions. Outer island branches of NU and the PNI favored structures that would represent the outer islands better, and this had the effect of toning down opposition to federalism generally. The PKI was the most vehement opponent of federalism among the parties. It should be mentioned, incidentally, that not even Masjumi leaders were entirely agreed on federalism; Noer notes that Yunan Nasution, a member of the Masjumi party council, was unwilling to go along with party opinion favoring a federal state ("Masjumi," p. 374).

would that favor Masjumi's position, but moreover anything less than a fully secular constitution might later be used to cause trouble by Islamic zealots who constantly threatened to ban atheistic Communism.[135]

Operating on a related but confusingly different plane in the Constituent Assembly was the ideological conflict itself, in part politically determined but having a life of its own. The acrimonious debates which had long been going on between secularists and their Islamic challengers found their institutional focus in the Constituent Assembly, which would determine once and for all whether the state should be based on the secular Pantjasila or on the tenets of Islam.[136] A fear-bred dislike of fervent Islam, shared by a large majority of inland Central and East Javanese, was a factor in the opposition to an Islamic state, but for the most part the secularists simply did not believe that Islam had anything to contribute to a modern Indonesian state. Both Soekarno and the devoutly Islamic Hatta openly expressed their conviction that the broadly conceived Pantjasila would unify the nation while Islam would divide it. A majority of army officers, including many who were otherwise sympathetic to Islam, were also committed to the Pantjasila, seeing in ideological Islam the origins of the Darul Islam, with which the army had had considerable bloody experience. Islamic leaders countered with the arguments that the Koran provided all the principles (including tolerance) that were needed to run a state, and that in any case this ideology was God's will.[137]

Yet despite the seemingly implacable opposition of these stands, an ideological compromise — though a very delicate matter — was possible, so long as a political agreement could be worked out. Moderate leaders of Masjumi and especially NU were not disposed to fight to the bitter and futile ideological end. Masjumi's greater interest in a favorable resolution

---

135 In religious Indonesia, the PKI was avoiding religious clashes. It took the view that although the PKI as a party was atheistic, its members could be believers and the party had nothing against religion. The PKI, said Aidit, only wanted freedom of religion and no forcing of religion; *Harian Rakjat*, Oct. 22, 1957.

136 Although the ideological battle in the Konstituante centered on the content of the preamble to the new constitution, more was involved. Questions of Islamic law, courts, and other institutions also hinged on the final outcome of the debate. In the various sub-committees of the Konstituante's constitutional preparatory commission, these other issues did arise, and proposals were submitted with respect to them.

137 Speeches on ideology in the Konstituante are compiled in the three volume collection, *Tentang Dasar Negara Republik Indonesia dalam Konstituante* (On the Basis of the State of the Republic of Indonesia in the Konstituante; Bandung or Djakarta: no publisher, 1958?).

of political issues than in ideological purity is indicated, for example, by Moh. Natsir's speech on the twelfth anniversary of the party in October 1957, wherein his total concern was with Masjumi's political demands.[138] Nor was this a matter of taking party ideology for granted; rather — without implying that Islamic leaders were weak on conviction — the point is that ideologies in Indonesia were to a large extent convenient symbols of competing groups within the national elite, who could sacrifice parts of the dogma in exchange for political concessions.

An important qualification is in order here, however, for the freedom of Islamic leaders to compromise was critically limited by the ideological character of their parties. Islamic parties depended for their cohesion on ideological Islam. The importance of Islam in the political motivation of the ranks of the Islamic parties (and certainly for the fanatic fringe) was of course great; their attachment to national party leaders was articulated in terms of the ideology. Therefore any ideological compromise would require a substantial obeisance to Islam, for otherwise the bond between the Islamic political elite and its followers would be threatened. A compromise would also have to be quick, because of the constant danger that pressure from within their parties might force Islamic leaders into a defense of principle. Similarly, one of the Islamic parties could not accept a compromise while others valiantly carried on the struggle. Masjumi was on guard against the possibility that NU might come to an agreement with the secular parties, and was able to nip such inclinations in the bud by bringing moral pressure to bear on NU members in the Constituent Assembly. Masjumi itself stuck to its ideological guns tenaciously in the hope of winning a favorable compromise on both political and ideological questions — a strategy that never proved successful.

---

138 See *Hikmah*, Nov. 9, 1957, pp. 4-8. Another illustration of the intricate connection between political and ideological interests is the response of Djerman Prawiradinata, a West Javanese Masjumi MP, to Hatta's support of the Pantjasila. Hatta had said that he would gladly serve as Prime Minister in a state based on the Pantjasila. Djerman's comment on this was that Hatta would naturally interpret the Pantjasila correctly: his Pantjasila state would pay prime attention to the first *sila*, Belief in God, and of course there would be no place in it for atheistic groups like the Communists. Masjumi, said Djerman (and others), had never argued that the Pantjasila was no good; it was only feared that in the hands of the wrong groups "the altogether neutral Pantjasila" might swerve from the right ideas (*PIA*, Nov. 21, 1957). Masjumi continually argued that it was willing to accept the Pantjasila, but with an elaboration of it — particularly the first *sila* — in Islamic terms.

The plenary debates on ideology were to begin in November 1957.[139] In August, when talk of a PNI-Masjumi-NU alliance was rife, PNI and Masjumi leaders in the Konstituante began to make conciliatory motions towards one another, the initiative apparently being taken by Central Javanese PNI members, including Sarino Mangunpranoto, chairman of the PNI delegation.[140] Vaguely worded political promises were frequent. Masjumi offered the tempting bait that if the PNI would incorporate Islamic principles into the Pantjasila, the Konstituante would undoubtedly finish its work in two years instead of four.[141] Sarino told the press that an ideological compromise would have "broader influence in the form of concrete cooperation between the Religious and Nationalist groups in facing the future building of the state."[142] In October, the advocates of a compromise were delighted by an obvious PNI slap at the PKI in the Konstituante subcommittee dealing with ideology. The PKI had proposed that the Pantjasila incorporate a statement recognizing the existence of "all forms and currents of political opinion in Indonesia," an attempt to erect a safeguard against anti-Communist threats and to make Communism respectable. Members of the PNI, Parkindo, and the Catholic party rejected the suggestion and shunted it aside from the Pantjasila category of ideological proposals. This did not, however, alter the PKI's commitment in the Constituent Assembly to the Pantjasila.[143]

Specific compromise solutions were proposed. One is discussed briefly here because it turns up again in 1959, when the Constituent Assembly held its last, and again unproductive, ideological debate. This was the idea of basing the constitution on the original Djakarta Charter of 1945, a result of the first compromise efforts by nationalist and Islamic leaders two months before Soekarno and Hatta proclaimed

---

139 Between plenary sessions, held twice yearly, the work of the Konstituante was done by a Constitutional Preparatory Commission. This commission was divided into several temporary subcommittees, each dealing with a part of the Constitution: ideology (subcommittee I), government structure, human rights, economy, and so on. Most sizeable parties were represented on each subcommittee. See Simorangkir and Mang Reng Say, *Konstitusi dan Konstituante*.

140 See *PIA*, Aug. 28; *Keng Po*, Sept. 13, 22, 1957.

141 *Java Bode*, Oct. 7, 1958.

142 *Keng Po*, Sept. 22, 1957. Sarino also pointed out that if there was no compromise, the PNI would be the beneficiary, because the provisional constitution would remain in effect and its ideological guide was the Pantjasila, Secular groups did have the important tactical advantage of defending the status quo on ideology.

143 *PIA*, Oct. 4, 1957.

independence. At that time Soekarno and the secular nationalist group initially made two concessions to Moslem leaders. The first was to change the order of the five points of the Pantjasila (which Soekarno had only recently enunciated) to put Belief in God first.[144] The second was to add an interpretive phrase to the first *sila* in the document that was called the Djakarta Charter-it read: "[The] Republic of Indonesia...[is] based on: Belief in God, with the obligation of practicing the Islamic Sjariah for the adherents of Islam."[145] Islamic groups were not strong enough to insist on the retention of this provision, and within a few days it was removed from the Djakarta Charter, Soekarno arguing that it would drive Christians and other religious minorities away.[146] The Djakarta Charter, without the Islamic injunction, became the preamble of the 1945 Constitution. In 1957 Islamic groups proposed that the phrase be readopted — as an elaboration of the Pantjasila — in the interests of compromise.[147] Apparently several members of Masjumi and the PNI found the original Djakarta Charter to be an acceptable solution, partly because there was little agreement on the meaning of the Sjariah clause. Sarino mentioned such a course as a possibility in September, when he said that an ideological compromise might be a "national state in which the Islamic law was guaranteed."[148]

---

144 The original order of the Pantjasila was: 1) nationalism, 2) humanitarianism, 3) people's sovereignty, 4) social justice, and 5) belief in God. See Soekarno, *Lahirnja Pantjasila* (The Birth of the Pantjasila; Djakarta: Ministry of Information). Prof. Moh. Yamin published the minutes of discussions in the two successive preparatory committees set up during the last three months of the Japanese occupation to consider problems of independence and to draft a constitution. See *Naskah Persiapan Undang-Undang Dasar 1945* (Documents on the Preparation of the 1945 Constitution; Djakarta: Jajasan Prapantja, 1959), vol. 1.

145 For the full text of the Djakarta Charter in English, see The *Indonesian Revolution: Basic Documents and the Idea of Guided Democracy* (Djakarta: Ministry of Information, special issue 65, 1960), pp. 53-54.

146 In his speech to the Konstituante in December, Roeslan Abdulgani (PNI) presented an excellent discussion of the origins and significance of the Djakarta Charter and the Sjariah phrase from a secularist point of view. He said that he had discussed the matter with Soekarno before drafting his speech. The speech is also a powerful statement of the secular argument in general. See *Tentang Dasar Negara*, III, 348-372. Roeslan concluded by saying, in effect, that the compromise of making Belief in God the first *sila* was enough.

147 *PIA*, Sept. 11; *Keng Po*, Sept. 13, 1957.

148 *Keng Po*, Sept. 22, 1957. For Islamic groups, the Islamic law was the logical core of their argument; without it, an "Islamic State" or a "state based on Islam" was meaningless. Yet among university-trained Masjumi leaders, especially some of the lawyers, there was considerable doubt about the usefulness of the Islamic law in a modern state, though it was not a doubt that could be expressed easily in public.

But the Djakarta Charter remained only a possible compromise. Within the PNI there were some members — especially Christians — who would not go that far under any circumstances.[149] Moreover, although Konstituante members could approach one another to some extent, this was less true of national party leaders, who assumed the leading role when the plenary debates began. The PNI soon began to feel uncomfortable about the fact that while the PKI staunchly defended the Pantjasila, it was members of the PNI, the original party of the Pantjasila, who were contemplating compromise. Also Soekarno displayed no sympathy for compromise efforts.[150] Masjumi later blamed the PNI and Soekarno for scuttling all attempts to resolve the ideological conflict, but by the time the Konstituante debates began in mid-November Masjumi leaders themselves had begun to lose interest in a compromise. They were increasingly frustrated in their opposition to the Government's regional, economic, and foreign policies. The Tjikini assassination attempt and the take-over of Dutch enterprises at the end of November and early December threw the whole political situation out of kilter. For Masjumi a single dimension compromise on ideology was meaningless while no concessions were forthcoming from the Government or from other parties on more imperative political questions.

The NU waited almost passively in the wings for an unmistakable cue. When it appeared unlikely that the PNI and Masjumi would in fact come together, NU quickly followed Masjumi towards a stand on principle. On the first day of the debate, November 10th, Suwirjo told the Constituent Assembly that any state philosophy other than the Pantjasila would endanger the well-being of the nation.[151] Natsir attacked secularism, insisting that only Islam could fulfill all the requirements of Indonesian statehood.[152] A few days later, partly in response to Masjumi pressure, the Moslem League declared that "an independent Indonesia based on Islam

149 See the speech of Arnold Mononutu, a Christian PNI member from North Sulawesi, in *Tentang Dasar Negara*, II, 341-352.
150 In the Catholic island of Flores, Soekarno said that Catholics would have complete freedom of religion under the Pantjasila. He reminded his audience of the treacherous Kartosuwirjo, leader of the West Javanese Darul Islam (*Antara*, Nov. 6, 1957). Islamic groups protested Soekarno's statements supporting the Pantjasila.
151 *Tentang Dasar Negara*, I, 1-12. The substance of the ideological debates will not be dealt with here.
152 *Ibid.*, pp. 109-141.

is the responsibility of all Moslems, especially those in the Konstituante."[153] NU secretary-general Zuhri said a week afterwards that the impression was incorrect that Islamic leaders were actively seeking a compromise on ideology outside of the Constituent Assembly. For NU, Zuhri stated, to carry on the Islamic struggle was an obligation that could not be evaded, even if the Pantjasila was a necessary precondition for restoring the Dwitunggal.[154] The PKI drove the wedge more deeply between Islamic and secular groups by connecting the Tjikini Affair with Masjumi's effort to make Islam the state philosophy, an accusation to which both NU and Masjumi reacted sharply, moving towards an even firmer defense of their ideology. *Duta Masjarakat*, the NU paper, reminded the PKI that it was not only Masjumi which supported Islam but also NU.[155]

In December there was still talk of a compromise, and members of the PNI and Masjumi as well as a few minor parties proposed various "middle-ways."[156] But it was obvious that the major parties had failed to resolve the conflict. There was sporadic talk of abolishing the deadlocked Konstituante — a suggestion that understandably dismayed party leaders.[157] Disappointed at the failure to overcome the impasse, most parties sought to save the situation by holding the ideological debate in abeyance until a more favorable time. The PSI and others proposed that the Constituent Assembly turn to the rest of the constitution and come back to ideology later. The Assembly decided not to take a vote at this session, in the hope that a compromise could yet be worked out before the next plenary debates.

On this discouraging note, the ideological discussions ended in 1957, giving further proof that the Constituent Assembly was no more capable

---

153 *Duta Masjarakat*, Nov. 19, 1957.

154 *Ibid.*, Nov. 23, 1957. This was in response to the speech of Sakirman (PKI), who proposed that the Pantjasila be accepted by acclamation and said that this would help efforts to restore the Dwitunggal, a point that angered members of both Masjumi and NU. Zuhri insisted that the Hatta issue must be separated completely from the question of ideology.

155 *Duta Masjarakat*, Dec. 3, 4, 1957. For the PKI comment, see *Harian Rakjat Sport dan Film*, Dec. 1, 1957.

156 In a second speech, Suwirjo appealed for an effort to seek a compromise, but did not suggest a basis for one (*Antara*, Nov. 22, 1957). Masjumi members felt at this point that everything depended upon the PNI's willingness to make a concession. Bahrum Djamil of Masjumi said in response to Suwirjo's speech that the balance of power was clear and that it was up to the PNI to choose with whom it wanted to cooperate.

157 See *Abadi*, Nov. 12, 1957.

of achieving results than Parliament. The debates also made it clearer that there would be no anti-Communist alliance.

Discussion of a PNI-Masjumi-NU coalition continued into January, however, stimulated by the great boost which the PKI enjoyed after the Tjikini Affair and the take-over of Dutch firms. But as the regional crisis began to come to a head, the PNI and NU drew further away from Masjumi. Masjumi and the PSI renewed their attacks on the Government in January, accusing it of handling the West Irian issue badly, the regional crisis worse, and economic conditions hopelessly. Both parties demanded a new cabinet with adequate moral authority to deal with the nation's crises. But the PNI and NU rushed to the defense of the Government. When at the end of January regionalist leaders in Padang insisted that the cabinet resign, Wahab Chasbullah of NU stated flatly that his party did not believe a new cabinet would be better than the existing one, even if Hatta were to lead it.[158] The PKI also affirmed its support of the Kabinet Karya, praising it as second best only to a Government with Communists in it.[159] In February all hopes of a three party alliance were shattered by the rebellion, which stigmatized Masjumi as treasonable and made it impossible for PNI and NU leaders to consider any working arrangements with it at all on the national level.

But, after all, the alliance had been a mirage all along. From Masjumi's point of view, anti-Communism was only one goal. That alone would not bring Masjumi in out of the cold rain of opposition, and to be permanently out of the Government was a possibility that could not be accepted either by the party or by the regions which it represented. For the PNI and NU, however, there was no question of relinquishing their positions in the Kabinet Karya for the sake of Masjumi. Having no power to determine the course of events, they preferred security to chance. Indeed, the real community of interest in the party world in 1957 was between the leadership of the PNI and NU; their concern was to maintain the cabinet in which they exercised some authority and to assure themselves of a place in any future Government. So strong were the arguments of PNI and NU leaders on this score that such cries as

---

158 *Keng Po*, Jan. 30, 1958.
159 *Ibid.*

there were in those parties for a new cabinet were quickly drowned out.[160] Never did an alternative course offer sufficient attractions to make them alter their views. Persistently, from June 1957 onwards, the PNI and NU affirmed their determination to defend the Djuanda Cabinet, as they had the previous Ali Cabinet; and, as in the case of the Ali Cabinet, the PKI fully supported their determination. Masjumi banged against a door that would not open.

---

160 As early as June, NU leaders made their resolve to remain in the cabinet perfectly clear. See *Keng Po*, June 18; *Duta Masjarakat*, July 11, 1957. In July, Suwirjo declared, in connection with rumors that the PNI, NU, and Masjumi might cooperate to form a new cabinet, that the PNI would not cooperate with anyone for the purpose of unseating the existing cabinet (*Keng Po*, July 11, 1957).

CHAPTER FOUR
THE REBELLION AND THE POLITICAL SYSTEM

The PRRI rebellion acted as a political catalyst to make permanent the trends begun tentatively in 1956 and 1957. Were it not for the temptation to call nearly every major event since 1956 a watershed in Indonesian politics, one might be justified in so labelling the rebellion. Eliminating the regional challenge to Java was only one of its significant consequences. A second was that it greatly strengthened the two partners of the anti-party alliance — Soekarno and the army.

The President's strongest opponents were eliminated or tainted by the rebellion. The fact that Soekarno had himself been something of a major issue in the regional crisis meant that the decision to confront the PRRI was also a defense of his position. Those who remained loyal to the Government were largely committed to supporting Soekarno's right — indeed, his responsibility — to lead the nation. The hostility of the United States to Soekarno, by arousing nationalist sentiment, also served to strengthen him. No longer was it necessary for him to make even a gesture of compromise towards Hatta, who now became an important but passive symbol of the opposition.

Similarly, the army drew political benefit from the rebellion. The civil war emphasized its role as protector of the nation, giving officers an even greater sense of their importance to the state. Moreover, the officer corps was purged of its most "radical" members, achieving in the process a greater degree of unity than it had ever before enjoyed. Nasution's position was secured, for the rebellion removed both his primary opposition and most of the potentially competitive chief-of-staff material within the officer corps at that time. Lubis, Simbolon, and Kawilarang, once considered as possible successors to Nasution, were now in the jungle. There remained Brigadier General Gatot Soebroto, second in command of the army; but he was then in his fifties, and had not the political sagacity of Nasution. Nor was any threat presented by either of the other two Brigadier Generals, Soengkono and Djatikusumo.[1] Finally, the rebellion offered an excellent excuse for maintaining martial law despite the insistent demands of civilian politicians that it be lifted.

A third major consequence of the rebellion, and a primary theme of this chapter, was that the political party system was restructured and the parties forced to mesh gears more intimately with the non-parliamentary power structure. The importance of this lies in the fact that the evolution of Guided Democracy was very much dependent on the interweaving of the anti-party and inter-party conflicts. It was not merely a case of Soekarno and the army suppressing the old system. Except for the PKI, nearly all the parties energetically helped to emasculate themselves. There were two key elements in this process. First, the decline of the parliamentary system, accelerated by the political impact of the rebellion, reinforced the tendency of the PNI and NU to work for political advantages within the new structure. The second element, related to the first, was the growing fear of most parties that they would finally be overwhelmed by the PKI. Here too the rebellion was important. It completed the process, in course since the first Ali Cabinet (1953-55), of isolating Masjumi and strengthening the PKI. Within the party system, the latter now faced only the inadequately equipped PNI and NU.

The discussion that follows will deal with the party system after the outbreak of the rebellion, the cabinet reshuffle of June 1958, and the rapid disintegration of the parties' position vis-a-vis the anti-party forces.

The Parties After the Rebellion

The rebellion and its rapid reduction placed several parties in jeopardy. All those who had opposed the Government in the regional crisis were left out on a limb. Four or five of the parties were in danger of reprisals as

---

1 Gatot Soebroto was promoted to Brig. Gen. in July 1957, Soengkono and Djatikusumo in November. Nasution was promoted to Lt. Gen. in July 1958, becoming the first Lt. Gen. since the late Sudirman, first commander of the army during the revolution. Along with Nasution, Navy Chief-of-Staff Subijakto and Air Force Chief-of-Staff Suryadarma were promoted to Vice-Admiral and Vice-Commodore respectively. See *Pesat*, XIV, no. 29 (July 19, 1958), 16.

some of their members had actually joined the PRRI. They all certainly stood to lose political influence; their views automatically counted for much less than previously. Any hope for a comeback depended on a compromise by the Government with the PRRI. But compromise was an unacceptable solution to Soekarno, to the PKI, to many in the PNI, and to some in the army. Therefore, even apart from the fact that anger against the PRRI generally ran very high, a compromise was unlikely, and indeed did not come about. As a result, a large segment of Indonesia's political spectrum was eclipsed.

Masjumi's decline after the rebellion began was final. It continued to exist as a party, to exercise its strength in Parliament, and to speak out in opposition to the Government, but its political influence was irredeemably diminished. Identified with the PRRI through the participation of Natsir, Sjafruddin, and Burhanuddin, it was tagged the party of rebellion, separatism, and foreign intervention. The leverage which it had enjoyed as the party of the outer islands disappeared the moment the decision was taken to meet the regional challenge with force. Whatever influence Masjumi might have regained was lost after February 1958 because of the ambivalent attitude the party took towards the rebellion. Stunned by the events of February-April and under severe attack by NU, the PKI, the PNI, and independent nationalist opinion (including the army), Masjumi faced a crisis of survival. Political wisdom counseled denunciation of the PRRI and all party members connected with it.[2] Parkindo, IPKI, and the PSI chose this course, though the PSI refused to take special measures against Soemitro Djojohadi-kusumo.[3]

---

2 For a comment on Masjumi's dilemma and a demand that it renounce Natsir, Sjafruddin, and Burhanuddin, see *Pesat*, XIV, no. 18 (May 13, 1958), 10-11. *Merdeka*, July 1, 1958, warned that only a convincing rejection by Masjumi of the PRRI, or the rise of a new group within Masjumi which could adapt to present conditions, would save the party from the dangers created by some of its leaders.

3 Each of these three parties denied any complicity in the rebellion, refusing to hold itself responsible for the acts of individual members. The PSI refused to mete out special punishment for Soemitro on the grounds that he had already removed himself from the party by disobeying it. To go further than this would have been to admit party responsibility, and this the PSI would not do. It came under harsher attack than the other minor parties because Soemitro was so important a figure and one as closely identified with the PSI leadership as Sjafruddin was with Masjumi. Parkindo and IPKI involvement in the PRRI was almost entirely limited to local members in Sumatra.

   Parkindo, as a religious minority party, was safer from attack than some of the other parties connected with the PRRI. Moreover, it did not present a serious political threat to anyone, though Soekarno found some of its leaders objectionable because of their opposition to him.

But what was left of Masjumi's leadership disagreed on what course to follow.

A minority of Masjumi leaders, including first vice-chairman Sukiman and Jusuf Wibisono, believed that the party must act quickly to avoid losing all national influence or possibly suffering outright suppression. According to their view, Natsir, Sjafruddin, and Burhanuddin had jeopardized Masjumi's existence and must be expelled from the party. The Sukiman group advocated a policy of peaceful compromise with the PRRI, but insisted that Masjumi must condemn the rebellion in order to be rehabilitated. Any other posture, they argued, was inconsistent; to refuse to denounce the rebellion and yet to continue to participate in legal politics was two-faced and debilitating.[4] The inevitable outcome of such a course would be that Masjumi's power would disappear altogether, imperiling the entire Islamic cause in Indonesia.

The prevailing group in the party, however, was that led by second vice-chairman Prawoto Mangkusasmito and, among others, Kasman Singodimedjo.[5] It was, for the most part, the old Natsir wing of the party — or at least closer to it than to the Sukiman wing. Basically their view

---

Also, Parkindo had an important protector in the cabinet in the person of Third Vice-Premier Leimena. The PSI had none of these benefits, and it suffered somewhat more than the others. A move was already underway in the government to reduce PSI influence in the top levels of the bureaucracy — e.g., ministerial secretary-generals associated with the PSI were forced into retirement by ex-post-facto limitation of the tenure of high level bureaucrats. The PSI was not deeply hurt, however, for its leaders remained influential among highly educated intellectuals in the government and, to some extent, in the army. Moreover, in many ways PSI leaders had stopped thinking of themselves as a party, regarding their political role — sometimes pretentiously — as one of intellectual guidance.

4   This point was made by H. Firdaus, a young Masjumi leader, in an attack on Kasman Singodimedjo. See *Pos Indonesia*, Sept. 8, 1958. (*Pos Indonesia*, begun in August 1958, succeeded in its high standard of reporting to the place of *Keng Po*, which was banned in February.) Firdaus declared that Masjumi's refusal to condemn the rebellion was in violation of parliamentary principles. Indeed, although the course of events obscured the logic of the matter, it was ironic that Masjumi, which had condemned the PKI for being anti-parliamentary, should now condone the ultimate contradiction of parliamentary government. The reply to this, of course, was that Soekarno had already violated the Constitution in 1957 — a reply that was regarded as pouting, and one that did nothing to help Masjumi's position.

5   The party division on this issue did not follow Java-outer island lines. Firdaus is a Sumatran; Sukiman, Wibisono, Prawoto, and Kasman are Javanese. Nor were generational lines the determining factor. Partly however, the division can be understood in terms of the differences between the Sukiman and Natsir wings of the party. The former, having always been able to communicate better with the "Javanese parties" and older nationalist leaders, had some trust in there still being grounds for working with some of the other parties to influence the course of politics.

was that an unequivocal denunciation of the PRRI by Masjumi would demolish the last bridge between the two camps in the civil war and make a compromise impossible. To this analysis was added a sense of righteous indignation with Soekarno and the Government and a conviction that Masjumi would never regain its former position without a total reversal of all political trends; therefore, why go along with the victorious enemy? Moreover, there was a reluctance to commit so flagrant an act of disloyalty as the renunciation of Natsir et al., with whom ties of friendship and respect remained strong. Possibly this sentiment was compounded by feelings of guilt among a few Masjumi leaders at not having joined a good cause in the jungle. Some were loathe to hurt the PRRI's chances, hoping that it might yet win in the long run, either through a reversal of the trend of Djakarta politics or through the economic ruin which Soemitro predicted would bring the central government to its knees.

After the outbreak of the rebellion, the Prawoto group determined Masjumi's posture — one of implacable stands on principle which made the party difficult to approach. In early March, before the Government began full-scale military operations in Sumatra, Firdaus — a second echelon national Masjumi leader — tried to call an emergency session of the party council to choose a new chairman to replace Natsir, but the proposal was blocked by Prawoto and a majority of the council. Natsir therefore remained Masjumi's party chairman *in absentia* until April 1959, when Prawoto was elected to the position; Sukiman, as interim leader in 1958, was unable to exercise much authority.[6] The anomaly of Natsir's retaining the chairmanship and the reluctance of party leaders to adjust to political realities left Masjumi in a very vulnerable position. On August 31st, at a party meeting in a Magelang movie house, Kasman Singodimedjo declared that the central government was as much to blame for the rebellion as were PRRI leaders and as deserving of punishment. There was no reason, he went on, for Masjumi to punish its leaders who had joined the rebellion, for they had done the party no wrong. Military authorities arrested Kasman within a few days, and he was later arraigned

---

6   The tension between the Sukiman and Prawoto groups was obvious throughout 1958. Wibisono resigned from the party executive council in December because of "differences of opinion" within the party. (See *Pos Indonesia*, Jan. 2, 1959.)

on charges of abetting the enemy.[7] The speech opened Masjumi to attack on all sides. Firdaus called it a trumpet of Masjumi's death, accusing those who refused to take a consistent stand on the rebellion of sacrificing the interests of the Islamic *ummat*.[8] Similarly, Masjumi's continued demand for compromise with the PRRI — a demand supported by the whole party — called forth government reprisals and renewed attacks by the PKI, the PNI, and NU. In October, a meeting of Masjumi-related *alim ulama* in West Java issued a resolution proposing *islah* (peaceful reconciliation) with the rebels. Masjumi gave the resolution its unqualified blessing, and consequently suffered a flood of abuse in the press, the arrest of several West Javanese Masjumi leaders by the army, and an accusation by NU leaders that Masjumi was damaging the cause of Islam.[9]

After the PRRI's military retreat the dominant mood in Masjumi approached defeatism. Government action to abolish the party, frequently rumored in 1958, would not have been a surprise to Masjumi. The party lost its dynamism and showed signs of disintegration. On May 8, the party newspaper, *Abadi*, ceased publication until September 26, ostensibly because of financial difficulties.[10] Masjumi's constituent member organizations, which had always been a problem in terms of party structure, started thinking more seriously about leaving the party in order to protect themselves. A debate on this question in Muhammadijah, from which much of Masjumi's leadership had been drawn, had begun again in 1957 and became more strident in 1958.[11] The Masjumi labor organization, SBII, which split in early 1958, and the youth movement, GPII, began gradually to assert their independence of the party, though there was no formal break. In July, a group of young Masjumi leaders in

---

7   Court report of the trial of Kasman beginning in September 1960 (typescript). Kasman lost his case and was sentenced to prison.

8   *Pos Indonesia*, Sept. 8, 1958. Firdaus, at the same time, proposed a "holy mission" from the Government to the rebels to seek a peaceful settlement.

9   The *alim ulama* meeting also took on an anti-Soekarno and anti-Guided Democracy cast. See *Pos Indonesia*, Oct. 13, 1958. The arrest of five West Javanese Masjumi leaders shortly afterwards was connected also with a statement by the regional party in July demanding that, in the interests of national peace, Soekarno should stop violating the constitution. Civil war, said the statement, must be ended peacefully. *Pos Indonesia*, Oct. 28; *Abadi*, Oct. 27, 28, Nov. 4, 1958.

10 *Abadi*, May 8, 1958; and *Kronik Pers*, 1958, p. 51.

11 Some proposed that Muhammadijah run in the next elections under its own symbol. Most Muhammadijah members opposed direct involvement in politics, however, for fear that the organization's other functions would suffer. See *Nusantara*, June 26, 1958.

East Java met to discuss the possibility of forming a new Islamic party under "progressive Masjumi leaders."[12] In the position of permanent opposition towards which Masjumi was moving, there was little to attract and hold a following. Ideology alone seems to have been largely responsible for keeping the party together after mid-1958.

It must not be supposed, however, that an about-face on the rebellion would have allowed Masjumi to go on as if nothing had happened. By being more flexible it might have added strength to those groups, particularly within the army, that were equally interested in bringing the rebellion to a peaceful end through compromise; and therein lay Masjumi's only hope, however slight, for a comeback. As it was, Masjumi hurt its own cause and assured its own isolation by persevering in a political stance that others, no matter how sympathetic, could espouse openly only at the risk of being similarly tainted. But even had Masjumi been more flexible, it would have been at a great political disadvantage, for it had lost its outer-island leverage and had been defeated on all the important issues of 1957.

The implications of Masjumi's decline for the course of Indonesian politics were manifold. For one thing, it presaged an end to the basic ideological struggle which had gone on since the revolution — indeed, since the coming of age of the nationalist movement under the Dutch. Political Islam was crippled. As many in the Islamic elite feared, Masjumi's political failure could not but affect in direct proportion the outcome of the Islam-Pantjasila debate — hence the plea of Firdaus and several NU leaders that for the sake of Islam Masjumi must denounce the PRRI and Natsir. In December 1958, two well-known Masjumi leaders wrote, for limited circulation, an assessment of the Islamic struggle which portrayed the utter failure of the Darul Islam, the PRRI, and all previous legal parliamentary efforts to advance the cause of Islam. Their pessimistic analysis, tempered by a call for renewed dedication, was clearly predicated on the expected collapse of Masjumi.

---

12 *Trompet Masjarakat*, July 10, 1958. The name of the new party was to be Masjumi Ahli Sunnah wal Djamaah. Nothing came of it, but many devout modernist Moslems were beginning to worry that political Islam must seek a more powerful expression than Masjumi could offer after the rebellion began. NU was regarded by these groups as unsatisfactory because of its Java-centric traditionalism.

From another point of view, that of the defense of parliamentary institutions, Masjumi's decline weakened the entire party system. Partly this was because the unrepented involvement of Masjumi in the PRRI added another tangible blemish to the party system and to parliamentary government.[13] But more important, the forces of anti-partyism now had one less party to deal with. Masjumi's opposition to Guided Democracy was no longer a factor to be reckoned with; nor was its hostility to Soekarno. This meant that for practical purposes the party side of the Guided Democracy conflict consisted of only three major parties, two of which — the PKI and the PNI — had symbiotic political relationships with Soekarno; and the third, NU, was not constituted to act with great firmness or to carry much political weight alone.

Complicating this picture was the effect of Masjumi's decline on the structure of the party system. This became a central political consideration, appearing to different groups as either promising or threatening.[14] For example, NU might hope to gain in stature by succeeding to Masjumi's place as the chief Islamic party. With Masjumi no longer in the government, NU might also hope to lure away Masjumi support in the outer islands, where NU was generally weak. Balanced against this, however, was the loss of Masjumi to the ideological struggle and the loss of the additional bargaining power NU had enjoyed while Masjumi had posed a threat to the PNI, the PKI, and Soekarno. The opposition which NU leaders expressed to the idea of abolishing Masjumi sprang not only from the fear, shared by others, that banning any party was a dangerous precedent, but also from concern that no Masjumi would mean a much weaker NU. The PNI also hoped for much benefit from the decline of its traditional opponent. To PNI leaders it seemed that without the political and ideological challenge of Masjumi, the PNI would loom large as the

13 In an editorial of August 23, 1958, *Suluh Indonesia* (PNI) noted that Djuanda's admonition in Parliament (on August 16) that all groups should take a firm stand in condemning their members who had joined the PRRI, applied directly to Masjumi and the PSI. If these parties rejected the advice, said *Suluh Indonesia*, it would mean that they were not "in tune with the ideals which presented the opportunity to establish political parties in 1945." Chief Prosecutor Soeprapto threatened to undertake an investigation of "PRRI pockets" in Parliament (*Nusantara*, Sept. 2, 1958).

14 In January 1959, Suwirjo said in Makassar that as a result of the rebellion there would be a major shift in the balance of political power, which would be indicated in the next elections; *Pos Indonesia*, Jan. 21, 1959.

fortress of victorious nationalism, assuming the core position in every Government. The one element, however, that threatened to upset this profit-loss balancing was the growing power of the PKI. Assuming, as the parties did, that the parliamentary system would continue, the vigorous PKI was the primary challenge to the PNI and every other party.

With the weakening of Masjumi, the balance among political parties was thrown to the left, and the powerful position achieved by the PKI in 1957 seemed to be even further enhanced. Having already emerged from the regional elections as the nation's number one party, the PKI was now favored by other factors. Not only did the rebellion discredit Masjumi and eliminate the major threat of the anti-Communist regional movements, but it also thoroughly discredited the United States, because of its support of the PRRI. At the same time, the sympathies of the Soviet bloc and new aid agreements with the USSR, China, Poland, and Czechoslovakia highlighted a move by the country towards the left internationally that appeared to favor the PKI domestically. The PKI's determined opposition to the regionalists stood the party in good stead with the Government in late 1957 and the trying early months of 1958. Even the General Staff valued the PKI's cooperation. So subdued was PKI-army antagonism for a few brief months, from December until about March, that Nasution felt obliged in January to deny the charges of some foreign newsmen that the army was Communist-influenced.[15]

Moreover, certain side-effects of the rebellion benefitted the PKI. One was the unexpected stimulus to the expansion of Communist strength in Sumatra. On the invasion of West Sumatra, an area of powerful Masjumi support, the Diponegoro division command found Communists the most trustworthy candidates to run the civil administration of the occupied territory. Nearly everyone else could be shown to be connected with or, because of the clan kinship system, to have a relative connected with the PRRI. Only the PKI had consistently and outspokenly opposed — long before the rebellion was proclaimed — Husein and other local leaders involved in the PRRI. Consequently, PKI members were appointed by the

---

15 *Abadi*, Jan. 14, 1958. Nasution stated that the army was committed to the independent foreign policy of the government and ideologically to the Pantjasila. Only a few weeks later, after the rebellion began, foreign newspapers were reporting the essential conflict of views between Soekarno and Nasution over the Communist issue.

military command to positions of power throughout the area, in villages as well as in the regional administration.[16]

Another development that seemed to favor the PKI was the crackdown on the Kuomintang in Indonesia following disclosures of Taiwan's sympathy and aid for the rebels. The PKI led the campaign against the KMT but was supported by the PNI, NU, and many others. However, the latter groups acted on anti-Chinese as well as anti-Taiwan grounds, threatening the position of Chinese groups other than those connected with the KMT.[17] Thus in April, all Chinese language newspapers were banned, and the PKI had to leap to the defense of those papers which supported the Government.[18] KMT social, educational, and business organizations were restricted, closed, or harassed. Finally, in August, the KMT was banned altogether in Indonesia.[19]

These developments all helped to improve the position of the PKI, but there were dangers inherent in this improvement, and overall the party's situation was more menacing than promising. PKI leaders recognized the problems with crystal clarity at the sixth plenary session of the CCPKI

---

16 There were several indications of the PKI's attempt to consolidate its successes in West Sumatra. *Harian Rakjat*, May 27, 1958, reported that a PKI parliamentary delegation had seen the Minister of Internal Affairs to urge him to confirm permanently in their posts leaders of the popular resistance in Sumatra who had been appointed to the regional administration by the army. The delegation also urged that Nursuhud, a West Sumatran PKI leader, be appointed to the regional government advisory board. See also *Harian Rakjat*, April 17, 1959. The PKI's influence in West Sumatra was not permanently on the rise, however. When the rebellion came to an end in 1961 and the administrative autonomy of villages began to be restored, PKI leaders in the villages found that their authority began to decline quite rapidly, often because they did not enjoy traditional customary sanctions.

17 There was always a danger that an attack on one group of Chinese would spread to include all Chinese. Memories were still fresh of the Assaat movement against Chinese commercial power in 1956 and the anti-Chinese activities it set off. See Herbert Feith, *The Decline of Constitutional Democracy in Indonesia* (Ithaca, N.Y.: Cornell University Press, 1962), pp. 481-487. See also, G. William Skinner, "The Chinese Minority," in Ruth T. McVey, ed., *Indonesia* (New Haven: HRAF, 1963), pp. 97-118. What reduced the risk of a renewed wave of anti-Sinicism in 1958 was, again, the overwhelming predominance of the regional issue. Chinese groups and organizations — e.g., the Baperki — which stood firmly on the side of the government in the regional crisis had a sound defense at the time.

18 See *Harian Rakjat*, April 22, 1958, for an attack on the order (from Nasution's headquarters) forbidding the use of non-Latin or Arabic alphabets in all publications. The editorial warned against chauvinism, and argued that groups loyal to the government should not be made to suffer. A new regulation permitting some Chinese papers to publish was later issued.

19 On the anti-KMT campaign, see V. Hanssens, "The Campaign Against Nationalist Chinese in Indonesia," in B. M. Vlekke, *Indonesia's Struggle 1957-1958* (The Hague: Netherlands Institute of International Affairs, 1959), pp. 56-76.

from March 31 to April 3, 1958.[20] Aidit entitled one part of his report to the Central Committee "Not Communist and Anti-Communist, but Democracy and Anti-Democracy, National and Anti-National," and here he touched on the primary dangers which the party faced:[21] anti-Communism, anti-partyism, and the army. Two of these were shared by the other parties, but all three were significantly related, mutually reinforcing, and especially threatening in the case of the PKI.

Putting aside anti-partyism for a while, the chief hazard for the PKI in the first half of 1958 was that its very strength made it a focus of attention. Although this had been equally true in 1957, the regional crisis had then had the effect of dividing anti-Communist potential. The rebellion had removed the threat of the anti-Communist regionalist movements, but it left behind an equally anti-Communist army more unified and less distracted than before.[22] Quite apart from the possibility of a coup, which

---

20 For the documents of the sixth plenum of the CCPKI, see *Bintang Merah*, vol. XIV, no. 3-4 (March-April 1958). Aidit's report to the meeting, "Fase Baru dan Penjesuaian Organisasi dengan Situasi" (The New Phase and Bringing the Organization into Line with the Situation), is also in his *Pilihan Tulisan* (Selected Writings; Djakarta: Jajasan "Pembaruan," 1959-1960), II, 378-443. See also Arnold Brackman, *Indonesian Communism* (New York: Praeger, 1963), pp. 249-254. The new phase refers to the turn of political developments beginning with the Tjikini Affair, the take-over of Dutch firms, and the outbreak of the rebellion, a turn which the PKI justifiably considered as being favorable to its position because it was unfavorable to that of the right wing.
To adjust to the potentialities of the new phase, the CCPKI undertook at this meeting to tighten up party organization and to intensify efforts to broaden the party's popular support — an indication also, perhaps, of concern for dangers yet to be faced. At this time, a small executive board (Dewan Harian) of the CCPKI was chosen, consisting of Aidit, Lukman, Njoto, and Sudisman (*Bintang Merah*, cited above, p. 153).
21 "Bukan Komunis dan Anti-Komunis, Tetapi Demokrasi dan Anti-Demokrasi, Nasional dan Anti-Nasional," in *Pilihan Tulisan*, II, 412-420. See also the speech by Jusuf Adjitoropu, elected to the politbureau at this meeting: "Apakah Arti Penjesuaian Organisasi dengan Situasi?" (What is the Meaning of Bringing the Organization into Line with the Situation?), *Harian Rakjat*, April 11, 1958.
22 The opening remarks of Aidit's report to the CCPKI may have significance with respect to the PKI's concern for the role of the army, as well as for numerous other possible developments. If efforts to crush the rebels in Sumatra and Sulawesi achieved rapid success, said Aidit, "it will stimulate more advanced development of the revolutionary situation in our country. If crushing the rebels can be accomplished in a short time, the reactionaries and imperialists will lose an important base of theirs, and better conditions will be created for carrying out the President's Konsepsi 100% and for fulfilling the demands of the August Revolution completely. But on the other hand, if the rebellion is not settled quickly, this critical situation will end up by adding a new chronic sickness in the body of the Republic of Indonesia, which can only be cured after a long time, as we have experienced with the DI-TII [Darul Islam-Tentara Islam Indonesia, Islamic Army of Indonesia]"; *Pilihan Tulisan*, II, 378. There are several possibilities that Aidit might have had in mind, among them the likelihood that the army would continue to exercise great authority as long as the rebellion dragged on.

imperiled all parties,[23] there was also the danger that the officer corps would soon begin to turn on the PKI. The latter's support of the army in the regional crisis, and its willing participation in the Civil-Military Cooperation Bodies, offered the party no insurance once the regional challenge was subdued. For protection, the PKI had to rely on Soekarno, and in order to avoid being isolated, it was also imperative to continue to maintain the united front. At the party meeting in April, however, Aidit warned that the right wing of the nationalist middle-group had been taken in by the "anti-Communism" slogan of Masjumi-PSI.[24]

Indeed, with more PNI regional leaders joining in the open condemnation of the PKI, there was increased pressure within the PNI for it to undertake an all-out attack on the Communists.[25] Anti-PKI arguments received a boost from the rebellion, for both national and regional leaders now began to fear that with the weakening of Masjumi the PKI would turn all its energies to destroying the PNI, a possibility that seemed quite real after the regional elections. Two weeks after the PRRI ultimatum, Suwirjo himself fired a short volley at the PKI by comparing the PRRI with the Madiun rebellion as a national disaster.[26]

Despite the PKI spectre, however, the PNI remained optimistic about its position in the government. This was mainly due, perhaps, to a misreading of Soekarno's intentions. Many assumed that once the rebellion was suppressed there would be a partial return to party government, with the PNI succeeding to the central place in the cabinet. For with Masjumi out of the way, it was supposed that ultimately Soekarno would not permit the PKI to occupy too powerful a position. According to this view, it followed that he would turn to the PNI to develop a radical nationalist governing force. In April and May a cabinet reshuffle appeared possible,

---

23 Aidit approached the army problem by attacking those who looked to Egypt as their example. He warned against an uncritical imitation of the Egyptian experience: "The PKI and the Indonesian people will oppose with all their might...any policy which increases the possibility of extra-parliamentary activity and coups"; *Pilihan Tulisan*, II, 417.

24 *Ibid.*, p. 415.

25 In January, A. K. Gani, newly elected chairman of the South Sumatran PNI regional council, declared that the PKI's support of the Pantjasila was nonsense. It was merely a tactic, for Communists would obey only the commands of the USSR (*Mimbar Umum*, Jan. 11, 1958). In November 1957, an anonymous PNI leader told *Pedoman* (Nov. 15), that he believed the PNI party council would finally be forced to follow the party's regional branches against the PKI.

26 *Abadi*, Feb. 27, 1958. Suwirjo also included the Republic of the South Moluccas rebellion, the Andi Aziz (Sulawesi) rebellion, and the Darul Islam in his condemnation.

in which the PNI was generally expected to be the main beneficiary. PNI-sympathizing journals, among them the weekly Pesat and the daily *Merdeka*, began to refer to the PNI as the chief supporter of the cabinet and the key party for determining government policy. The importance the party was assumed to have is indicated by the fact that two formerly non-party Ministers — Subandrio and Sadjarwo — joined the PNI sometime in the first half of 1958.[27]

Enjoying these apparent advantages, the PNI became more assertive in April and May, moving at the same time to strengthen its position in the Government and to pull away from the PKI, hoping somehow to set the latter up for an eventual deadly attack. The PNI's growing open hostility to the PKI was probably encouraged by what seemed to be a Government swing to the right as the rebellion declined in April — reducing the PKI's political leverage[28] — and as efforts began in May to improve Djakarta-Washington relations.

From the 27th to the 30th of April the executive committee of the PNI National Congress met in Semarang, Hadisubeno's home ground, to discuss party policy. The meeting was generally regarded as an important one, for, as *Merdeka* put it, with the decline of Masjumi the influence of the PNI would certainly grow; its decisions in Semarang would therefore have significance not only for the Government, but for the future of the party system as well.[29] PNI leaders easily affirmed their support of the Government's policies against the rebellion and also produced an unconvincing statement on party self-correction.[30] On the PKI issue, the advantage had by this time shifted to the regional PNI view, and

---

27 *Mimbar Umum*, May 22, 1958. That Sadjarwo joined the party is especially significant. As a former member of the Communist peasant organization, BTI, he was one of those whom anti-Communist groups wanted out of the cabinet. Foreign Minister Subandrio was brought into the party and given a seat on the party council on the decision of Suwirjo himself, on the supposition that this would not only enhance the PNI's position in the cabinet but also make several ambassadorships available to the party faithful. Several PNI leaders were angered by Suwirjo's action, because he had failed to consult the party council on the matter and, too, because some felt Subandrio ought to work his way up in the party.

The PNI's apparent strength was also illustrated in the number of central positions which its members held in the government: Sartono, Speaker of Parliament; Hardi, First Vice-Premier; Wilopo, Chairman of the Konstituante; Roeslan Abdulgani, Vice-chairman of the National Council.

28 See Feith, *Decline of Constitutional Democracy*, pp. 589-590.

29 *Merdeka*, April 26, 1958.

30 See *Marhaenis Bergerak* (Marhaenists on the Move, PNI journal), III, 34-36.

the Congress finally issued a formal slap at the PKI by condemning the Madiun rebellion. It also carefully condemned all foreign intervention in terms broad enough to include both blocs.[31] In June, Slamat Ginting of the PNI was to assert that there was no longer any reason for confusion about the PNI's attitude towards the PKI, for never, before the Semarang conference, he said, had there been an official PNI resolution branding the Madiun rebellion as a national betrayal.[32]

But, as many in the anti-Communist camp asked: so what? Masjumi, NU, the PSI, Christian parties, and much of the independent press were delighted at the growing split between the PNI and the PKI, but they also pointed out that anti-Communist verbiage alone was hardly enough. They continued to press the PNI for an anti-Communist alliance or for some indication of just what the PNI intended to do about the PKI. The PNI, however, had chosen to stand squarely in the middle of a polarized situation. From February through June it staked all its chips on acquiring a fortress position in the Government, from whence it would be easier to deal with the PKI. But the PNI grossly overestimated its political advantages, underestimated Soekarno's pique with the party, and misinterpreted the new conditions arising from the rebellion. The Cabinet reshuffle of June, which brought the PNI and PKI to blows, showed the former to be much weaker than was expected, with significant consequences for the PNI and for the entire party world thereafter.

The Cabinet Reshuffle of June

The rebellion saved the Kabinet Karya, capping a year of failure with great success. From April 1957 until February 1958 it had accomplished very little. Quite apart from the regional crisis, economic conditions had grown steadily worse; shortages of essential goods, particularly rice, and rising prices grew constantly more serious. Inflation was spurred on by the budget deficit policy resorted to in 1957 and the increasing volume of

---

31 For the full resolution of the Semarang meeting, see *Marhaenis Bergerak*, III, 30-33. For other comments on the conference, which was discussed in the press mainly in terms of the PNI's support of the government, see *Pesat*, XIV, no. 18 (May 3, 1958), 3; *Basis* (Catholic Monthly), VII, no. 9 (June 1958), 317.

32 *Pikiran Rakjat*, June 7, 1958.

money in circulation. The Government's financial resources were depleted. On the political right the cabinet faced an "I told you so" attitude towards the effects of the December take-overs. From both the left and the right there were demands for more goods at lower prices, demands which even the Government-supporting parties took up, thus dissociating themselves from the cabinet's responsibility for economic conditions. Even so, it is not likely that the cabinet would have resigned so long as the regional crisis continued; for those who supported the Government against the regions had too much at stake. But the authority of the cabinet suffered, enough for *Siasat* to suggest in early February that the cabinet might be seeking a more honorable issue than economic failure upon which eventually to resign.[33] However, the Padang ultimatum of February 10, the Government's forceful response in March, and the course of the rebellion thereafter changed the outlook completely. Economic decline continued after February, and in fact became worse, but such considerations were overshadowed by the successful prosecution of the war against the PRRI in the face of foreign hostility.[34] Masjumi and the PSI continued to demand the cabinet's resignation after the PRRI rebellion began, but this position was politically meaningless. By removing the primary opposition to the Government and to Soekarno, the rebellion strengthened both.

This new-found security made possible consideration of revising the cabinet. Besides marking the end of a period, there were several other reasons for doing so. As a cabinet of experts, it had shown technical weaknesses deserving of criticism. One weak link was the NU Minister of Trade, Soenardjo, who it was generally agreed (outside of NU circles) should be dropped. For those, like Djuanda, who wanted the Government to turn to economic problems once the rebellion was under control, a cabinet revision to improve its personnel was necessary and would symbolize new priorities. It was the hope of such men that making changes in the cabinet would involve a minimum of political bargaining

---

33 "Kabinet Djuanda dapat bertahan terus, tapi..." (The Djuanda Cabinet can hold on, but...) in *Siasat*, XII, no. 556 (Feb. 5, 1958), 3.

34 *Merdeka*, April 10, 1958, summed up the new position of strength of the Kabinet Karya. Admitting that the cabinet had displayed some weaknesses in the past, *Merdeka* thanked God that it had come through in the final crisis: "as a result the Kabinet Karya has found its proper character — as a cabinet of struggle, confronting challenges from within and without, which, it is hoped will clear the way hereafter for the development of the state and the nation."

and that it would remain primarily a business cabinet intended to deal with national problems, free of narrow political considerations. These hopes were to be disappointed.

One of Soekarno's aims in the reshuffle was to bring the Sultan of Jogjakarta into the cabinet, in order to buttress the government's authority and help cement national unity. If the Sultan accepted, this would belie the PRRI's claim that the Djakarta Government was supported only by groups dependent upon Soekarno and that it was therefore not truly a national government. For the Sultan was an important, though not very outspoken, symbol of opposition to Djakarta's policies in the regional crisis. Moreover, he had the additional advantage of being trusted in American circles at a time when it was highly desirable to ease relations with the United States. Sometime in May and again in June, Djuanda and Soekarno invited the Sultan to accept the post of Minister of Trade. They had been led to believe that he would agree, apparently because of an ambiguous remark that he had made. But in fact he was unwilling, partly because of his disapproval of the Government's uncompromising policy on the rebellion. His refusal was a disappointment to the right wing, for it meant that there probably would not be an effort to come to terms with the rebels. PNI leaders, who had supported the Sultan, and many in the army were also disappointed.[35]

It is not clear what else Soekarno wanted to achieve in a reshuffle. It is unlikely that he considered a *gotong-rojong* cabinet — i.e., one with the PKI in it. For one thing, the army was opposed to this. Second, it would not help to relax tensions with America. And third, a four-party cabinet would have to include Masjumi, which Soekarno did not want in the Government. Possibly, therefore, he saw the advantages of a cabinet

---

35 The offer to the Sultan was muted in the press. He himself later denied that he had refused for policy reasons, stating that his reasons were the same as when he last withdrew from a cabinet. That had been in 1952, after the October 17th Affair, when he decided that he would not again become embroiled in cabinet politics. See *Siasat*, XII, no. 579 (July 16, 1958), 5. It is possible that another reason for Soekarno's desire to bring the Sultan into the cabinet was that the Sultan's immense prestige and popularity in ethnic Java (and his acceptability in other areas) made him a potential rival whom it would be better to have associated with the government than outside of it. Soekarno, Hatta, and the Sultan had always been the three best known leaders in the country. For a roundabout comment with the above implication, see *Sikap*, July 3, 1958, p. 1: "Hamengkubuwono is not only important as a single individual, but also he represents a certain political force that bears weight." See also *Siasat*, XII, no. 577 (July 2, 1958), 3, and *Surabaja Post*, July 2, 1958, for comments on the absence of the Sultan in the reshuffled cabinet.

revision in terms of consolidation, improvement, and a new program to signify political graduation to a new stage of development. But the politics of the reshuffle quickly became complicated.

The possibility of a cabinet change immediately became entangled with the possibility of a change in policy towards the rebellion. Groups which had opposed the Government since early 1957 saw this as their last chance to force a reversal of Djakarta politics by achieving a new cabinet committed to compromise with the PRRI. Nasution and the General Staff wanted a revision that would at least make the cabinet acceptable to rebel army leaders and encourage them to give up their fight.

Partly connected with this, the anti-Communist parties and army leaders sought to eliminate all Ministers considered to be Communist or simply too far to the left. These included, most prominently, Sadjarwo, Prijono, Chaerul Saleh, Hanafi (particularly) — all of them on the radical left but non-Communist — and to a lesser extent Tobing and Sudibjo. In late May and June there were rumors that Tobing's Ministry of State for Inter-regional Relations — especially galling to the regions — and Hanafi's Ministry would be abolished.[36] Djuanda seems to have wanted to drop Hanafi at least, both because of his political views and because his ministry was in no way useful. Vehement anti-Communist groups insisted that all these men be removed from the cabinet to prove that Indonesia was not becoming a Communist state.[37]

Understandably, the strongest opposition to a cabinet revision came from the PKI, for whom any prospect of a reshuffle appeared to be immensely dangerous, coming as it did at a time when the PNI was hostile, the Government was seeking to reduce tensions with the U.S., and there was considerable pressure to end the rebellion by compromise. So far as the possible removal of Hanafi and others was concerned, this was alarming to the PKI not because these men were Communists, but rather because

---

36 *Pesat*, XIV, no. 25 (June 21, 1958), 7.
37 See *Pemuda*, June 3, 1958. In May, an anti-Communist organization called the LAKRI (Liga Anti-Komunis Rakjat Indonesia, Anti-Communist League of the Indonesian People) called for a cabinet reshuffle in which Soekarno should replace "several Ministers suspected of being Communists or who benefit the Communists." This was necessary, said LAKRI, to restore the confidence of the world in Indonesia, and especially that of Indonesia's neighbors, such as Singapore, Malaya, Australia, and the Philippines. See *Pemandangan*, May 31, 1958. *Pemuda* denied there were Communists in the cabinet.

any marked shift to the right was inherently perilous to the party.[38] To prevent a reshuffle, the PKI undertook a campaign beginning in late April and May to identify efforts in that direction as pro-PRRI and pro-United States. On May 1, Aidit accused America of trying to establish a Masjumi-NU Cabinet which, when the PRRI challenge had been overcome, would be able to force the PKI and the PNI into opposition; alternatively, the United States would try, said Aidit, by establishing a Masjumi-NU-PNI Cabinet, to divide the nation — i.e., to isolate the PKI. At the same time, according to Aidit, the U.S. was encouraging certain groups in the army to force Soekarno to accept this new cabinet.[39] Conditions would thus be created, he said, for replacing the present army leadership with officers trusted by America, for reestablishing Masjumi and the PSI, and for strengthening colonialism in West Irian. He declared that the PKI wanted the Kabinet Karya to continue as it was. The only acceptable alternative was a *gotong-rojong* cabinet — which Aidit undoubtedly realized was an unlikely possibility.[40]

The PNI and NU regarded the prospect of a cabinet reshuffle from a traditional parliamentary point of view. Once the momentary unity forged by the regional crisis disappeared, they were again competitive, and questions of bargaining strength and the number of available portfolios became crucial. In late March and April the two parties began to make their bids. On March 24th NU handed the cabinet a memorandum of policy proposals on economic problems and government organization — a remarkable display of initiative by any party in the Kabinet Karya, but especially so for NU. Nothing came of the note, but it served to emphasize that NU was in the cabinet and would work to stay there.[41] On April 8th,

---

38 Of the six ministers under attack for their political views, the PKI defended all but Chaerul Saleh; between Chaerul and the Communists no love was lost. See *Harian Rakjat*, June 26, 1958.

39 "Kalahkan Konsepsi Politik Amerika Serikat" (Defeat the Political Conception of the United States), in *Pilihan Tulisan*, II, 444-454, at p. 450. Although for obvious reasons Aidit overemphasized the role of the United States, his analysis was on the right track.

40 *Ibid*. Raising the spectre of a Hatta or Masjumi Cabinet, Aidit said: "In the present situation no Indonesian patriot is willing to see Masjumi and PSI leaders, who have led the PRRI or who at least have not condemned the PRRI, sit at the top of the government. Also, men like Hatta who oppose the struggle to liberate West Irian, and who have given great moral support to the PRRI rebels, cannot be expected by the majority of the Indonesian people to stand at the helm of the Indonesian government" (p. 451). On the PKI attitude towards the Kabinet Karya, see also the speech by Sakirman on the 38th anniversary of the PKI, *Harian Rakjat*, May 28, 1958.

41 *Surabaja Post*, March 28, 1958. The memorandum suggested, *inter alia*, that to conserve funds

the PNI issued its first comprehensive policy statement since 1956. Unlike the NU note, which in several respects seemed to be a serious effort to cope with outstanding economic problems, the PNI statement was more like an old party platform. In addition to laying down party policy on everything from forestry to external affairs, it also promised a struggle against inefficiency, bureaucracy, and colonial laws — clichéd negative symbols in use since the revolution.[42] Both parties made a point of stressing the continuation of parliamentary institutions and their improvement.

It soon appeared, however, that the PNI held the political advantage. Having some confidence in achieving a position of political primacy within the government, it is not surprising that the PNI was the first to propose a cabinet reshuffle to Soekarno — probably after the Semarang meeting at the end of April.[43] But if the PNI's optimism was justified, NU was in danger of losing out; and at the very least, NU stood to lose the profitable Ministry of Trade, if not to the Sultan, then to the PNI. Thus there seemed nothing to be gained by NU in a reshuffle, and it joined the PKI in opposing it. Of the government-supporting parties, therefore, only the PNI was strongly in favor of a reshuffle.

In mid-May, the PKI anti-reshuffle campaign went into high gear and ran right over the PNI. The PKI had ignored the PNI's hostile gesticulations of April, but Communist restraint came to an end under the threat they saw in new diplomatic approaches between Djakarta and Washington.

---

the cabinet ought to be simplified, with less important ministries being merged into larger ones. It also proposed that the government speed up implementation of regional autonomy laws, allow free importation of goods for a limited period of time to build up government rupiah holdings for development, centralize economic and financial policy-making responsibilities, and create new regulations on the transferral of Dutch property rights. There were, of course, important economic advantages to be gained from some of these measures by NU clientele. Generally on economic policy, the NU note said that more economic activity should be left to community initiative, with the government's role being limited to guidance. This position was out of line with predominant government economic thinking. NU supporters, primarily Islamic merchants and landholders in East Java, were beginning to feel something of an economic squeeze, and the threat of more extensive government economic control was not greeted favorably.

42 See *Marhaenis Bergerak*, III, 4-29.

43 In his party anniversary speech of July 3, 1958, Suwirjo said: "possibly it was the PNI which first of all proposed to the Formateur (at the beginning of 1958) that the Kabinet Karya be reshuffled after…working for about 10 months. This proposal was based on considerations of strengthening the Cabinet." See *Almanak Umum Nasional 1959* (Djakarta: Endang, 1959), p. 393. However, *Pedoman* reported in May that Suwirjo told Soekarno after the Semarang meeting that the party leadership was divided, some wanting a reshuffle — evidently the majority — and some not. See *Basis*, VII, no. 4 (June 1958), 317-318.

On May 12th, Ambassador Jones visited Suwirjo at the latter's home for a long talk. The next day, the PNI announced that it would not take part in an anti-foreign intervention demonstration organized by the PKI for May 16th.[44] A day later, the Djakarta military administration forbade the demonstration on grounds that it came too near National Awakening Day (May 20th).[45] On the 20th, Dulles made his conciliatory remark, on the 21st came the announcement that the U.S. would send small arms, and on the 22nd Soekarno and Jones had lunch together.[46] The ominous atmosphere which these events created for the PKI prompted it finally to launch an attack on the PNI, immediately after Suwirjo's talk with Jones and the PNI's withdrawal from the demonstration. Mainly through a whisper campaign, the PKI charged the PNI with deceit, disregard of the national interest, and indecision on the rebellion. Suwirjo was accused of having talked with Jones about compromise with the rebels, and it was said that Jones had influenced the PNI decision not to join the demonstration.[47] At the same time, the United States was accused of working to create a new right wing cabinet which would overturn all that had been achieved in defeating the PRRI's goals.[48]

As nearly the entire left-wing press took up these cries, the PNI found itself identified with pro-United States and -PRRI views. The newspaper *Pemuda*, a sensationalist sheet which tried hard and often successfully to reflect Soekarno's point of view, all but accused Suwirjo of intriguing with Jones to change the government — to restore party control — and to work out a compromise with the rebels, which Jones was widely believed to be urging upon the Government.[49] Neither Suwirjo nor Jones was

---

44 *Pesat*, XIV, no. 22 (May 31, 1958), 4. According to *Pesat*, the PKI had organized the demonstration without first consulting the PNI. It had simply announced that the "Big Four" parties would take part and then informed them later. For the announcement, see *Harian Rakjat*, May 9, 1958. Apparently the PKI had hoped thus to emphasize its own patiotic initiative, PKI-PNI-NU solidarity, and Masjumi's isolation, for the latter obviously would not participate.

45 For the PKI's resentful reactions, see *Harian Rakjat*, May 16, 1958.

46 See *Merdeka*, May 23, 1958, under the headline "Diplomatic Activity Coming to a Head." In the same issue, *Merdeka* reported without comment a statement by Deputy Secretary of State Robert Murphy to the effect that the PKI parroted the line of the Soviet Union in its attacks on the United States.

47 See *Pesat*, XIV, no. 22 (May 31, 1958), 4, for a defense of the PNI against these charges.

48 *Harian Rakjat*, May 22, 1958.

49 *Pemuda*, May 16, 1958, an editorial entitled "Tukar Fikiran?" (Exchanging Ideas?), and *Pesat*, cited *supra*, n. 47. *Pemuda* was known until late in 1959 as the closest thing to being Soekarno's mouthpiece. Its editor, Notosoetardjo, was a leading member of the Djakarta PNI until July 1958,

in a position to do much intriguing at this time, but *Pemuda*'s attack illustrates the awkward corner into which the PNI was drifting. Soekarno did not want an unrestrained rush to the right either internationally or domestically, but that is where the PNI seemed definitely to be heading. On June 9th, Soekarno made a gesture towards restoring the cold war balance by lunching with Soviet Ambassador Zhukov.[50] (Suwirjo followed suit late in June, after the reshuffle, by meeting with Zhukov.) And in any case if Soekarno sought to relax tensions with the United States, that did not mean he was willing to see the PKI seriously weakened, for the party remained important to him in the balance of internal forces. By its animosity towards the PKI, the PNI proved itself to be "Communistophobic" — Soekarno's caustic characterization of those who feared the left — and threatened to create a split among the elements supporting Soekarno.

The PNI was compelled to respond to the accusations levelled against it, and in a formal reply published on May 24th made its view of the PKI perfectly clear. It reiterated the decisions of the Semarang conference which rejected compromise with the PRRI — thus fulfilling at least one objective of the PKI — but it also condemned all foreign intervention, now adding specifically, "from the American bloc, or from the Soviet bloc." The statement further warned the public that the PKI ("a group") considered that it was time to direct its efforts against the PNI, now "that the right wing in the political party world of Indonesia has experienced decline and political bankruptcy."[51] Finally, PNI leaders affirmed their determination to stand in the middle, fighting off the dangers to the state from the liberal-capitalistic-reactionary right wing and the totalitarian-internationalistic left.[52]

---

when he was dismissed from the party as a result of his frequent attacks on the Suwirjo leadership. Actually it was *Pemuda* and other journals which carried the attack on the PNI in May more than *Harian Rakjat*; the latter seldom used overly harsh words in referring to the PNI.

50 *Merdeka*, June 10, 1958. During the whole period of working out the Djakarta-Washington rapprochement, *Harian Rakjat, Bintang Timur, Sin Po*, and *Pemuda* demanded great caution in dealing with America, reminding the nation of American support of the PRRI and displaying deep distrust of Washington's apparent about-face. See *Pemuda*, May 10, 23, 1958.

51 According to the statement, "This destruction of the right-wing has created a propitious situation for a certain group...to direct its attention, energy, and attacks towards the PNI in a frontal and systematic way."

52 For the full statement, "PNI Mendjawab" (The PNI Answers), see *Marhaenis Bergerak*, III, 39-42. See also *Suluh Indonesia*, May 24; *Nusantara*, May 28, 1958.

A series of blistering attacks on the PKI followed. In early June the East Javanese PNI demonstrated astounding in-sensitivity to the nuances of Indonesian foreign policy and the predilections of Soekarno by declaring that the PKI's campaign for abolition of SEATO (in connection with foreign intervention) proved the Communists were a channel for foreign propaganda, because SEATO was not an internal affair of the Indonesian Government.[53] The PKI declined to reply, leaving it to national PNI leaders to qualify the awkward position of their own branch.[54] On June 14th, the PNI affiliated student organization, GMNI, also warned the nation against Communism, though in a more reasoned statement than that of the East Javanese PNI.[55] Masjumi, NU, the PSI, and Christian parties heaped accolades upon the initiatives of the East Javanese PNI and the GMNI, calling at the same time, however, for PNI deeds as well as words.[56]

Meanwhile, in late May and June, the politics of the cabinet reshuffle became more tense. Soekarno had made no public commitment at all to revise the cabinet, and until about the second week in June it was assumed that he was open to persuasion from either side. From the Communist and allied press poured forth a constant stream of vituperation against those who wanted a reshuffle and accusations that they were inspired by the United States and the PRRI.[57] The American press was reporting at the time that Djakarta had given assurances to Washington on the Communist problem; on May 28th, Allan Pope's capture in the Moluccas was announced, and in June (just a few days before the reshuffle was completed) the daily press published a pro-PRRI letter allegedly written by Admiral Frost to Alex Kawilarang. Taking advantage of the anti-American ire aroused by these events, the PKI raised blunt questions

---

53 *Pedoman*, June 3; *Pemuda*, June 3, 1958.
54 Suwirjo said on July 4 that the PNI could not condone such military pacts as NATO and SEATO. See *Almanak Umum Nasional 1959*, p. 389.
55 *Pedoman*, June 17, 1958. The GMNI (Gerakan Mahasiswa Nasional Indonesia, Indonesian National Student Movement) said, among other things, that to prevent Indonesia from becoming a Communist state the government must effect rapid economic development. But it recognized this to be difficult in times that were not politically calm. K. Werdojo, a SOBSI leader, replied with the argument that emphasis should be on national problems, not international ones, and that the Communists did not have ulterior motives. *Pedoman*, June 18, 1958.
56 See *Pedoman*, June 20, 28; *Pikiran Rakjat*, June 12, 18; *Nusantara*, June 8; *Mimbar Umum*, June 13, 1958.
57 See, for example, *Harian Rakjat*, June 9, 1958; *Pesat*, XIV, no. 25 (June 21, 1958), 5-6.

about U.S. motives in finally extending arms aid. On May 23rd and again on June 9th, Djuanda felt constrained to deny that any concessions had been made to the U.S.[58] The PKI was thus able to make any attempt to eliminate the left wing ministers of the cabinet seem like a giving-in to American demands.[59] NU leaders picked up most of the PKI's themes. Wahib Wahab declared that the real purpose of changing the cabinet would be to benefit the PRRI. Those who were intriguing with foreigners to force a reshuffle, he charged, were covering up their intentions by claiming that the cabinet needed improving or that weak ministers must be replaced.[60] Over the din of this PKI-NU opposition, the PNI and its supporters tried to argue that a reshuffle would only mean strengthening the cabinet, not altering the Government's policies.[61]

While the PNI press reported the imminence of a reshuffle and the PKI and NU denied every such intimation, Soekarno said nothing until June 14th. On that day, in Surabaja, he was greeted by an anti-reshuffle demonstration, probably organized by the PKI. Speaking to the crowd he made it clear that there would be no change of policy on the rebellion; but he hinted broadly that there would be changes in the cabinet, and the people need only wait and see the results of his consideration of all the problems involved.[62]

The effectiveness of the PKI campaign, together with his own reluctance to deflect policy on the rebellion or drastically to weaken his support from the left and his growing discouragement with the

---

58 *Merdeka*, June 10; *Harian Rakjat*, June 10, 1958.
59 On June 23, Djody Gondokusumo, speaking on behalf of the National Progressive parliamentary fraction, told the press that in the event of a reshuffle, it should not be based on American desires. To avoid the impression that it was — and this was the same argument used by the PKI — weak ministers should be replaced with "progressives," not "reactionaries" (*Pemuda*, June 24, 1958).
60 *Harian Rakjat*, June 6, 11, 1958.
61 *Suluh Indonesia*, *Merdeka*, and the weekly *Pesat* campaigned in favor of a reshuffle. For the best discussions of the pro-reshuffle point of view, see *Pesat*, XIV, no. 22 (May 31, 1958), 3; no. 24 (June 14), p. 3; no. 25 (June 21), pp. 3 and 5; no. 2 6 (June 28), p. 3; and no. 27 (July 5), p. 3.
62 *Merdeka*, June 16, 1958; *Pesat*, XIV, no. 25 (June 21, 1958), 3-4. The day after the Surabaja episode, *Antara* News bureau reported that Soekarno had said that he would neither dissolve nor reshuffle the cabinet. *Harian Rakjat* ran the report triumphantly on June 16. *Antara* later corrected its report, possibly after a word from the Palace, but *Harian Rakjat* did not. Whether this was a last minute effort to block the reshuffle is not clear, but some, including *Pesat*, thought so. In his remarks to the crowd, Soekarno also said that many had asked him about the reshuffle, even some army officers who feared that there would be a change in policy favoring the rebels. This may have been a warning by Soekarno to those in the army who wanted a softer policy on the rebellion.

PNI, evidently all worked together to decide Soekarno on keeping the cabinet much as it was. But the political negotiations involved in the reshuffle were as tough as in any party cabinet of previous years. Soekarno's intention of maintaining the PNI-NU balance in the cabinet gave NU leaders an unexpected advantage during the last hectic days of bargaining.[63] They agreed to relinquish Soenardjo, who was later given an ambassadorship, so long as he was replaced by another NU appointee. In addition, they insisted on another cabinet post to redress the PNI-NU balance, upset when Subandrio and Sadjarwo joined the PNI. Adding two new NU ministers appeared to some observers to be also an effort to balance the influence of the Communists. The "leftist" ministers were all retained, although Hanafi's ministry was abolished and Tobing's had its name changed. Soekarno himself decided to bring into the cabinet Moh. Yamin, the historian and longtime radical-nationalist ideologue. A ministry was also given to the army in the person of Col. Suprajogi, formerly regional commander of West Java. On June 25th, the reshuffled cabinet was announced as follows:

Prime Minister	Ir. H. Djuanda (non-party)
First Vice-Prime Minister	Mr. Hardi (PNI)
Second Vice-Prime Minister	K. H. Idham Chalid (NU)
Third Vice-Prime Minister	Dr. J. Leimena (Parkindo)
Foreign Affairs	Dr. Subandrio (PNI)
Internal Affairs	Sanusi Hardjadinata (PNI)
Defense	Ir. H. Djuanda
Justice	Maengkom (PNI)
Information	Sudibjo (PSII)
Finance	Mr. Sutikno Slamet (PNI)
Industry	Ir. F. J. Inkiriwang (non-party)
Trade	*Rachmat Muljoamiseno (NU)

---

63 On June 23, one of a few such days, Soekarno met with a wide range of men in connection with the reshuffle. They included Djuanda, Roeslan Abdulgani, Subandrio, and Nasution. Political attention was centered on PNI and NU leaders by this time, Soekarno seeing a delegation of the former led by Suwirjo and Hardi, and of the latter led by Idham Chalid, Wahab Chasbullah, Wahib Wahab, and Zainul Arifin. (*Harian Rakjat*, June 24, 1958).

Agriculture	Mr. Sadjarwo (PNI)
Navigation	Commodore (Navy) Nazir
Public Works and Power	Ir. Pangeran Moh. Noor (formerly Masjumi)
Labor	Mr. Samjono (non-party)
Health	Dr. Col. Aziz Saleh (IPKI)
Religion	K. H. Iljas (NU)
Education and Culture	Prof. Dr. Prijono (Murba)
Agrarian Affairs	Mr. Sunarjo (NU)
Communications	Mr. Sukardan (non-party)
Veterans Affairs	Chaerul Saleh (non-party)
Social Affairs	Muljadi Djojomartono (formerly Masjumi)
Ministry of State for Transmigration Affairs	**Dr. F. L. Tobing (SKI)
Ministry of State for Economic Stabilization	*Col. (Army) Suprajogi
Ministry of State for Civil Military Relations	*Wahib Wahab (NU)
Minister of State without Portfolio	**A.M. Hanafi (non-party)
Minister of State without Portfolio	*Mr. Moh. Yamin (GPPS)[64]

* New minister
** In previous cabinet with different portfolio

The army's role in this cabinet requires some comment. Wahib Wahab's primary function was to maintain contact with the National Front for the Liberation of West Irian (FNPIB) and the civil-military cooperation bodies, which Djuanda said would now be used for purposes of economic

---

64 Yamin was given the task of liaison with the Konstituante, and Hanafi with Parliament and the National Council. Neither function had a great deal of significance, but both men were close to Soekarno, and this meant that they would be more his representatives than the cabinet's.

development under the Government's direction.[65] These bodies were in fact in no state to be really useful; nor was Wahab able to assert effective control over the military-run organizations. But the establishment of this ministry did create a formal tie between the Government and the army's political brainchild, constituting a kind of recognition of the legitimacy of the endeavor. Suprajogi's appointment was more important. In part, the Government hoped that through him the army would be able to end the illegal smuggling and barter activities of military commanders in the outer islands; in this Suprajogi did not enjoy complete success, though smuggling operations did diminish somewhat by 1959.[66] The new minister was also to lead the Bureau for Economic Stabilization, which Djuanda created on May 19, 1958, in part at least on the urging of army leaders. Its functions were less important ultimately than the fact that the army was now in the cabinet and had specific responsibilities, for the execution of which it could be blamed or praised. Economic conditions were to grow worse, not better.

Like the reshuffled cabinet itself, the new Government program was nearly the same as the old one. Only the first item of the program was changed, from establishment of the National Council to establishment of a National Planning Council, which Soekarno regarded as a significant step towards the planned economy part of Guided Democracy. The rest of the program was as before: 2) to normalize the situation of the republic — i.e., to end the rebellion; 3) to continue the struggle for West Irian; and 4) to speed up development. It remained Soekarno's program.

The cabinet also remained Soekarno's, and this was perhaps the most significant, though not surprising, political aspect of the reshuffle. In effect, the process of the cabinet revision formalized the conclusion to which the rebellion had brought the political battles of 1957. The system

---

65 See Djuanda's statement to Parliament on July 4, 1958, in *Ichtisar Parlemen* (IP, Summaries of Parliamentary Debates), 1958, p. 741.
66 Smuggling at Atjeh was particularly troublesome. In the second half of 1958, the Atjehnese military command agreed to an arrangement whereby it would keep only 30 per cent of the foreign exchange realized from local exports — an arrangement similar to the one Atjeh had enjoyed before it decided to keep all the foreign exchange in 1957. But the new agreement was not carried out completely. Moreover, despite the assurances of Col. Sjamaun Gaharu, commandant of Atjeh, following a new regulation in September that no more barter licenses would be issued as of September 10th, "technical difficulties" prevented complete prohibition of barter. See *Nusantara*, Aug. 27; *Siong Po* (Atjeh), Sept. 22; *Patriot*, Oct. 24; *Tjerdas*, Nov. 29, 1958.

of the Kabinet Karya, and all that it implied — non-parliamentarianism, anti-parliamentarianism, Soekarno's accession to power without constitutional investiture, the freezing of the parties out of power — was consolidated. Diffusion of authority and a certain political tentativeness, however, continued to characterize the Kabinet Karya system, which was so well suited to this politically transitional period of 1957-1958. Along with Soekarno's, Djuanda's position was spotlighted by the reshuffle. Although his restrained political style and views made him seem neither more nor less influential than he was in 1957, he was in fact stronger, more assertive, and more confident. That he remained both Prime Minister and Minister of Defense indicated his usefulness and acceptability to Soekarno and army leaders. He drew strength from having led the cabinet through Indonesia's most challenging trial. In his statement to Parliament after the reshuffle, Djuanda devoted almost the entire speech to a review of the rebellion, foreign hostility and intervention, and the Government's firm response.[67] He rightly shared the credit for keeping the state together, and now that his office was renewed, he consequently was able to speak with greater confidence. Within the limits of political possibility, he attempted with some success to lead the Government authoritatively after the reshuffle, acting as something of a brake on Soekarno and army leaders and as a moderator between the various foci of political power.

Party reactions to the reshuffle were naturally varied. Its earlier opponents switched grounds and — as the PNI press pointed out with profound resentment[68] — praised the revision now as having strengthened and improved the cabinet. The PKI was satisfied that there had been no change in the direction of the cabinet's policies. As for the NU, it had not only maintained but also, indeed, improved its position in the cabinet; and afterwards, Kiaji Muslich, an NU parliamentary leader who had ridiculed reshuffle efforts in early June, said he felt more responsible than ever for defending the Kabinet Karya to the very end.[69] On the other hand, Masjumi, the PSI, and other groups who had vainly hoped the reshuffle would signify a political reversal, saw it as a

---

67 IP/1958, pp. 728-741, session of July 4, 1958.
68 See especially *Pesat*, XIV, no. 27 (July 5, 1958), 3-4; Suwirjo's speech of July 3 in *Almanak Umum Nasional 1959*, pp. 385-395.
69 *Pesat*, cited *supra*, n. 68, p. 4.

confirmation of their worst fears: there would be no compromise with the rebels; Soekarno was stronger, not weaker; and the star of the PKI still seemed to be rising.

The PNI and the Re-emergence of Partindo

The PNI was bitterly disappointed and hurt by the results of the reshuffle, which to many seemed brilliantly to illustrate the futility of the course PNI leaders had chosen to follow since 1957. Not only had the party failed to regain primacy in the government, but it was also out-maneuvered by the PKI and out of touch with Soekarno. The PNI's apparent centrality to the crucial issues of Communism and Guided Democracy increased the frustration of other groups with it. More than ever it seemed a weak and vacillating body, lacking discipline, firm leadership, integrity, and direction. Its failure to undertake any meaningful reform called down upon PNI leaders a barrage of abuse in the daily press after June. The party was attacked, with considerable justification, for harboring corruptors and profit-seekers, for the emptiness of its ideological professions, and for its utter paralysis in the middle of the road.[70] It is indicative that those who, on the one hand, called it to the defense of parliamentary democracy and those who, on the other, demanded of it an unhesitating commitment to Soekarno, all agreed that the PNI must reform itself into a progressive, revolutionary, radical, and dedicated party.[71] This it proved incapable of doing.

Long smoldering tensions within the PNI finally burst into flame in July and August. Dependent for its binding force more on common interest and mutual benefit than on ideology, the party was never able to remain united out of power for more than a short while; in the past it had suffered several minor splits. In 1958, however, an eruption occurred that was more serious both because of the PNI's critical lack of initiative and because Soekarno appeared to have an active part in it.

In May, soon after the PNI meeting in Semarang, there was a move to resuscitate the pre-war Partindo (Partai Indonesia), which Soekarno

---

70 See *Basis*, VII, no. 10 (July 1958), 352; *Indonesia Raja*, July 7, 10; *Harian Umum*, July 8; *Java Post*, July 9; *Trompet Masjarakat*, July 31, 1958.
71 See *Merdeka*, July 3; *Indonesia Raja*, July 10, 1958.

had led after the demise of the original PNI in the early 1930's.[72] Although personal grudges and ambitions were also involved, the stated purpose of the effort was to return to the nationalist principles which Soekarno had enunciated in the 1930's and which the present PNI was accused of having abandoned.[73] Among those involved in the move were two respected PNI leaders, Winoto Danuasmoro, who at the time worked in the palace secretariat, and Winarno Danuatmodjo, governor of South Sumatra until February 1958. Winarno had been elected to the executive board of the PNI party congress in Semarang (possibly to assuage his resentment at party leaders for having supported his recall from Palembang in 1957, following regionalist protests against him). Others initially connected with the Partindo effort were Moh. Yamin, Asmara Hadi, related by marriage to Soekarno, and Gatot Mangkupradja, leader of the West Javanese Movement to Defend the Pantjasila (GPPS) and Soekarno's co-defendant before the colonial court in 1930.[74] Of these three, however, only Asmara Hadi finally joined the new party.

In July Winarno and Winoto left the PNI, amidst blaring headlines, in order to organize the Partindo openly. Early in August, Winarno

---

72 The symbolic potential of Partindo was considerable. When the original PNI was dissolved after Soekarno's imprisonment in 1931, it was succeeded by two new organizations: the Partindo, led by Sartono, and the PNI-Baru (New PNI) led first by Sjahrir, then by Hatta. The PNI-Baru stood on a more radical socialist and class struggle platform than the Partindo, emphasizing the need for cadre formation and political education. The Partindo, on the other hand, was explicitly a mass party. It defined its struggle as that of the Indonesian People vs. Colonialism, while the PNI-Baru denied that all Indonesian classes could be made to work together, because of the inherent opposition of class interests in Indonesian society. On his release from prison, and after much soul-searching, Soekarno, having failed to unite the two organizations, decided to join the mass party Partindo. Partindo, too, later dissolved itself after Soekarno's arrest for the second time. Soekarno's views have consistently remained the same in preferring the mass organization approach. See Jan M. Pluvier, *Overzicht van de Ontwikkeling der Nationalistische Beweging in Indonesie* ('s-Gravenhage, Bandung, 1953), pp. 49-50; A. K. Pringgodigdo, *Sedjarah Pergerakan Rakjat Indonesia* (A History of the Movement of the Indonesian People; Djakarta: Pustaka Rakjat, 1960), pp. 123-128.

73 See *Kuang Po*, May 10; *Kedaulatan Rakjat*, May 13, June 3; *Pikiran Rakjat*, May 17, June 11; *Pedoman*, May 28, 1958, for developments related to the establishment of Partindo.

74 The GPPS (Gerakan Pembela Pantjasila) was originally related to the PNI and designed to attract voters who thought well of the ideology but were uncertain about the party. In most areas the GPPS remained connected with the PNI, but in West Java, for various personal and political reasons, Gatot Mangkupradja pulled away from the parent party and ran the GPPS as an independent organization — though he continued to profess agreement with PNI principles. It was for this latter reason, he said later, that he did not join Partindo (*Pos Indonesia*, Aug. 6, 1958).

announced its rebirth; its leaders were Winarno, Winoto, Asmara Hadi, Dr. Buntaran, Budiarto Martoatmodjo, and several other long-time radical nationalists.[75] During the following months branches were set up in several regions of Java and Sumatra, drawing a varied membership from the PNI and a few other parties. Some no doubt joined because they believed Partindo to be a new and clean movement. Many more joined because there was no way up for them in their former parties or because they were convinced that Partindo was closely associated with Soekarno and therefore a wave of the future. Indeed, for a while in July and August there were rumors that Soekarno would organize a single state party and abolish all the rest; emerging when it did, Partindo seemed to be that party, and as a result it attracted great attention.

Soekarno never admitted having anything to do with the new party, and he assured Suwirjo that he remained independent;[76] nevertheless, nothing would have come of Partindo without his encouragement. Despite his own protest against the great number of parties, he did not condemn the creation of yet another one.[77] Like the PNI, Partindo claimed Marhaenism — Soekarno's concept of Indonesian proletarianism — as its official ideology. A debate ensued over which party espoused the true Marhaenism. Partindo leaders argued that Marhaenism was Marxism adjusted to Indonesian conditions. PNI leaders, denying Partindo's accusation that they rejected Marxism, also denied that Marhaenism was simply Marxism applied to Indonesia.[78]
At the end of August, Soekarno gave the nod to Partindo: Marhaenism, said its creator, was Marxism adjusted to Indonesian circumstances.[79]

---

75 *Pos Indonesia*, Aug. 6, 1958.

76 *Pos Indonesia*, Aug. 23; *Suluh Indonesia*, Aug. 27, 1958.

77 *Pemuda*, however, Aug. 28, 1958, attacked Partindo because it turned out to be just another party, rather than a fusion of parties. The paper pointed out that Soekarno wanted fewer parties, not more. It is possible that Soekarno did not intend Partindo to emerge as a new party, but rather sought to use the threat to goad the PNI into reform and unity behind his program. As was often the experience in Indonesia, however, leaders of the new party leapt at the chance to create a wholly new organization with the prospects of even a little political profit.

78 For the fullest statement of the PNI position in this curiously ethereal debate, see the series of articles by Juti (Sajuti) in *Pesat* beginning with the issue of Sept. 6, 1958 (Vol. XIV, no. 32); "Persamaan dan Perbedaan antara Marhaenisme dan Marxisme" (Similarities and Differences between Marhaenism and Marxism).

79 *Pos Indonesia*, Aug. 25, 1958. Soekarno said this to participants in a conference on Marhaenist education who came to visit him at the Bogor palace. The group was headed by the PNI leader, Mrs. Supeni.

Some PNI leaders took this as a hard slap from the man whom many in the party looked upon as their spiritual guide.

Partindo did not become a large party, despite its later and electorally untested claims; nor did it cut seriously into the top leadership of the PNI, who angrily regarded Partindo as mainly an exercise in ambition. The slight influence which it acquired was due almost entirely to the informal association of its leaders with Soekarno. It was in effect a patronage party, without political dynamism of its own; it never developed effective party, labor, and peasant organizations. In several regions it received considerable help from the PKI, with whom Partindo leaders were committed to cooperate. Indeed, the growing unwillingness of PNI leaders to work with the PKI was one of the essential reasons for the Partindo break.[80] Eventually, by 1960-1961, the PKI came to wield predominant influence over Partindo. Some PKI followers joined Partindo, giving the latter bulk and enabling it to meet the requirements laid down by a new law on political parties drafted in 1959. Men with PKI connections in time assumed the leadership of the party.

Besides indicating Soekarno's displeasure with the PNI, the immediate significance of Partindo's establishment was to illustrate the serious decline and vulnerability of the PNI. In early August, another (though minor) revolt in the PNI broke out in Medan.[81] Although there was no question that the PNI would survive, it was in no condition to assert itself either within or outside the government. Under attack for its decrepitude and its failure to do anything about declining economic and political conditions, the increasingly demoralized PNI could only say — as it had said in the past — that it was no more to blame than the other Government-supporting parties.[82]

In mid-1958, when Guided Democracy re-emerged as a primary issue, the weakness of both Masjumi and the PNI made the defense

---

80 Asmara Hadi was one of those who in 1957 praised the PKI as working for a social revolution and insisted that the PNI should work with it as long as there were similarities between Marxism and Marhaenism. See *Harian Rakjat*, Aug. 20, 1957.

81 See *Tjerdas*, Aug. 3; *Mimbur Umum*, Aug. 6; *Harian Umum*, Aug. 8, 1958. The founders of the splinter group said that past experience had shown the PNI to be a tool of personal interests, and the new party would serve as a channel for the views of its members. Ironically, the new splinter group was named PNI-Baru (New PNI); see *supra*, n. 72.

82 *Suluh Indonesia*, Aug. 8, 1958.

of parliamentary institutions seem a poor cause.[83] They gave no hope that a healthy parliamentary system could yet be developed. Nor were these parties themselves capable of putting up an effective defense of parliamentary democracy. In contrast, the strength and dynamism of the PKI stood out in nearly hypnotic relief. And when the parliamentary system came under concerted attack in the second half of 1958, it was the PKI which emerged as its staunchest defender.

Postponement of the Elections

The cabinet reshuffle of June marked the end of the critical phase of the rebellion and the beginning of the drive to develop Guided Democracy. By July and August, attention was again focussed on the need to reform the political system, with the political parties distinctly on the defensive against the initiative of the National Council. At about the same time, the question of holding the next parliamentary elections — due in September 1959 — was under consideration. In March the national elections committee had announced that preparations were to begin in May 1958.[84] The prospect of an election within a year and a half gave rise to grave concerns in the party world and obvious doubts among anti-party groups, particularly the army. It was here that the multiple forces which produced Guided Democracy became most evident. For had the conflict of parties vs. anti-parties been a simple one, the former might have been expected to make a determined stand on holding elections in 1959. As it was, however, at a time when they were trying to save the principle of representative government, upon which their existence depended, most of the parties felt compelled to sacrifice elections — the

---

83 Soon after the cabinet reshuffle, the *Surabaja Post*, July 2, 1958, noted the disappointment of Western diplomats that the left-wing ministers were still in the cabinet. In a nicely reasoned comment on this, the *Post* said that this disappointment followed from a failure to understand all the considerations operative for the Indonesian people, including Soekarno. One of these was the weakness of the middle of the road (PNI) and right wing parties. It was dangerous to drive the PKI into the opposition because the non-Communist parties were not confident of their ability to improve deplorable conditions in the country. If they failed, the Communists would be the alternative leadership. The *Post* went on to advise Western help for the democratic parties to enable them to improve the welfare of the people, thus reducing the chances for the PKI.

84 The national elections committee (Panitia Pemilihan Indonesia, PPI) consisted of representatives of several parties, including the four major ones. A new committee, with S. Hadi-kusumo (PNI) as chairman, was appointed early in 1958 (*Nusantara*, Feb. 5, 1958).

substance of the system — primarily out of fear of the PKI's popular strength.

The essential fact about elections in 1959, from one point of view, was that an overwhelming Communist victory seemed inevitable. Only the PKI looked forward eagerly to an electoral test. Its organization was in excellent shape, party morale was high after the regional elections, and the PKI was on the popular side of most significant national issues. Never having been in the Government, it shared no responsibility for deteriorating economic conditions in the country. At the CCPKI meeting in early April, considerable emphasis was given to the parliamentary struggle and to the need quickly to expand party membership and electoral support.[85] From a huge vote the party could expect not only increased political leverage but, it followed, a better chance of forcing a coalition government.[86]

Conversely, the other parties had little to look forward to from elections. Masjumi's prospects seemed hopeless, for even had the party been otherwise capable of mounting a strong campaign — which it was not — the areas of its strength in Sumatra were in rebellion. The PNI, though in better shape than Masjumi, clearly could not be optimistic, considering the outcome of the regional elections and the continuing decline of party organization and morale. NU might have been able to hold its own, and perhaps even to pick up some of Masjumi's support, but that too was questionable. In any event, it was evident that neither the PNI nor NU, nor possibly even the two together, could hold the PKI in check. Among anti-Communist groups there was some fear that the PKI might win an absolute majority in the next elections; thus the other parties would be left collectively to enjoy the support of only a minority of the electorate before being swept away completely in a Communist deluge.

There were evident dangers for the PKI in these assessments, One was that the other parties, the PNI and NU in particular, would not be disposed to face elections in 1959. Another was that army leaders, not well disposed to elections in any case, would bring pressure against holding

---

85 See *Harian Rakjat*, April 8, 1958, for the resolutions of the April plenum.
86 Aidit told an AP reporter in January that with an election victory the PKI could hope for a coalition government with several Communist ministers in the cabinet (*Pedoman*, April 23, 1958).

them. Furthermore, the likelihood of a Communist victory might also reinforce an inclination elsewhere in the government — in the cabinet and the National Council — to put off elections until a new electoral system (less advantageous to the PKI) could be devised.

The PSI was the first to propose reconsideration of the elections, though others, most prominently Masjumi and the Christian parties, were quick to follow. In April, soon after the announcement of the new election schedule, the PSI press launched a two pronged campaign. On the one hand, it argued, reasonably, that there ought to be a new election system; for it was, after all, the breakdown of the parliamentary system, based on the elections of 1955, which had given rise to the regional crisis, military dissidence, and President Soekarno's Konsepsi and Guided Democracy. Elections under the old procedure would not produce a more stable polity with a government better able to reflect the will of the people. It was proposed that proportional representation with multi-member districts be eliminated in favor of the single member district, for the ostensible reason that this would reduce the number of parties and forge a closer relationship between constituent and repre-sentative. A less public argument was that the single member district system would work against the PKI — assuming the non-Communist parties might join together in support of common candidates in many districts.[87] Later, accepting a tenet of Guided Democracy, the PSI also proposed that attention should be paid to the election of functional group representatives, from the army among others.[88]

Also in April, the PSI-sympathizing daily, *Pedoman*, pointed in warning at the victory of the Indian Communist Party in Kerala. Accusing the PKI of the same sort of "trickery" — posing as a respectable defender of parliamentary democracy in order to grab power via elections — *Pedoman* clearly invited others to draw the necessary conclusion in favor of delaying the elections. Economic conditions, it argued, were bad and declining, and the Government had begun to depend on the Communist bloc for credits, thereby giving the PKI a boost. The PNI and NU were no longer really electorally competitive with the PKI because they had

---

87 *Pedoman*, April 16, 1958; *Sikap*, XI, no. 19 (July 31, 1958), 1. Army leaders were in time captivated by the single member district idea, primarily for its potential usefulness against the PKI.
88 *Sikap*, cited *supra*, n. 87.

ignored the people's problems. The PKI vote had risen from six to eight million between 1955 and 1957, ran the argument, and it would not be surprising should it become an absolute majority in 1959.[89]

Fearing that such views extended beyond the PSI and Masjumi, as indeed they did, the PKI replied immediately, starting a campaign of its own to head off efforts to postpone the elections. It condemned all proposals to change the electoral system, calling the idea of single member districts obsolete and a tool of imperialist countries. In this it found common ground with the PNI and NU, as well as many smaller parties, which also saw a threat in the elimination of proportional representation. The PKI charged, moreover, that any delay in holding the elections would be an attack on the basic constitutional rights and democratic freedoms of the people.[90] And, as with the cabinet reshuffle, all attempts to postpone the elections were loudly blamed on the United States and supporters of the PRRI.[91] At the same time, Communist leaders denied predictions that the PKI would be the only victor at the polls and greatly played down the party's strength. Aidit told the Hungarian party newspaper, *Nepszabadsag*, that the PKI would not try to win more than 25 per cent of the next Parliament, and Lukman declared that rightist forces still balanced the PKI and other democratic forces.[92] *Harian Rakjat*'s modest prognosis was that Masjumi voters would shift to the PNI and NU, provided these parties continued to oppose imperialism, while the PKI's support would also increase.[93]

In June and July there were rumors that the elections would be postponed. Local authorities in charge of registration and other pre-election matters were without funds, and apparently their requests to Djakarta went unheeded.[94] Masjumi members of regional assemblies in a few areas, such as North Sumatra, frantically urged resolutions against holding the elections.[95] In an effort swiftly to develop popular

---

89 *Pedoman*, April 23; see also May 12, 1958.
90 *Harian Rakjat*, issues of April 24, May 13, May 17, May 20, May 28 (Sakirman's speech), and June 10, 1958.
91 *Harian Rakjat*, April 25, May 13, 1958.
92 Aidit, *Pilihan Tulisan*, II, 462. *Harian Rakjat*, May 12; *Pedoman*, May 9, 1958.
93 *Harian Rakjat*, May 13, 1958.
94 *Suara Rakjat*, July 16; *Surabaja Post*, Aug. 28, 1958.
95 *Lembaga*, Aug. 5, 1958. The North Sumatran PNI was on the verge of joining Masjumi's stand against holding the elections when the government finally postponed them. *Tjerdas*, Sept. 22,

pro-election momentum, the PKI determinedly prepared registration campaigns, while regional Communist leaders pushed very hard to get election machinery in their areas moving.

But the PKI was virtually alone in these labors, the PNI and NU showing little enthusiasm. A few leaders of these two parties initially joined with the PKI in defending the elections and attacking the *Pedoman* proposals.[96] By August and September, however, the PNI and to a lesser extent NU were willing to see the elections postponed. When the PKI started its registration campaign in Djakarta at the end of July, it was obvious that neither the PNI nor NU had made any preparations for the coming election. It is quite possible that their treasuries were nearly empty.[97] Moreover, it is likely that the PNI's view was influenced by the outcome of the cabinet reshuffle and by the emergence of Partindo, which not only depressed the party but threatened further to divide PNI support. Consequently neither the PNI nor NU made a real effort to defend holding the next elections, and within government councils it is likely that leaders of both parties agreed with arguments against holding them.

There were many such arguments and quite a few of them seemed strong. On May 27th, Djuanda had requested the cabinet's ad hoc committee, led by Leimena, to review the election law of 1953, ostensibly in order to bring it into line with the new regional government structure created by Law 1/1957.[98] But by this time certain members of the cabinet were already beginning to wonder whether it would not be best to postpone the elections, and in the following months army leaders suggested many good reasons for doing so.[99] For one thing, they argued, security conditions were bad and the shock of the rebellion had not yet worn off. Second, the

---

1958. See also *Lembaga*, July 21; *Mestika*, Aug. 13, Sept. 16, 1958.

96 See S. Djaka, "Laksanakan Pemilihan Umum Parlemen ke-II" (Carry out the Second Parliamentary Elections) in *Pesat*, XIV, No. 28 (July 12, 1958), 12. Also *Duta Masjarakat*, Sept. 4, 1958.

97 The NU newspaper, *Duta Masjarakat*, like Masjumi's *Abadi*, did not publish for a few months, from the end of May until August 17. The reason, presumably, was lack of funds.

98 *Pedoman*, May 29, 1958. Information Minister Sudibjo said at the time that the Government still intended to hold the elections.

99 On July 16 there was a meeting between Soekarno, Djuanda, Hardi, Idham, Leimena, Subandrio, and the Chiefs-of-Staff, in which, according to Djuanda, discussions were held concerning the military, economic, and financial situations, the problem of political parties, the Konstituante, and the second parliamentary elections (*Republik*, July 17, 1958).

conflict of election campaigning would only make the security situation worse. Third, in some areas of Sumatra and Sulawesi, elections could not be held at all because of the rebellion. Another argument that may have been advanced was that funds were in dangerously short supply, and the elections would be extremely expensive.

Besides these considerations — and the very important factor of a possible Communist victory — the issue of elections *per se* raised basic questions about the political system and the ultimate role of the political parties. In July, August, and September, the National Council was deep in discussion of Guided Democracy, and Djakarta was ablaze with rumors about abolition of political parties, creation of a single party, and simplification of the party system. To hold elections, at least under the old system, would simply restore the old style Parliament, then under attack. Therefore the whole question of elections was anomalous.

This appears to have been felt by the public. In view of the apparent weakness of Parliament and the tentativeness of the existing political system, elections did not seem urgent, and several newspapers — mostly anti-Communist — encouraged the view that they were unnecessary. As one Surabaja daily put it, the money needed for elections might be better used for national development.[100] Thus, except for the PKI and a few allied groups, such as Baperki, no one brought significant pressure to bear on the Government to hold the elections.

On September 22, Djuanda informed Parliament that because of poor security conditions, inadequate communications, and the fear that a free and secret vote could not be guaranteed, the Government had decided to postpone the elections for at most one year. In the meantime, to prevent a legislative vacuum, it was felt that the present Parliament should continue until a new one was elected.[101] Support for and justification of the postponement came from Masjumi, the PNI, NU, the PSI, and several other minor parties.[102] Only the PKI seriously objected, pointing out the

---

100 *Harian Umum*, July 28, 1958.
101 *Pos Indonesia*, Sept. 22; *Merdeka*, Sept. 23, 1958.
102 *Nusantara*, Sept. 23; *Suluh Indonesia*, Sept. 24; *Duta Masjarakat*, Sept. 22; *Merdeka*, Sept. 23, an especially interesting and informative editorial; *Suara Rakjat*, Sept. 25; *Harian Umum*, Sept. 25, 1958. For a representative PNI view, see also *Pesat*, XIV, no. 39 (Sept. 27, 1958), 3-5, which defended the PNI against accusations by *Pemuda* — now called a trumpet of Partindo — that it feared elections and felt safer with the pontponement. See also *Pemuda*, Sept. 23, 1958.

constitutional violation; in a few regions PKI leaders were so frustrated that they insisted, in vain, that the elections must go on anyway.[103]

The inevitable consequence of postponing the elections was to weaken Parliament further. Already under attack for its lack of moral authority and the decline of its influence in national problems, Parliament's very legality now came to be questioned. Some argued that without elections — the essential basis of representative government — the entire status of Parliament must become constitutionally suspect.[104] Postponing the elections similarly affected the position of the political parties, whose legitimacy necessarily depended to a great extent upon a popular mandate. Without elections, the parties were not extraordinary, for the main source of their justification and significance disappeared. Increasingly, they had to fall back on another, and narrower, source of legitimacy — the mere fact that they constituted organizations of the elite whose authority in a traditionally inclined society was respected simply because they existed as an adjunct of the government. The parties' defense of parliamentarianism was fought from a vulnerable corner; at the same time, the postponement of the elections gave the opponents of the parliamentary system more time to work for its replacement.

The willingness of the PNI and NU, as well as Masjumi, the PSI, and most smaller parties to put off the elections was consistent with the process of political disintegration and recreation that had begun in early 1957. After the proclamation of martial law and the formation of the Kabinet Karya and the National Council, there were two overlapping political systems in force: one represented by the parties and Parliament, the other by Soekarno and the army. To put it another way, one system was based on the Constitution of 1950, the other on martial law — and the latter was in the ascendancy. Gradually but irrevocably the exponents of the weaker system were drawn towards the stronger.

Quite apart from their loss of initiative in 1957, most of the parties — excepting only the PKI — were already seriously degenerated, unreformed, out of touch with the electorate, and unsure of their abilities to deal effectively with the nation's problems. Party reform, were it

---

103 *Pos Indonesia*, Sept. 23, 1958.
104 See the discussion by Soedarisman Purwokusumo reported in *Nusantara*, Nov. 6, 1958.

possible, would have threatened the pre-war generation leaders who were still in control of most parties, particularly the PNI and NU. Moreover, elections, had they been held, would in any case have greatly reduced the parliamentary power of these parties in favor of the PKI. Consequently there was a tendency for leaders of the PNI and NU to accept the new power structure, and to work within it to secure whatever advantages they could. In the cabinet reshuffle neither of these parties demanded a restoration of party control of the government; rather they fought to maintain or improve their positions within the Kabinet Karya, to which they continued thereafter to pledge their support. As for the elections, there was no powerful urge to defend them. For more obvious reasons, Masjumi, the PSI, and similarly inclined parties had little to gain from the parliamentary system as it then stood.

By far the strongest and most vital party, the PKI lost most from the postponement of the elections, for with deferral the bed began to wash away from underneath the parliamentary road.[105] The power of the PKI was one of the basic reasons for delaying a vote — the other being that the anti-party forces could not permit the party system generally to renew its legitimacy — and the same reason obtained when elections were put off again and again in the following years. This suggests another facet of the analysis above: that is, the PKI threatened not only the other parties, but the entire social and political order. It was not simply that everyone feared that the Communists, once in power, would overthrow the existing political organization, eliminate the old elite, and invoke their own exclusive ideology. That clearly was the crux of the matter, but it cannot be too strongly emphasized that the social force mobilized by the PKI could not be matched by any of the other parties, by the army, or even (in organizational terms) by President Soekarno. Thus, it was necessary — taking the broadest view of social conflict — to limit the PKI's opportunities to use its power fully. By containing the truly radical PKI, the elite whom it challenged, both party and non-party, was able to maintain its hopes for the future. It is important to point out that this elite did in fact remain in power under Guided Democracy and that it

---

105 See Ruth T. McVey, "Indonesian Communism and the Transition to Guided Democracy," in A. Doak Barnett, *Communist Strategies in Asia* (New York, London: Praeger, 1963), pp. 162-167.

did so by shifting away from a broader electoral basis of politics towards a narrower and more traditional elite basis.

In the meantime, while the PNI and NU adjusted themselves to the new developing political system, Masjumi and its allies turned to the army for help against the PKI, which in turn was then forced to seek protection from Soekarno. It is clear that after the rebellion no one was looking essentially to the parliamentary system for political sustenance. The parties defended it tenaciously from 1958 to 1960, but it had become, in terms of political power, a shell.

CHAPTER FIVE
THE DRIVE TO GUIDED DEMOCRACY (I)

During 1957 and early 1958 the hopes of party leaders for an eventual return to political normality were encouraged by the absence of concrete alternatives to the parliamentary system. Soekarno had been consistently radical in word but vague in deed, proposing little that made a lasting impression on politicans long inured to ideological pronouncements and impossibly broad statements of ideals. But the respite enjoyed by the parties was the gift of the PRRI; Soekarno and army leaders had tacitly declared a truce in their conflict with the parties pending an outcome of the rebellion. In early June, when the double threat of rebellion and foreign intervention had begun to recede, Soekarno for the first time focussed the attention of the National Council on Guided Democracy. After an interruption while he tended to the cabinet reshuffle, the discussions were resumed in late July, and from then until July 1959 Guided Democracy was the main concern of nearly everyone.

Conditions were ripe in mid-1958 for further consideration of the political system, or rather conditions made it impossible to avoid the matter. The rebellion had been a great shock to the nation, loosening many of the remaining underpinnings of the old constitutional order and accelerating the search for new pillars of society. A few very calm thinkers, like Moh. Said, a Djakarta leader of the nationalist educational foundation, Taman Siswa, could infuse only a little moderation into the national discussion, which ranged far beyond politics to education, public morality, and the social order. Within the politically conscious elite, the serious doubts which had arisen after the 1955 elections about the validity of the political system were exacerbated, and the proclivity for social introspection which particularly characterizes the Javanese became more pronounced, making the atmosphere of general malaise plain. The debate begun in 1956, never having stopped, grew in intensity as men tried to analyze all the failings of post-revolutionary society and the disintegration of revolutionary ideals. Some flatly condemned the entire older generation, as having failed miserably and dragged down democracy in its failure.[1] Others turned to total solutions: at a symposium in Jogjakarta in September 1958, for example, Prof. Sigit of the pedagogical faculty argued that only a restoration of the Soekarno-Hatta duumvirate could assure Indonesia of unity and integrity, and he proposed, with considerable support, that the two men be appointed President and Vice-President for life and given rather full powers.[2] Indeed, there was an identifiable consensus that for at least a number of years Indonesia needed a determined and authoritarian government, perhaps a strong man, capable of molding the nation into a politically disciplined and economically viable entity.

In this turmoil of sensitive probing into national political and social ills, Guided Democracy had an immense appeal.[3] It offered solutions, however vague, that were not to be found elsewhere, and they were solutions that struck numerous sympathetic chords, especially in Java. Moreover, the profound popular trust in Soekarno's leadership was matched by an equally profound deprecation of the political parties, which were too demoralized, disunited, and disoriented to put up an effective defense of the parliamentary system. Party leaders feebly parried all challenges to their formal hegemony with hollow praises of democracy, the Constitutional Assembly, and Parliament, or the defensive promise that although the parties had done wrong in the past they would do better in the future.

Nevertheless, Guided Democracy did not have an easy time in the making. Despite the general agreement in principle that a more

---

1 See the statement by Soebadio Sastrosatomo, a PSI leader, before a meeting of the Socialist Youth Movement, *Pos Indonesia*, Dec. 2, 1958.

2 *Pos Indonesia*, Sept. 29, Oct. 2, 1958. The symposium, sponsored by the Institute for Press and Public Opinion, found wide agreement that Indonesia suffered from a profound moral confusion, as evidenced by the growing number of political and social *aliran* — literally "currents" of alignment. This was largely the result, said several participants, of the great influence of foreign ideologies, "as if Indonesia were simply parroting" everything that went on abroad. Among such sentiments, it is easy to see, Soekarno's stress on national identity found welcoming responses.

3 By mid-1958 the "guided" idea had sprouted various shoots. "Guided study" described efforts to tighten up lax rules for university students. "Guided economy" represented the demand for a more thoroughgoing state socialism.

authoritarian political system was needed, there was in practice considerable ambivalence about the matter. The parties were unwilling to make any sacrifice that might endanger their claims on the right to govern. Moreover, there was some concern, especially among the intellectual public, over what a more authoritarian system might lead to. Frequently the fear was expressed that Guided Democracy might become either a personal or a military dictatorship. Especially for those who distrusted Soekarno and saw danger in his willingness to deal with the PKI, Guided Democracy had ominous overtones.[4] Clearly the constitutional issues of Guided Democracy were thoroughly mixed up with the political issues and alignments that preceded the idea, vastly complicating the further development of the new system.

Basically, this further development must be understood as a mopping up operation against the parties, in which Soekarno and the army leadership fortified the positions they had captured in 1957 and consolidated as a result of the rebellion. But this was an exceedingly difficult process. First of all, the National Council, starting with the ideas enunciated by Soekarno in 1957 and 1958, had to develop the new system from the ground up, seeking constitutional bases as it went. The supporters of Soekarno were themselves uncertain of what would finally come out of the process.[5] And as for Soekarno, the utmost care was required on his part to guard against the possibility of his partner in the alliance of Guided Democracy, the army, running rampant.

Nothing could have been done to alter the political system without the support of the army, which simultaneously was the prime mover behind

---

4 Consistently the most vociferous opposition to Guided Democracy on the grounds that it was anti-democratic and favorable to the Communists came from East Java, where the local press was far less hampered than in other regions by the local commandant, Col. Sarbini. Hostility to Guided Democracy became so outspoken in East Java during the second half of 1958 that Soekarno was said to have postponed a trip to Surabaja at the beginning of 1959 as a result. See *Suara Rakjat*, Feb. 7, 1959. He finally did go, however, for the celebration of Mohammad's ascension day in early February. While there he spoke of the need for a national will and spirit to rise politically, economically, and culturally. The empire of Madjapahit (based in East Java), he said, collapsed in the 15th century because it had no such will. One wonders whether he intended this as a subtle dig at his antagonists. See *Java Post*, Feb. 9, 1959.

5 Foreign Minister Subandrio told Parliament in October that Guided Democracy would comprise the Parliament plus the parties plus X — i.e., presumably, the functional groups. The PKI quickly responded that the X in the equation was the National Council and a *gotong-rojong* cabinet with the PKI in it. *Harian Rakjat*, Oct. 14, 1958.

Guided Democracy and the main threat which both the parties and Soekarno had to face. For the parties, the choice in 1958 seemed to be less one between Guided Democracy and parliamentary democracy as one between Guided Democracy and military rule, and the latter appeared to be the less desirable. For Soekarno, who was as much a follower as a leader in his alliance with the army, the problem was to find an institutional solution that would incapacitate the parties without leaving himself and the nation at the mercy of the army. This was the essence of the politics of Guided Democracy in 1958, and the intricate nature of the aims and fears on all sides helps to explain why it took so long, nearly a year, for Guided Democracy to materialize into anything resembling a systematic alternative to parliamentary government. Even then, the solution was a compromise.

This chapter is concerned with the evolution of Guided Democracy in the second half of 1958, leaving the grand compromise for the next chapter. The discussion that follows covers the position of Djuanda, the momentum of the army, the deliberations of the National Council, and the response of the political parties to the threat of Guided Democracy.

Djuanda

A special comment about Djuanda is needed because his role and views would otherwise be obscured by the confusion of political events in 1958. Acting as buffer and moderator between the contending party and anti-party forces, he emerges as a figure of considerable stature, not only for the trust that nearly everyone had in him, but also for the independent course he tried, quite without success, to follow.[6]

Djuanda was in the difficult position of heading a cabinet, partly representing the parties, which would be responsible for dealing with

---

6　This quiet man, almost the ideal type of Feith's "administrator," was not bound to the parties, to Soekarno, or to the army, but depended on all three. He and Nasution got along very well and on many policy matters stood quite close together. Djuanda was not loathe to refer to the army for help in getting a program off the ground against the will of the parties. Soekarno respected the Prime Minister, who in turn realized that it was due to Soekarno's figure that the cabinet's authority was respected. The parties worked with Djuanda because they did not fear him, and he treated them with the respect necessary to maintain parliamentary support for the economic measures he wished to promote.

any anti-party proposals made by the National Council. Never having committed himself unequivocally to Guided Democracy, Djuanda was not in sympathy with the initiative taken by the National Council against the parties, and he greatly feared any hint of radicalism. In mid-July 1958, before the National Council met again, the combination of a coup scare, set off by reports of Kassim's coup in Iraq, and the prospect of further discussions on Guided Democracy led by Soekarno provoked wild rumors that the parties would be abolished or drastically reformed.

Djuanda attended the National Council session on July 22nd to warn against extremism.[7] There were two alternatives, he said, one of which was revolutionary — i.e., the abolition of all parties and Parliament. The inherent danger of this was that one group would be imposing its views by force on all other groups, the kind of situation in which dictatorships arose. In the circumstances, a dictatorship would have to be based on the power of the army, and Djuanda declared that an army-backed dictatorship would meet with the strongest opposition throughout the country. The second alternative, which Djuanda espoused, was to accept the existing situation as a starting point and improve it within limits defined by law. Warning against optimistic expectations with respect to any of the nation's political institutions, he implied that the lack of agreement on basic issues of interest — which plagued not only Parliament and the Constituent Assembly, but also the National Council itself — was simply a fact of Indonesian political life which would not change whatever the system. Djuanda went further to ask, given these differences of view between various groups, who could say what was right or wrong. Without glossing over the deficiencies of the Constituent Assembly and Parliament, he noted that those two bodies were elected by the people, institutional inadequacies to the contrary notwithstanding. On the other hand, the National Council, which was now discussing profound constitutional changes, was chosen only by the cabinet and the President; was it not possible, asked Djuanda, that these latter were more liable to error than the elected bodies?[8] He argued that most national difficulties

---

7 Djuanda's remarks to the Council were not made public, but his views were generally known among Djakarta politicians. I have seen a typescript copy of his statement.

8 This question was of course as unanswerable as it was fundamental, for it went to the heart of the crisis of political legitimacy, confronting philosophically a conflict that basically

could be solved through compromise and friendly give and take. If the Konstituante remained deadlocked, then a referendum might settle the ideological question once and for all. As for the need to reform political institutions, improvements would best be pursued through Parliament itself. This could be achieved, he believed, rather optimistically, by gradually convincing the parties of the need for change.

Djuanda himself set out on this course, moving with deliberate speed to spur the Constituent Assembly to action. Under fierce attack for its general malfunctioning, the Assembly encouraged few to believe that it would ever get over the ideological impasse and finish its work.[9] On July 31st, a week after he had spoken in the National Council, Djuanda appealed to the Assembly to streamline its procedures, to settle the ideological question soon, and to set a deadline for completing its task in order to avoid "serious problems."[10] He also admonished the members not to ignore the issues raised by Guided Democracy with respect to political parties and the electoral system. Two weeks later, Soekarno made the same point more pointedly in his Independence Day speech, when he accused the Konstituante of working nonsensically and urged it to pay heed to the revolutionary needs of the people.[11] The PKI added to the pressure on the Assembly by threatening to submit a resolution that the body dissolve itself unless its procedures were drastically amended.[12]

---

involved power. But it was a question that many asked. See, for example, *Harian Umum*, July 25, 1958, which argued that the Konstituante was the proper place to discuss Guided Democracy, not the National Council.

Djuanda's is one of the best statements I have seen representing the conservative view of the state, as compared with Soekarno's approach to nation-building. To the one, law and order were essential to progress; for the other, law at least was an obstruction which could not be permitted so to bind the state's leadership that the nation could not be pushed over the hump to greatness.

9 See *Pesat*, XIV, no. 4 (Jan. 25, 1958), 16, criticizing the Konstituante for its failure to convene a quorum at the opening of the first biannual plenum of 1958; see also *Harian Rakjat*, July 30, 1958.

10 *Pesat*, XIV, no. 32 (Aug. 9, 1958), 3-5. Djuanda's speech can be found in English translation in the Ministry of Information's Special Release No. 39, 1958.

11 See the collection of Soekarno's August 17th speeches, from 1945 through 1961, *Dari Proklamasi sampai Resopim* (Ministry of Information), p. 372.

12 Many took the threat seriously, reacting to it favorably or leaping to the defense of the Konstituante with renewed attacks on the Communists. Islamic groups were particularly upset. But, though the effort almost backfired, the PKI was trying to goad the other parties into action. See *Pos Indonesia*, Aug. 22, 25, 26; *Pemuda*, Aug. 25; *Trompet Masjarakat*, Sept. 3, 1958. In the latter (a left-wing Surabaja daily), an article signed G. H. G. pointed out that the PKI threat was actually no more than a warning to the Konstituante to improve its methods.

Djuanda had promised more effective cooperation from the Government to help the Constituent Assembly. In late August, meetings were begun by cabinet representatives and Assembly leaders, and a special state commission on constitutional matters was appointed by Djuanda to advise both the cabinet and the Assembly.[13] A few procedural improvements were actually accepted by the Konstituante: for example, a simple majority replaced the two-thirds rule on procedural though not on substantive questions. Many party followers were encouraged by Assembly Chairman Wilopo's statement that, with some procedural changes, a new constitution could be finished by March 1960. The outlook for an ideological compromise remained discouraging, however. In late August, Mr. Sartono, the highly respected Speaker of Parliament and a leading PNI member, told a mixed civilian and military audience in Magelang that if he were in the army, he would not obey any decision of the Konstituante that eliminated the Pantjasila from the constitution.[14] The Islamic parties were incensed by this and the likelihood of a compromise receded further.

At the same time, Djuanda firmly defended the integrity of the cabinet and pursued his own policies, despite occasionally serious disagreements with Soekarno. The resulting tensions were exacerbated by the efforts of both the PKI and the PNI to emphasize their support of Soekarno in nearly all policy matters. One illustration of this was the debate over the National Planning Council bill, the first point of the cabinet's new program, for which Djuanda had requested parliamentary priority.[15]

---

13 *Pos Indonesia*, Aug. 23, 28, 30, and Sept. 9, 1958. The state committee consisted of several legal and constitutional experts, including Prof. Supomo, who died a short time later, Prof. Djokosoetono, A. G. Pringgodigdo, Moh. Nasroen, and Sudarman Gandasoebrata. Apparently the committee was unable to make a substantial contribution to the Konstituante's work.

14 Sartono also proposed — and this may have been a key element in his thinking at the time — that the Konstituante adopt the existing provisional constitution without further ado. Had they been able to put their ideological differences aside for a while, this would have been the most astute political move the parties could have made. For they would then have been armed at least with a permanent constitution that embodied the parliamentary system. The provisional character of the 1950 constitution left a legitimate opening for the anti-party forces, who were themselves reluctant (but perhaps not in the last resort unwilling) to use unquestionably unconstitutional measures. See *Pos Indonesia*, Aug. 25; *Pedoman*, Aug. 27, 1958; *Pesat*, XIV, no. 37 (Sept. 13, 1958), 3-4.

15 The National Planning Council bill was drafted by the cabinet and the National Council shortly after the cabinet reshuffle. The Planning Council was to consist of functional group representatives, experts in various fields, and other civil and military officials. In the parliamentary

Basic as the idea of planning was to Guided Democracy, Soekarno felt that the Planning Council should stand above the cabinet and beyond its authority. Djuanda would not countenance this, both because it would make coordination difficult and because the cabinet must ultimately assume responsibility for executing a development plan. In Parliament he insisted that the new body should be subordinate to the cabinet, not above or even on the same level with it.[16] Meanwhile the PKI and the PNI raced one another to propose that Soekarno should become chairman of the National Planning Council. Djuanda replied that this would be improper because of Soekarno's position as a constitutional and non-responsible president.[17] The bill was passed in late September without significant amendment.

Another issue that caused Djuanda discomfort was the foreign investment bill, which Parliament debated in August and September. Although foreign investment had always been a sensitive matter in post-revolutionary Indonesia, Djuanda was determined to encourage it, albeit with proper controls. Soekarno distrusted and opposed this policy, fearing that it would open the way for European capital to reassert its grasp on the Indonesian economy. He favored government-to-government loans or grants, not investment, and in this he was joined by the radical nationalist left. In Parliament, Soekarno's views were quoted in extensio by the PKI

---

debates, the Government was asked to define what the functional groups were and how they would be constituted, but no one was clear on this as yet; see *Risalah Perundingan D. P. R. 1958* (Minutes of Parliamentary Debates), session of Sept. 16, pp. 3338 ff. For the text of the law on the National Planning Council (80/ 1958), later amendments, and other materials relating to the functions of the body, see "Peraturan Depernas" (National Planning Council Regulations) compiled for the Planning Council by Moh. Yamin. The law and its clarification are interesting for their illustration of the views current on the need for and role of planning.

16 *Risalah Perundingan 1958*, session of Sept. 19, p. 3463; see also *Nusantara*, Sept. 20, 1958. The Chairman of the Planning Council would have protocol rank as Minister, but would not sit in the cabinet.

17 *Risalah Perundingan 1958*, session of Sept. 19, p. 3464. Djuanda said that the President would be able to present major addresses to the Planning Council. Unlike most others, Djuanda continued to lay stress on the point that the President's position remained constitutionally limited. Soekarno himself occasionally issued a reminder to the same effect, partly in order to ward off the various pressures brought to bear upon him.
Who would become chairman of the National Planning Council was being considered — and rumored about — at this time. Those proposed at first included Hatta, who had already rejected the possibility in 1957, and the Sultan of Jogjakarta. Later in the year Yamin's name came up, though the suggestion was vehemently attacked in Parliament, especially by Soetomo (Bung Tomo) of the PRI. Yamin was Soekarno's choice, however, and in mid-1959, when the Planning Council was officially appointed, he became its chairman.

and allied groups.[18] Djuanda replied firmly that he would not allow the cabinet to be confronted by the President or anyone else on this bill; for it was the cabinet, he said, which was responsible to Parliament. The bill was passed — though it never had any real effect — with support from the PNI, NU, and Masjumi.[19] Djuanda's attitude won the praise of those who had once feared that he would be a sycophant to the President.[20]

Other parts of Djuanda's economic program were passed by Parliament without great difficulty, though the Government did face considerable opposition on the 1959 budget. The Five Year Plan, which had been drafted before the second Ali Cabinet took office but had not yet been debated in Parliament, was finally accepted in November.[21] But many of the cabinet's economic goals were long range. Over the immediate conditions of inflation, food shortages, and inadequate foreign exchange, the Government had little control, and whatever remedies were tried met with obstruction. In October an attempt to raise the official price of rice met with so much opposition, including a parliamentary resolution and the refusal of the army command in East Java to implement the

---

18 See especially the statement by R. W. Probosuprodjo, *Risalah Perundingan 1958*, session of Aug. 26, pp. 2743-44. Soekarno had made his antipathy to foreign investment clear in several speeches during the year, one of them to the Engineers' Association Congress on July 24. On the foreign investment bill, see A. Laksmi, "Politik Penanaman Modal Asing" (Foreign Investment Policy), in *Mimbar Indonesia*, XII, no. 36 (Sept. 6, 1958), 5, 20-21.

19 A few PNI leaders were tempted to come out against the bill, but for the party to have done so would have put the cabinet, which it supported, in an awkward position. The support of NU, Masjumi, and the PNI for the bill can be understood partly in terms of the fact that foreign aid and private foreign business operations were important sources of party funds. Some party leaders justified this (privately) by arguing that a way had to be found to counter the PKI's alleged foreign sources of income. Nay votes on the foreign investment bill were cast by the PKI and the PSI, partly on the same grounds that foreign investment encouraged corruption. See *Pedoman*, Sept. 17, 1958.

20 See *Suara Rakjat*, Sept. 4, 1958.

21 On the Five Year Plan, see Douglas Paauw, *Financing Economic Development* (Glencoe: Free Press, 1960), and Benjamin Higgins, *Indonesia's Economic Stabilization and Development* (New York: Institute of Pacific Relations, 1957). The plan, which was supposed to run from 1956 through 1960, could not, obviously, be put into full effect; Djuanda said it would be executed as far as possible in 1959 and 1960, while the National Planning Council was drawing up a new plan, but he admitted frankly that the primary importance of the plan was to prove to the world that the government was seriously concerned to undertake long term development, thus encouraging foreign trust and facilitating foreign loans and other aid. The Five Year Plan, he said, was considered a realistic one and not overly ambitious. Internally, according to Djuanda, the plan would have the effect of compelling the government to carry out development. See *Pos Indonesia*, Nov. 12, 1958. On the latter score he was wrong. The course of events after 1958 buried the Five Year Plan. Its place was taken by the grandiose, unsystematic, and unattainable Eight Year Plan announced by the National Planning Council in 1960.

price increase, that it finally had to be rescinded.[22] At the same time a Government purchase of rice from the Soviet Union came under prolonged attack by anti-Communist parties.[23]

It was under these conditions that Djuanda had to deal also with the National Council on the issues of Guided Democracy.

The Army Initiative

The influence of the rebellion on the role of the army has already been discussed in the last chapter. Inevitably the already extensive authority exercised by the officer corps under martial law was greatly expanded. Security became the chief concern of the government, a rock-hard fact against which the political parties continually bumped in their attacks on martial law and in their efforts to alter the budget. The demands of the General Staff for more funds had to be met, and more than ever before the military became its own master.[24] But the additional significance of the rebellion, as has been mentioned, was that it erupted at a time when the army had already succeeded partially in establishing its political rights under martial law and when parliamentary institutions were clearly in decline. With the eclipse of the rebellion in mid-1958, army leaders set out to achieve two basic political aims: 1) to reduce the role of the parties to a minimum, to create a more authoritarian and stable government — often conceived in terms carried over from military experience[25] —

---

22 See *Nusantara*, Nov. 6, 1958.

23 *Abadi*, Oct. 28; *Harian Rakjat*, Nov. 5; *Suluh Indonesia*, Nov. 6, 1958. Masjumi, the PNI, and other non-Communist parties attacked the purchase partly on the grounds that the price of Soviet rice was higher than any other which Indonesia had bought. The purchase price was later lowered by Moscow.

24 In his Armed Forces Day (Oct. 5) message in 1958, Nasution noted that for the first time since 1945 the government was paying attention to the development of the army with respect to personnel and equipment. See *Pesat*, XV, no. 41 (Oct. 11, 1958), 5-6.

25 Nasution and other officers frequently spoke of organizing the government on military lines in one sense or another, and their conceptions of structure, hierarchy, and function were understandably drawn from patterns which they knew and in which, as they compared them with the civilian government, they had considerable pride and confidence.
Mention might be made here of the lingering influence of the Japanese occupation on officers whose first military experience was in the para-military organizations established by the Japanese army from 1943 through 1945. Many officers were deeply impressed by the rigorous discipline and martial determination of the Japanese soldier, and, though the occupation was recalled with distaste and antipathy, the impressions showed through. For example, in connection with a national physical education program in which the army would participate, Nasution wrote some

and to deal with the evils that had led to the rebellion; 2) to work out a permanent political role for the army independent of the temporary martial law, a role that would satisfy both the mission and the ambitions of the politically conscious army elite, and allow it to enjoy the fruits of the revolution and to participate responsibly in the political life of the nation on some basis short of a military regime.[26]

By mid-1958 the mood and intentions of the army were a chief topic of political discussion. Officers were outspoken in their disdain for the parties and their confidence in the army.[27] In mid-July Kassim's coup in Iraq abruptly called attention to the same possibility in Indonesia. The press pointed out that nothing had improved in the last year and a half; economically the country was in a worse condition, the reshuffled cabinet had not yet produced any economic plans or gained control of the situation, and the parties were still dipping into government coffers and hungrily bargaining for diplomatic posts as if the rebellion had never happened.[28] There were warnings that the army would not put up with

---

comments to the Minister of Education, remarking, inter alia, on the need to make the people defense-minded and militant: "When the revolution broke out in 1945 young people were ready and ripe to perform their defense tasks as a consequence of the Japanese system of education which earlier had prepared them for this both in the schools and in the community at large. Apart from the 'ism' which was implanted at that time, such a system should be established again and its benefits should always be realized." *Risalah Perundingan 1958*, appendix of Djuanda's statement before Parliament on the extension of martial law, session of Dec. 8, pp. 5183-5184.

26 See Daniel S. Lev, "The Political Role of the Army in Indonesia," *Pacific Affairs*, XXXVI, no. 4 (Winter 1963-64), for a discussion of the army's search for a formula justifying its political participation independent of martial law.

27 In April, before the effort to reshuffle the cabinet had got fully underway, Brig. Gen. Djatikusumo, a dashing officer with the confidence of noble birth and a proclivity for speaking out, said that the nation needed "a non-party government backed by the army with elections suspended for six years." And "there should be an army man in the government. There are too many small men and not enough big men. The army is the source of good leaders." *Indonesian Observer*, April 24, 1958. A few days later Nasution ordered his officers to control themselves in giving political interviews to the press. But it was difficult to restrain many in the officer corps, for the rebellion trained a spotlight on the army, into which its leaders stepped with considerable confidence and a heightened sense of importance.

28 *Merdeka*, July 16, 1958. *Merdeka* proposed that Soekarno meet with the Prime Minister, the three vice-premiers, and the chiefs-of-staff to outline a firm policy to restrict the political parties. They did meet at the time, along with Foreign Minister Subandrio, apparently to discuss the Middle-Eastern crisis. *Nusantara*, July 24, 1958, noted that the Iraqi crisis and de Gaulle's re-emergence in France indicated that other countries were experiencing difficulties like Indonesia's and were beginning to settle them.

The Iraqi coup was accompanied by the dispatch of American troops to Lebanon. At the same time there were reports that some ships of the Seventh Fleet were in Singapore waters. The foreign intervention issue being still very much alive, the United States came in for angry condemnation

this much longer; it was at this time that the party system began to come under renewed and sustained condemnation in the press.

In early August, at about the same time that he was submitting to the National Council a new proposal on Guided Democracy, Nasution convened in Djakarta the first conference of army commanders to be held since April 1957, ostensibly to discuss operations against the PRRI.[29] This was the first of a series of such meetings in 1958 and 1959 that were concerned quite as much with politics as with technical military problems. Serving as informal political forums and sounding boards, they were the inexperienced equivalent of political party council meetings. They also served to bring pressure to bear on the government at strategic moments. The resolution adopted by the August 1958 conference, addressed clearly to all national leaders, expressed the temper of the officer corps:

1. In suppressing the rebellion, the Armed Forces of the Republic of Indonesia base the performance of their task on the conviction that when it is done, there will be no repetition of the political excesses of the past — such as 'cow-trading,' the politicization of economic problems and the civil service, and so on. It is these rotton excesses that are the basic cause of our troubles.

2. The TNI [army] is determined, after this rebellion, to concentrate its power on putting law and discipline in order, and on cleaning up the state's organization, both civil and military.

3. The government must guarantee that after the rebellion is suppressed it will intensify efforts [to improve] regional autonomy and national development, using as a guide, inter

---

in paint on many walls for its action in Lebanon. The issue of early recognition of the new leftist regime in Iraq, against which the right-wing press campaigned unsuccessfully, was so hotly debated that at length Nasution forbade further discussion in the press of the Middle-Eastern crisis, partly no doubt also to put a damper on the speculation about a coup in Indonesia. See A. Laksmi, "Krisis Timur Tengah dan Faktor dalam Negeri Kita" (The Middle-Eastern Crisis and Our Internal Factors), in *Mimbar Indonesia*, XII, no. 30 (July 26, 1958), 3-5.

29 *Pos Indonesia*, Aug. 4, 1958. Djuanda and Suprajogi attended, the former in his capacity as Minister of Defense.

alia, the results of the National Conference and the National Conference on Development [of 1957].

4. The TNI hopes that an expression of gratitude will be made to the soldiers who have fulfilled their duties loyally and to their suffering families.[30]

Soon afterwards, the impatience of army headquarters for reform became apparent. A long-standing complaint — not of the army alone — against party government was the politicization of the civil service.[31] On August 9th, without consulting the cabinet beforehand, Nasution issued a directive aimed at correcting this problem. On the flimsy grounds that martial law authority required the army to obtain information from civil servants in the interests of public order, he instructed all government personnel offices to compile reports on the political affiliations of rank F officials (the highest rank in the bureaucracy, covering every significant staff position in national and regional government).[32] The reports were to be sent directly to the army intelligence chief, Col. Soekendro, a politically active officer who may have been one of the masterminds behind the move.

Nasution's order received considerable support in the press, but it shocked the parties and the cabinet, not to mention the bureaucracy. Coming at a time when the party system was everywhere under attack and men were becoming shy about their party membership, the mere promulgation of the measure had the effect of weakening party loyalties further.[33] No one pretended that it was anything but the first step in an eventual prohibition against civil servants joining political parties.

---

30 Quoted in Thalib Ma'azis, "Reorganisasi," *Mimbar Indonesia*, XII, no. 44 (Nov. 1, 1958), 6. See also *Siasat*, XII, no. 588 (Sept. 17, 1958), 8. Soekarno gave the resolution prominence in his August 17th speech.

31 See *Mimbar Indonesia*, XII, no. 33 (Aug. 17, 1958), 7; *Pesat*, XIV, no. 33 (Aug. 16, 1958), 4, for comments on the destructive influence of the parties in the bureaucracy.

32 *Pos Indonesia*, Aug. 9, 1958. There were about 5000 rank F civil servants out of an approximate total of 1,000,000, as nearly as anyone could tell (*Pos Indonesia*, Oct. 2, 1958). See also Roeslan Abdulgani, "Kepimpinan dalam dinas Pemerintahan" (Leadership in the Government Service), *Mimbar Indonesia*, XII, no. 45 (Nov. 10, 1958), 9-11. Nasution's order also applied to other organizations than parties, such as labor unions.

33 *Siasat*, XII, no. 591 (Oct. 8, 1958), 12, noted that, in contrast to a decade earlier, men were no longer proud to be members of political parties, for they now realized that it was not necessary to belong to a party in order to contribute to society.

Only the PKI, with little strength in the bureaucracy, did not face a loss of patronage, funds, and prestige. This, indeed, was one illustration of the sometimes perplexing contradictoriness of the army's political involvement; pursuing the one objective of destroying the party system, army leaders often succeeded in weakening only the non-Communist parties, thus making their other — and increasingly important — objective of destroying the PKI in particular more difficult to prosecute. At this time, however, Nasution and other officers were concentrating on the party system generally. Aidit praised Nasution's order but suggested that it should have been issued by the cabinet; the threatening aggressiveness of the army outweighed any advantage that might accrue to the PKI from further weakening the already flabby non-Communist parties.

Djuanda was also concerned, for apart from the tension which the army measure created, it also bypassed the cabinet's authority over the civil service, something that had never been questioned even under martial law. Djuanda made his objections clear to Nasution, who agreed to draft a new order and to submit it first to the cabinet for pro-forma approval. The revision, promulgated over Nasution's signature on September 13, provided that the reports on party affiliations should be sent to Prime Minister cum Defense Minister Djuanda, whose jurisdiction over the bureaucracy was thereby recognized.[34] But army intelligence continued to be the driving force behind the regulation, subsequent developments of which in mid-1959 were to fulfill the parties' every fear.[35]

Other actions initiated by Nasution were equally upsetting to the parties. The ultimate threat of the army was that it might decide to abolish the parties outright; it was this that made the waxing and waning rumors about drastic reform seem real. On September 5th, Nasution suddenly banned Masjumi, the PSI, Parkindo, and IPKI in those regions where they were accused of having supported the rebellion.[36] The order appeared

---

34 *Pos Indonesia*, Sept. 6, 19; *Nusantara*, Sept. 20; *Merdeka*, Sept. 19, 1958.

35 Civil servants were understandably reluctant to report their party connections, and army intelligence resorted to bluffs and threats to force them to do so. In the past, new civil service regulations had been used to get rid of political enemies; Nasution's order was regarded somewhat in the same light. See *Pos Indonesia*, Sept. 18, 1958.

36 *Pos Indonesia*, Sept. 5, 1958. The areas were Tapanuli, West Sumatra, Riauw, North and Central Sulawesi, the Moluccas, the Islands off the coast of Irian, and Nusatenggara. Members of the banned parties were made to register with the local prosecution offices. See *Nusantara*, Oct. 17; *Abadi*, Oct. 29, 1958. Immediately after the order was promulgated, PSI and Masjumi

on the same day that the Masjumi leader, Kasman Singodimedjo, was arrested for a pro-PRRI speech delivered in Magelang on August 31st, and it was commonly supposed that the two events were connected.[37] The banned parties immediately protested their innocence, denying any organizational responsibility for the PRRI. Other parties — including the PNI, NU, and the PKI — publicly acclaimed Nasution's decision and condemned Kasman, Masjumi, the PSI, and the PRRI with renewed vigor. Beneath the public reaction, however, was another feeling less indignant and more distraught, in which all the parties, those struck and those applauding, shared equally. For it was a long jump, as the PSI-leaning *Siasat* pointed out, from a general prohibition of political activities to a specific prohibition of political parties.[38] The anti-Soekarno press, particularly in East Java, charged that the implementation of Guided Democracy was being begun by means of military regulations, and many party leaders shared this view.[39] Nasution himself took advantage of the anxiety by saying that he was still considering what to do about the other parties. The ban on the parties in rebel areas had some influence on the Government's decision to postpone the elections, and this indeed may have been a factor in Nasution's action.

In October, the army spectre grew to enormous proportions as a result of the bumper crop of coups during late 1958 in Southeast Asia and the Middle-East. Following Kassim's coup in July, in October the civilian regimes of Pakistan and Burma fell to Generals Ayub Khan and Ne Win respectively. A new coup also struck Thailand, replacing one military regime with another. Soon afterwards rumors of a coup plot were heard

---

delegations pleaded their cases with Djuanda, but to no avail. *Pos Indonesia*, Sept. 17, 1958.

37 An earlier order, in mid-June, forbade all political activity in disturbed areas. This caused something of a stir among the political parties, but it was easy to argue that such a measure might be necessary for the sake of military operations. See *Nusantara*, June 17; *Pedoman*, June 18, 1958. The June order permitted "political activity" in support of the government; *Bintang Timur*, July 8, 1958. After the September order had been issued, the army information officer of North Sumatra stated that political and ideological differences caused conflict and therefore made military operations more difficult; *Waspada*, Sept. 9, 1958. See also *Waspada*, Sept. 26, 1958, for a list of 11 other organizations banned subsequent to the Sept. 13 order in Tapanuli (North Sumatra).

38 *Siasat*, XII, no. 587 (Sept. 10, 1958), 3. The magazine blamed the banning on the "martial law-Guided Democracy atmosphere." *Pesat*, XIV, no. 37 (Sept. 13, 1958), 3-4, observed that members of the untouched major parties — PNI, NU, PKI — were privately agreeing with what the right wing press was saying openly, i.e., that the army was setting an extremely unhappy precedent.

39 See *Suara Rakjat*, Sept. 9, 1958. *Surabaja Post*, Sept. 9, 1958, hoped editorially that the measure would not be extended to other parties.

from the Philippines, and in November the Sudan was taken over by the military. On each occasion a shock wave of anxiety pulsed through Djakarta and every other major city, exciting worried reactions from the parties, the Government, and the independent press.[40] Numerous comparisons were made between the situations in those other states and in Indonesia, where it was feared army leaders would be tempted by the initiative of their foreign counterparts. The omnipresent fear of a coup dovetailed with the raging discussion about Guided Democracy to throw the whole political future into question. Time and again it was pointed out in the press that everywhere in the new states civilian regimes were under pressure by militaries because of corruption, "cow-trading," economic decline, and insensitivity to the needs of the people.[41] Were not all these evils still evident in Indonesia, despite the warnings sounded since 1956? In early November fuel was added to the fire by a *New Leader* article, picked up by the Djakarta press, which propounded the simplistic thesis that in the underdeveloped states of Asia dictators were necessary in order to save them from Communism.[42]

With considerable trepidation the parties warned against emulating foreign examples; the suspension of political parties in Pakistan provoked worried assurances from party headquarters that in Indonesia the situation the different.[43] The PKI declared that a coup would be a betrayal of the Indonesian national character and that the leaders of a coup would surely be thrown out by the people, who in Indonesia, unlike Thailand and Pakistan, knew the meaning of revolution.[44] Throughout the rain of coups, army leaders assured the Government that they had no similar intentions.[45] After each new foreign report Nasution publicly

---

40 See, for example, *Pesat*, XIV, no. 42 (Oct. 18, 1958), 3-5, and *Star Weekly*, XIII, no. 673 (Nov. 22, 1958), 1, 46-47.

41 See *Indonesia Raja*, Oct. 29; *Java Post*, Oct. 22, 1958.

42 The article was by John Scott. "Whose Dictators in Asia," *New Leader* (Nov. 3, 1958), pp. 14-16.

43 See *Duta Masjarakat*, Oct. 10, and, following the Sudan coup in mid-November, *Suluh Indonesia*, Nov. 19, 1958. The PNI press pointed to Ayub Khan's decision to drop the Islamic state in Pakistan as a meaningful lesson for Indonesian Islamic parties. In general the party press did not contribute a great deal to the depth of discussions about the army challenge.

44 *Harian Rakjat*, Oct. 22, 1958. The CCPKI had made the same warning at its sixth plenum in March-April. *Harian Rakjat* compared the Thai coup with the periodical upheavals in South America as proof of the destruction of democracy in this SEATO country.

45 Within a few days of the coups in Pakistan and Burma, Subandrio and Nasution talked

emphasized that he, Soekarno, and Djuanda were solidly united and that efforts to divide them would be dealt with sternly.[46] Djuanda and other Government leaders somewhat anxiously de-emphasized the possibility of a coup, but public concern was not greatly ameliorated, and the threat seemed to hang like an axe ready to fall at almost any time.

The significance of this threat had to do mainly with the negotiations then developing in the Guided Democracy arena. Soekarno used it to force concessions from the parties, which were in effect presented with the choice: accede to the National Council demands, which would weaken the parties, or be obliterated by the army. In September, after Nasution had begun to move on his own against the party system, the weekly *Pesat* had put it to the parties that they must either give Soekarno full support or confront a military dictatorship.[47] By October this choice was in even sharper focus. Following a meeting with Nasution in which the foreign coups were discussed, Subandrio said that the crisis of liberal democracy in Indonesia would be solved differently from the way taken in other countries; there was an alternative to a choice between liberal democracy and dictatorship, he insisted — Guided Democracy.[48] Party leaders were aware of the dilemma.[49] They were able to stop short of surrendering entirely to the National Council only because Soekarno himself feared the army and was reluctant to eliminate the support that the parties could give him.

The Guided Democracy or military rule alternatives were real ones. For although the army was not at this time inclined towards a coup, the guarantee that it would not become so depended on a revision of the

---

about developments in "neighboring countries." Djuanda was away on a trip to Yugoslavia and elsewhere during much of October. When he returned at the end of the month he expressed his relief that nothing untoward had happened in his absence. *Surabaja Post*, Oct. 30, 1958.

46 See the statement by army information officer Harsono, *Pos Indonesia*, Oct. 10, 1958. Deputy Chief-of-Staff Gatot Soebroto said in early December that Indonesia was unsuited for a coup, because its people were different in character and the situation was different from the other countries in which armies had taken over. *Pos Indonesia*, Dec. 5, 1958.

47 "Menudju ke Demokrasi Terpimpin atau ke-Diktatur" (Towards Guided Democracy or Dictatorship), *Pesat*, XIV, no. 37 (Sept. 13, 1958), 3-4.

48 *Surabaja Post*, Oct. 13, 1958.

49 The NU daily, *Duta Masjarakat*, Oct. 10, 1958, argued angrily that it would be altogether improper and unfair if the suspension of political parties in Pakistan were used as an opportunity to bulldoze the parties with Guided Democracy and such ideas as functional representation in Parliament.

political system that would satisfy its interests and demands. Events in Pakistan, Burma, and Thailand gave army leaders an advantage in the National Council discussions of late 1958. But it was necessary for them to define their demands and to explicate the role which they believed the army must play. Nasution was one of the very few officers equal to this task.

The reasons why a coup was not likely then in Indonesia should be emphasized, for they also explain the difficulties which army leaders faced in working out their political position. Although some officers, particularly in the intelligence branches, were in fact beginning to think favorably of the possibility of a coup, the predominant view of the officer corps remained that this would cause more problems than it would solve. Most Javanese officers remained loyal to Soekarno as national leader and symbol of national unity. Equally important was the fact that the unpopularity of the army was too great, its image too sullied by commercialism, corruption, profiteering, and coercion; to consider a coup seriously, officers would have to have been entirely insensitive or profoundly cynical. If the army had the political advantage of physical power, it did not have the advantage of legitimacy. This belonged to Soekarno, and army leaders therefore chose, in a sense, to ride his coattails.

Officers, however, were by no means inclined to surrender any of the authority which had been put in their hands since 1957; on the contrary, they wished to extend it. Not only were they convinced that the army had more to contribute to national development than civilian politicians, but they had also become too engaged in the political, economic, and social life of the country to be willing to withdraw into the barracks. Yet, unless they were to stage a coup, the only existing basis for military participation in the political life of the country was martial law, and that was temporary and under attack.

In the midst of the furor over foreign coups, discussions in the National Council, and renewed assaults on martial law, Nasution attempted to formulate the army's position in a speech that deserves to be called a basic document in Indonesian constitutional and political development. It was delivered on November 12th, on the occasion of the first anniversary of the National Military Academy in Magelang.[50] The Indonesian army, said Nasution, could not follow the course of Latin American armies, which played direct political roles; nor should it emulate the passive role prescribed for the military establishments in Western Europe.[51] Rather, the Indonesian army must pursue a "middle-way" between these extremes; the army *qua* army would not involve itself in political affairs — i.e., there would be no coup — yet neither would it be purely a spectator. Officers must be granted the opportunity to participate in the government on an individual basis and to make use of their non-military skills in helping to develop the nation. At the highest levels of government, argued Nasution, officers must be permitted to participate in determining economic, financial, international, and other policies. Therefore they must have a place in all the institutions of the state, not only in the National Council and the cabinet, as was already the case, but also in the National Planning Council, the diplomatic corps,[52] Parliament, and elsewhere in the government. If this were not granted, Nasution threatened, it could not be guaranteed that the army would

---

50 See *Pos Indonesia*, Nov. 13; *Pesat*, XIV, no. 47 (Nov. 22, 1958), 4-5; *Siasat*, XII, no. 597 (Nov. 19, 1958), 3.
   In late September, Nasution had given an interview to a Turkish free-lance reporter, Arslan Humbarachi, in which he presaged his November speech but with heavier emphasis on more immediate problems. He lashed out at those — Americans and others — who believed that the Indonesian army could be influenced, as in Latin America, through its personally ambitious officers. Nasution also stressed the army's support of an independent foreign policy and of the Pantjasila. As evidence of the army's dedication to the Pantjasila, he mentioned the suppression of the Madiun rebellion and the fight against the Darul Islam. See *Nusantara* and *Pos Indonesia*, Sept. 27, 1958; also Nasution's Army Day message, *Pos Indonesia*, Oct. 4, 1958. It is interesting to note, incidentally, with respect to Nasution's statement about being pro-Pantjasila, that in the National Council in June Soekarno had also said that a consensus must be created on the Pantjasila; no one, said Soekarno, should try to change the Red and White flag into a Green one or a Red one. The ideological alliance of the army and Soekarno against the right and left extremes is here evident.
51 Nasution said that Eastern European armies had much to offer by way of example, although their role also did not completely satisfy the Indonesian case. The Yugoslav experience was regarded with some favor by Nasution and other officers, partly because of the common partisan origins.
52 In early October Lt. Col. Isman, the first army officer assigned specifically to diplomatic work, was sent to the U.N. as an advisor to the Indonesian delegation. See *Siasat*, XII, no. 591 (Oct. 8, 1958), 5. Brig. Gen. Djatikusumo was later appointed Consul-General in Singapore, where he remained until he joined the cabinet in July 1959. Soon numerous officers were sent to embassies abroad. As in the case of the army's involvement in the Dutch firms seized in 1957, it was not always the most able officers who were chosen for these posts. Army leaders, like party leaders before them, often used appointments abroad as a means of easing men from the domestic scene.

eschew violence to prevent discrimination against its officers.

This speech represented a major effort to redefine civil-military relations, and in general the response to it was favorable — if for no other reason than its assurance that there would be no coup in the near future. Djuanda was quick to praise the middle-way, declaring that Indonesia would not go the way of military dictatorship.[53] In the press Nasution was hailed as a statesman, as well as a skillful military leader, who had laid the army's cards on the table with restraint and clarity and had kept the national interest in mind throughout.[54] There were doubts, however, about what the proper role of an army was. The officer corps had displayed the same symptoms of deterioration as the political parties before them; army leaders were called upon to eliminate corruption and high living from the army itself if they were to make a real contribution.[55]

Nasution's purpose in giving the middle-way speech at this time was to make the army's position clear in the negotiations then in progress in the National Council. The issue at stake was the army's status as a functional group, which would permit officers legitimately to take their places in the government with or without martial law. Pending the outcome of those negotiations, however, martial law remained the basis of the army's political rights.

The issue of extending martial law arose again in November-December, by which time the parties and the National Council had reached an impasse over the latter's proposals to the cabinet on revision of Parliament, functional groups, and the establishment of a national front. Martial law was due to lapse on December 17, 1958, unless Parliament extended it for another year. Just as the basic conflict of Guided Democracy was, in many ways, that between the army and the parties, martial law was the basic issue on which the conflict turned. That is to say, for the army martial law

---

53 *Pedoman*, Nov. 15, 1958; *Siasat*, XII, no. 597 (Nov. 19, 1958), 3. Djuanda's remarks were made at the ceremony officially transferring control over the ex-Dutch firms, now nationalized, from the army to various ministries. He replied here to the *New Leader* article mentioned above, denying vehemently that Scott's ideas applied to Indonesia.

54 See *Pedoman*, Nov. 14; *Merdeka*, Nov. 14; *Surabaja Post*, Nov. 17, 1958.

55 *Pedoman*, Nov. 14, 1958, said that the middle-way could be guaranteed only if army excesses were eliminated and the army cleaned up. An editorial in *Suara Rakjat*, Nov. 17, 1958, was more skeptical: the problem, it said, was whether the army, now participating actively in political, economic, and social affairs, could prevent itself from being influenced by civilian political groups which also had a say in determining state policy. See also *Mimbar Umum*, Nov. 15, 1958.

was the fundamental prerequisite for continuing to be politically active until a permanent arrangement could be worked out; for the parties, it was the insuperable obstacle preventing their return to authority and, furthermore, the chief threat to their very survival.

After almost two years of martial law, the army was vulnerable to accusations of having vastly exceeded its authority. Such "excesses" as military detention without indictment or trial and the growing suppression and control of the press continued to call forth vigorous protests that the rule of law was crumbling — as indeed it was — and that free expression and democracy were being destroyed.[56] Party leaders protested against oppressive restrictions on political activities, harassment by local commanders, and interference with Mosque services. In Parliament, during the budget debates in late 1958, these and numerous other charges were levelled against the army. In the press there were angry complaints that the army was too quick to use force rather than persuasion in exercising its authority. At the same time many pointed to symptoms of military indiscipline and warlordism, the most vivid example being the refusal of Col. Sarbini in East Java to implement Government economic regulations.[57]

Moreover, military involvement in a myriad profitable aspects of government administration and economic policy exposed the army to the attack that not only was it transgressing the proper limits of its functions but the economic and administrative ills which army leaders had set out to remedy so long ago were instead being aggravated under martial law. Having assumed authority with gusto, the officer corps now found itself held partly responsible for bureaucratic malfeasance and economic decline, and justly so. Army leaders were on the defensive on all of these

---

56 On October 1, 1958, a new regulation of the Djakarta commandant required all newspapers and magazines to request a permit to publish. The reason given was the need for control over journals that were sensationalist and "in conflict with morality and public order." *Pos Indonesia*, Oct. 2, 1958. Permits to publish in Djakarta — the registration numbers had to be printed on each issue — were given to 21 dailies, 57 weeklies, 40 fortnightlies, 11 monthlies, 11 bimonthlies, 21 quarterlies, 14 irregulars, and 4 news bureaus. *Pos Indonesia*, Feb. 23, 1959.

57 See *Harian Umum*, Oct. 29; *Surabaja Post*, Nov. 3; *Nusantara*, Nov. 6; *Merdeka*, Nov. 24, 1958. Sarbini had refused to implement not only the rice price increase decided upon by the Government but also other economic measures of the cabinet. This direct challenge to Djakarta's authority was played down with considerable discomfort by the cabinet and by the General Staff. It is one of the more obvious illustrations of the informal federal system operating through the structure and authority of the army under martial law.

scores. They were constrained to agree that the army did not belong in the economy and promised that it would withdraw as soon as economic conditions were improved.[58] In late December, Nasution gave assurances that, contrary to popular suspicion, the army did not intend to hold power forever; its temporary task under martial law was to stimulate civilian officials to work better.[59] Nasution and other officers were dismayed by the increasing evidence of military corruption and commercialism, and they frequently insisted that the officer corps must be purged of all corrupt elements.[60] Yet matters grew continually worse as new horizons of gain appeared and the social expectations of officers ballooned.

In November and December, news leaked out of a major scandal involving rubber smuggling — which the army was in charge of eradicating throughout the archipelago — in the Djakarta harbor of Tandjung Priok. Those implicated included Col. Dachjar, commandant of Djakarta, Col. Ibnu Sutowo, inspector-general for people's defense, Lt. Col. Soekendro, army intelligence chief, and a senior officer in the military police. In fact the Tandjung Priok smuggling was not as serious a matter as it was made out to be, for it at least originated in an attempt to buy badly needed arms in Singapore for which there was inadequate foreign exchange.[61] But

---

58 See *Pos Indonesia*, Oct. 25, 1958. There were frequent objections within the officer corps to economic activity by army members. In October, Col. Jusuf, commandant of South Sulawesi, ordered his officers and troops to choose between the army and commerce. *Harian Umum*, Oct. 31, 1958. The transfer of the nationalized Dutch firms to civilian control in November encouraged some observers, but it should be remembered that individual officers remained attached to the firms even after the latter had passed from direct army control. See *Abadi*, Nov. 3; *Merdeka*, Nov. 15; *Suara Rakjat*, Nov. 18; *Pos Indonesia*, Dec. 26, 1958. It was not until much later that these officers were released from active military service and made subject to the civil and criminal codes applicable to business concerns generally.

59 *Pos Indonesia*, Dec. 24, 1958. This was a speech in Atjeh to which reactions were favorable but skeptical. Nasution denied that the army was governing the country: "we only exercise control, give guidance, and offer stimulation to civil offices to work harder and take steps against matters that are not right.11 But all this, he emphasized, was only temporary.

60 See statement by Nasution, *Mimbar Umum*, July 3, 1958; also *Indonesian Observer*, Sept. 10, 1958.

61 See Bustanil Arifin, "Beberapa segi dari praktek Undang-undang Keadaan Bahaja tahun 1957" (Aspects of the Operation of the State of Emergency Law of 1957) in *Padjadjaran*, II, no. 2 (Feb. 1960), 67-94, at p. 91. See also Djuanda's statement before Parliament, *Pos Indonesia*, Dec. 11, 1958; *Abadi*, Dec. 16, 1958. The official story on the "Priok barter" was that Col. Ibnu Sutowo, a General Staff officer, seeing the need for more material in operations against the rebels, ordered Soekendro, Dachjar, and several others to establish control over the rubber smuggling to Singapore in order to obtain foreign exchange with which to buy equipment. Nasution ordered the barter stopped on discovering it. *Pos Indonesia*, Jan. 6, 1959. But it was not in fact halted immediately, despite Nasution's claims to the contrary, and various difficulties arising from it continued into 1959. The

when it was discovered, Djuanda quickly condemned the smuggling; he and Nasution asserted that although there were mitigating circumstances in the case the officers had nevertheless violated the law and therefore must be punished.[62]

Various attempts to improve the public image of the army met with no success,[63] which meant that in the parliamentary debates on martial law the officer corps suffered a moral disadvantage. This was balanced, however, by the low public regard for the parties, which were blamed for poor political conditions in the first place. Few people looked forward to a restoration of party government, even if they also regarded the army as an incubus.[64] Moreover, the moral disadvantage of the army had little significance when it came to the essential issues involved, for the officer corps was simply not prepared to surrender the authority it then possessed.

Djuanda had proposed earlier in the year that martial law might be gradually lifted as security conditions improved. By September and October the parties had begun to demand that martial law be lifted immediately in areas where no rebellion or other threat to security existed — for example, East and Central Java, and parts of West Java, Kalimantan, Sumatra, and Sulawesi.[65] Local party branches were trying

---

officers involved in the smuggling no doubt enjoyed some personal profit from it. Djuanda stated that all foreign exchange realized from the smuggling would be turned over to the Government, but it is unlikely that all of it was.

62 Col. Ibnu was temporarily suspended from active duty, his post being transferred to Col. Jani. Dachjar was relieved of his position and sent to the staff school. See *Abadi*, Jan. 7, 1958.

63 For example, the Djakarta military administration established a special bureau to receive public claims against abusive and damaging acts by members of the army. But most persons either feared to make charges or were not used to the idea of openly claiming against constituted authority. See *Pos Indonesia*, Oct. 29; *Abadi*, Dec. 9, 1958. Concern with the public image of the army was often in evidence. One illustration was army information's reminder that the martial law statute of 1957 was a new and national law, not the colonial State of Law and Siege (SOB) statute. As the parliamentary debates on martial law extension neared, the public was asked to stop referring to martial law as the SOB, which, it was said, was buried, and to use KB (Keadaan Bahaja, state of emergency) instead. *Pos Indonesia*, Oct. 28, 1958. But for most it remained the SOB.

64 See *Surabaja Post*, Nov. 22, 1958.

65 All the major parties were agreed that the country would be much better off without martial law, though their emphases differed somewhat. See *Pos Indonesia*, Sept. 29, Oct. 23; *Suluh Indonesia*, Nov. 12, 20; *Harian Umum*, Nov. 22, 1958. Masjumi objected in principle to martial law and sarcastically reminded the other parties that it had opposed the proclamation of the state of siege in 1957 when they had supported it. But Masjumi too went along with the Government's later decision on extension. *Abadi*, Dec. 1, 1958.

to elude the restraints imposed by local army commands, who were equally determined not to relinquish the reins of authority. The General Staff and regional commanders were unanimously agreed that martial law must remain in force everywhere. Nasution convened a second major conference of commanding officers on October 23rd-25th. The key decision of this meeting was that martial law must be extended for another year throughout the country; a partial lifting was unacceptable.[66] Army leaders countered the parties' anti-extension efforts with the argument that security in one area affected all other areas, and therefore martial law must remain in force everywhere. They also emphasized the need to guard against subversive activities, to carry on the West Irian campaign, to control cold-war influences, to attend to the exigencies of economic and social development, and to follow up the army's victories against the rebellion.[67] Regional commanders in some cases stated simply — as did Col. Sjamaun Gaharu of Atjeh — that martial law would be maintained for the sake of security and development, and that the people did not want it to be lifted.[68]

Army leaders were faced with opposition not only from the parties but also from within the armed forces, by the air-force. Air-Commodore Suryadarma supported the parties' case for lifting martial law in secure areas, and a special meeting of air-force officers in November reported the same view to the Government.[69] Rivalry between the air-force and the army had been in evidence for some time, and was gradually incorporated into the remarkably intricate set of checks and balances of the Guided Democracy political system. In army circles Suryadarma was regarded with suspicion because of the closeness of his and his wife's relations with the PKI. What is more important, in assessing the position of the air-force, is the feeling that many of its officers had of being very much out of things in contrast with the politically active and powerful army, particularly since the proclamation of martial law in 1957.[70] Soekarno

---

66 *Pos Indonesia*, Oct. 19, 26, Nov. 8.

67 *Pos Indonesia*, Oct. 28, Nov. 8, 1958; *Pesat*, XIV, no. 44 (Nov. 1, 1958), 3-4.

68 *Nusantara*, Nov. 10, 1958.

69 See *Pesat*, XIV, no. 46 (Nov. 15, 1958), 3-5; *Pos Indonesia*, Nov. 8, 1958. See also Suryadarma's message on Armed Forces Day, *Pos Indonesia*, Oct. 6, 1958.

70 The navy, least political of the armed services, took no strong stand on martial law. Under martial law, the air-force was given full authority over the air space of the country, the navy over

used this tension to help keep the army in check, and he may indeed have encouraged Suryadarma's opposition to martial law. But the air-force and the parties together were no match for the army.

The cabinet decided in early November to request Parliament to extend national martial law for one year.[71] The National Council also advised extension. In effect, there was no other decision that could be made, for rejection of the army's demand for extension would have made the threat of a coup more real; and an attempt to take away the authority of a few regional commanders might have created a situation in which they would ignore the central government's decision. In addition, martial law was the basis also of the Kabinet Karya and of the effort to create a new political system. Even had it been possible to remove martial law entirely, Soekarno would not have wanted to do so, for that would have restored the pre-1957 situation, at least in formal terms.[72]

The parliamentary debates on martial law began on December 2nd and lasted for two strained weeks, during which every aspect of martial law came under scrutiny and attack.[73] The basic demand of most parties was that the Government remove martial law in at least some areas.[74] On December 8th, Djuanda promised Parliament that efforts would be made to reduce the army's role in the economy and to put a stop to martial law "excesses." He also reported on the army's activities with respect to the take-over of Dutch firms, control of the Kuomintang, and the anti-

---

the territorial waters.

71 In early November, after returning from abroad, Djuanda held several meetings on the very tense issue of martial law. On Nov. 6, he met with Suryadarma, Navy Chief Subijakto, and Lt. Col. Mashudi, representing Nasution, along with Hardi, Idham Chalid, Leimena, Suprajogi, Chief Prosecutor Soeprapto, and several other ministers. On the 7th the cabinet convened in Tjipanas, in the mountains to the south of Djakarta, to take its decision on extension. See *Pos Indonesia*, Nov. 7, 8; *Nusantara*, Nov. 7, 1958.

72 *Pemuda*, Oct. 22, 1958, the strongly pro-Soekarno paper, supported extension of martial law throughout the country, arguing, inter alia, that under martial law the government was able to promote the interests of the people and to move against oppressive and corrupt businessmen. The Partai Murba, on its 10th anniversary, issued a statement to the effect that national martial law remained necessary in the interests of carrying out Guided Democracy and creating a guided economy. *Pos Indonesia*, Nov. 7, 1958.

73 Djuanda's written statement on the bill to extend martial law for one year was delivered to Parliament on Nov. 25. When the debate began he asked that informal discussions be held with him on questions "too delicate" to be dealt with in open session. *Risalah Perundingan 1958*, session of Dec. 2, p. 5026.

74 See the speech by Slamat Ginting (PNI), *Risalah Perundingan 1958*, session of Dec. 22, pp. 5027 ff.

corruption campaign. In connection with the latter, the parties were rattled by Djuanda's release of a full list of persons charged with crimes of corruption. Several PNI, Masjumi, and NU leaders were included in the list.[75]

On December 15th Djuanda spoke once more in the debates, offering the parties a compromise that in fact gave them very little. The Government, he said, would review martial law within six months to determine its status in various areas; where conditions were normal or improved, a less drastic level of martial law might be implemented.[76] He also emphasized the point, as Soekarno had done at an army conference a few days earlier, that civilian functions should be handed back to civilians.[77] (This army conference, begun on December 10th, was the third conference in 1958 of national and regional commanders, and was undoubtedly intended to bring pressure to bear on Parliament.[78])

There was never any real doubt that martial law would be extended. Despite their reluctance, the PNI and NU were committed to the cabinet decision — though the PNI continued openly to favor a partial extension only — and the PKI was not likely by itself to oppose it unequivocally.[79] The

---

75 Following protests by the parties whose members' names were mentioned, Djuanda stated that the men were only accused, not yet proved guilty. Among those included in the list for various crimes were Dr. Ong Eng Die (PNI, former Minister of Finance), Mr. Iskaq Tjokrohadisurjo (PNI, former Minister of Economic Affairs), Dr. A. K. Gani (chairman, South Sumatra PNI), Soediro (PNI), Zainul Arifin (NU), Djamaludin Malik (NU), Jusuf Wibisono (Masjumi), R. Moch. Kaffrawi (Masjumi), and several others from such parties as the PSI, the PSII, the PIR, and even one from the PKI, Hutomo Supardan, in connection with the organization of an agricultural and industrial fair in Surabaja by the "Centre for Economical Fairs of Indonesia" (C.E.F.I.). See appendix to Djuanda's statement to Parliament, *Risalah Perundingan 1958*, pp. 5154-5156; also in Ministry of Information, *Djawaban Pemerintah mengenai R.U.U. Tentang Perpandjangan Djangka Waktu Keadaan Perang* (Government Reply on the Bill to Extend the Period of Application of the State of War), pp. 79-84. It should be emphasized that, as Djuanda said, not all those accused were in fact guilty, though a good number were. Not all those accused were actually prosecuted.

76 The Government, said Djuanda, was also prepared to draft several amendments to the existing martial law statute after Parliament recessed. The statute was not in fact amended, however, until the end of 1959, when it was fundamentally revised. For Djuanda's statement to Parliament, see *Risalah Perundingan 1958*, session of Dec. 15, pp. 5508-5515.

77 Soekarno's statement to the officers, on Dec. 11, was quoted by Djuanda, *Risalah Perundingan 1958*, Dec. 15, pp. 5514-5515. Stressing the need to restore security quickly, Soekarno also made a strong appeal to the conference for civilian functions to be quickly restored to civilian offices, and for the strengthening of discipline within the army itself.

78 See *Pos Indonesia*, Dec. 3, 13, 14, 1958. The conference also discussed the organization and expansion of the National Front for the Liberation of West Irian.

79 *Pedoman*, Nov. 27, 1958. Interpreting martial law as a response to the security problem, the PKI agreed to extension but insisted that efforts must be intensified to crush the rebellion as quickly

parties were afraid of provoking the army to a coup, a possibility of which Djuanda reminded them when the debates became too acrimonious. On December 15th Parliament voted to extend the state of emergency for one year, the four major parties concurring.[80]

With the extension of martial law, the battle of Guided Democracy was all but over. The parties could not hope ever to regain the initiative. They could only bargain within the martial law political system, in which Soekarno and the army were supreme.[81]

The National Council and Guided Democracy: First Phase

From July through November of 1958, the National Council developed a set of basic proposals on Guided Democracy. These proposals were primarily aimed at reducing the role of the party system and making room for functional representation and a new national front as the eventual replacement of the parties within the government.

Soekarno approached the National Council discussions with a characteristic mixture of outward radicalism and deliberate caution. In his public speeches, he continued to demand that the very roots of liberal democracy be torn out.[82] But apart from insisting that the Decree of November 3, 1945 — which had first encouraged the formation of parties — should be ripped to shreds, he made no concrete proposals. Soekarno portrayed himself as a begetter of broad ideas whose details others were better able to fill in. By thus sketching a profile and waiting for others to work out its details, Soekarno allowed himself time to assess the balance

---

as possible. As it had done in 1957 and 1958, the PKI also proposed that people's organizations be equipped to fight the rebels; but this the army rejected, as before, as an attempt by the PKI either to arm itself or to infiltrate the army. See speech by J. Piry (PKI) in the budget debates, *Risalah Perundingan 1958*, session of Nov. 27, at p. 4859.

80 *Risalah Perundingan 1958*, pp. 5516-5523.

81 As a final note on the role of the army and the threat of a coup, on Dec. 19, when Parliament finally passed the 1959 budget after long and tempestuous debate, Djuanda stated that the Government was always alert to avoid a coup and that Indonesia was not likely to succumb to one; but if the Government and Parliament were not careful, he said, it might happen. *Pos Indonesia*, Dec. 20, 1958. The remark was pertinent to the discussion then going on between the cabinet and the National Council with respect to revision of the parliamentary system. Djuanda was in effect warning the parties not to be obstinate about accepting some changes, lest the army take matters into its own hands.

82 See, for example, Soekarno's Independence Day (Aug. 17) address of 1958, *Dari Proklamasi sampai Resopim*, pp. 355-388. The speech was entitled "Tahun Tantangan" (A Year of Challenge).

of forces and pick out the best compromise between divergent views and interests. His ability to do this has been a necessary condition of leadership unsupported by a tightly organized political force. In 1958 this was all the more urgent as it seemed possible that the army might simply decide to trample the parties underfoot, leaving Soekarno powerless to control its actions. Soekarno's effort to lead the nation towards a wholly new political system was circumscribed not only by the limits of his imagination (though not his vision) but also, and more importantly, by the ever present danger that the system might pass out of his control.

Soekarno did not have a great deal to work with in developing Guided Democracy. Ultimately he hoped that Indonesia would be led by a national mass organization on the radical non-Communist left. But as yet not even the seeds of such an organization were discernable. Every party but the PKI was decrepit and basically conservative. Soekarno's anger with the PNI — ideologically his only choice among the parties — was partly traceable to its inability to serve as the foundation for the kind of organization which he admired in China and the Soviet Union. In the National Council, when asked about the possibility of creating a single state party or a "pioneer party" similar to the Indian Congress or the Burmese AFPFL, Soekarno curtly dismissed the idea by pointing out that if there were a party with the necessary dynamism, support, and ideological vigor, it would emerge naturally as the national pace-setter.[83] But it was the PKI that was doing precisely that, and, as has been argued, part of Soekarno's objective was to prevent it from so emerging. A possible alternative seemed to be the army's National Front for the Liberation of West Irian (FNPIB). Two factors worked against this, however. First, the army élite was basically as conservative as most party leaders, but second, and more decisive, Soekarno would not depend solely on the army's political organization any more than he would on the PKI; to do so would be to give the army almost uncontested power. For the same reason, to avoid depending on the army alone, the parties could not be abolished.

---

83 In July and August rumors about a pioneer party or a single state party (*staatspartij*) were going around Djakarta. The capital press made a good deal of a proposal by Gatot Mangkupradja that Indonesia should have a *staatspartij*, as in China. See *Siasat*, XII, no. 585 (Aug. 27, 1958), 8, 23.

THE DRIVE TO GUIDED DEMOCRACY (I)   221

Soekarno told the National Council that he did not believe the parties could be eliminated. However desirable that was, he said, one had to strike a balance between *das Sollen* and *das Sein*, a dichotomy that had become a popular cliché among national politicians. *Das Sein* was the many parties, which, because they represented social forces, could not be eliminated by snapping one's fingers.[84] Moreover, there was as yet nothing to replace them. Consequently, a beginning had to be made by drastically reforming existing institutions in deliberate steps towards Guided Democracy, now represented embryonically by the National Council and, when it was formed, the National Planning Council. Thus the party system must be "simplified" to reduce the number of parties and to lessen ideological conflict. A new elections law, then coming under cabinet consideration, together with a new political parties law would replace the Decree of November 3, 1945.

At the same time, functional groups must be introduced permanently into the Parliament. The main objective of Guided Democracy, said Soekarno, was a just and prosperous socialist society, to be achieved through planning in every field. The cabinet's acceptance of the National Council proposal to create a planning council was a healthy step in that direction; but what good would an effective socialist "blue-print" be if it were only to be destroyed by an ineffective liberal Parliament controlled by a party system whose essential characteristics were self-interest, multiplicity, and ideological conflict:

The operation of Guided Democracy will begin at the moment a basic development plan for the just and prosperous society is

---

84 Utrecht has said that Soekarno decided the parties could not be abolished, because they represented "social movements." "If the only function of the political parties was as an apparatus for selection (in the hands of a small group of men — i.e., party big-shots or political adventurers) then the parties could certainly be eradicated. In Indonesia, even though the selection apparatus character of the parties…is…conspicuous, yet it cannot be doubted that the large parties, like Masjumi, the PNI, and PKI are 'social movements'. (The NU, an extremely opportunistic political party, seems to be purely a selection apparatus in the hands of several kiaji and ulamas)." (*Pengantar Dalam Hukum Indonesia* [Djakarta: Ichtiar, 1959]), p. 456. To some extent, of course, this was true. The popular strength of the PKI, the religious zeal of many of Masjumi's members, the PNI's hold in the bureaucracy, and the NU's support among Javanese *kiaji* — Utrecht's remark notwithstanding — made it impossible to consider abolition seriously; not even army leaders, I think, actually did so in 1958. Rather, the objective of anti-party forces was to wear the parties down while building up a substitute for them.

completely finished. The evaluation of this plan cannot be entrusted to a Parliament which arose from the liberal system. Consequently a revision is necessary of the structure and procedure of selecting the next Parliament and also of the party system.

And, to be sure, the Parliament which decides upon this blue-print must be a Parliament which is no longer formed according to the procedure of or from the world of liberal democracy. Such a [liberal democratic] Parliament is not only incapable of understanding, but also might well twist and transform that socialist blue-print into a liberal blue-print.[85]

The new Parliament which Soekarno envisaged would not be based on political parties alone, but primarily on functional groups:

a technical prerequisite for the operation of Guided Democracy is a national Parliament consisting in particular of functional group representation — aided by regional legislatures consisting also primarily of functional group representatives, and acting as executive boards charged with responsibility for the blue-print allocations for the regions.[86]

The idea of functional representation remained unclear to most minds, and it was never developed with precision. What was clear was that Soekarno, Nasution, and other exponents of anti-party views regarded functional representation as the very antithesis of party representation. The latter divided society along ideological lines, and it was partly to eliminate ideological conflict that the new political order was conceived.[87]

---

85 The first paragraph above is Roeslan Abdulgani's paraphrasing of Soekarno's comments to the National Council; the second is a direct quote from Soekarno reported by Roeslan. See Roeslan's speech before the seminar on the Pantjasila in Jogjakarta in February 1959: "Pantja Sila sebagai Landasan Demokrasi Terpimpin" (The Pantja Sila as the Basis of Guided Democracy) in *Seminar Pantjasila ke-I* (Jogjakarta: Seminar Committee, 1959), p. 148. Several informative speeches by Roeslan provide the material on the National Council discussions.

86 Roeslan's paraphrasing of Soekarno, *ibid.*

87 See Achmadi (then vice-chairman of the FNPIB), "Kedudukan Dewan Nasional dan Front Nasional dalam Ketatanegaraan Republik Indonesia" (The Position of the National Council and the National Front in the Structure of the Republic of Indonesia), an article written for the

Moreover, functional groups were regarded by Soekarno as a source of new political leadership (and support) and political energy. They would serve to represent all those interests which the parties had failed to represent — particularly the army, whose exclusion from the political arena had threatened the state with disaster.

To mobilize the people and to consolidate the new forces represented by the functional groups, Soekarno and the radical nationalist Murba (or Murba sympathizing) group — including most prominently Sukarni and Chaerul Saleh — visualized a national front organization which would eventually become a huge state party and assume the role of the party organizations of the Soviet Union and China.

To formulate some of these ideas into tentative proposals to the cabinet, a committee of the National Council was appointed in July.[88] The committee was headed by Ahem Erning-pradja, as chairman, B. M. Diah, and J. K. Tumakaka.[89] Functioning as a subcommittee, these three and several others had the task of bringing together the various views represented by the large parent committee. This was a most difficult assignment, for the National Council itself enjoyed no consensus, and the minority of members representing party interests were hostile to all proposals seriously threatening the party system.

Because of this division between a minority representing the parties and a majority representing an anti-party view or amenable to Soekarno's influence, the National Council discussions took on the character of

anniversary in October of the Student Senate of the law faculty of the University of Indonesia in the Minister of Information's special issue no. 31, *Karya Sumbangsih*. Arguing the case of functional representation, Achmadi pointed out that the division of Indonesian society into ideological categories had proved not to be the proper and effective division, because it was a consequence of the colonial system. Ideological categories, he said, did not match the interests found in Indonesian society, and the result was considerable instability (p. 13).

88 Between plenums of the National Council, usually held for two or three days once late in the month, its procedure called for further consideration of important matters by ad hoc committees. Soekarno and Roeslan chose this committee to represent as many varying points of view as possible. The ad hoc committee on Guided Democracy consisted of twenty-eight members, including Nasution, Chief of Police Sukanto, Chief Prosecutor Soeprapto, and others of highly divergent political interests. A smaller subcommittee was responsible for working out the consensus of the large committee and drafting a set of proposals for consideration by the plenum. Once accepted, these proposals were sent to the cabinet as the advice of the National Council.

89 Ahem was a PNI labor leader; B. M. Diah was editor of the independent nationalist daily *Merdeka*; Tumakaka was a radical nationalist PNI member, though soon to leave the party, and a recent appointee to the National Council. See Tumakaka's short book, *Demokrasi Terpimpin*, published in early 1959 by the Ministry of Information.

tense constitutional debates. The differences of approach went deep on several issues. One conflict that was put aside for the sake of agreement concerned the economic basis of Guided Democracy. The Murba leader, Sukarni, and several others took a firm stand in favor of a radical socialist program. NU members on the committee quickly indicated their fears for the security of private property. But such issues were incidental to the main concern of the committee, namely the governmental system, where the major conflict centered around the role of functional groups. In the Ahem committee's deliberations party members partly succeeded in pushing this matter into the background. They also succeeded in watering down recommendations for a new national mass organization, on which radical nationalist members of the committee put considerable emphasis. These successes were temporary, however.

The chief point of interest in this phase of the National Council discussions was the conflict over the constitutional basis of Guided Democracy. Most members of the Ahem committee assumed, as Soekarno himself did, that until the Constituent Assembly completed its work, the 1950 provisional constitution would remain basically in effect. A majority of proposals to the committee favored simplification of the party system, more formal authority for Soekarno, and other piecemeal institutional revisions. The one fairly complete program, Nasution's, took a different tack befitting the novel course army leaders were following.

Nasution did not propose that the parties be abolished. He did suggest 1) that the President call all party leaders together in an effort to reduce tensions, 2) that a new law limit the number of parties and establish government control over their finances and membership, and 3) that the election system be revised to eliminate straight party lists, so that, as many others had proposed, the representative would be brought into closer contact with his constituents. But all civil servants should be prohibited from joining political parties; and the same rule, according to Nasution, must apply to the armed forces (including the police), who should also be denied the right to vote. The rationale behind this was to prevent further politicization of the military. To make up for the sacrifice of their political rights, however, representatives of the armed forces must be appointed to Parliament and other governmental bodies. This was one key item in Nasution's program. Its aim was to reduce the unstabilizing political role of the army in exchange for giving it a permanent place in the government. In a broader sense, it was also hoped that by bringing the army legitimately into the structure of the government, the officer corps would be made more responsible politically and better able to make a constructive contribution to the state. In support of military participation in the government, Nasution appealed to the history of the revolution, when both military and civilian leaders led the state to independence.

His second key proposal was also in the tradition of the revolution. This was that Indonesia's need for secure and stable leadership could best be satisfied by the 1945 Constitution. The revolutionary constitution incorporated an extremely strong executive system, in which the President was responsible only to an intermittently convened People's Consultative Assembly (Madjelis Permusjawaratan Rakjat). It had been in effect for only a short time, August, September, and October, 1945, before the government was changed *de facto* into a parliamentary form under the leadership of Prime Minister Sjahrir.[90] A major consideration in Nasution's preference for the 1945 Constitution was that, with Soekarno as the strong president, executive authority and nationwide popular trust were combined in the same man.[91] Moreover, parliamentary obstruction of the executive was eliminated, and for the period of at least five years between elections for the presidency, the Government could work free of interference.

Behind Nasution's proposal there were other important considerations of both constitutional and more immediate political significance. One was that certain articles of the 1945 Constitution could be interpreted as providing for representation of functional groups, thus eliminating the

---

90 On the 1945 Constitution see George McT. Kahin, "Indonesia," in Kahin, ed., *Major Governments of Asia* (Ithaca, N.Y.: Cornell University Press, 2nd ed., 1963), pp. 564 ff. For the text of this constitution, see the appendix to the present study.

91 Nasution's views on the 1945 Constitution can be found in his enlightening book, *Tjatatan2 sekitar Politik Militer Indonesia* (Djakarta: Pembimbing C.V., 1955), especially pp. 20, 99, and 194. Nasution told Louis Fischer that "I believe in the 1945 Constitution and never understood why it was scrapped." He said further that "We need a Parliament consisting of a body directly representing the electors and another body representing the regions and functional groups [thus in part a federal arrangement]. A conference of both would choose the president and vice-president and outline a five-year national program. This is what we had after 1945, but Sjahrir changed all that to prove that we were democratic. Dr. Hatta restored the 1945 system in 1948 [under a "presidential" emergency business cabinet]; then we dropped it in 1950. I would put it back again. But I haven't the power. The army has no power to make such a change and the Constituent Assembly will not consent." Fischer, *The Story of Indonesia* (New York: Harper and Brothers, 1959), pp. 291-292. Mr. Fischer has informed me that his interview with Nasution took place on May 15, 1958.

necessity of an artificial constitutional basis for this innovation. Another was that repromulgating the early constitution would eliminate the Constituent Assembly, the forum of ideological conflict; the preamble of the 1945 Constitution incorporated the ideas of the Pantjasila.[92] Finally, from another point of view, many officers, including those who had joined the rebellion, favored the 1945 Constitution.[93] Nasution and the General Staff may have hoped that its restoration would convince rebel officers of the basic similarity of views between all army members, and the PRRI officers would then be encouraged to end the rebellion.

Although there was some support for Nasution's proposal on the 1945 Constitution, the majority of the Ahem Committee did not accept it.[94] one reason was the fear generated by Nasution's initiative in the matter. In addition, however, it was felt that a precipitous restoration of the 1945 Constitution would have to be done forcibly and on the basis of martial law, leaving little room for compromise. The Constituent Assembly and Parliament would have to be abolished forthwith — so the committee assumed — because the 1945 Constitution provided for completely different institutions. Naturally party exponents on the National Council vehemently opposed this possibility. But Nasution remained as adamantly opposed to any other plan and expressed his reservations about the committee compromise by which the 1945 Constitution could be resorted to only in case other possibilities failed.

---

92 A year earlier, the 1945 Constitution made a little-noticed appearance in the Konstituante. In August 1957, the Front of Defenders of the 1945 Proclamation, a group of small parties in the Constituent Assembly whose combination had no significance beyond this act, introduced a resolution promoting the 1945 Constitution as the basis for a new constitution. The parties included, among others, Murba, GPPS, Labor, BTI, PPPRI (Persatuan Pegawai Polisi Republik Indonesia, Union of Police Officials of the Republic of Indonesia), and IPKI, Nasution's old party. See Konstituante, constitutional preparatory committee, session III, meeting 23, August 13, 1957, p. 10 (mimeo). The resolution reflected opposition to ideological Islam and bicameralism; both would suffer under the 1945 Constitution, which incorporated the Pantjasila and a unitary state structure.

93 Possibly the first significant mention of the 1945 Constitution in this period was made in December 1956, when several officers delivered a "political concept" (the December 4th Idea) to Col. Simbolon before the coup in North Sumatra. The officers expressed their dedication to the Proclamation of Independence of 1945 and to the Constitution of 1945. See IP 3/1957, p. 19, session of January 21, 1957, Prime Minister Ali's report on the regional crisis.

94 Others on the Ahem Committee made proposals based on parts of the 1945 Constitution. One who did so was Iwa Kusumasumantri, an old line left-wing nationalist who had been Minister of Defense in the first Ali Cabinet (1953-1955). He too favored the strong presidential aspect of the early constitution.

In view of the influence of Nasution's proposal on later developments, it is necessary to consider briefly Soekarno's probably attitude towards the 1945 Constitution. One can only speculate, for Soekarno, unlike nearly every other political leader, never made his attitude clear too early in the game. It seems likely that in 1958 he did not favor the 1945 Constitution. Apart from the consideration that the army might win too great an advantage from so fundamental a change, the 1945 Constitution would place an enormous burden of responsibility squarely on Soekarno's shoulders. He had never evidenced any desire for formal responsibility after the revolution. In 1957 he had evaded all proposals that he assume accountable authority — e.g., as head of the cabinet — in part because this was what his opponents wanted and he feared the vulnerability of such a position. In the National Council discussions of 1958 he made no attempt to fit himself into the structural picture of Guided Democracy; nor did he appear to want any real change in his role of authoritative but non-responsible leader. It is indicative that although he attacked the Decree of November 3, 1945, he did not mention the equally famous vice-presidential Decree no. X of October 16, 1945, which had transferred the powers of the President to the legislature (KNIP), thus creating a parliamentary system in spite of the constitution.[95] Similarly he did not respond enthusiastically to repeated proposals by the PNI and other groups that he head a presidential cabinet. The Ahem Committee's proposals were probably more in line with his thinking.

The Ahem Committee wrestled laboriously with the various ideas before it during the first two weeks of August, finally producing a tentative report only by means of painstaking compromises that left some room for interpretation. Much of the report was based on Soekarno's comments before the National Council: the bases of Guided Democracy were the Pantjasila, the struggle for a just and prosperous society,

---

95 For the text of the Decree — X, not 10, because at the time it was drafted it happened that no one knew where it belonged chronologically — see Koesnodiprodjo, *Himpunan Undang2, Peraturan2, Penetapan2, Pemerintah Republik Indonesia* (Compilation of the Laws, Regulations, and Decrees of the Government of the Republic of Indonesia), vol. for 1945, pp. 58-59. In the second half of 1958 there were occasional public references to Decree no. X and to the 1945 Constitution. See, e.g., *Pos Indonesia*, Aug. 13, 1958; Achmadi in *Karya Sumbangsih*, p. 14. But in general the 1945 Constitution did not receive a great deal of attention at this time. In his August 17th speech Soekarno mentioned the 1945 Constitution only indirectly in a reference to the preambles of all three constitutions.

national identity, planning, and a new parliament "not formed by liberal procedures." Djuanda, when he saw the report, insisted that the words "but still democratic" be added to this latter phrase. He was also skeptical about whether the political parties law proposed by the committee could be pushed through Parliament. The committee's proposals were as follows:[96]

I. Constitution: Guided Democracy can be carried out…within the framework of the existing provisional constitution, without foreclosing the possibility of turning…to the 1945 Constitution.

II. Parties and Mass Organizations:…the Government Decree of November 3 must be rescinded and replaced with a law on political parties and mass organizations…In this law…a) the parties and mass organizations must [agree with and support the basic ideas of Guided Democracy]…; b) [there must be] a proper categorization of the people according to interests and ideology…

III. Elections: The election law (7/1953) must be brought into line with…Guided Democracy in accordance with the following conditions:

1. [Only parties which fulfill the conditions in II above may put up candidates].

2. Conditions of candidature must be made more difficult.

3. Elections must be direct…

IV. The System of Government: In order to bring the governmental system…into line with Guided Democracy, the basic ideas on… the parties, mass organizations, and elections must be carried out first…Therefore during the present transitional period the Kabinet Karya and the National Council can be maintained, without excluding the possibility of improving them. In connection with this, it is extremely *important that the authority and prestige of his excellency President Soekarno must be brought to bear maximally*

---

96 The full report can be found in a speech by Roeslan Abdulgani delivered before a Ministry of Information conference on Sept. 13, later issued in mimeograph form by the National Council's offices.

as a catalyst in concentrating authority in order to achieve Guided Democracy. [My italics]

V. Konstituante:…the Konstituante must finish its task within a set time period, and produce a constitution not in conflict with the ideals of the Proclamation of August 17, 1945.

VI. [The Institutions of government must be cleaned up and improved in order to prepare a government apparatus to which the execution of Guided Democracy may be entrusted.]

The clarification of the report was far more radical in tone, putting considerable emphasis on the urgent need to develop a national front organization under Soekarno's leadership.

This first phase of the National Council discussions produced few definite conclusions. The Ahem Committee's task had been to explore basic ideas and to sound out attitudes. It admitted to a lack of unanimity in its report, which was sent to the cabinet as material for further consideration but not for action. The next phase of the Guided Democracy deliberations, during September and October, was more substantive.

Meanwhile, outside the National Council's closed doors, Soekarno banked on compelling the parties to accept peacefully whatever proposals the Council produced. The PNI, NU, and the PKI had all outwardly supported Guided Democracy since 1957 — as Masjumi frequently pointed out with weighty irony and sarcasm — and Soekarno attempted to hold them to their commitments and thus to assure a parliamentary majority for the National Council program. The three parties, however, refused to follow docilely to their own slaughter.

From July through August the parties were responding to only the wildest rumors — about abolition of the parties, formation of a *staatspartij*, and simplification of the party system. The fear of a final solution spearheaded by the army weighed heavily on them, seriously limiting their ability to maneuver. Without initiative, and uncertain of what to expect from the National Council, the parties tended to withdraw into an uncomfortable posture of defensive conservatism.[97] Almost unanimously

---

97 During most of this period the deliberations of the National Council were secret. In the capital city, however, political leaders were aware of what was being discussed and what views were being

they rejected radical solutions and defended the party system as the essential basis of government. Forced to consider simplification as the least drastic approach, the parties insisted that the best way to alter the party system was through Parliament; but they contributed little that was meaningful to a discussion of reform. The PKI, then trying to save the 1959 elections, was alone in arguing consistently that simplification must be accomplished through elections. The other parties, whose interest in elections was waning, tended to favor mechanical reforms. PNI and NU leaders, for example, proposed abolition of the smaller parties, thereby arousing the indignant ire of minor party leaders who argued that the big parties were much more responsible for the sorry conditions of the country than were the small ones.[98] A number of proposals were made by both Islamic and secular parties that the party system might be divided into two or three basic groups — Islamic, secular nationalist, and Communist — each of which would eventually consolidate. But few of these ideas were taken seriously; and in any case, as everyone knew, they missed the point of Guided Democracy.

The PNI, NU, and the PKI were in no position to take stands as consistent as that of Masjumi, which had refused from the start to pay even lip-service to Guided Democracy.[99] They continued pro-forma to aver their support of Soekarno and Guided Democracy but promptly hedged when it came down to brass tacks. The PKI insisted that Guided Democracy meant a *gotong-rojong* cabinet — which NU and, less openly, the PNI regarded as an obnoxious interpretation. But both of these parties, like the PKI, took stands that obstructed any program of

---

put forward. Not only were they kept informed by their own friends on the Council, but also a fairly constant stream of rumor leaked out of the Council, so that generally within the Djakarta elite — as was always the case-there was no lack of information. But outside of Djakarta political information was slower in getting about, with the result that estimations of what Soekarno might do, or the army might do, tended to extremes.

98 See the statement by Prof. Abidin (Labor Party) in the Konstituante, *Siasat*, XII, no. 586 (Sept. 3, 1958), 3; *Nusantara*, Aug. 15, 1958, blamed the PNI and NU especially for the national decline. See also *Suluh Indonesia*, Aug. 7, 1958, for an editorial proposing that parties without representation in Parliament might be abolished to reduce the number of parties. This was before a few PNI MP's joined Partindo. Suwirjo suggested that simplification should be undertaken by Parliament, or, alternatively, some parties could voluntarily dissolve and join like-minded parties. *Pos Indonesia*, Aug. 6, 1958.

99 For Masjumi statements on Guided Democracy, see *Indonesia Raja*, July 4; *Republik*, Aug. 21, 1958.

drastic change. In August, before Soekarno's Independence Day address — in which it was rumored that he would announce the abolition of Parliament and/or the parties — the PKI, NU, and the PNI made their views clear. Lukman affirmed the PKI's objections to any attempt to enforce simplification from above; if simplification were to succeed, he said, or if a *staatspartij* were to emerge, it would have to come from below, from the people, and therefore through elections.[100] Both NU and the PNI held party council meetings in August specifically to discuss party policy on Guided Democracy. NU issued the stronger statement, accepting Guided Democracy but only on the bewildering conditions that Parliament, the Konstituante, and the entire parliamentary system remain just as they were.[101] The PNI meeting was held under the worst circumstances. Battered unmercifully in the press and badly damaged only a few days earlier by the splitting-off of Partindo, the PNI was under great pressure to give its unequivocal support to Soekarno. But despite the fact that many older generation party leaders were discomfited by the loss of Soekarno's favor and eager to give him this support, a majority of the party council was unwilling to give carte blanche to the National Council in making its proposals. The final statement of the party council meeting was as equivocal as the National Council's intentions were uncertain. Just as NU supported Guided Democracy because it was "not in conflict with Islam," so the PNI supported it because it was "not in conflict with Marhaenism."[102] A special committee, headed by Hardi, was appointed by the party executive council to contribute new ideas to the formulation of Guided Democracy.

Thus, by mid-August the three principal party supporters of Guided Democracy had indicated their serious reservations, and it therefore seemed that Soekarno's drive must come to a halt — unless force were to be used.[103] The President's August 17th speech, in which he demanded

---

100 *Pos Indonesia*, Aug. 11; *Harian Rakjat*, July 7, 1958.

101 See *Pos Indonesia* and *Sin Po*, Aug. 14, 1958. See also *Suluh Indonesia*, Aug. 28, for a statement by Saifuddin Zuhri, NU secretary-general, that the party system was the best basis of democracy. Zuhri also said that the NU could accept Guided Democracy because it was in agreement with Islamic teachings, but in nearly the same breath he stated that Guided Democracy was not yet clear enough for NU members. "There is not yet any clarification concerning the form of Guided Democracy or how it will be put into effect." See also *Pos Indonesia*, Aug. 8, 1958.

102 *Pos Indonesia*, Aug. 16; *Nusantara*, Aug. 18; *Suluh Indonesia*, Aug. 14, 1958.

103 *Pedoman*, Aug. 8, 1958. The editorial, remarking upon Gatot Mangkupradja's campaign for a

a new election law, a faster working Constituent Assembly, and the destruction of the Decree of November 3, 1945 — but left all this up to the parties-encouraged the belief that he might wait, perhaps until the next election, before carrying Guided Democracy to a higher stage of development.[104] The possibility of abolishing the parties or creating a *staatspartij*, despite occasional new scares, seemed to go by the board.[105] In spite of the army's frightening moves against the party system in August and September and the continual pressure of the pro-Soekarno press, most parties relaxed slightly into talk about self-correction, reform, and "further consideration" of Guided Democracy in Parliament and in the Konstituante. The moderate press did the same, calling on the parties to reform now if they did not want to be swallowed up later.

This euphoria lasted less than a month. Having started the National Council in motion and finding it necessary continually to overtake Nasution's initiatives, Soekarno could not at this juncture accept a stalemate. In his August 17th speech he quoted the resolution of the army conference of early August and all but openly warned the parties that if they balked change, the army might not wait passively on the sidelines.[106]

---

staatspartij and upon the reemergence of Partindo, noted that among the supporters of Guided Democracy there was considerable difficulty. Moreover, parliamentary democracy being felt to have failed, the supporters of Guided Democracy still did not feel that Guided Democracy was satisfactory: what next? See also *Sin Po*, Aug. 8, noting that since the PNI, NU, and the PKI had come out against abolition, clearly Guided Democracy would proceed by way of simplification. The anti-Soekarno press took this as a sign that Guided Democracy had failed completely. *Suara Rakjat*, Aug. 20, 1958, an editorial entitled, "A Failure." Only one or two parties (Partindo and Murba, most importantly) had agreed to Guided Democracy, said the paper, possibly out of considerations of "right or wrong, Bung Karno." But the rest had rejected it. Now, said *Suara Rakjat*, it is necessary to discuss whether the Decree of Nov. 3, 1945, has to be torn up; it replied "No," for the parties had become part of the very flesh and blood of the state.

104 *Pedoman*, Aug. 18, 1958. Soekarno's speech excited considerable discussion, especially with respect to the Decree of Nov. 3. See A. Laksmi, "Antara Partai2 Politik dan Ideologi Negara" (Between the Political Parties and State Ideology), *Mimbar Indonesia*, XII, no. 34/35 (Aug. 27, 1958), 4-5, 8. Laksmi, taking a very moderate view, called upon Soekarno to stop blaming the parties entirely for national conditions. He insisted that Soekarno must assume part of the blame for the Decree of Nov. 3. In any case it was not the Decree alone, or the parties alone, that were to blame, Laksmi wrote, but the entire elite. Party leaders took the same view.

105 Vice-Premier Hardi assured Parliament on Sept. 2, in the course of defending the National Council from attack, that it had no intention of abolishing the parties. *Indonesia Raja*, Sept. 3, 1958. Agrarian Minister Sunarjo (NU) said the same thing in Medan shortly afterwards, pointing out that without parties the government could never know what society was doing and thinking. *Pos Indonesia*, Sept. 14, 1958.

106 *Dari Proklamasi sampai Resopim*, p. 375.

In mid-September the President's forces resumed the initiative against the parties by publicly raising new issues in the debate. Little had yet been said openly about the matters most central to the discussion in the National Council, particularly concerning functional groups and a new Parliament. The half-public, half-secret character of the National Council deliberations was for a while to everyone's advantage, for it lent time for negotiations and compromise. By opening up the files on Guided Democracy, however, Soekarno could catch the parties off guard and help crystallize views within the National Council itself. Thus on September 13th, before a conference of Ministry of Information officials, Roeslan Abdulgani set forth the whole of the National Council's discussions.[107]

Roeslan admitted that the National Council and the cabinet had not yet made any decisions and that his comments were by way of a problem-statement. The Ahem Committee report was incorporated into the speech along with many of Soekarno's comments in the National Council during June and July. After discussing the philosophical and political bases of Guided Democracy — that it was a democracy and not a dictatorship, that it was founded on the Pantjasila, and that it demanded a planned society and economy — Roeslan emphasized the need to create a new non-liberal parliament to pass on future plans:

> With [the assurance that] a National Planning Council will soon be formed which must produce a socialist plan, the National Council is now concentrating on the following problems:
>
> a.   How to obtain a new parliament which *consists primarily* of functional groups, and
> b.   How to obtain a new party system.

Roeslan then recounted the results of his conversations in early August with Professor Djokosoetono on how to achieve the goals of Guided

---

107 The conference was supposed to have been closed. The speech was partially reported in *Pos Indonesia*, Sept. 15, 1958, and a few other newspapers; within a week it received wide coverage in several magazines. After it had caused an uproar, the entire lecture was mimeographed and released by the National Council offices with a covering statement by Roeslan, who said that Soekarno agreed with the content of the speech and with the way in which it was presented. The mimeographed text is used here. See also *Pesat*, XIV, no. 38 (Sept. 20, 1958), 7-9.

234 THE TRANSITION TO GUIDED DEMOCRACY: INDONESIAN POLITICS, 1957-1959

Democracy, without, it was emphasized, violating the Constitution.[108] Here the idea of a national front was brought out forcefully.

First: The 'moderate' way, by: a) making the prerequisite conditions for existing as a party more difficult, b) making the conditions for candidature more difficult. These would be established by law.[109]

Second: The 'semi-radical' way: a) alongside the parties a 'Front' could be formed, consisting of a combination of functional groups, and it would be given the right to participate in elections. b) the parties could still enter candidates for election, but the conditions would be made tougher. c)...the above-mentioned Front would also enter candidates.

It would be best if 1) President Soekarno leads the Front, 2) all parties supporting the Pantjasila decline to run candidates on their own part, but voluntarily choose instead to nominate via the Front.

Third: The 'semi-radical plus' way: a) a Front would be created and the parties left as is. b) but the sole right to put up candidates in parliamentary elections would be given to the Front. The parties would not be permitted to put up candidates. President Bung Karno would lead the Front.

---

108 Professor Djokosoetono played the important role throughout the National Council discussions of providing justifications, constitutional formulas, and scholarly background materials for whatever the Council decided. He was for a while a one man legislative reference service. In October 1957, he had lectured to the National Council on functional representation and the shift of authority from the parties to Soekarno, the latter point being one to which he gave continual emphasis. Djokosoetono drew heavily on European and American scholarship, but his personal views were very much characterized by a strong Javanese philosophical and mystical bent. Many army officers also came to the highly respected Djokosoetono to ask his help in formulating their political views or developing a political philosophy for the officer corps. It is possible that he had something to do with working out the idea of the army's "middle-way" enunciated by Nasution. Djokosoetono himself eschewed direct political involvement of any kind.

109 According to Djokosoetono, in Western literature on the subject the following could be included in a political parties law: 1) prohibition of non-democratic parties; 2) a condition that every party must work towards carrying out state principles and not merely for material interests; 3) control over party finances; 4) a condition that parties must be organized democratically; 5) regulation of candidature; 6) a rule that only recognized parties might participate in elections (p. 7 of mimeo text). Djokosoetono was instrumental in drafting the political parties law in 1959.

Fourth: The 'radical' way: On the basis of a revolutionary situation and martial law…, along with the fact that there has been a shift of authority towards the President/Commander-in-Chief: President Bung Karno, a) could directly dissolve Parliament and the parties (thus reversing the Vice-Presidential Decree no. X of Oct. 16, 1945 and the Decree of Nov. 3, 1945); b) could directly form a new Parliament consisting primarily of representatives of functional groups (as, e.g., according to the procedure of Government Regulation no. 6,1946 of Dec. 29, 1946).[110]

Roeslan told the meeting that Soekarno had already chosen one of these alternatives, based on "a balance between *das Sein* and *das Sollen*." He declined to say which one, referring his audience to the President's August 17th speech. It was in fact the "semi-radical way"; but the threat of the most radical approach was held over the parties heads.[111]

Roeslan's speech hit the headlines almost immediately, exciting a powerful reaction in Parliament, the press, and party circles. Taken by surprise, party leaders tried to counter the impression that the National Council had already decided upon its course and that no negotiations were possible.[112] Djuanda, evidently as taken aback as party leaders were,

---

110 Presidential Regulation 6/1946 provided for the appointment of representatives of parties, regions, and "major groups in society" to the Central Indonesian National Committee (KNIP) — the legislative body. See Koesnodiprodjo, *Himpunan*, vol. for 1946, pp. 146-147.
Obviously this "radical" alternative could not be contained within the limits of constitutionalism, though Roeslan (and Djokosoetono) claimed that in none of the four alternatives were there any constitutional violations. In his talk with Roeslan, Djokosoetono said, with respect to the radical way, that it might be necessary to add the grounds of "returning to the situation and spirit of August 17, 1945, and the Constitution of 1945." But this comment by Djokosoetono was not included in Roeslan's lecture.

111 Roeslan went on deftly to answer all charges against Guided Democracy, attributing them to anti-Pantjasila sentiments, PRRI sympathies, foreign attachments, or plain ignorance. He noted that Western press reactions, like those of the PRRI, were opposed to Guided Democracy, and he quoted a mid-February statement by Dulles that was contemptuous of Guided Democracy. Fears and resentments of foreign influence and judgments were used to good effect by the proponents of Guided Democracy. Roeslan ended by saying that "We cannot retreat one bit before…any opposition. For the Guided Democracy idea is an extension of the Pantjasila idea. More than that, Guided Democracy is one of the best means of guaranteeing a just and prosperous society."

112 *Duta Masjarakat*, Sept. 16, 1958, declared that as the National Council's proposals were not yet official, there was still room for other views on Guided Democracy. The NU paper also suggested testily that Roeslan should have waited until the National Council had come to definite conclusions before making its discussions public.

declined to make a statement to Parliament on grounds that Roeslan had spoken in his own name, not as vice-chairman of the National Council.[113] Roeslan himself reiterated that he had presented only a personal analysis. The parties, however, were made fully aware that they were not off the hook of Guided Democracy; and the postponement of the elections a few days later reinforced the impression that the party system was in fast and disorganized retreat. Moreover, largely as a consequence of Roeslan's talk, it was at this time that the public debate on Guided Democracy reached its highest point, while the National Council moved into the second phase of its discussions.

This debate, however, produced little that was new, which is perhaps the most telling point to be made about it. The pro-Guided Democracy press tended to offer its support almost wholly in anti-party, pro-Soekarno terms; and the parties, fighting for their lives in a battle that was perceived as involving power more than reason, contributed little more to a thorough examination and defense of parliamentary democracy than they had in 1956-1957.[114] They offered nothing in the way of positive alternatives to radical reform. As has been mentioned, the parties, taking their cue from the National Council, proposed simplification, but never in terms that hinted of sincerity. To deflect the major challenge of Guided Democracy to the party system, the PNI, for one, continued to suggest that Soekarno take the leadership of a presidential cabinet. In general the parties were intent upon maintaining the status quo, decorated to some extent with promises of reform.

In their attack on functional groups, the parties were joined by

---

113 *Risalah Perundingan 1958*, session of Sept. 19, p. 3471.
114 The parliamentary forum was hardly used by the parties for this purpose. Rather, most MP's made piecemeal attacks on proposals made by the National Council or Guided Democracy supporters, with the result that parliamentary discussions of political reform took on a highly negativist aspect. There were only a few exceptions to this, frequently PKI members. One of the better discussions of the issues posed by Guided Democracy and the decline of parliamentary democracy was by Memet Tanumidjaja, a police official and parliamentary leader of the PPPRI, an organization that was in fact more of a "functional group" than a party. See *Risalah Perundingan 1958*, session of Nov. 28, pp. 4908-4913. Memet, like other party leaders, argued that the parties performed an important leadership selection function and that they served to exercise control over the national political elite, whose members would otherwise be on their own, subject to no discipline. But Memet also went on to propose definite reforms of the party system by Parliament — e.g., with respect to party finances and the like. It is important to note that Parliament at no time during this period tried to take the initiative in revising the political system.

independent moderates. Besides the implicit threat to the party system, it was feared that functional representation would lead to a copy of fascism.[115] Party leaders argued that functional interests in society were already adequately represented by the parties, both within themselves and through their subsidiary labor, peasant, student, and other organizations. Much more to the point, some reasoned sharply that functional groups no less than parties would reflect political differences, for they enjoyed no intrinsic consensus; the mere displacement of parties by functional groups could not therefore guarantee the greater stability and reduced conflict promised by Soekarno.[116] But it was difficult to debate the issues posed by functional representation, for it became increasingly apparent that the idea had not been developed much further since 1957, when it appeared as a simple alternative to the party system. In 1958 it was still uncertain precisely what constituted functional groups and how they were to be organized.[117]

The "front" conception was attacked on similar grounds. The point made with greatest force was that a political system without parties or one based essentially on a single legitimate party, whatever it was called, would be a dictatorship.[118] Soekarno denied this time and again, and proponents of Guided Democracy prefaced their discussions with the comment that it was democracy, not dictatorship. It was also argued by the antagonists of the National Council that a front led by Soekarno would inevitably depend entirely upon Soekarno. Some in the intellectual elite were openly doubtful on precisely these grounds, fearing that Soekarno's immensely powerful personal hold on the nation would lead to a political structure in which he would be the keystone. The Ahem Committee's point, repeated by Roeslan, that Soekarno's personal authority must be

---

115 Cf. Achmadi in *Karya Sumbangsih*, p. 13, where he agreed that the functional representation idea reflected a European background but argued that its application in Indonesia had altogether different purposes, primarily to seek out the unity which ideological representation had prevented.

116 See *Harian Umum*, Sept. 16, Oct. 10, 1958.

117 See A. Laksmi's article in *Mimbar Indonesia*, XII, no. 39 (Sept. 27, 1958), 3-4, the best piece on Roeslan's speech and the issues it raised. Laksmi (a pseudonym), a keen and usually profound political analyst, was deeply skeptical about the development of Guided Democracy, questioning whether enough thinking had been done about such basic issues as the meaning of the Pantjasila and the role of functional groups.

118 See, for example, *Harian Umum*, Sept. 17, 1958.

made full use of in attaining Guided Democracy, reinforced these fears. Skeptical observers asked what would happen when Soekarno was no more; would Guided Democracy also then cease to exist?[119] But this was decidedly a minority view. The more common one was that Soekarno must assume full leadership. The nationalist weekly *Pesat* called for Soekarno to take upon himself the leadership of the revolution and to play in Indonesia the role filled by state parties in the Soviet Union and other people's democracies.[120]

The National Council: Second Phase

During October and November the National Council moved quickly towards formulating its deliberations into definite proposals to the cabinet. The speed of the process was due in part to pressure from army leaders and to the anxiety felt by many on the council as a result of the coup scare. It also sprang, however, from the desire of Soekarno and his supporters on the council, as well as Nasution, to take advantage of the momentum built up against party government. Possibly the fact that Djuanda was abroad during much of October had something to do with both the character of the National Council proposals and the rapidity with which Soekarno forced a Council decision upon them; when Djuanda returned at the end of October, he was faced with a *fait accompli*, though it is by no means certain that he could have headed it off had he remained in Djakarta.

In late August or early September the Ahem Committee was replaced by a new ad hoc committee on Guided Democracy under the chairmanship of Tumakaka.[121] Its task was to consider 1) simplification of the party system, and 2) improvement of the system of representation.[122]

---

119 Laksmi, cited *supra*, n. 117, p. 3; *Surabaja Post*, Sept. 16, 1958.
120 "Juti" (Sajuti), part IV of a series on Guided Democracy, *Pesat*, XIV, no. 34 (Aug. 23, 1958), 11-12, and the same journal, no. 37 (Sept. 13, 1958), p. 4.
121 Among the members of the Tumakaka committee were Iwa Kusumasumantri, Baramuli, Sugriwa, Tjan Tju Som, Nja Diwan, Sitor Situmorang (PNI, a recent appointee to the Council to represent artists), Ahem, Munir, Fatah Jasin, Moh. Padang, Rangkaju Rasuna Said, and Trimurti. *Pos Indonesia*, Sept. 19, 1958.
122 See Roeslan's speech of September 13 and his speech in *Seminar Pantjasila*, pp. 150-151; also Ministry of Information, *Dua Tahun Kabinet Karya* (Two Years of the Kabinet Karya; Djakarta, 1959), pp. 752-755.

Under this latter rubric, the chief interest focussed on how to form a new parliament based primarily on functional groups. The question of creating a new national front was also under consideration.

Like the Ahem Committee, the Tumakaka Committee was unable to deliver a unanimous report to the National Council plenum. Party representatives, in a disadvantageous bargaining position and faced by an unmistakable threat, would not go along with the proposals. The Committee agreed that a share of Parliament's seats should be given to functional groups, but the alarming demand of the anti-party group was that that share be 50 per cent. Party exponents refused to acquiesce in more than 33 1/3 per cent. Similarly, on the national front issue, the anti-party group insisted that the front be led directly by Soekarno and that the parties not be allowed to participate in it. The parties, perceiving that a national front led by Soekarno would soon push them entirely out of the political picture, argued that they must have a role in the front. These were the substantial questions brought before the National Council at its session of October 21st, 22nd, and 23rd.

For the first and only time in its short history, the National Council took a vote, putting aside the consensus-seeking *musjawarah-mufakat* procedure; it was obvious that otherwise no decision would be taken, for the interests at stake were too great. With the armed forces' representatives, particularly Nasution, pushing hardest for functional groups, the Council voted approximately 25 to 8 in favor of functional groups making up 50 per cent of Parliament. The same vote favored excluding parties from the national front. Thus the October session of the National Council produced the following proposals to be sent to the cabinet for action:[123]

First: The matters which must be included in a political parties
　　　 law are as follows:

a)　 Parties are agencies of democracy in the form of organizations of Indonesian citizens according to political ideologies, whose purpose is to support and defend the Unitary Republic of Indonesia and to work for the ideals of the Indonesian people

---

123 See Roeslan, in *Seminar Pantjasila*, pp. 151-152.

towards a just and prosperous society, based on the Proclamation
of Independence of August 17, 1945.

b) Functional groups are agencies of democracy in the form of
organizations of Indonesian citizens according to their function
in production and social services, which contribute to the
development of a just and prosperous society based on the ideals
of the Indonesian people [as expressed] in the Proclamation of
Independence of August 17, 1945.

c) The National Front is an agency of democracy in the form of an
organization that mobilizes national potential for the purpose
of collectively striving after the just and prosperous society in
accord with the ideals of the Indonesian people and the goals of
the Unitary State of the Republic of Indonesia.

Second: Changes which must be incorporated in a new Elections
Law are, inter alia:

a) One half of the total membership of the next Parliament will
represent functional groups of the Indonesian People.

b) Candidacy of functional groups will be via the National Front,
which will be led by the President.

c) Conditions of candidacy will be made more demanding.

d) The method of election will be based on a double-choice system;
that is, the voter will vote once for a party symbol and once again
for a functional group symbol.

The objective of this program was to recognize the parties only as a
transitional element that would soon fade out of the political system.
In the next national elections, the parties would already have lost
control of the Parliament to functional groups. The functional groups'
independence from political party influence would be assured by: 1) their
separate election, and 2) their organization within the National Front,
which would enjoy the prestige of Soekarno's leadership. Functional
group candidates would be chosen by Soekarno himself. Thus the parties
would be forced to engage in a competition which they could not hope
to win. Eventually the National Front would develop into a nationwide
mass organization on the radical nationalist left, absorbing the support

once given to political parties. It would then become the single legitimate political organization in the country, performing the major functions of political tutelage and mobilization.

Soekarno's role in this reorganized system would clearly be much greater than any he had previously played, but it fitted his view of what that role should be.[124] He would guide the government, select its leaders, and offer new ideas, but he would not assume a position of daily administrative responsibility. Nor would he occupy a position of constitutional responsibility; that would be assumed by a cabinet chosen by him and supported by a Parliament also subject to his influence. No attempt will be made here to discuss the constitutional uncertainties implicit in this, because in fact it did not work out quite that way. But it is important to make the general point that the National Council proposals of October visualized a monolithic political system in which Soekarno would provide the chief inspiration and legitimation.

For Soekarno, the major problem posed by the National Front concept in 1958 was that army leaders might seize control of it by way of the FNPIB, which Nasution hoped would be the basis of any future National Front. Increasingly since June he had concentrated on developing it into a more effective counterpoise to the parties and an incipient mass mobilization organization. In late September Nasution issued a directive declaring the FNPIB to be the only legitimate mass organization and stating its functions to be, in particular, to restore West Irian to Indonesia and, in general, to complete the revolution.[125] The organization itself

---

124 See Kahin, *Major Governments*, p. 640, n. 4. Soekarno told Kahin in March 1959 that "Under the new system I will have to carry a great deal more weight upon my shoulders." By March the decision had been taken to restore the 1945 Constitution, and Soekarno was referring partly to the fact that he would have to assume the constitutional duties of president. But much of the National Council's earlier program still obtained, especially with respect to the National Front, of which Soekarno said that "to lead the National Front will require much work and energy from me." See also the rest of Kahin's discussion of Soekarno's views, pp. 636-640.

125 *Pos Indonesia*, Sept. 29, 1958. Various instructions were issued during the year by Nasution to clarify the connection between the FNPIB, the civil-military co-operation bodies, and national and regional army commanders. *Pos Indonesia*, Oct. 25, 1958. See also Ministry of State for Civil-Military Cooperation Affairs, *Karya Kerdja Sama Sipil Mlliter* (Civil-Military Cooperation; Djakarta, 1959). Brig. Gen. Moestopo was Secretary-General of the FNPIB until November, when he was replaced by Lt. Col. Achmadi (*Pos Indonesia*, Nov. 22, 1958). Achmadi, former leader of the revolutionary "student army" (*tentara peladjar*) and one of the radical young men whom Soekarno was sponsoring, was quite close to Soekarno, who may have been instrumental in his appointment as FNPIB secretary-general.

was revised to bring the civil-military cooperation bodies under tighter control.[126] Nasution's efforts to improve the FNPIB did not meet with noticeable success, however, largely because of tacit opposition from both the parties and Soekarno. Despite its expansion into the lower levels of regional government and the formation of new civil-military cooperation bodies, outside of Djakarta the FNPIB remained loosely structured and organizationally nondescript. Its regional officer leaders were sometimes politically incompetent and sometimes corrupt, and above all they seem not to have understood fully the purpose of the organization or how it could be directed to political ends. These deficiencies made it possible for Soekarno to elude army pressure for the FNPIB to be used as the National Front. It could also be argued that the FNPIB already had a narrowly defined function — with respect to West Irian — and that therefore a much broader and differently organized front was necessary. Nasution lost out on this question, and the National Council emphatically stated in November that the future National Front would be a new one.

On the issue of functional representation, however, Nasution made rapid progress. This, indeed, was the focus of his attention, for, in the development of Guided Democracy, it was this issue which would most clearly determine the outcome of the clash of interests between the army and the political parties. Not only were functional groups intended to displace the parties, but moreover functional representation was the only plausible concept that would permit the legitimate participation of the officer corps in the government. Just when the military won the status of functional group is not clear, but the process illustrates the basic evolutionary theme of the army's political development. For neither in 1945, when a kind of functional group concept was first introduced into the constitution, nor in 1957, when Soekarno revived the concept, were

---

126 In mid-1958, the FNPIB had seven civil-military cooperation bodies organized under it: youth, women, labor, peasants, religious leaders (*ulama*), and two special bodies, one of them connected entirely with the Veterans' Legion. More were organized in 1959. Only the civil-military cooperation bodies were permitted as constituent members of the FNPIB, and it is clear that they were regarded by Nasution and others as potential organizations of the functional groups. See *Pos Indonesia*, Aug. 5, 1958. In the reorganization of the FNPIB in mid-1958, an honorary council was established which included Soekarno, as Chairman, Roeslan, Sudibjo, Chaerul Saleh, and Wahib Wahab. Neither Roeslan nor Chaerul was appreciated in army leadership circles; their appointments are evidence of Soekarno's constant attempt to increase his influence within the organization.

the armed forces considered a functional group.[127] They were regarded as being properly outside of the political arena, subject to the will of civilian government; and though some leaders had come to recognize that it was impossible to deny the political interests of the army, many more still would not agree to the military enjoying the right of political participation.[128] It was to this lingering view that Nasution addressed himself in November at the National Military Academy.

Nasution's basic demands in the National Council were that the army must be recognized as a functional group, but unlike other functional groups its representatives would be appointed, not elected, and the army as a whole would be disenfranchised. The point of this, as has been mentioned, was to give the army a responsible role while eliminating politically unstabilizing influences on it. Soekarno agreed with Nasution on this issue, for it would be far safer to have the army represented in the Government, where it could be controlled, than to attempt to keep it in the barracks, from which it might well burst out violently with disastrous consequences for the state.[129] There was opposition in the National Council, however, against granting the army functional group status, though by mid-1958 the press was already beginning to refer to the military as a functional group.[130] The National Council session of October did not specify which functional groups would be formally represented in Parliament, and it may be that a major reason for this was the problem of Nasution's demands. But the coup scares of October and

---

127 In the 1945 Constitution, article 2 provides that the People's Consultative Assembly, the highest constitutional body, will consist of the members of Parliament, representatives of the regions, and "groups which shall be determined by law." Those who saw in the 1945 Constitution a basis for functional representation looked to this article. The clarification of the 1945 Constitution stated that "What are called 'groups' are such bodies as cooperatives, labor unions and other collective bodies," — in other words, economic organizations. The military was not included in this understanding. See Moh. Yamin, *Naskah Persiapan Undang-Undang Dasar 1945* (Documents on the Preparation of the 1945 Constitution; Djakarta: Jajasan Prapantja, 1959), I, 40.

128 For a clear statement of the view opposing an army that would be active in politics, see Prime Minister Ali Sastroamidjojo's reply to questions in Parliament on the regional crisis on February 4, 1957, IP/1957, pp. 84-85.

129 To put this another way — as suggested to me by Prof. Kahin — Soekarno sought to bring the army into the structure of the government for the reason that its representation in the government would necessarily be far less than the extent of its actual power.

130 *Sikap* (PSI), XI, no. 19 (July 31, 1958), 1, mentions the military as a functional group along with labor, peasants, youth, women, and intellectuals, in connection with devising a new election law.

November worked to the army's bargaining advantage, and Nasution's middle-way speech in mid-November put the issue squarely before the Council and the political parties: either the army's officers must be given an opportunity to take part in the government, or they might be forced to seize that opportunity.

The party response to Nasution's proposals was ambivalent. On the one hand, the parties breathed a sigh of relief that nothing worse was in store.[131] On the other, they regarded the middle-way notion as another major challenge to the party system; for by formally entering the political arena, the army threatened to squeeze the parties out. The PKI, having most to fear from an expansion of the army's role, was the party most hostile to Nasution's ideas. After expressing its satisfaction that there would be no coup, the PKI quickly suggested numerous reservations about greater political participation by the army. Thus the Communist press insisted that if — despite their reluctance — the army's representation in the government were to be enlarged, it should be on the same basis as other functional groups, that is by election and not appointment. *Harian Rakjat* also issued a reminder, in an effort to de-emphasize the role of the army, that the latter was only one part of the armed forces.[132]

When the National Council session of November 21st-23rd finally agreed on a list of functional groups, the armed forces were among them.

---

131 See *Abadi*, Nov. 15; *Suluh Indonesia*, Nov. 17, 1958. *Suluh Indonesia*'s (PNI) initial reaction to Nasution's middle-way speech was one of full support. The Indonesian national identity, it said, made the middle-way acceptable. Both civil and military leaders being children of the revolution, both could participate in the government. This daily repeated its frequent admonition not to look to events abroad and declared that military juntas do no good.

132 *Harian Rakjat*, Nov. 14, 17, 1958. The PKI observed that the middle-way was not really new; the Chiefs-of-Staff were in the National Council, Suprajogi was in the cabinet, and in Parliament and the Constituent Assembly the army was represented by some members of IPKI. *Harian Rakjat* suggested that the middle-way meant that various groups ought not to interfere in one another's jurisdictions — e.g., the military ought to stick to the military field and stop getting involved in politics and trade, just as politicians should not interfere in military affairs. The PKI also suggested that the participation of military leaders in the political life of the nation might be limited to their presence in the highest bodies of the government — implying that they should not have a vote, however, See also *Republik*, the Baperki daily, for Nov. 14, 1958, which to some extent followed *Harian Rakjat*'s position.

If the PKI was most hostile to the prospect of greater military participation in the government, conversely, the right-wing was most favorable, and the acquiescence of the PNI and NU was due not only to their concern to avoid a coup but also to their willingness to rely on the army to keep the PKI at bay. However, army leaders encountered some opposition among older leaders of the PNI and NU to a greater role for the army.

The list was as follows:

1. Labor/Officials
2. Peasantry
3. National Businessmen
4. Armed Forces

    a.Army   c.Air Force

    b. Navy   d. Veterans, OPR, and OKD[133]

5. Religious leaders

    a. Islamic   c. Catholic

    b. Protestant   d. Hindu-Bali

6. Generation of the Proclamation of August 17, 1945
7. (Other) groups

    a. Intellectuals   e. Regions

    b. Teachers and educators   f. Youth

    c. Artists   g. Women

    d. Journalists   h. Citizens of foreign descent

It will be noticed that these functional groups were, with two minor exceptions, the same ones that were represented in the National Council.[134] The major difference was that in 1957 the armed forces representatives had been appointed ex-officio (the chiefs-of-staff) rather than in recognition of the military as a functional group.

Nasution went a step further in demanding a sizeable representation for the military functional group. According to the National Council plan, 50 per cent of the next Parliament would consist of functional groups; of this proportion Nasution requested 50 per cent for the armed forces, or in other words 25 per cent of the Parliament. This was a matter for negotiation, however, both with the parties and within the National

---

133 The OPR (Organisasi Pertahanan Rakjat, People's Defense Organization) and OKD (Organisasi Keamanan Desa, Village Security Organization) were voluntary uniformed paramilitary organizations under army control. In the National Council the army was challenged over the question of its right to represent the veterans. It is probably for this reason that the veterans constitute a separate category of representation.

134 The ex-armed fighters category in the National Council was not included in this list, but intellectuals, who were not formally represented in the National Council, were constituted as a new group.

Council, and Nasution agreed in early 1959 to take a rather smaller quota of 35 seats in a Parliament of approximately 260. The army, of course, would receive the largest share of the military representation.

The National Council proposals of October and November were presented to the cabinet, where they were received, understandably, with some shock. Neither the party leaders nor Djuanda — who had already warned of the impossibility of the Government asking Parliament to work against its own interests — could accept the proposals. Djuanda may have offered his resignation to the President at this time, but, if so, Soekarno would not accept it. At the end of November Djuanda announced that the cabinet, the President, and the National Council would hold a frank discussion — an "Open Talk," as it was promptly labelled — of the Council's proposals on Guided Democracy.[135] The first meeting was held on December 5th, making little headway; and two more were held in January, following state visits by Marshal Tito and President Prasad. The results of the Open Talks will be discussed in the next chapter. The last few pages of this chapter will deal with the party response in late 1958 to the threat of Guided Democracy. The major parties were unanimously opposed to the National Council proposals, but they remained at odds on nearly everything else. Divided they were to fall.

Indeed, each party was not so much defending the political system which sustained it as trying to protect its own position in whatever system happened to emerge. To repeat a point already made in the last chapter, the leaders of the PNI and NU were seeking a comfortable niche in the new power structure, while the PKI was trying to maintain some basis of independent power from which to continue its growth; and Masjumi, having nothing to gain from any developments in existing circumstances, was very much at sea. The minor parties were distributed over this spectrum of big party positions, having no significant say in the politics of Guided Democracy, yet unhappily dependent upon whatever solution the major parties worked out with the anti-party forces.

The postponement of the elections in September and the coup scare of October-November decided the PKI upon accepting part of the National

---

135 See *Pos Indonesia*, Nov. 11, 27, 29; *Nusantara*, Nov. 28; *Merdeka*, Nov. 29; *Republik*, Nov. 28, Dec. 4, 1958.

Council program while pushing closer to Soekarno. At the 7th plenum of the CCPKI on November 19th-21st, Aidit stated that:

> the leadership in executing the Guided Democracy idea must rest with President Soekarno, as the originator of the Guided Democracy idea and of the President's Konsepsi, and as a democrat whose courage was tested when he rejected the militarists' attempt to make him a dictator in the 17 October 1952 Affair. As a consequence of this view, the President must be given the extraordinary right according to democratic procedures and according to law to fill part of the Parliament with patriots who have won the faith of the people.[136]

The PKI thus pinned its hopes for the evolving political system not only on Soekarno's ability to control the army but also on the likelihood that he would rely on the left-wing for support.

The hopes of Masjumi, on the other hand, were pinned on less realistic objectives. Some Masjumi leaders of the Sukiman-Wibisono group were convinced that both the party and Islam faced a double threat, from Guided Democracy and Communism, which could be overcome only with a drastically revised political approach. Wibisono argued in October that the long term strategy of the Islamic parties must be based on the assumption that there would be no radical change in the comparative strength of Islamic and secular groups during the next decade. Therefore,

---

136 "Bersatu Menempuh Djalan Demokrasi Terpimpin Menadju Pelaksanaan Konsepsi Presiden Sukarno 100%" (With Unity Tread the Path of Guided Democracy towards a 100% Implementation of the President's Konsepsi), Aidit's report to the seventh plenum of the CCPKI, in his *Pilihan Tulisan* (Selected Writings; Djakarta: Jajasan "Pembaruan," 1959-1960), II, 526-556, at pp. 548-550. In this report considerable attention is paid to the foreign coups, the possibility of a coup in Indonesia, and the threat of the army generally. The October 17th Affair, it will be remembered, was the attempt of a group of officers led by Nasution to force Soekarno to assume greater executive power vis-a-vis Parliament.

In October Aidit said the PKI supported Guided Democracy because it was anti-military dictatorship, anti-personal dictatorship, and anti-liberalism. See "Mendukung Demokrasi Terpimpin adalah politik jang paling revolusioner" (To Support Guided Democracy is the most revolutionary policy), statement of October 24, 1958, *Pilihan Tulisan*, II, 518-522, at p. 520. PKI, NU, and PNI leaders were all made distinctly uncomfortable during these months by criticism of the hypocritical positions they were compelled to take with respect to Guided Democracy. The PKI was the only major party to go beyond the usual statement of "Of course we accept Guided Democracy fully, but…" See also *Sin Po*, Oct. 13, 25, 1958.

he proposed, the Islamic parties should form a Democratic Front with the nationalist parties against Communism, accepting the Pantjasila as the state ideology. Meanwhile, Islamic groups should study the conditions of society and adjust themselves to the national stage of development.[137] This, of course, was the strategy which the PKI had successfully employed, but it was too late for Masjumi to do the same. Moreover, a majority of Masjumi's leadership was not amenable to this kind of reasoning.

At the same time, in October and November, Masjumi leaders of both wings proposed the formation of a new cabinet — one in which Masjumi would be happy to serve — capable of dealing with national economic and political problems.[138] This caused a considerable stir. The PNI and NU immediately rushed to the defense of the Kabinet Karya. Masjumi accused these parties of being influenced by the PKI in their opposition to a cabinet revision, but the fact of the matter was that the PNI and NU were in constant fear of losing their holds in the Government. Wahab Chasbullah (NU) put the case best for both parties. Rejecting Sukiman's proposal of a new cabinet and the PKI's demand for a four-legged-horse cabinet based on the President's Konsepsi, Wahab said that the best cabinet was like a two-legged man, with the PNI and NU as its core representing the major political trends, Religion and Nationalism.[139] A Duta Masjarakat editorial added that it would be best not to think of the Konsepsi or a new cabinet but rather to try to try to open the way for Guided Democracy, and this would best be done by the Constituent Assembly — which was to ask for the best of all worlds.[140]

The PNI's position was not noticeably different. But caught as usual between Soekarno and a divided assessment of party interests, the PNI was under intense pressure to come out strongly for Guided Democracy

---

137 See *Pos Indonesia*, Sept. 27, Oct. 5, 1958.

138 *Pemuda*, Oct. 17; *Pos Indonesia*, Nov. 8; *Nusantara*, Nov. 10, 1958. See also *Pesat*, XIV, no. 43 (Oct. 25, 1958), 3-4. *Pesat* admonished Masjumi to clean up its own backyard before trying to clean up the nation. The magazine also called upon Sukiman — who was regarded with much more favor than the Prawoto group by older generation PNI and NU leaders — to assume the leadership of his party and bring it back to the proper rails of Indonesian political life.

139 *Abadi*, Dec. 3, 1958. Wahib Wahab stated that only if Masjumi supported the cabinet policy on the rebellion and, emphatically, if it agreed that the Kabinet Karya was constitutional, would the door be open for it to join the cabinet. Zainul Arifin said flatly that cabinets should not be changed in mid-stream. See also *Pos Indonesia*, Oct. 18; *Nusantara*, Oct. 20, 1958.

140 *Duta Masjarakat*, Dec. 8, 1958.

as interpreted by Soekarno. Supporters of the President accused the PNI of having left the revolutionary rails and warned that without Soekarno the party would disintegrate into insignificance.[141] On November 1st and 2nd the PNI executive council met to discuss the National Council' proposals of October. It was unable to offer more than pro-forma support of the "principles"of Guided Democracy and declared that it was necessary to think further about the matter.[142]

To meet the vociferous criticism of the pro-Soekarno press following this party conference, and in an attempt to head off the National Council's onslaught, the PNI suddenly leapt to an interesting but belated and hopelessly ill-conceived initiative. On November 25th, following discussions with Roeslan and Djuanda, Suwirjo announced, with suitable fanfare, the creation of a new Front Pantjasila. Its purpose was to save the state from attempts to subvert it, such as the Madiun rebellion and the PRRI, and from efforts to pull Indonesia towards one bloc or another. The Front Pantjasila would include all groups truly dedicated to the Proclamation of August 1945, said Suwirjo, and it would thus form a strong basis for carrying out Guided Democracy. Such evils as political "cow-trading" would be eliminated, because every cabinet would henceforth consist only of true followers of the Pantjasila.[143]

This suggestion obviously represented a blind rush by the PNI to grasp a central position in the Government and to circumvent the threat of Guided Democracy by co-opting the function of the National Front

---

141 The daily *Pemuda* carried on an incessant drumbeat of vituperation against the PNI during these months, insisting that the party must attach itself to Soekarno. It accused the PNI of having lost its dynamism since the deaths of Sidik Djojosukarto and Mangunsarkoro. See *Pemuda*, Nov. 1, 1958.

142 See *Suluh Indonesia*, Nov. 4, 21; *Pemuda*, Nov. 4, 22, 1958, for an exchange concerning the PNI's stand. *Pemuda* pointed out that while the PKI was beginning to give support to Soekarno, the nationalist group kept quiet in a thousand different languages.

143 *Pos Indonesia*, Nov. 26, 1958, *Pesat*, XIV, no. 49 (Dec. 6, 1958), 3-4, 12, and same, no. 50 (Dec. 13, 1958), pp. 3-4. A. Laksmi, "Sekitar Pembentukan Front Pantjasila" (On the Formation of the Front Pantjasila), in *Mimbar Indonesia*, XII, no. 49 (Dec. 6, 1958), 3-4, 18. Initially, some optimism was expressed about the potentiality of the Front Pantjasila, primarily by groups which hoped that this might be a way of eluding the proposals of the National Council, but the optimism faded quickly.

In his announcement of the Front, Suwirjo said that he would soon contact the leaders of the FNPIB to hold discussions about the new organization. It was clear, however, that he had not discussed the idea with the other parties.

proposed by the National Council.[144] It was doomed to failure from the beginning. The PNI had neither the energy nor the support to develop such a front. Army leaders, having little respect for many older PNI leaders, were not impressed and offered no assistance from the FNPIB. Moreover, if the Front idea were to have any hope of success, it must incorporate the other major parties on the premise that this was their only chance to undercut the challenge of the National Council. But every other party correctly judged that the PNI had chosen to grasp all the profits for itself. The PKI warned the PNI that its Front Pantjasila could not succeed without the support of the fifteen million voters represented by the PKI and NU; and it accused the PNI of wanting to establish another Front Anti-Komunis.[145] NU leaders also rejected the Front Pantjasila immediately, for they could hardly condone the proposal that the Government should be chosen from men who were "truly of the Pantjasila spirit," and instead Wahab Chasbullah launched an attack on the Pantjasila.[146] Regarded by nearly everyone as essentially a Front PNI, the Front Pantjasila drew no support, and within a few weeks the idea faded completely from the scene.

Before fading, however, the Front Pantjasila proposal helped to negate any hope of achieving an ideological compromise.

The Constituent Assembly was in any case encountering increasing difficulties in its deliberations during late 1958, largely because the issues of Guided Democracy were continually intruding themselves in the committee discussions. But the question of ideology remained the chief stumbling block. Compromise efforts became somewhat more sedulous

---

144 In Roeslan's speech of September 13, he mentioned the possibility of a Front consisting of a party or combination of parties dedicated to the Pantjasila. This was the likely origin of the Front Pantjasila idea. It is not clear what Soekarno thought of the effort, but if he was not skeptical from the start, he undoubtedly became so once it was clear that the Front Pantjasila had little backing outside of the PNI.

145 *Harian Rakjat*, Dec. 4, 1958. The Front Anti-Komunis (FAK), was an ineffective organization led by Isa Anshary, the West Javanese Masjumi leader. Aidit also warned that the Front Pantjasila would only discredit the PNI if it became a minority organization.

146 *Pedoman*, Dec. 1, 1958. See also *Duta Masjarakat*, Dec. 11; *Pemuda*, Dec. 11, 1958. *Pemuda*, repeating a comment by Gatot Mangkupradja that the Front would at most become a weak federation because the PNI had not contacted other parties first, noted also that the Front could not succeed as a PNI organization because many men no longer wanted to admit they were PNI members. The PNI tried unsuccessfully to defend itself against the accusation that it wanted to run the whole show alone. See *Suluh Indonesia*, Dec. 10, 1958.

in the anti-party atmosphere of late 1958, however, for it became clearer that a successful Konstituante was imperative in the interest of saving the party system. NU leaders especially were anxious to find a compromise. In October, K. Masjkur, the NU Konstituante leader, announced that the NU would propose a formula for bringing Islam and the Pantjasila together.[147] On October 15th this formula was introduced to the Konstituante session: it was called "Pantjasila-Islam," without any further clarification. The NU advocated this solution fervently until Suwirjo announced the ill-fated Front Pantjasila. Startled and angered by what appeared to be a PNI effort to push them aside, NU leaders rapidly retreated to a stand of solidarity on Islam with the other Islamic parties. Masjumi hailed this as proof that the Pantjasila-Islam notion was not a matter of principle for NU; and to confirm NU's new position, the Masjumi press published statements by Wahab Chasbullah and Idham Chalid from as early as 1955 showing their dedication to Islam as the essential corrective to the Pantjasila as the state ideology.[148] Meanwhile the PSII called a meeting of the Islamic parties to take their stand on the ideology question before the Konstituante, and NU reluctantly accepted.

All this made some contribution to one accomplishment in the Assembly on the ideology problem. On December 11th, the parties supporting the Pantjasila withdrew their various proposals (seven in all) on the constitutional preamble and united behind a single proposal: the preamble of the Constitution of 1945.[149] The Islamic parties decided to follow suit, introducing in mid-January a united proposal for an Islamic preamble.[150] Thus ideological lines were drawn firmly and with less chance

---

147 *Pos Indonesia*, Oct. 10, 1958.
148 *Abadi*, Dec. 12, 1958.
149 The preamble of the 1945 Constitution is included in the Appendix following Chapter VI.
150 The preamble proposal put forward by the Islamic parties read as follows:
"Whereas: The Independence of every people and their right of self-determination is the teaching of Islam, therefore colonialism in any form must be eliminated from the face of the earth.
"Whereas: In the struggle for Indonesian independence Islam has been the primary stimulus of the Indonesian people.
"Whereas: The Indonesian nation, the major part of which belongs to the Islamic community (ummat), has always been united in that struggle for independence. Praised be to God, by the Grace and Mercy of Almighty God the independence of Indonesia was proclaimed on 17 August 1945. To make that independence secure, we the people of Indonesia are resolved to establish the state of Indonesia as a sovereign Republic based on Islam.
"In this, we the people of Indonesia do maintain a state based on the rule of law, which guarantees

of a compromise, for never before had the parties united completely within their own camps.

Two or three points should be made about this development. First, in their divided state the parties were not prepared — and never had been — to confront Soekarno and the National Council in an all-out defense of the parliamentary system. Second, the ideological conflict between the parties in the Constituent Assembly came to a head precisely when the ideologically-based party system was threatened with annihilation by the demands of Guided Democracy. Unable to give promise of a permanent constitution in the near future, the parties yet again demonstrated their ineffectiveness.

Finally, the facing-off of the Pantjasila and Islamic groups in the Constituent Assembly symbolized the last stand of Islam as an organized political force in independent Indonesia against the triumphant forces of nationalist secularism. For the attack of Guided Democracy on the ideological party system was also an attack on Islamic ideology, which after a few years of apparent strength was succumbing to the real strength of other trends.

---

justice and prosperity for the whole people, and holds high the principles of mankind in the relations of all nations.

"To this end, we the people of Indonesia do accept and promulgate this constitution…"

For original text, see Ministry of Information, special issue 48, *Kembali ke Undang-Undang Dasar 1945* (The Return to the Constitution of 1945), Appendix XIII.

CHAPTER SIX
THE DRIVE TO GUIDED DEMOCRACY (II)

What little bargaining power the parties had in their negotiations with the National Council derived primarily from two factors. First, Soekarno did not want to resort to a blatantly unconstitutional solution; he preferred a decision that had the appearance of unanimity. Second, Soekarno was unwilling to resort to force, because in doing so he must rely upon the army, and at this stage he did not want to reduce the parties' strength so greatly that he would have no effective assistance in controlling the army. But there was no question of Soekarno's abandoning the drive against the party system; even if he were inclined to do so, army leaders would not permit a relaxation of the conflict. As for the parties, they would not surrender to the National Council without some guarantee of their survival. The result was a compromise, though one of little advantage to the party system. This initial settlement of the parties-National Council conflict was accompanied by the formal conclusion of the ideological debate in the Constituent Assembly.

This concluding chapter will deal with the Open Talks, the Constituent Assembly debates that followed, and the restoration of the 1945 Constitution.

The Open Talks and the Decision to Return to 1945

On November 7, 1958, the cabinet decided that it must agree to the introduction of functional groups into Parliament. This was reported to Soekarno in the first Open Talk on December 5th; there was no further agreement, however, except upon the necessity for further discussion.[1]

---

1 See the address by Soekarno at the Pantjasila Seminar on Feb. 20, 1959, in *Seminar Pantjasila*

Essentially, the matter now depended upon the PNI and NU, as the primary supporters of the cabinet, accepting, rejecting, or offering a compromise on the National Council's proposals. The PKI's views were important in the negotiations, but its influence was less because it was not in the cabinet. Army officers were trying, to some extent, to make common cause with the PNI and NU against the PKI, which left the latter somewhat at the mercy of the other two parties, even though it was their defense of the party system that the PKI was continually attempting to shore up.

The PNI and NU needed no great prodding, however, for the National Council proposals were unacceptable to them from the beginning. To sum up again briefly, these proposals were: 1) that 50 per cent of Parliament be turned over to functional groups, 2) that functional group candidates should be chosen by a National Front established by law and led by Soekarno, 3) that Soekarno should determine the list of functional group candidates, 4) that election ballots should comprise two lists — one of parties, one of functional groups — and that voting should be done by puncturing the ballot twice, once on the party side and once on the functional group side, and 5) that representatives of the armed forces functional group be appointed, not elected, to Parliament.

Having reluctantly accepted the principle of functional representation, the parties were forced to bargain for better proportions and, more important, for the right to exercise some control over functional groups in the electoral process. Roeslan explained in February that the essential problem lay in finding a balance between: 1) the armed forces functional group and the other functional groups, 2) the function of the National Front and the authority of the President as its chairman, and 3) the position of the parties and the National Front in choosing candidates and electing functional representatives in Parliament.[2] Though it does not entirely represent the views of the PKI and NU, the following comment from a semiofficial history of the PNI (published in 1959) lays down the party case:[3]

---

ke-I (Jogjakarta, Seminar Committee, 1959), p. 212. See also A. Laksmi, "Open Talk," in *Mimbar Indonesia*, XII, no. 50 (Dec. 13, 1958), 3-4, 18.

2 See Roeslan's address in *Seminar Pantjasila ke-I*, pp. 153-154.

3 *Empat Windu Partai Nasional Indonesia* (Four *Windus* [a *windu* is eight years] of the PNI;

The PNI Party Council did not accept — not entirely — the above conception of the National Council, particularly with respect to the method of introducing functional groups into Parliament. In broad outline the objections of the Party Council were as follows:

On the method of election...The functional group candidates with their own electoral symbols would not enter the Parliament as candidates put forward by the parties, and therefore would be free of all ties and party discipline in Parliament. The parties... would compete for only one-half of the Parliament, so that the representation of any party would be at a minimum (the 50 per cent would be further divided). This would mean 'emasculating' the parties. And it is only logical that no party, all the more so a major party, would be prepared to 'emasculate itself.'

...The multi-party system in Indonesia has evidently brought... damaging consequences for the nation...so that there must be a simplification of the parties achieved by law. But Guided Democracy must not...emasculate the parties. Because Guided Democracy is democracy! If the parties are not healthy they should be made healthy, and if there are too many parties their number should be simplified.

Similarly another National Council conception which the Party Council could not accept was that the functional group electoral list would be determined by the president...

This was unacceptable to the Party Council, in addition to other reasons because Bung Karno, whom we love very much, cannot remain President forever...Moreover, the PNI could not accept a law brought before Parliament which provided: 'The list of functional group candidates would be determined by President Soekarno [personally]...' What would the whole world then say about Indonesia? If the PNI agreed to such a law, its reputation

published by the PNI regional council of Central Java, n.d.), pp. 251-253.

would be shattered. And not only the PNI, but also Bung Karno's name would be sullied. And the PNI does not want Bung Karno's name to be sullied.

The PNI and NU would not agree to more than a one-third functional representation, but the more important question was how functional group representatives should be selected. Party leaders counter-proposed that functional representatives should be chosen via the parties themselves on a single list ballot.[4] Functional groups would thus be brought under the wing of the parties, preventing their appearance as an alternative to the party system. This obviously was unacceptable to the National Council, for it would negate the anti-party intentions of the original proposals; the National Front would be rendered ineffectual, and the parties would remain the core of the electoral system. Between the two poles there appeared to be no grounds for compromise. In addition, the PKI objected strenuously to the provision that representatives of the army be appointed to Parliament, and the PNI and NU objected to the large number of representatives demanded by the army.

The second and third Open Talks (January 15th and January 26th) proceeded under great tension, for questions began to be asked about the outcome should the parties refuse to go along with Soekarno. There were rumors that the cabinet would resign to be reshuffled, but this gave no hope that the situation would change later. Masjumi and the rest of the right-wing renewed their demand that the Dwitunggal be restored, with Hatta as prime minister. Within the cabinet, friction resulted from a speech broadcast in mid-January by Minister of Information Soedibjo in which he praised Guided Democracy and disparaged Parliament, provoking counter-attacks in the party press and an interpellation in Parliament.[5] At the same time maneuvering began, within both party and

---

4 *Ibid.*, p. 253. Both the PNI and NU maintained consistently from 1957 through the early months of 1959 that the parties already adequately represented functional interests; therefore functional groups were unnecessary. But both, like the PKI, reluctantly accepted the idea in recognition of the fact that this was less a matter of principle than of bargaining position, and their bargaining position was not excellent. See also "Perwakilan Golongan Funksionil Parlemen" (The Representation of Functional Groups in Parliament) in *Pesat*, XV, no. 6 (Feb. 7, 1959), 3-7.

5 See *Suluh Indonesia*, Jan. 16, 1959. Soedibjo had said that Parliament was infected by the disease of liberalism, which the PNI daily countered by declaring that every other governing institution, including the planning council yet to be formed, also suffered from various ailments. Moreover,

non-party groups, for positions in the new National Planning Council, whose composition was being considered by the cabinet during January and February.[6] But the Open Talks held the center of the stage, as the pro-Soekarno press demanded the immediate acquiescence of the parties in the National Council's program, while the parties advised against any precipitant action. *Harian Rakjat*, involved in a feud with *Merdeka*, the paper of the National Council member B. M. Diah, commented that the National Council should reconsider its proposals if no agreement were reached in the Open Talks.[7] But the anti-party press, deriding the hypocrisy of the "so-called supporters of Guided Democracy," warned that unless the parties gave in the country would suffer. The inclination to put everything into Soekarno's hands in order to find a solution to the conflict grew noticeably.

Taking matters into his own hands, then, Soekarno summoned the leaders of the PNI, NU, and the PKI — not, conspicuously, Masjumi — for private discussions on January 11th, before the second Open Talk.[8] He was unable to change their positions, however, and afterwards the party delegations admitted to the press that some difference of views remained concerning the size of functional representation in Parliament. NU leaders, fearing perhaps that the PNI and the PKI might make separate deals with Soekarno, insisted that Masjumi should be invited to join the discussion in order to make its views known.[9] But Soekarno continued to ignore Masjumi.

---

said *Suluh Indonesia*, the Ministry of Information (which also controlled the national radio network), as the spokesman of the cabinet, should reflect the cabinet's views — which in the Guided Democracy conflict it never did, Soedibjo enthusiastically allying himself with Soekarno. Later Soedibjo tried to explain his attack away in answer to the parliamentary interpellation.

6 See *Pos Indonesia*, Jan. 13, 1959. The cabinet planned hearings with organizations of youth, women, labor, etc., in order to select the sixty-six members of the National Planning Council. As the trend of the times became clearer, various organizations began to stake out claims to functional group status; thus in late January the Union of Internal Affairs Officials demanded to know why the *pamong pradja* administrative corps was not considered a functional group. The rush was on. *Pos Indonesia*, Jan. 24, 1959.

7 See *Harian Rakjat*, Jan. 14; and *Abadi*, Jan. 15, 1959, which argued the Masjumi view that there was no need for major institutional changes — the system is all right, it said, only the leaders are no good.

8 *Pos Indonesia*, Jan. 9, 1959. See also Ministry of Information, Kronik Dokumentasi, *Demokrasi Terpimpin*, pp. 220 ff. Aidit, Lukman, and Njoto represented the PKI; Wahab Chasbullah, Idham Chalid, Djamaluddin Malik, and Zainul Arifin represented NU; and Suwirjo, Manuaba, S. Hadikusumo, and Mrs. Supeni represented the PNI.

9 *Pos Indonesia*, Jan. 12, 1959.

The second Open Talk was held on January 15th, after Djuanda had received several proposals from a new National Council committee, one of whose members was Nasution. Djuanda spoke optimistically of the meeting before it began, partly no doubt to dispel the atmosphere of desperation. But he may also have been encouraged by the cabinet's acceptance of a quota for armed forces representatives in Parliament. The National Council apparently succeeded in reducing Nasution's demand for one-fourth of the Parliament to 35 appointive seats, to which the PNI and NU agreed.[10] At the second Open Talk this item was approved, but although Djuanda reaffirmed his optimism afterwards, it is unlikely that much else was settled.

Following this second round of discussions, the cabinet established a committee to formulate a set of compromise proposals before the next Open Talk.[11] Strained optimism preceded this third meeting, held in Bogor, but in the event the discussion broke down completely.[12] From available evidence, it seems likely that the cabinet parties continued to argue for a one-third functional group quota in Parliament, a single list ballot controlled by the parties, and, possibly, for functional candidates to be chosen by the functional groups themselves rather than by the National Front.[13] This latter was the least the parties could demand in the hope of assuring themselves some influence over the functional candidates and stunting the growth of a Front led by Soekarno. At the end of the ten hour meeting, it is possible that Soekarno angrily offered the original National Council proposals, as amended in the second Open Talk, and told the cabinet that everything now depended on its finding a solution. Later Roeslan was to say that this set of proposals, called the Bogor Formula, was a compromise agreed to by the cabinet; but this it decidedly was not.

---

10 See *Pos Indonesia*, Jan. 19 and 22, 1959. On Jan. 13th, the PNI party council accepted the idea of appointive seats for the armed forces but still insisted that the total functional group representation of Parliament should not exceed one-third and that it should be under the parties' aegis; *Pesat*, XV, no. 10 (March 7, 1959), 6.

11 *Pos Indonesia*, Jan. 16, 1959. The committee consisted of Djuanda, Leimena, Hardi, Idham, and Yamin.

12 At this meeting, Muljadi, Soekardan, Sadjarwo, and Sanusi did not attend. Idham Chalid left in the early afternoon, complaining that he did not feel well (*Pos Indonesia*, Jan. 27, 1959). In the Open Talks probably only a few ministers took active part, and of course the cabinet was quite divided, several members — including Yamin, Chaerul Saleh, Prijono, Soedibjo, and Hanafi — being firmly on the President's side.

13 See *Pos Indonesia*, Jan. 23, 1959.

The Bogor Formula provided first of all that the armed forces would be given 35 appointive seats in Parliament and that functional groups would have neither more nor less than 50 per cent of the total seats in Parliament. Second, a National Front would be established by law which, in addition to putting up candidates in elections, would "buttress the unity of functional groups for the purpose of over-all development." Third, except for appointive members, functional group candidates would be chosen "through and/or *by* the National Front." The ballot would comprise a double list, with each party and functional group having its own symbol, and the ballot *must* be punctured twice.[14] The list of functional group candidates would be determined by the President after consultation with the political parties and other electoral associations. Clearly the parties had had little success in softening the National Council's demands.

Following the third Open Talk, a sense of "anything can happen" pervaded the capital.[15] There were new rumors of a coup, of abolition of the parties, and of a cabinet overhaul. The pro-Soekarno press demanded that the Bogor Formula be announced immediately — it had been kept secret — and put into effect. But to have done this would have been to throw Soekarno and the parties into a direct public confrontation, from which Soekarno could not easily have backed down. The parties one by one clarified their views, at the end of January and the beginning of February, and it was obvious that the impasse had not been overcome. On the 30th, after a party executive council meeting on the 28th, Idham said that the NU could accept functional representation in Parliament only with the agreement of Parliament and on condition that the functional groups were connected with the parties.[16] Lukman said on behalf of the

---

14 Failure to puncture the ballot twice — once on the party side, once on the functional group side — would render it invalid. This was intended to prevent the parties from telling their followers not to vote at all on the functional group side. See Roeslan in *Seminar Pantjasila ke-I*, pp. 153-154, for the Bogor Formula.

15 In the provinces, however, there was increasingly noticeable indifference to the confusing intricacies of Djakarta politics, partly at least because restraints on the Djakarta press made it more difficult to get straight news. But also economic conditions in some regions received more attention than events in the capital. See *Java Post*, Feb. 17, 1959. Moreover, it may also be that the greater independence enjoyed by the regions under martial law was having the effect of turning provincial attention slightly more inward. Unlike the period before 1957, it became easier for men to say "to hell with Djakarta" and tend their local concerns with somewhat less fear of interference from the capital.

16 *Pesat*, XV, no. 6 (Feb. 7, 1959), 6; *Pos Indonesia*, Jan. 28 and 31, 1959.

PKI (Aidit being in Moscow at the time) that the party approved Guided Democracy but opposed the appointment of members of the armed forces to Parliament; they should be elected, he said, for otherwise they would not have the support of the people.[17] The PNI, racked by internal dissent and indecision, met several times in late January and early February without defining its stand clearly, but it was evident that the party could not agree to the Bogor Formula. Soekarno, who had declared after the January 26th meeting that there would be no more Open Talks, was informed of the parties' positions while he was on tour through Java. The deadlock remained and the cabinet had to find a way out or face the indeterminate consequences.

With remarkable quietude for Djakarta politics, in January and February a new line of compromise was developing that finally broke the deadlock. This was the possibility of adopting the 1945 Constitution, which Nasution had continued to espouse since proposing it to the National Council in August 1958. (For reference the text of this brief constitution is included as an appendix, following the end of this chapter, though it should by no means be taken as a guide to the actual workings or operative structure of the government either during the revolution or after July 1959.) As a compromise solution it had numerous advantages, several of which were referred to in the last chapter.

The 1945 Constitution would put dominant formal authority in Soekarno's hands, and since 1957 most parties had agreed on the merits of a stronger executive led by Soekarno. Probably the PKI had the most (tacit) reservations about such a course, primarily because a stronger executive must mean a weaker Parliament. But Soekarno's own reservations were also considerable, for the reasons discussed in Chapter V. In addition, the idea of restoring the 1945 Constitution was less attractive because it was Nasution's brainchild, and the army's political power was becoming more menacing by the day. The President finally agreed, however, because of the lack of any other practicable compromise and because of increasing pressure within the National Council to take

---

17 *Harian Rakjat*, Feb. 1, 1959. Lukman also said that the PKI would oppose Guided Democracy if it were used to dissolve the parties and eliminate democracy. The anti-Communist press quickly emphasized the PKI's opposition to military representation. *Pedoman*, Feb. 2 and 10, 1959.

this step. It will be remembered that in August 1958 the National Council had agreed upon the 1945 Constitution as an alternative course of action should other efforts fail.

Adopting this constitution would help solve the functional group problem. Allowing for great freedom of interpretation, article 2 of the 1945 Constitution could be construed as providing for functional representation. The Open Talk differences could be partially side-tracked for the sake of institutional recognition of functional representation, and the question of proportions of party and functional group membership in Parliament could be held in abeyance.

Moreover, it could also be argued in defense of the 1945 Constitution that, in providing specifically for regional representation (art. 2), it would work to satisfy regional aspirations. At the same time, it would establish a unitary state, nipping in the bud the evidently growing federalist sentiment in the Constituent Assembly. Nasution and other officers probably also argued that adoption of the 1945 Constitution would, by restoring the spirit of 1945, encourage all rebels to return to the fold.[18] On another level of argument, adopting the 1945 Constitution would bring the Konstituante to an end and settle the Islam-Pantjasila conflict in favor of the latter. This argument undoubtedly appealed to Soekarno and others in the National Council, but it could not of course appeal to NU, whose lack of enthusiasm later caused the effort to restore the 1945 Constitution much grief.

Other advantages of the 1945 Constitution were mainly symbolic. It was suited to the revival of the revolutionary temper best articulated by Soekarno himself. The "Return to the Spirit of 1945" was a banner that waved daily, and as political malaise increased the words assumed more significance for those dismayed by the confusion of the state. Army officers were most enthusiastic about a return to the Spirit of 1945, for the revolution symbolized their important contribution to the birth of independent Indonesia. But other groups also benefitted. The Generation of 1945, hardly an organization before, suddenly began to take shape in

---

18 See *supra*, p. 207, on Nasution's proposal in the National Council that the 1945 Constitution be restored. The arguments are repeated here because they probably became operative for a wider group of National Council members in early 1959 once the notion of resuscitating the early constitution took hold.

early 1959. Under the leadership of Chaerul Saleh, who sought to create a personal following from it, a major organization meeting was called in Djakarta of selected claimants to a place in revolutionary history. Vaguely conceived and without specific purpose, the Generation of 1945 was never to amount to much as a political force, but whatever chance it had depended largely on the symbolism of 1945. For others, the Spirit of 1945 took on the anti-party aspect of Guided Democracy, offering an escape from misgovernment and political disunity.[19] In any event, the important point is that revolutionary symbolism had widespread appeal, and in this environment the 1945 Constitution always seemed just around the corner.

It is not clear when the cabinet began to consider the 1945 Constitution seriously. It is likely that it was being discussed again by the National Council during its session of January 12th-13th following Soekarno's abortive talks with PNI, NU, and PKI leaders on the 11th. Adoption of the 1945 Constitution may have been proposed to the cabinet during the second Open Talk, and it was certainly one topic of discussion at the third Open Talk on January 26th. From then until February 20th, the 1945 Constitution was as lively an issue within the cabinet as functional representation and the National Front. Unlike the latter two problems, however, on which the PNI and NU were agreed, the 1945 Constitution divided them.

The PNI accepted it more quickly; in fact the party claims to have proposed its adoption at a party council meeting on January 13th.[20] Not only was it seen by PNI leaders as an acceptable compromise, but also they were convinced that giving Soekarno a more prominent formal role must redound to their advantage. Many in the party had already concluded that

---

19 Similarly the later restoration of the 1945 Constitution was seen popularly also as an anti-party move. A public official in Surabaja said to me in November 1959 that "The 1945 Constitution is a symbol of revolutionary struggle. People want to return to the period of the revolution, to start at the beginning again, and to reduce the part played by political parties…The country has. to stop the political parties, which favor only their own interests, from ruining the state." The sentiment was commonly expressed.

20 See *Pesat*, XV, no. 10 (March 7, 1959), 6, and *Empat Windu*, pp. 253-254. PNI leaders noted that they had proposed a presidential cabinet at the party congress executive meeting in Semarang in April 1958. The PNI, like several other groups, has staked out rather extravagant claims to the honor of having been the first to think of the 1945 Constitution. If the 1945 Constitution was actually discussed at the PNI meeting on Jan. 13, 1959, then it is likely that Soekarno talked about it with PNI, NU, and PKI leaders on Jan. 11.

the threat of the PKI was greater than the threat posed by Soekarno to parliamentary institutions. They (and many others on the left and right) believed that only Soekarno, with his immense popular support, could hold the Communists in check. In addition, PNI leaders also assumed, as always, that Soekarno would ultimately turn more towards the PNI than to any other party. At the same time, a toned-down Guided Democracy, with the Pantjasila as its ideological component, could be seen as the fulfillment of the PNI cause.

Initially, NU leaders refused unequivocally even to consider the possibility of adopting the 1945 Constitution. For, unlike the PNI, the NU could not view with equanimity the demise of the Constituent Assembly and the abandonment of the Islamic struggle; nor could much political compensation be expected were they to agree. The NU did not have all of the PNI's reasons for welcoming Soekarno's assumption of a stronger role; and being somewhat more confident in its electoral strength, the NU was more worried that Parliament would suffer. On January 30th, Idham Chalid said that NU acceptance of functional representation depended among other things, on maintenance of "the provisional constitution [of 1950]…and the authority of the President given him by the provisional constitution."[21]

The three weeks following the third Open Talk were spent in intense maneuvering as the parties worked assiduously to head off any decision by Soekarno to announce the Bogor Formula. While pressure built up in the press for the parties to accept the National Council proposals on functional representation, Nasution urged the cabinet to accept the 1945 Constitution. On January 30th, IPKI, whose connections with the army were bringing it increasingly into prominence, publicly proposed a return to the 1945 Constitution.[22] Suwirjo followed suit for the PNI on February 13th.[23] In mid-February political activity became even more

21 *Pos Indonesia*, Jan. 31, 1959. This was at the celebration of NU's 34th anniversary, following a party council meeting on Jan. 28th. See also *Pesat*, XV, no. 10 (March 7, 1959), 7.
22 *Suluh Indonesia*, Jan. 31, 1959.
23 *Bintang Timur*, Feb. 14, 1959. On Feb. 11, *Suluh Indonesia* declared in an editorial that the time had come for Soekarno to say the final word and assume "total leadership in the people's struggle." The PNI-leaning weekly *Pesat*, XV, no. 7 (Feb. 14, 1959), 3-4, proposed a return to the 1945 Constitution as a way out of national difficulties and claimed to be the first to propose this solution publicly. Murba issued a statement favoring the 1945 Constitution on Feb. 19th, when the cabinet had already decided upon this course. By this time, the 1945 Constitution was something

intense as the National Council met on the 12th to hear Soekarno's report on the third Open Talk. The cabinet met the next day. And at the same time, in a move aimed at bringing pressure to bear on both the National Council and the cabinet, Nasution called another conference of military commanders to meet in Djakarta on the 13th and 14th. This conference was frankly devoted to political matters, producing statements of support for Soekarno in his attempts to implement Guided Democracy and promises of backing for the Government in stabilizing the economy. In reporting the conference conclusions to Soekarno and Djuanda, it is likely that Nasution told them that the officer corps was fully committed to the 1945 Constitution.[24]

Throughout these weeks the NU cabinet ministers were under powerful pressure to accept the 1945 Constitution. There were several meetings between Soekarno and NU leaders,[25] and in addition Djuanda, PNI leaders, and army officers were all urging them to accede. Finally they were brought round, sometime before February 19th, by the highly persuasive argument that if they did not corruption charges pending against several top echelon NU leaders would be prosecuted. As was indicated in Djuanda's report during the debates on martial law in December, Zainul Arifin and Djamaluddin Malik were actually awaiting trial in cases begun under the army's anti-corruption campaign, and others

---

of a topic of rumor-ridden conversation. *Bintang Timur*, frequently close to *Harian Rakjat* in its views, on Feb. 16, 1959, noted the trend with disfavor, fearing that the 1945 Constitution might be "an easy way" to settle the functional group problem and to give the President absolute powers. The Constitution, said *Bintang Timur*, was not set up for that purpose but to protect the rights of the people. It warned that if there were to be a return to the 1945 Constitution, it must be done constitutionally, and therefore the two-thirds rule in the Konstituante should be reconsidered. This turned out to be prophetic.

24 In a message sent to a civilian-military meeting of some sort in West Sumatra on Feb. 13, Nasution said, "it is commonly known that the TNI (army) is pioneering the effort to return to the Constitution of the Proclamation of '45" (*Pos Indonesia*, Feb. 13, 1959). This was one of the few occasions on which Nasution publicly claimed credit on behalf of the army for the move to revive the revolutionary constitution. Nasution's statement may have been directed towards the rebel officers, for he said at the same time that the door was open for the rebels to return. Later, army sources denied that the effort to restore the 1945 Constitution was connected with attempts to end the rebellion. On the army conference in Djakarta, see *Pos Indonesia*, Feb. 19, and *Pedoman*, Feb. 13, 1959, which noted that the conference was probably connected with the cabinet discussions on functional group representation. Nasution went to West Sumatra on Feb. 15 and was back in Djakarta on the 17th, when he met with Djuanda for a talk that undoubtedly touched on the 1945 Constitution; *Pos Indonesia*, Feb. 18, 1959.

25 See *Pos Indonesia*, Feb. 13 and 17, 1959.

were under investigation.[26] Reluctantly, Idham therefore committed the NU to support a cabinet decision adopting the 1945 Constitution, even though this would mean victory for the Pantjasila in the Constituante. He and other NU ministers insisted only upon the face-saving proviso that their acceptance was with the understanding that the Djakarta Charter of 1945 was the "burden and soul" of the 1945 Constitution.[27] Despite their evident discomfort, however, it should be pointed out that an element in the NU leaders' support of the 1945 Constitution was a willingness to go along for the quid pro quo of remaining in the government.

Once the NU had given its assent, the cabinet sat down to a hurried and strained session on February 18th and 19th to work out a full compromise proposal for Soekarno, At this time a seminar on the Pantjasila was in progress in Jogjakarta, and on the night of the 16th Roeslan — as he had done on September 13th, 1958, with the National Council discussions — publicly released the Bogor Formula, undoubtedly in order to spur the cabinet and particularly the PNI and NU into action. Djuanda and the party leaders were infuriated, fearing that the gigantic leak would scotch the compromise effort; but it turned out to be mainly an irritating incident.[28] The cabinet completed its proposal on the 19th and sent it

---

26 Besides Zainul and Djamaluddin, an extraordinary number of the highest NU leaders was known to be involved in various brands of corruption — including, for example, illegal gold imports, manipulations in the purchase of foreign printed Korans, and so on.

27 *Pesat*, XV, no. 10 (March 7, 1959), 7. In a statement on Feb. 21, the NU noted that it had tried to speed up the work of the Konstituante; thus it had proposed the "Pantjasila-Islam" compromise to overcome the deadlock. In the conviction that its proposal would not be accepted, the NU then went on to say that if the 1945 Constitution were then proposed to the Konstituante, "in all sincerity [the NU] will be prepared to accept it with the understanding that this acceptance of the 1945 Constitution also means accepting everything connected with 'the historical documents,' including also the Djakarta Charter (Piagam Djakarta) as the burden and soul of the 1945 Constitution." The NU statement did not insist, however, that the Djakarta Charter be incorporated into the Constitution. See also Utrecht, *Pengantar Dalam Hukum Indonesia* (Djakarta: Ichtiar, 1959), pp. 439-440, n. 237. See *supra*, p. 128 on the Djakarta Charter.

28 Djuanda attacked Roeslan on the 20th for creating tensions between the cabinet and the National Council. He pointed out that to disclose the National Council's discussions was a violation of the law which established the Council as an advisory body to the cabinet. Djuanda also denied that the Bogor Formula was a compromise. See *Pesat*, XV, no. 9 (Feb. 28, 1959), 4-5. See also *Empat Windu*, p. 254.

In the same forum in Jogjakarta, Roeslan and Moh. Yamin campaigned for the 1945 Constitution. Yamin described the growing "movement to return to the 1945 Constitution" as a matter of principle transcending mere questions of compromise; to return to the first constitution, he said, was not to turn back the clock but rather to return to proper origins. Yamin, a practiced nationalist ideologue, declared that with the 1945 Constitution the Unitary Republic of Indonesia would be recreated on the basis of a doctrine consisting of three principles: The pantjasila, Guided

immediately to Soekarno, who announced his acceptance of it on the 20th at the Pantjasila Seminar.[29]

The cabinet proposal was in many ways a classic in the genus of political compromise. Attention should be called to three points in it. First, it was decided to follow constitutional procedures, although some consideration was given to the possibility of simply asking Parliament to approve the 1945 Constitution. Prof. Yamin was responsible for the formula that President Soekarno should "go in through the front door of the Konstituante" to ask it to accept the 1945 Constitution. The second point was that the Constituent Assembly would be requested to accept the 1945 Constitution unchanged, thus avoiding Islamic amendments and a prolonged and acrimonious debate. Third, the Djakarta Charter would be formally acknowledged, but no more than that; the reasoning of the cabinet decision on this point was seriously wanting in diplomacy. The compromise is summarized below.[30] Items of particular importance or interest are underscored.

On the 1945 Constitution: It is an "historical document" on the basis of which the revolution was begun and which can be used to complete the revolution. It is adequately democratic and in tune with the national identity. It guarantees the implementation of Guided Democracy. "Guided Democracy is democracy." The 1945 Constitution guarantees stable government for at least five years. The amendment procedure is flexible, though it is best that amending it be held off for several years pending political and economic stabilization. Functional groups can be introduced into Parliament, the Supreme Advisory Council, and the People's Consultative Assembly. Guided economy can be implemented on the basis of art. 33, after explication by the National Planning Council.

Democracy, and functionalism. See *Seminar Pantjasila ke-I*, pp. 28-46; *Pos Indonesia*, Feb. 19, 1959.

29 *Seminar Pantjasila ke-I*, pp. 209-222.

30 See Ministry of Information, *Kembali ke Undang-Undang Dasar 1945* (Return to the Constitution of 1945; Djakarta, 1959), pp. 5-10. See also Notosoetarjo, *Kembali kepada Djiwa Proklamasi 1945* (Return to the Spirit of the Proclamation of 1945) published in 1959 by the daily, *Pemuda*. Also Simorangkir and Mang Reng Say, *Tentang dan Sekitar Undang-Undang Dasar 1945* (On the 1945 Constitution; Djakarta: Djambatan, 1959). Subsequent events nullified much of this compromise, but the principle points are still of considerable interest.

"The 1945 Constitution will be adopted as a whole." [i.e., without change for the present.]

"In order to approach the desires of Islamic groups, in connection with restoring and maintaining security, the existence is recognized of the 'Djakarta Charter' of 22 June 1945, signed by Soekarno, Moh. Hatta, A. A. Maramis, Abikusno Tjokrosujoso, A. K. Muzakir, Agus Salim. A. Subardjo, Wahid Hasjim and Muh. Yamin."[31]

On the procedure for returning to the 1945 Constitution: *This will be done constitutionally.* It will be taken to the Konstituante, where the President will speak in the name of the Government to request that the 1945 Constitution be adopted. If accepted, the 1945 Constitution, according to art. 137 of the provisional constitution [on the Konstituante and the new constitution], will be proclaimed "with grandeur." The proclamation will be accompanied by a "Bandung Charter" [*Piagam Bandung*] signed in the Konstituante by the President, Ministers, and members of the Konstituante. The Bandung Charter will contain these provisions: a) on the existence of the Djakarta Charter, b) that the results of the Konstituante's work to date will be given to the Government,[32] c) that the Government will form a committee to bring existing laws into line with the 1945 Constitution, d) the promulgation of the 1945 Constitution for the entire nation.

Upon promulgation of the new constitution the Kabinet Karya will return its mandate. Beforehand the Kabinet Karya will prepare draft

---

31 The threat is explicitly recognized here that to ignore Islam entirely might lead to defections by devout Moslems and the consequent strengthening of the Darul Islam or the PRRI. As it was, however, the wording angered many Islamic leaders who were simply not satisfied to have their sentiments "approached." Army leaders argued that restoring the 1945 Constitution would offer an excuse for Darul Islam members who wanted to stop fighting to do so; for many who had joined the Darul Islam in 1948 had done so because they felt that the Republic was giving up the battle against the Dutch and forsaking the revolutionary struggle.

32 This was an attempt to head off criticism and rebellion in the Konstituante. The implicit promise was that the Konstituante's work would not go to waste. The results of the Konstituante's labors from 1956 through early 1959 can be found in Ministry of Information, *Kembali ke Undang-Undang Dasar 1945*, pp. 137-214, an appendix to Djuanda's report to Parliament in March.

laws on the party system and elections; these will be put before the present Parliament, which will continue until a new Parliament is formed following the next elections. The new Parliament will consider draft laws on the Supreme Advisory Council and the People's Consultative Assembly.[33] The People's Consultative Assembly will then select a President and vice-President according to art. 6.

On functional groups in Parliament: It is agreed that to make the party system healthy it must be simplified on the basis of new laws on the party system and elections. The parties will not be abolished.

Functional groups will be included in one list of parties and electoral associations under one symbol, alternating on the ballot with the party candidates, without further consideration of whether the total functional group contingent should comprise one-third or one-half of Parliament.

The President may participate in compiling the lists of candidates with the understanding that; a) he will be assisted by a new National Front established by law, b) his consultations will be by *musjawarah* [full discussion] and kebidjaksanaan [judiciousness], c) the National Front will have the right to put forward its own list of functional group candidates.[34]

---

33 In the interim, however, it was assumed by supporters of Soekarno that he would appoint these bodies; thus he would have tremendous authority for about two years. And that is the way it happened, with the result that the parties ultimately were unable to get the benefit they hoped for from the compromise.

34 This is not altogether clear, but the interpretation of Soekarno and those close to him was that he would discuss the ballot lists with the parties and that he would decide upon the relative ranking of the functional group candidates. One consequence of this would be that Soekarno would be given an opportunity to mix in party affairs. Moreover, Soekarno seemed to think that the system might result in a Parliament consisting of even more than 50 per cent functional representatives. In his Feb. 20 address in Jogjakarta, he stated, "With this system which I have decided to accept [from the Cabinet proposal] even though it is a single list and not a double list system, the Parliament will have even more functional representatives than 50% of the total. This is very joyous news." See *Seminar Pantjasila ke-I*, pp. 217-219. See also George McT. Kahin, "Indonesia," in Kahin, ed., *Major Governments of Asia* (Ithaca, N.Y.: Cornell University Press, 2d ed., 1963), p. 663, n. 15.

The President/Commander-in-Chief will appoint the armed forces representatives to Parliament — i.e., the army, navy, air-force, police, OKD [Village Security] and OPR [People's Defense]. The total armed forces representation will be 35. Members of the armed forces will be disenfranchised.[35]

An enormous campaign — led almost entirely by the army — to mobilize and dramatize public fervor behind the "Return to 1945" was launched immediately. Banners were strung everywhere, and there was even a special train decked out for the purpose in April. Mass rallies were organized under army auspices by the FNPIB, with demonstrations and parades by the civil-military cooperation bodies. Soekarno spoke to one such meeting on March 8th, military and commandeered private trucks transporting people from surrounding areas to the huge field in front of the palace. In general, however, Soekarno did not play an active part in the campaign; after a few speeches, he said he would speak no more and the people would make up their own minds. Nasution cracked down on the press, threatening repressive action, already commonplace, against "tendentious" reporting on the return to the 1945 Constitution. In several regions, particularly in the outer islands, army commanders told military and civilian officials to support the 1945 Constitution or give up their positions.

The strained atmosphere of the discussions on the 1945 Constitution did not allow the issue to be viewed with appreciable depth and imagination. Many serious questions were raised, it is true, both in Parliament and the Constituent Assembly, about constitutional structure and substance; and there was great concern over the kind of governmental system that would evolve. Parliamentary debates touched on the point that the early constitution contained no list of human rights, that it provided only very limited controls on the government, and that it was inadequate in other respects.[36] These inadequacies Djuanda

---

35 It was recognized, of course, that the General Staff would select its own representatives for appointment.
36 See Ministry of Information, *Kembali ke Undang-Undang Dasar 1945*, pp. 37-132, for Parliamentary questions on the 1945 Constitution and Djuanda's reply. Most questions had to do with functional groups, the role of Soekarno, the National Front, elections, and what would happen to the Konstituante if it refused to approve the 1945 Constitution.

admitted, promising that they would be corrected in time. The main concern of the Government, however, was to get the 1945 Constitution accepted by the Constituent Assembly. On March 2nd Djuanda reported to Parliament on the cabinet decision; and on March 25th he replied to questions, amidst growing public interest. Discussions were quickly held between the cabinet and the Konstituante leadership to set an early date for Soekarno's speech. After some opposition from Prawoto, one of the vice-chairmen of the Konstituante, it was agreed that Soekarno should address the Assembly on April 22nd, the day prior to departure on a two-month world trip. Konstituante Chairman Wilopo was at first reluctant to bring the 1945 Constitution before the body, fearing that it would not get the required two-thirds majority; he agreed only after Djuanda's assurance of NU support, which would give the proposal more than enough votes.

The dramatic cabinet decision of February 19th won quick approval from most parties. Statements of support were forthcoming from PNI and NU headquarters almost immediately. Many minor parties — including the PSI, Parkindo, the PSII, IPKI, Murba, Partindo, and a dozen others — also expressed their approval of the 1945 Constitution, though some of them attached conditions. It was generally agreed that Soekarno's assumption of formal authority would be a healthy development. Moreover, leaders of several of the non-Communist parties concurred in the view that the return to the 1945 Constitution would considerably damage the PKI.

PKI leaders also feared this might be the case. Adopting the 1945 Constitution was another step towards destruction of the parliamentary road to government. Furthermore, the army had won a favored and permanent role in the political system. But the only practicable choice for the PKI was to adjust to the new situation, and it was fortunate to possess the vitality, flexibility, and adequate mass support to do so. At the announcement of the cabinet decision, the PKI hesitated and then agreed, with evident reluctance; the party withheld judgment, however, on the projected election and parties laws until they could be examined. The CCPKI statement also emphasized that the return to the 1945 Constitution meant that Soekarno would assume both executive and legislative leadership, and it renewed its demand for admission to the cabinet.[37] Thereafter the PKI became one of the chief advocates of the 1945 Constitution, solidly supporting the course which it knew to be inevitable.

Masjumi's initial response to the decision on the 1945 Constitution was equivocal. The party had always favored a strong executive government, but at this time there was nothing politically favorable for it in the decision. Masjumi leaders demanded that Hatta return to the government, on the grounds that the Dwitunggal was an essential part of the 1945 picture.[38] But neither this nor any of Masjumi's other interests were to be satisfied. Furthermore, the Constituent Assembly was to be eliminated and with it the Islamic struggle at that level, and aside from objections of principle on this score Masjumi leaders did not want the ideological issue to come to a head before the rebellion was ended and the party was in a much better bargaining position.

Masjumi was by no means united in facing these problems, however. The division in the party was seen in clear relief at the Masjumi national congress held in Jogjakarta from April 23rd to 27th, just before the Konstituante debates on the 1945 Constitution. A serious battle — which the press, hostile as it was to Masjumi, did not allow to pass unnoticed — took place between the Sukiman group on the one hand and the Prawoto group on the other. And this battle covered the whole range of Masjumi policies: the party stand on the rebellion, the problem of constituent organizations of the party, and the issue of the 1945 Constitution. With dominant support from East and Central Java branches and from a few younger leaders, Sukiman was intent on bringing Masjumi back from the brink of oblivion and forcing it to adjust to the turn of national politics. He and Wibisono attacked the party view of the rebellion defended by Prawoto and quietly sought a relaxation of the Islamic struggle in the Konstituante for the sake of a political detente with other non-Communist parties. At the same time they argued vigorously that Masjumi must support the return to the 1945 Constitution, for the Sukiman group saw

---

37 *Pos Indonesia*, Feb. 24 and 25, 1959.
38 The reply from Soekarno circles was that the People's Consultative Assembly would later elect the President and Vice-President; see the statement by Chaerul Saleh in *Pos Indonesia*, March 2, 1959. Others either attacked Hatta, as the PKI did, or argued that it was no longer necessary to have a vice-president, as some PNI members did in the Konstituante.

this as the last hope for the party to remain alive.[39] Masjumi opposition to the return would be unlikely to prevent it and would only result in pushing the party further beyond the political pale.

The conflict over these issues ran deep and quickly took on the character of a Java-outer islands split. Several party leaders, including Prawoto, were convinced that the future of Masjumi lay in the powerfully Islamic outer islands, not in Java. Therefore the rebellion could not be condemned, for that would be a betrayal of strong Masjumi areas. Moreover, several of the outer island delegations to the congress — particularly from Atjeh, South Sulawesi, and South Kalimantan — as well as part of the West Javanese group, insisted that the Islamic struggle must be prosecuted with more, not less, determination. Thus a majority of the congress inclined towards a stand on principle, and many members privately accused the NU of opportunism in abandoning the interests of Islam and accepting the cabinet decision. When it came to Guided Democracy and Soekarno, the Prawoto group, unlike Sukiman, Wibisono, and their associates, found it nearly impossible to accept or trust either one.

Prawoto was elected party chairman, defeating Sukiman by a narrow majority.[40] At the same time, the meeting voted down an attempt by Wibisono to separate the SBII, Masjumi's labor organization, from the party.[41] But Wibisono and the SBII took an independent stand in favor of

---

39 When the cabinet decision was first announced, a press report said that Sukiman's reaction was truly enthusiastic; he expressed his delight that a presidential cabinet would be formed under the 1945 Constitution; he also said that the Pantjasila was not in conflict with the teachings of Islam. See *Pos Indonesia*, Feb. 24; *Pesat*, XV, no. 10 (March 7, 1959), 7. Soon afterwards, however, Sukiman sent a telegram to Yunan Nasution of the Masjumi party council declaring that he had not said everything that was reported in the press; see *Pos Indonesia*, Feb. 26, 1959. These were his views, nevertheless. For rather full but biased reports on the conflicts at the Masjumi congress, see *Bintang Timur*, April 29, May 2, 4, and 6; *Sin Po*, April 29, 1959. Masjumi's replies to *Bintang Timur* are in *Abadi*, May 8 and 12, 1959.

40 *Abadi*, April 30, 1959. Sukiman was elected first vice-chairman, Fakih Usman second vice-chairman, Moh. Roem third vice-chairman. Yunan Nasution was elected secretary. Other members included Anwar Harjono, Hasan Basri, and Osman Raliby. The party council was heavily weighted in favor of the Prawoto group.

41 It was generally agreed in the party that eventually the constituent organizations should separate, but the issue was always a matter of timing. Wibisono continued to insist that the SBII would leave the party organization — as it eventually did — though it would still cooperate with and support Masjumi. *Pedoman*, May 11, 1959. Anwar Harjono debated the question with Wibisono; see *Pedoman*, May 12; *Abadi*, May 12, 1959. Harjono's view was essentially that no one should leave the party in time of crisis. Wibisono felt that the SBII should be saved from the fate of the party. Muhammadijah, the Islamic educational foundation, was also anxious to leave the party organization, and soon did. When Masjumi was finally banned in August 1960, both the

the 1945 Constitution. There was a good deal of feeling among Javanese members of the party that Masjumi was a lost cause. To avoid an open split, the congress worked out a compromise on policy that left the party's position vague, as the PNI and others protested, though still clear enough to place Masjumi firmly in the opposition to the government. On the cabinet decision, the congress resolution stated that there were three elements in the spirit of the 1945 Constitution: "1) the Dwitunggal of Soekarno and Hatta, 2) national unity, and 3) national peace" — the last two meaning compromise with the rebels. The congress also demanded that the Konstituante be allowed to continue its work of creating a new constitution. All Islamic parties were called upon to unify their policies, "especially in carrying out the struggle for the ideals of Islamic ideology." And, last, all Islamic parties and other democratic parties were admonished to work together to save democracy in Indonesia.[42] Masjumi thus entered the Constituent Assembly debates on the 1945 Constitution prepared to make something of a last-ditch stand.

Meanwhile, the public response to the proposal to restore the 1945 Constitution was ambivalent. On the one hand, though the country (or, better, the capital) was tense, divided, and dismayed over the six months of bickering that had preceded resolution of the crisis, on the whole the cabinet decision evoked a favorable reaction. There was widespread feeling that this was, as Yamin put it, a return to proper origins, and there was a noticeable optimism that the Spirit of '45 might yet revive and turn men to clean and honest living, unity, progress, discipline, and idealism. Many were confident, many others hopeful, that Soekarno, Nasution, and the leaders around them were sincere in their promises to reform and revitalize the nation. Even among the opposition to Soekarno, within Masjumi and the PSI for example, there were those who said that if this was an honest effort to get the country back on the right track, they would support the President.

On the other hand, there were grave fears among the politically conscious that this was just another play in the game of politics, whose

---

Muhammadijah and the SBII were permitted to continue.
42 *Abadi*, April 30; *Pedoman*, April 29, 1959. In Bandung, from April 27 to April 30, the Masjumi-related All Indonesian Association of Former Armed Islamic Fighters [of the Revolution] also held a conference in which the Islamic struggle was emphasized. See *Abadi*, May 15, 1959.

rules had been in force too long to be changed. It quickly became apparent that there would be no transformation of political behavior. Groups began frenziedly to maneuver for advantageous positions before the impending restructuring of the government. The rush to Soekarno's side, in part compulsive but also largely opportunistic, proceeded apace. When before the end of February it became clear that the cabinet would return its mandate in July, the scramble started for places in the new cabinet. In March and April secret lists of prospective cabinet members were in circulation, arousing the indignation of the independent press and evoking an admonition from Information Minister Soedibjo that everyone ought to be thinking about the return to 1945 rather than the new cabinet that would follow. Some suspected that the restoration of the 1945 Constitution was simply another ploy to avoid the tough work of economic development. The doubts of commercial circles were partially reflected in continued speculation and rising prices. Party leaders — except from the PKI — seldom talked about the people's suffering, as the press occasionally pointed out, but rather resorted to ideological shibboleths that contributed little to practical policy decisions.

No relaxation in tension followed the cabinet decision. The "Return to 1945" campaign combined with a high pitch of nationalist sentiment to create a volatile political temper. Soekarno's appeals to radical and revolutionary symbolism were repeated in the left-wing and radical nationalist press. Nasution and other officers insisted that ideological uniformity was essential, that loyalty to the revolution should be rewarded, and that those who had cooperated with the Dutch should be weeded out of the government.[43] The old order was constantly under attack, and the new standards of political good came increasingly into play.

An example of the temper of the times was the Schmidt affair, which produced an uproar in Djakarta in March and April. Schmidt was a Dutchman and an ex-member of the Netherlands-Indies army who had been sentenced in 1956 to several years imprisonment for subversive activities. At the time, his case and that of Jungschlager, who died before serving his sentence, had created a furor in the national press and to

---

43 *Waspada*, April 13, 1959, a speech in Padang during the celebration of the end of Ramadan, the month of fast.

some extent in the world press. In March 1959, the Djakarta appeals court reviewed the evidence in Schmidt's case and reduced his sentence to the time already served. On direction of the Chief Prosecutor's office Schmidt was therefore released and, in order to avoid a public reaction, he was quickly and secretly flown to Holland with the help of the Dutch Consul, Ravensteyn. The matter became a *cause célèbre* as soon as it was uncovered. The court and Chief Prosecutor Soeprapto, a highly effective and judicious official of long experience (and a member of the National Council), were subjected to a merciless lashing in the left-wing press for letting Schmidt go. Djuanda ordered a government investigation, and Soeprapto was relieved of his office as of April 1st, partly as a scapegoat.[44] In his report to Parliament on the affair, Djuanda declared that the Government would use martial law powers to act against courts when their decisions endangered national security.[45] This was the first time the courts, generally respected and honest but a distinct part of the old order, had come under such an attack by the Government. Some defended the judiciary and Soeprapto, but something of a pall set in around the often praised symbol of "rule of law" (*negara hukum*). With the new Chief Prosecutor, Gatot Tarunamihardja, appointed by Soekarno in mid-April, the public prosecution began to lose its semi-independent character.

---

44 But not entirely; Soeprapto had long aroused antagonism among cabinet leaders, at least since 1953 or 1954, for his refusal to subordinate the public prosecution to political ministries. In 1956-1957, his prosecution of Roeslan Abdulgani on charges of foreign exchange violations, over the objections of the Ali Cabinet, made him the object of considerable PNI resentment. On the Schmidt affair see Ministry of Information, *Keterangan Pemerintah mengenai Penjelesaian Soal Schmidt* (Government statement on the disposition of the Schmidt problem; Djakarta, 1959). See also, *Abadi*, April 25, and *Sin Po*, April 1, 3, 8, 24, 1959; *Sin Po* carried on the most determined campaign against Soeprapto, the appeals court, and the courts generally.

45 *Sin Po*, April 24, 1959. At the same time, however, Djuanda said that as the executive the cabinet had no authority to interfere with the courts, though it expected the Supreme Court would in future take all necessary steps to keep the lower courts in line. Djuanda's statement was a strange mixture of approaches to the position of the judiciary, reflecting, I think, a transitionally ambivalent attitude towards the court system during a time of "revolution." Partly of course he was recognizing and accepting the powerful sentiments against the courts aroused by the Schmidt case. The courts were not in fact bothered a great deal afterwards until about the end of the year, when increasing pressure was brought to bear on judges to conform to the official ideology. Judges by and large resisted these pressures longer than other official groups. Partly at least this was because judges were as a group rather skilled and confident practitioners with considerable pride in their functions.

The Constituent Assembly Debates and the Decree of July 5th

Soekarno addressed the Constituent Assembly on April 22nd, as Bandung rocked with demonstrations of support for the return to 1945. He warned against expecting too much from the 1945 Constitution. But this was a time, said Soekarno, to leave text-book thinking, to return to the revolution, and to listen to the Message of the People's Suffering.[46] The 1945 Constitution would give Indonesia a permanent unitary state. And it would eliminate dualism, especially the dualism of thought regarding whether or not the revolution was complete; it was not, he declared, and the 1945 Constitution would in effect give form to the ongoing revolution. It would lay the basis for the implementation of Guided Democracy in which leadership would be unified and government would be by *musjawarah*. The past ten years of deviation and error would be cast aside. Soekarno asked the Konstituante to accept the 1945 Constitution as it was, preamble and body both, without any change.[47]

The next day Soekarno left the country on a two-month world trip, provoking a few accusations that he was running away precisely when his presence was most needed.[48] His departure also chagrined the cabinet

---

46 Increasingly in 1959, as Soekarno rose more sharply towards the peak of authority, and ideology became more important, these phrases — text-book thinking, the Message of the People's Suffering (Amanat Penderitaan Rakjat, abbreviated to AMPERA) and many more — quickly became common catchwords and slogans, spread far and wide by the Ministry of Information and the daily press. Another term of importance later in the year, though Soekarno had used it in 1958, was "retooling," which referred to the need to rework government structure, try new approaches, and obtain new and better personnel. Possibly he took the phrase — retooling for the future — from Vera Micheles Dean's book, *The Nature of the Non-Western World*.

47 Soekarno's speech, entitled "Res Publica! Sekali Lagi, Res Publica!" (Res Publica! Once Again, Res Publica!), was published by the Ministry of Information in both Indonesian and English (Djakarta, 1959). The speech was drafted with the help of a National Council committee headed by Sukarni, and it was discussed by the National Council.

48 The trip had been planned a few months earlier, but it is likely that Soekarno did in fact prefer being away during crises of this sort. In the first place, he could thus avoid the burden of responsibility for turns of events over which he could not exercise full control. Second, he may have felt that being out of the country made it easier to assess possibilities as they developed at home. Third, by removing himself from the scene, Soekarno could let contending forces battle it out among themselves without using him as a weapon, sometimes against his will. Soekarno's yearly trips, aside from affording him an opportunity to meet and be met by foreign leaders, and aside from being good entertainment for the fun-loving President, also served other useful political functions. The choice of the entourage — membership in which offered prestige — was one means of building new political loyalties or influencing potential opponents. On this trip, thirty-one men joined the President, including Subandrio, Supreme Court Chairman Wirjono Prodjodikoro, Chaerul Saleh, and Col. Harun Sohar, commandant of South Sumatra. See *Pedoman*, April 24;

and Constituent Assembly leaders, who felt that he ought to see the 1945 Constitution safely through the Assembly. Soekarno rejected these protests, arguing that the trip constituted an important effort to make Indonesia known to the world and that he also needed a rest. Speaker of Parliament Sartono became acting president, but he declared that significant measures could not be expected from him; he was an acting constitutional president, said Sartono, not an acting President Soekarno.[49]

With Soekarno's speech as their focus, the debates in the Assembly began April 29-30, continued May 4-6 and 11-13, and ended May 25-26, the issue being put to a vote at the end of the month. The debates were more tense and bitter than vigorous. The commitments of the PNI and the PKI to the 1945 Constitution were mainly political, so that neither of these parties had a great deal to say, though PKI speakers did ask for guarantees of elections and the rights of Parliament. Among other parties officially supporting the 1945 Constitution there was considerable antagonism towards the Government, whose refusal to consider amendments aroused in the Constituent Assembly institutional pride and anger at the thought of two years work going for nothing. The Government was attacked for making the Constituent Assembly the scapegoat for its own failures. There were lengthy comments on the inadequacies of the 1945 Constitution, and Soekarno was accused of desiring to create an authoritarian or totalitarian state. On these questions individual members of the Christian parties, Labor, and a few others spoke out in defiance of party discipline, but it was Masjumi which provided solidest opposition. Continuing their demands for Islamic principles, federalism, Hatta, and a new cabinet, Masjumi leaders, fresh from the party conference a few days earlier, assaulted Guided Democracy and with it the 1945 Constitution, which the prominent party leader Hamka called the road to hell for Indonesia.[50] Prawoto demanded that the Assembly, as a democratically elected body, be permitted to complete its work in peace regardless of the fate of the 1945 Constitution.[51]

Pos Indonesia, April 20, 1959. The countries visited on this trip included Turkey, Poland, Sweden, Denmark, the Vatican, Brazil, Argentina, Mexico, North Vietnam — Ho Chi Minh had visited Indonesia in March — Japan, and Cambodia, with side trips to South Russia and California. His earlier trips had covered the giants: the United States, the Soviet Union, and China.

49 *Sin Po*, April 23, 1959.

50 See *Abadi*, May 9; *Bintang Timur*, May 8, 9, 1959.

51 *Abadi*, May 6, 1959. Masjumi, said Prawoto, took its stand on the defense of a State based on

The Government was sure, however, of a solid core of support — more than 280 seats out of less than 500 — and a favorable vote by NU, with 90 seats, would push the total well past the two-thirds majority required.[52] Masjumi's 114 votes were not enough to threaten the Government, and a few hostile minor parties could also be ignored, including all the minor Islamic parties (and of these the PSII even seemed likely, for a while, to join NU in voting with the pro-1945 group). But these calculations necessarily depended on NU support, and it soon became clear that this was not as secure as Djuanda and others had hoped.

The reason was that the issue of conflict in the Constituent Assembly shifted almost immediately from the 1945 Constitution to Islam, and once ideology held the center of the stage, the 1945 Constitution became a highly questionable proposition. At the time, many Assembly leaders were convinced that the Government had wrecked its chances by permitting this to happen.[53] It is true that during this period the Government's

---

Law (*rechtstaat*) and rejected a State based on Power (*Machstaat*). Summaries of the Konstituante debates were published in two mimeographed volumes by the Ministry of Information: *Inti Sari pidato-pidato anggauta* Konstituante berkenaan dengan amanat President tanggal 22 April 1959 (Summaries of Speeches by Konstituante Members in Connection with the Presidential Address of April 22, 1959; Djakarta, 1959). The first volume covers speeches made during the first round of debates from April 29 through May 13, the second volume the second round of May 25-26. See also Notosoetardjo, *Kembali kepada Djiwa Proklamasi 1945*, pp. 259-298, 522-554. The debates received full and excited coverage in the daily press, the arguments raging outside as well as inside the Konstituante.

52 No more than 470 of the more than 500 elected to the Konstituante participated in these debates. The majority required for passage of substantive issues was two-thirds of those attending and fulfilling a quorum. Parties expected definitely to vote for the 1945 Constitution were the PNI (117), the PKI (59), Republic Proklamasi (a combination of parties) (21), Parkindo (18), Katholik (11), PSI (8), Persatuan Irian Barat (5), GPPS (4), and several other minor parties, some of which, however, were divided on the issue. Of the Islamic parties other than Masjumi and NU, the PSII had 17 seats, Perti 7, Akui 1, PPTI 1. See *Suluh Indonesia*, May 16, 1959.

53 The following comment, paraphrased, was made to me by a PSI leader in the Konstituante on June 1st, while the 1945 Constitution was still being voted on: "The whole of the politics of the Konstituante with respect to the return to 1945 plan has been badly mismanaged by the Government. The issue of Islam vs. Pantjasila should never have been raised or allowed to become crucial. The Government doesn't realize its own limitations. They've seen the Darul Islam trouble go as yet unsolved. The PRRI broke out and the government is still trying to push the Moslems further. Once the Islamic groups began to see the 'return' plan as a move against the Moslems, they of course had to stand on principle. And this includes the NU." It is with this view, held by many, that I take issue. Another comment by a long time government official, who had for many years served close to Soekarno but no longer agreed with him, seems to me to be closer to the truth: "Soekarno knew that the Pantjasila-Islam dispute would arise again the Konstituante, but he had to send it through that body to eliminate the last of the obstacles in his way by proving that it [the Konstituante] could only obstruct and procrastinate and not get anything done." Sept. 2, 1959.

strategy with respect to Islam was blundering and insensitive, both in and out of the Assembly. But one has to ask whether it was really possible to avoid the religious-ideological issue, and the answer seems to be no. For not only was the Konstituante the very forum of ideological debate, the altar of Islamic hopes and the Islamic struggle, but moreover the ideological debate itself was ripe for resolution. That is to say, the Islamic parties were politically weak — Masjumi's strength was sapped by its connection with the PRRI and NU's leadership was manipulable — and the sources of Islamic power, though potentially great, were otherwise unarticulated. Therefore the time had come for political Islam to give way before the power of political secularism. However vaguely others may have perceived this dialectic, Soekarno probably understood it and was prepared to follow it. The impotence of Islam as a political force at this time made compromise with it unnecessary, and none came about in the Constituent Assembly. But the result, perceived in historical perspective, probably differed little from what would have ensued had the Constituent Assembly followed another course in 1959.

Idham had agreed to the cabinet decision of February 19th without consulting the party council; nor, apparently, were any of the NU ministers frank in discussing the matter outside of the innermost circle of the party leadership. They appear to have reckoned on party adherence to the decision out of faith in Idham, Wahab Chasbullah, and Zainul Arifin; and if any serious doubts arose, an appeal could be made to the necessity that NU not allow itself to be isolated out of the government. NU had never had serious trouble with factionalism or party revolts, for it was too solidly based on interest and suffered none of the schisms of principle that result from intellectual leadership. But this time the opportunism of national NU leaders overreached itself. Their apparently sudden willingness to surrender the Islamic struggle threatened to dissolve entirely the essential ideological bond that permitted NU to justify itself as a party. In late February and March several NU regional leaders protested that Idham had no right to take so important a decision without consulting them first.[54] The East Javanese NU, most powerful branch in the party, was joined by such of the younger national party leaders as Imron Rosjadi to demand

54 *Java Post*, March 20, 1959.

that an emergency session of the party council be called to discuss the issue. This meeting was held in Patjet (Tjiandjur) on March 26-29, with about 80 council members, MP's, Konstituante members, and Ministers attending. Over the opposition of a large and vociferous minority who insisted that NU must press for an Islamic constitution, Idham was able to get the party council's endorsement of his commitment to the cabinet.[55] But the endorsement was no carte blanche, several regional leaders demurring tentatively while they "sent out feelers" into the party ranks. Idham, however, satisfied that NU members in the Konstituante would vote as directed, or perhaps afraid that they would not, went off on a *hadj* trip to Mecca while the party cauldron began to boil.

With Idham away, NU's lack of enthusiasm for the secular constitution of 1945 became glaringly obvious. Fearing lower echelon reactions, NU leaders urged the Government to tone down the campaign to return to 1945. In East Java, NU joined with Masjumi in refusing to participate in a mass rally supporting the return to 1945.[56] Regional NU leaders were apparently assured by the army command in East Java, however, that their opposition to the 1945 Constitution on religious grounds would not bring harm to the party.[57] Meanwhile, in and out of the Konstituante, NU was under dogged and fervent pressure from Masjumi to obey the call of the Faith. The accusations frequently heard about NU opportunism, and Masjumi charges that Idham and NU were selling Islam down the river, appear to have stung painfully, particularly as it seemed to many NU members that this was in fact the case.[58] This pressure was much

---

55 For this NU won the praise of the PNI, the PKI, and several government leaders, including Roeslan Abdulgani, all of whom were anxious to keep NU from being influenced by Masjumi. See *Duta Masjarakat*, March 31; *Suluh Indonesia*, March 31; *Harian Rakjat*, April 1; *Sin Po*, April 17, 1959.

56 See *Perdamaian*, April 15; *Trompet Masjarakat*, April 17; *Suara Rakjat*, April 18, 1959. It was in response to an invitation to speak at this rally that Soekarno, in refusing, said he would not attempt to influence the people one way or the other. Apart from other reasons of limited time, the President probably did not want to go to East Java, where the opposition to him continued to be disturbingly vociferous. In any event, NU praised Soekarno's attitude, agreeing that the people's spirit should not be set ablaze while the Konstituante was discussing the 1945 Constitution.

57 This at least was rumored by different sources during the Konstituante debates, which I attended in late May. It is quite possible that Col. Sarbini, who was more sympathetic to the parties generally (except for the PKI) than most officers and apparently got on very well with East Javanese NU leaders, told them that their position in the Konstituante was their own affair, and that it would make no difference in their relations in East Java.

58 During the Masjumi conference in April the left-wing news service, INPS, reported

stronger than the *sotto voce* threats from government and army circles against NU members who refused to support the 1945 Constitution without amendments.[59] In April, Wilopo received indications from NU members in the Konstituante that the party might not honor Idham's commitment.

By the beginning of May, the Government was still confident that NU leaders were too well aware of the possible consequences to allow their party to vote against the 1945 Constitution. But when the Constituent Assembly debates began, the fires of the Islamic issue, with fuel poured on by Masjumi, were blazing within the NU representation. NU leaders who wanted to support the Government were compelled to join their lower echelons in defending the ideology; otherwise they risked being trampled underfoot in a rank and file revolt led by those few leaders who had disagreed with Idham from the start. Anxious to avoid identification with Masjumi, however, several NU leaders went out of their way in late April and May to attack that party, to speak out more loudly than usual against compromise with the PRRI, and to emphasize their indifference to Hatta.[60] But although Masjumi spoke more vehemently on more issues — at times Islam hardly seemed the chief interest of Masjumi leaders, while for the NU it was the central issue[61] — on Islam the parties of the

---

remarks by Masjumi members that the NU's support of the cabinet decision proved that party's utter opportunism. See *Bintang Timur*, May 2, 1959. One or two NU leaders, including K. H. Muslich, parliamentary leader and member of the party council, immediately replied with attacks on Masjumi's involvement in the rebellion and, going much further, warned Masjumi that if it refused to accept the President's proposal to return to 1945 it would place itself forever outside the pale. On behalf of the executive council of NU, however, Achmad Sjaichu disavowed Muslich's views, saying that they would divide the Islamic parties. Sjaichu declared that the NU would not heed the INPS reports until proved. *Abadi*, May 6, 1959.

59 See speech by K. H. M. Sjukri (NU) in the Konstituante, *Abadi*, May 2. On May 28 *Abadi* reported rumors of blackmailing activities against opponents of the 1945 Constitution and called on the Government for appropriate preventive measures. Pro-Government newspapers kept up constant pressure on NU to honor its commitment. On March 15 the Sunday newspaper, *Berita Minggu*, had revealed charges of corruption against NU cabinet ministers, to which *Duta Masjarakat*, March 19, replied defensively to the effect that precisely at this critical time when the nation wanted to restore the 1945 Constitution and the Djakarta Charter, and when the fate of 85 million Indonesians hung in the balance, slanderous campaigns were begun against two ministers of the Kabinet Karya. See also *Duta Masjarakat*, March 17, 1959, which accused *Berita Minggu* of resorting to blackmail.

60 Statement by Wahab Chasbullah (Rois Aam) in reponse to the decisions of the Masjumi conference in April. *Suluh Indonesia*, April 30, 1959.

61 A symbolic compromise on Islam might have satisfied many NU members, but it would have been meaningless for Masjumi, which was threatened with permanent political displacement.

Faith came together. The PSII, which had wavered, joined the Islamic camp again in May.[62]

The immediate issue on which the Assembly debates turned was the significance to be given to the Djakarta Charter, with its command that Moslems practice the Islamic Sjariah. As Djuanda had somewhat evasively defined it, the Government's position was that the Djakarta Charter would be recognized as an historical document, prior in date to the Constitution itself and having an influence on the spirit of the constitution, but it would have no organic relation to the constitution and therefore would be without imperative legal force.[63] Islamic groups, however, demanded a substantive expression of the role of Islam in the state — in other words that the Djakarta Charter be incorporated as the preamble to the constitution. To avoid the interpretation that preambles are not binding, NU members stood in the Konstituante in May to insist that the obligation of Moslems to follow the Islamic law must be fitted into article 29 of the 1945 Constitution, dealing with religion.[64] This single concession would enable NU to vote for the 1945 Constitution. But for secular groups, and especially the Catholics and Protestants, this prospect immediately conjured up visions of religious oppression and Islamic fanaticism.[65] The Islamic law clause in the Djakarta Charter was not interpreted by Islamic leaders as a permissive rule, and it was for this reason that the many nominal Moslems of the secular parties objected to

---

For an illustration of the differences between Masjumi and NU on the proposal to restore the 1945 Constitution, see the questions of Anwar Harjono (Masjumi) and Achmad Sjaichu (NU) in Parliament in March in Ministry of Information, *Kembali ke Undang-Undang Dasar 1945*, pp. 73-87, 127-131.

62 *Antara*, May 25, 1959. The PSII, like NU and unlike Masjumi, emphasized its support of the 1945 Constitution, but insisted that the Djakarta Charter must be part of it.

63 See Djuanda's replies to questions in Parliament in Ministry of Information, *Kembali ke Undang-Undang Dasar 1945*, pp. 82, 129. One of Djuanda's carefully drafted points was that "on the basis of [the 'obligation' clause in the Djakarta Charter] laws can be made for the adherents of Islam which can be brought into line with the Islamic Sjariah."

64 See the speech by H. Saifuddin Zuhri in Ministry of Information, *Inti Sari Pidato*, pp. 43-46; see also *Suluh Indonesia*, May 6, 1959. Article 29 said: (1) The State shall be based upon Belief in the One, Supreme God. (2) The State shall guarantee freedom to every resident to adhere to his respective religion and to perform his religious duties in conformity with that religion and that faith. (Department of Information translation, in *The Indonesian Revolution: Basic Documents and the Idea of Guided Democracy* [Djakarta, 1960?], a very useful collection, with comments on the origins of the documents included.)

65 See *Sin Po*, May 6; *Suluh Indonesia*, May 13, 1959.

giving it legal force.[66] Thus within a short time the Constituent Assembly was back on familiar ground debating the great issues of ideology, while the 1945 Constitution's two-thirds majority melted away into improbability.

The Government became frantic when it realized this, and Djuanda rushed to Bandung to cajole, discuss, and argue with NU leaders. But on May 12th Zainul Arifin, joining the tide that he had been unable to stem, presented the definitive party stand in the Constituent Assembly. Rejecting the notion that the Djakarta Charter was merely an historical document, Zainul argued on the contrary that it was the prime document, the very source of the fundamental norms of the state. He proposed that the Djakarta Charter be incorporated into the Bandung Charter — the already drafted instrument of promulgation of the 1945 Constitution — and made binding for the government in the creation of new law.[67] This was too much for secular groups to accept. On May 21st Djuanda replied to questions raised during the debates, going as far as he believed possible in offering concessions to Islam.[68] He went about a fourth of the way to meeting Zainul Arifin's demands by agreeing to incorporate the Djakarta Charter in full into the Bandung Charter, but without the dictum that it

---

66 The official translation of the Djakarta Charter puts the pertinent clause this way: "the structure of Indonesia's National Independence shall be formulated in a Fundamental Law of the Indonesian State which shall have the structural state form of a Republic of Indonesia with sovereignty of the People, and which shall be based upon: *Belief in God, with the obligation of practising the laws of Islam for the adherents of that religion.*" See Ministry of Information, *The Indonesian Revolution: Basic Documents*, p. 54. The precise meaning of this clause has been argued. The original Indonesian (*dengan kewadjiban mendjalankan sjari'at Islam bagi pemeluk-pemeluknja*) seems to imply that the obligation is encumbent upon each Moslem himself; thus, as most non-Islamic party leaders argued, it was moral and unenforceable. Islamic leaders assumed, on the other hand, that the obligation must be enforced by the state, so that a closer translation of the clause as they understood it would be: "with the obligation to apply the *sjari'at* to the adherents of Islam."

67 *Abadi*, May 13, 14, 15, 1959. Ministry of Information, *Inti Sari Pidato*, pp. 134-135. Actually this may have been intended as a subtle compromise; for the 1945 Constitution would not have to be amended, and the Bandung Charter could later be relegated to a position of symbolic significance. But Zainul's "fundamental norm" notion worried secular groups.

68 See Notosoetardjo, *Kembali kepada Djiwa Proklamasi 1945*, pp. 324-382, for Djuanda's speech; also *Pedoman*, May 22; *Sin Po*, May 21; *Pos Indonesia*, May 21, 1959. As in Parliament, Djuanda dealt with a broad range of questions posed by the Konstituante members, including those concerned with Guided Democracy, Hatta — with respect to whom Djuanda said that it was well known that the Government had done all it could to bring Hatta back into the government, but without success — and the past difficulties of the government. He assured the members that the Government was determined to restore the 1945 Constitution by constitutional means, and that it had never considered simply decreeing the early constitution into effect. It was a moderate speech, but a firm one.

284 THE TRANSITION TO GUIDED DEMOCRACY: INDONESIAN POLITICS, 1957-1959

must comprise the fundamental source of law in the state.[69] This symbolic gesture did not satisfy Islamic leaders, who continued during the second round of debates, on May 25-26, to demand substantive significance for the Djakarta Charter.

By this time the ideological issue had precedence over all others, and the daily press was filled with the contending arguments and a feverish counting of likely votes. Immense pressure was brought to bear on NU, which the pro-Government press accused of giving in to Masjumi and of defaulting on Idham's commitment to the cabinet.[70] Outside the Assembly, IPKI, at this time working quite closely with a number of army officers, concluded a party conference in Lembang with the threat that if the Konstituante did not accept the 1945 Constitution IPKI would take revolutionary steps — i.e., it would approach the President and the army to urge abolition of the Konstituante and the decreeing of the 1945 Constitution into effect.[71] While Masjumi leaders rushed about stiffening the Islamic line before the voting began on May 29th, Nasution called yet another military conference to decide what measures should be taken in the event of an impasse in the Constituent Assembly.[72] Djuanda sent out a call to Idham, who had just returned from Mecca, to hurry to Bandung to corral his party. But Idham could do nothing. On May 27th, Djuanda delivered another and very strongly worded plea to the Constituent Assembly. Before a tense overflow crowd, he warned that unless the 1945 Constitution were accepted, the nation faced grave possibilities: that the

---

69 See *Sin Po*, May 21, 1959, for the new draft of the Bandung Charter. Konstituante decisions on the territory of the state, the flag, national language, national anthem, and a few other matters were also to be incorporated into the Bandung Charter in an attempt to assuage the anger of those who felt that the Konstituante was being treated shoddily.

70 See, e.g., *Sin Po*, May 19, 28, 29, 1959.

71 *Pedoman*, May 25; *Sin Po*, May 23, 1959; see also *Pesat*, XV, no. 22 (May 30, 1959). The IPKI conference decisions made the headlines just before the second round of debates began in the Konstituante and were played up in the pro-Government press as a warning to NU, whose leaders were worrying quite a lot about what would happen to them if the party voted against the 1945 Constitution.

At the IPKI conference Dr. Gunawan was elected party chairman and Soegirman first vice-chairman. Less a party than a collection of men with old army ties and no structured program, IPKI was vehemently anti-Communist and, so to speak, pro-army. To some extent, army leaders used it as a vehicle for initiating new political moves, with the result that it began to play a more important role in Djakarta politics. Soegirman, a Djakarta building contractor and an old friend of Nasution, though the two men were no longer extremely close, was especially active politically during these months.

72 *Pos Indonesia, Bintang Timur, Sin Po*, May 29, 1959.

cabinet would resign, with nothing better in sight; that Parliament might be dissolved, with elections unlikely to be held; that even if Parliament continued, relations between it and the Government would suffer because of the Konstituante tensions; and, finally, that under these conditions Indonesia might have the same experience as "several neighboring states" — again the threat of a coup — which no lover of democracy wanted.[73] The speech had an impressive impact on the audience. Kiaji Masjkur of NU stood up immediately afterwards and shook hands with Djuanda and the other ministers present at the podium, causing some confusion as to whether this meant NU would or would not support the 1945 Constitution. The Constituent Assembly parties held hurried caucuses the same night, NU being the first to do so. But the hope that NU might yet swing around under pressure proved groundless when the voting began two days later.

Following a long hassle on procedure, in which the pro-1945 parties dominated by simple majority, the Konstituante decided to vote first on an amendment proposal by NU, supported by Masjumi and the other Islamic parties, that the Djakarta Charter be incorporated as the preamble and into the body of the constitution. Thereafter three votes would be taken on the constitution, the hope being that this would offer NU members time to change their minds.[74] On the night of the 29th, however, when the Islamic proposal was before the Assembly, Wahab Chasbullah made an emotional appeal to the Konstituante that the amendment was not much to ask, but it was the minimum that Islamic groups could accept. If it were rejected, he warned, the Islamic bloc would vote against the 1945 Constitution 100 per cent, even should that mean "inviting a military junta, if that is really what is desired."[75] But the amendment was still defeated, 265 against 201, and this, for all practical purposes, sealed the fate of the 1945 Constitution in the Constituent Assembly. On the next day, in the

---

73 *Pos Indonesia, Sin Po*, May 28, 1959.
74 For the best discussion of procedural maneuvers in the Konstituante before the balloting, see *Pesat*, XV, no. 23 (June 6, 1959), 3-6. See also Ministry of Information, special issue 57, *Keterangan Pemerintah tentang penjelesaian andjuran Presiden/Pemerintah untuk kembali kepada Undang-Undang Dasar 1945* (Djuanda's report to Parliament on July 6; Djakarta, 1959).
75 *Pos Indonesia, Sin Po*, May 30, 1959. Possibly, Masjumi joined in sponsoring the amendment proposal in the realization that it would be defeated, and that this would make certain the rejection of the 1945 Constitution. See *Pesat*, cited *supra*, n. 74, p. 5.

286 THE TRANSITION TO GUIDED DEMOCRACY: INDONESIAN POLITICS, 1957-1959

packed and excited hall, the first vote was taken on the Constitution: 269 were in favor, 199 opposed, the two-thirds majority nowhere in sight.[76] The vote was made an open one, in the hope that NU members would be too fearful of retaliation to cast their ballots against the Government. This strategy having failed, the second vote, on June 1st, was closed, so that NU could turn under the cover of secrecy. The result was even worse; 264 in favor, 204 opposed. On June 2nd the last vote was public again: 263 supported the 1945 Constitution, 203 opposed it, and two abstained.[77] All last minute efforts to reverse the NU stand had failed.

Following this final vote, a proposal by the GPPS, IPKI, Murba, and the PKI to dissolve the Constituent Assembly was turned down, and by acclamation it was decided to recess for a few weeks.[78] Wilopo said that discussions would be held with the Government concerning future sessions, but although some members, particularly from Masjumi and NU, believed that the Konstituante would go on to complete its work, many others doubted that it would ever meet again. Before the members departed for home within the next few days, Masjumi took the initiative in getting an agreement among the Islamic parties that they would stick together, whatever the consequences, to continue the Islamic struggle. But Masjumi alone left the session feeling victorious in the defense of principle, secure in the knowledge that the next step was up to the Government. NU leaders, fearful of their political future, called for renewed efforts to seek a compromise; and Idham, admitting to some strain in his relations with the Government and with his own party, publicly denied that he would resign the leadership of NU.[79]

The outcome of the Constituent Assembly debates created a new and delicate situation. With the failure of the constitutional solution, the supporters of the return to 1945 were faced with the alternatives of extra-constitutionalism or defeat. This was a particularly painful choice for the

---

76 *Pos Indonesia, Sin Po,* May 30, 1959.
77 *Suluh Indonesia, Pedoman,* June 3, 1959.
78 *Suluh Indonesia,* June 3, 1959. The PKI was more conservative in its language than the GPPS, IPKI, and Murba, each of which demanded outright that the Konstituante abolish itself in view of its failure to break the impasse. Anwar Sanusi said that the PKI still wanted to restore the 1945 Constitution by constitutional means, but if the two contending sides continued to face one another off, there would be no other choice than abolition of the Konstituante.
79 *Abadi,* June 3, 1959.

parties, whose ambivalence was obvious during much of June. On the one hand they did not want to see the elected assembly ignored, because of the precedent this would create, but on the other hand this was a secondary political consideration for those fully committed to Soekarno's program. Although the PNI was at first relatively uncertain and cautious, the PKI joined others on the radical nationalist left in demanding popular action to retrieve the 1945 Constitution, arguing that it had been approved by a majority of the Konstituante and that this was enough to make it valid, procedural niceties notwithstanding.[80] Against this, the PSI for one protested that to foresake constitutional procedures would open up a pandora's box in which would be found, among other evils, the isolation of the Islamic parties to the advantage of the PKI; moreover, it would wreck any chance of achieving the political stability which had been hoped from the return to the 1945 Constitution, and the political tension that must result would hardly guarantee a return to the spirit of 1945.[81]

There was really no question, however, of the Government, Soekarno, and army leaders bowing stoically to the setback. Quite apart from the momentum the return to 1945 campaign had achieved and the fact that Soekarno's prestige was at stake, the factors at work in producing the compromise of February still obtained, and the decision to submit the matter to the Constituent Assembly was one even then of discretion. The cabinet, army officers, and acting President Sartono continued to speak of the return to 1945 as the only effective answer to national decline. But there was no immediate consensus on how to get around the impasse. Roeslan and Djuanda tortuously denied that the Assembly

---

80 See *Harian Rakjat, Pemuda, Bintang Timur, Sin Po,* June 1, 1959. But see also *Bintang Timur,* June 4, for the view that despite its deficiencies the Konstituante was an elected body and that its fate ought not to be considered too quickly or lightly. PKI leaders, despite their surface radicalism, took the same view. Apart from the precedent abolition of the Konstituante might set, there was also the consideration that the PKI, as well as other parties, did not want the result of past deliberations forgotten, especially with respect to constitutional guarantees of civil and political rights.

81 *Pedoman,* June 3, 1959. *Pedoman* and similarly inclined journals called for a careful reconsideration of the entire 1945 Constitution issue with calm and concern for legality. Masjumi continued to hold the Konstituante up as the apotheosis of democracy in action, proposing that the only course to follow, once the Konstituante had made its decision, was for the cabinet to resign, so that the Government could set about dealing with pressing economic problems. *Abadi,* June 6, 1959. Masjumi leaders realized, however, that this was unlikely to happen, and few other parties considered the idea seriously.

had actually rejected all of the President's proposal, Roeslan warning that the consequences of such a view were too inimical to contemplate.[82] With Soekarno away, however, the Government, not having made plans to cover all eventualities, was unable to do much more than discuss the problem and counsel calm. Following the first vote in the Konstituante, Roeslan had flown to report to Soekarno, who made it clear that even in this situation he would not cut his trip short and so would not be back in Djakarta before the end of June.[83]

Meanwhile the army assumed control of events. As had apparently been decided a few days earlier at the army conference, on June 3rd Nasution slapped a formidable prohibition on all political activities, partly to prevent frayed political tempers from bursting out into violence but primarily in order to freeze the situation.[84] Political organizations were not outlawed — as the PKI was quick to emphasize — but all political meetings were banned, the parties were enjoined from ideological propaganda of any kind and from discussing the pros and cons of the return to 1945, religious leaders were ordered to keep their sermons religious, and although Parliament was permitted to sit, the press was told to be selective in reporting its debates.[85] Constituent Assembly members

---

82 *Pos Indonesia*, June 3; *Suluh Indonesia*, June 8, 1959. Roeslan offered the argument that since a two-thirds vote was necessary to reject the 1945 Constitution, it could not be said to have been rejected. This statement was given while Roeslan was in Manila. Djuanda restricted himself to saying that the Konstituante action was not the final end of the matter.

83 The Government and Roeslan were reluctant to ask Soekarno to come back, feeling that he was not yet prepared to do so. From Hollywood Soekarno let it be known that if he had thought the situation at home was urgent he would not have left in the first place. There was still much time, said his aide, to discuss the return to 1945 when he returned (*PIA*, June 4, 1959). On June 6th Soekarno arrived in Tokyo, to stay until the 20th, the first four days being an official visit. It was in Tokyo that he received most reports from Djakarta and made his decisions about what to do on his return. From Tokyo he was to go to Cambodia. Many felt strongly that Soekarno ought to return quickly. See *Trompet Masjarakat*, June 3. The PNI paper, *Suluh Indonesia*, June 2, objected to various ministers being abroad and away from their offices at this critical time.

84 The threat of violence was real, particularly in Bandung, where local and area PKI and Masjumi youth groups had moved into the city during the final stages of the Konstituante debates. Col. Kosasih, commandant of West Java, ordered posters put up by the PKI to be torn down, both in order to prevent the GPII (Masjumi youth organization) from doing so and also to try and deter the PKI from taking any initiative in post-Konstituante developments. There were frequent warnings from the Government about permitting tensions to get out of hand. Before he left for a conference on cooperatives in Sweden, Hatta advised the nation to keep a cool head in the tense conditions following the Konstituante session (*Sin Po*, June 7, 1959).

85 Major Harsono, army information officer, stated that party newspapers were forbidden to discuss ideological matters, whether Marxism-Leninism, Islam — as a political ideology, not as a religion, it was carefully explained — or the Pantjasila. *Pedoman*, *Sin Po*, June 4, 1959. But in fact the

left Bandung on the warning that to remain there might be construed as political activity. Press restrictions were tightened. Djuanda said that Nasution had acted with the Government's knowledge; and the parties ordered their ranks to comply fully with the regulation.[86] The drastic measure was greeted with some approval, even by a few party leaders, for it did have the effect of slightly relieving tension; but it also encouraged new speculation, already rife, about a coup.

Many people had half expected army leaders to choose this time for a coup, and within Masjumi, the PSI, IPKI, and related regional groups sentiment was growing that this might be a welcome development in that it would force a rapid showdown with the PKI and swing the pendulum back to the right.[87]

The fact that several officers, particularly in the regions, had given assurances that no harm would befall the Islamic parties, combined with the anti-PKI bent of the officer corps, daily in evidence, increasingly encouraged right-wing groups to see their future as dependent upon the army. But as before, the officer corps remained divided on political issues of the highest magnitude — the position of Soekarno most of all — and Nasution himself was reluctant even to consider taking over the

---

Pantjasila was tacitly excepted, and Nasution himself continued to praise it as the best of all ideologies, for example on Pantjasila Day (*Suluh Indonesia*, June 8).

86 *Duta Masjarakat*, June 3; *Suluh Indonesia*, June 6; *Bintang Timur*, June 9, 1959. On the Central Military Authority Regulation, see *Pos Indonesia*, June 3; *Pesat*, XV, no. 24 (June 13, 1959), 3; *Himpunan Lembaran Penguasa Perang Pusat* (Gazette of the Central Military Authority), no. 24, 1959, for the full text. In the elucidation of this regulation, it was stated that "the Army Chief-of-Staff is aware that the provisional constitution guarantees basic rights, the freedom of a person to embrace an ideology, to choose a political line of thought [*aliran*], to become a member of a political party, and to undertake political activities. But in connection with the debates in the Konstituante on the return to the 1945 Constitution, it is clear that those political activities have had undesirable effects on public order and security, for there were intimidations and threats."

87 Whereas the PKI frequently and anxiously denied that army leaders wanted a coup, several Masjumi editorials during June hinted at the possibility of a coup in terms that were not entirely unfavorable. See *Abadi*, June 5, 6. Later in the month, partly in reaction to the (sometimes fulsome) praise that was being heaped on Soekarno and the Government's tendency to put everything in Soekarno's hands, *Abadi* ran a long editorial on June 23, the anniversary of Napoleon's fall from power, which *Abadi* ascribed to his deviation — albeit with a desire to save France — from the constitution. See also *Surabaja Post* and *Suara Rakjat*, June 1, for comments on the possibility of a coup. *Suara Rakjat* doubted that there would be a coup but eschewed prediction: "So far as we are concerned, be it a military government or parliamentary government, it will not be objectionable provided it consists of good, capable men." (USIS Surabaja Press Summary.) Few, however, were convinced that a military government would necessarily bring vast improvements, though many were satisfied that it would at least reduce the power of the PKI and restrict Soekarno.

government. In Soekarno's absence, however, Nasution was prepared to maintain a tight grip on all developments, to keep the parties caged up, to make it impossible not to adopt the 1945 Constitution, and to put the army in a position of great influence in the Government that would follow. In response to the undercurrent of coup scare during June, army officers reiterated their support of Soekarno — the captain of the ship, one announcement called him — and of the return to 1945.[88]

Under the surface calm enforced by the ban on political activities, Nasution stepped into the breach to rescue the 1945 Constitution, maintaining the year-long army initiative in this quest. As soon as the Konstituante stalled, he turned to the alternative of forcing Soekarno to decree the constitution into effect. The possibility of a decree had been mentioned by pro-Government groups during the debates, and the PKI seemed on the verge of starting a campaign to that end when all political activities were banned.[89] But Nasution was apparently determined that the army should take the credit and reap the political benefit of pushing the 1945 Constitution through. Within the officer corps, opinion in favor of a decree was rapidly built up. On June 3rd, a day after the Constituent Assembly recessed, the Military-Youth Cooperation Body resolved that Soekarno should resort to a decree, and on the same day an Inter-Generation of '45 Action Committee, of which Brig. Gen. Soengkono was a prominent member, cabled Soekarno to the same effect.[90] A few days later, probably on his own initiative, Brig. Gen. Djatikusumo declared in Singapore that the time had come to stop fooling around and, for the sake of political stability, to decree the 1945 Constitution into effect.[91] In early

---

88 See *Suluh Indonesia*, June 4, 6, 13, 1959. See also *Pos Indonesia*, June 14, 1959, for a statement by Col. Jani in Karachi that the army did not intend a coup.

89 The alternative of using a decree had been mentioned as early as April by Soedarisman Poerwokoesoemo, the PNI mayor of Jogjakarta. See his articles in *Pesat*, XV, no. 16 (April 18, 1959), 10-12, and *Mimbar Indonesia*, XIII, no. 22/23 (June 3, 1959), 3-6. Like many others, Soedarisman had praised the Government's decision to restore the 1945 Constitution by constitutional procedures but then saw no alternative but a decree when the Konstituante bogged down. The June seminar on the 1945 Constitution held in Jogjakarta also suggested that a decree be used following the Konstituante decision.

90 See *B.K.S.-P.M. Menjongsong Kembali ke U.U.D. '45* (The Military-Youth Cooperation Body Supports the Return to the Constitution of '45; published in Djakarta by the executive board of the PKS-PM, 1959), pp. 156-167. The cable was sent before the third vote in the Konstituante. See also *Suluh Indonesia*, June 3, 1959.

91 *Suluh Indonesia*, June 8, 1959.

June, Nasution and Deputy Chief-of-Staff Gatot Soebroto held talks with party leaders to win their backing for this course.

They did not have a great deal of difficulty in convincing the parties. Masjumi of course did not approve the idea and, with the failing enthusiasm of a lost cause, continued to speak of the Constituent Assembly as the place to decide all constitutional issues. But NU leaders looked upon a decree as an admirable solution to their problems, for it would rescue them from another round in the Konstituante. Just after the vote in the Assembly, Wahab Chasbullah himself had suggested that two courses of action were possible — a military junta or a decree — making NU one of the earliest parties to mention a decree.[92] Having served its obligation to defend Islam in the Konstituante, NU, by supporting a decree, could still hope to retain a place in the Government, thus enjoying the best of both worlds.[93] Idham was advised by Djuanda and Nasution to say nothing more for the duration about the Konstituante debacle or the Islamic issue, and in this NU leaders complied, concentrating their attention on the future cabinet. As for the PNI and the PKI, both were already agreed in principle on abandoning the Constituent Assembly, for they had to continue to support the 1945 Constitution. Moreover, they may have

---

92 *Duta Masjarakat*, June 1, 1959. *Harian Rakjat*, June 3, commented on Wahab's remark in an editorial entitled "Is NU's Rois Aam Proposing a Way Out?" It stated that Wahab must prefer a presidential decree to a military junta, and then said that a decree by the President would be a responsible and constitutional action.

93 The agreement forged by Masjumi among the Islamic parties after the Konstituante debates was ignored both by NU and the PSII. Some in Masjumi had feared this would happen. As one Masjumi leader told me: "Masjumi was able to keep NU in line on the return to the 1945 issue despite the position of its leadership. But then when the Konstituante recessed, the NU people got back to Djakarta and were influenced by the situation there; and so they finally agreed to work in the Cabinet...Masjumi wanted to keep all the Islamic groups in Bandung pending settlement of the whole conflict, knowing that...in Bandung it was easy to keep the spirit of the fight up...but not when the groups dispersed" (conversation of Oct. 22, 1961).

Not all NU members were aware of the situation that was developing. One leader of NU who had opposed Idham's commitment to the cabinet explained: "the party council was kept completely in the dark about what was happening in the cabinet [from February through May] and about what the Government's thinking was on the issue of the return to 1945...The NU ministers didn't fully report on the matter to the party, with the result that it made very serious miscalculations in dealing with the issue later on. [That is to say, this informant miscalculated and damaged his position on the party council.] I myself completely misjudged how the Government would react if a two-thirds vote were not given to the 1945 Constitution by the Konstituante. I assumed, like many others, especially in Masjumi, that if the issue failed, then the Konstituante would simply go on and finish its work, or at most that there would be a new Konstituante election. But I certainly didn't expect the Konstituante to be abolished" (conversation of Oct. 26, 1961).

feared that unless the 1945 Constitution were soon put into effect, a coup would be in the offing. None of the parties wanted to resort to extra-constitutional means, but by this time the greater misgivings of the PKI and the PNI arose from the fact that Nasution was firmly in the driver's seat, preventing them from establishing their own claims to benefit from the return to 1945. On June 16th, Suwirjo hurriedly cabled Soekarno expressing PNI support for abolishing the Konstituante, decreeing the 1945 Constitution into effect, and forming a presidential cabinet.[94] Fearing that the PNI would grab an advantage and that NU regional leaders might be roused to oppose a decree, NU protested, and no further cables to the president were countenanced by the martial law authority.[95] In any event, by mid-June Nasution had the assurances of the PNI, NU, and the PKI that they would not oppose a decree.

A proper formula was needed to justify a major deviation from the existing constitution, and Nasution was again instrumental in finding one. Emergency conditions would serve to satisfy the legal requirements of a decree, but dispensing with the Konstituante was more delicate. In some furtive political byplay, in which IPKI played a superficially key role, Nasution helped to work out the idea that if a majority of Constituent Assembly members refused to convene, the Assembly would automatically cease to exist. In mid-June IPKI organized a Front for the Defense of the Pantjasila (Front Pembela Pantjasila) consisting of 17 minor parties which would decline to meet again in the Assembly.[96] IPKI vice-chairman Soegirman was able to convince Suwirjo and Aidit to sign a resolution to this effect only with some difficulty; it is likely that they did not enjoy IPKI's getting such a jump on them, but they could hardly refuse to support the Pantjasila and the return to 1945. Both the PNI and the PKI later declared that they would attend the Constituent Assembly only to vote for its dissolution, but that proved unnecessary.

---

94 *Pos Indonesia*, June 18, 1959.
95 *Duta Masjarakat*, June 19, 1959. Army information officer, Major Harsono, stated at first that Suwirjo's cable did not violate the ban on political activities because it was constructive, not destructive. *Sin Po*, June 20. The next day, however, Harsono told the press that no more cables should be sent, because they would give rise to "various interpretations." *Sin Po*, June 21.
96 Most of this information comes from an interview with the IPKI leader, Soegirman, on July 27, 1960.

On June 15th, the cabinet advised Soekarno, still abroad, of three alternative plans of action, one of which was to use a decree.[97] Though noncommittal at first, perhaps for tactical reasons, the President soon indicated that this was the course he would follow. Roeslan told the press that Soekarno was determined on the return to 1945 and that the Government and the President were agreed on the way to achieve this.[98] Indeed, even had Soekarno come to another conclusion, by late June Djakarta had become, as some put it, "decree minded."

While he was away, Soekarno's position was greatly strengthened, for all attention and political maneuvers were focused intently upon his return. Pro-Government parties — including the PNI, the PKI, Partindo, and Murba — took the view, amidst renewed professions of loyalty, that everything was now up to him, and even the hostile press agreed that the determining role was his. Acting President Sartono and ministers of the cabinet called upon the people to await Soekarno's command, assuring them that he would be able to overcome all difficulties.[99] Most important, the army waited for Soekarno, Nasution and other officers reiterating time and again their loyalty and obedience to the President/ Commander-in-Chief. But it is clear that Soekarno was deeply concerned over the role being played by Nasution, and many of the reports which he received from Djakarta sources probably stressed the danger of the position of personal power which Nasution seemed to be developing for himself. In the third week of June, Col. Djuhartono was sent to deliver a message to the President, provoking rumors, first reported in foreign newspapers, that Nasution had proposed a military government with

---

97 It is not clear what the others were, but they may have involved either reshuffling the cabinet or returning the 1945 Constitution proposal to the Konstituante for further consideration. In Jogjakarta on June 13, vice-premier Hardi stated that the cabinet was still committed to carrying out Guided Democracy within the framework of a return to the 1945 Constitution, and that there was another means of accomplishing this than the Konstituante. *Pos Indonesia*, June 14, 1959. By this time both the PNI and NU were agreed to a decree. See also *Sin Po*, June 20; *Suluh Indonesia*, June 20, 1959. On June 20, Djuanda told the press that Soekarno had not yet made his intentions clear. *Pos Indonesia*, June 21, 1959.

98 *Suluh Indonesia*, June 23, 26, 1959.

99 *Suluh Indonesia*, June 10; *Bintang Timur*, June 26, 1959. As acting president, and as a political leader of considerable prestige himself, Sartono took part in Government discussions on post-Konstituante policy and took the initiative in consulting with party leaders about their positions.

himself as premier.[100] Army headquarters denied this, but whatever the case Soekarno came back to Djakarta with profound misgivings about Nasution's strength.

Soekarno was to return on June 29th. In celebration of his homecoming, the army ordered flags flown for ten days and prescribed the slogans and cheers to be used in greeting him, including "Long Live the Proclamation and the Constitution of 1945" and "Bung Karno, Act Firmly."[101] At the same time, Nasution called another conference of all military commanders to begin on the 29th, confronting Soekarno with a united army front favoring the 1945 Constitution and providing Nasution with an effective platform from which to negotiate in the formation of a new Government. Soekarno arrived that evening, amidst great fanfare. He stated that he would have a major announcement to make in a few days. He also declared that he did not intend to become a dictator; he had proved that, said Soekarno, in an obvious swipe at Nasution, in October 1952 — i.e., when Nasution had tried to force him to assume greater executive powers.[102] But it must have seemed both to Soekarno and Nasution that the latter had finally achieved the goals of the October 17th Affair.

On July 2nd, Soekarno resumed the presidency, and on the 3rd he informed the cabinet that he would promulgate the 1945 Constitution by decree. On July 5th, in front of the Djakarta Palace, Soekarno read a proclamation which abolished the Konstituante, decreed the 1945 Constitution into effect, and promised that the institutions of that constitution would be formed in the shortest possible time. In the considerations of the proclamation, Soekarno indicated that because most of the members of the Constituent Assembly refused to convene again it could not complete its work. The Djakarta Charter was said to inspire the constitution of 1945 and to make up, with the constitution,

---

100 *Sin Po*, June 22; *Pedoman*, June 23, 1959. Col. Djuhartono was sent, according to official reports, not as an army courier, but as a Government courier. Roeslan, in Hongkong after leaving the President in Tokyo, also said that Djuhartono had not discussed a military government with Soekarno. *Pos Indonesia*, June 24, 1959. Nasution sent his own reports to Soekarno.

101 *Pos Indonesia*, June 25, 1959. The designation of proper slogans and cheers was a relatively new phenomenon which served as an excellent means of forming and channelling public opinion. It also allowed the army to keep control over public demonstrations, particularly those sponsored by the PKI, for whom demonstrations were an important political tool.

102 Notosoetardjo, *Kembali kepada Djiwa Proklamasi 1945*, pp. 585-590; *Pos Indonesia*, June 30, 1959.

one whole; but this bow to Islam did not change the constitution.[103]

On July 6th, after more than two years as Prime Minister — longer than any other man had held that office — Djuanda returned the Kabinet Karya's mandate to Soekarno and then delivered his final report to Parliament, thanking it and begging forgiveness for all faults.[104] Meanwhile, the negotiations leading to a new cabinet had already begun.

The general reaction to the decree was one of acceptance of the inevitable. Most people believed it to be for the best, hoping that a new Government under the revolutionary constitution would show a perceptible improvement and that a new and clean sheet of history would be begun. But optimism was guarded pending results. Of the parties, most were prepared to accept this formal mark of the passing of the parliamentary system. Among the opposition parties there were some who said that they would be willing to give Soekarno whatever help they could to refashion the nation. Masjumi leaders, however, feared that the end of their party was in sight.

The New Government and the Developing System

Soekarno promised a cabinet chosen for the sake of efficiency, effectiveness, and capacity to deal with national problems. There would be no more lengthy cabinet crises as in the past and, as an indication that national and not narrow political interests would determine the makeup of the Government, Soekarno publicly eschewed hearings with the political parties. He succeeded in producing a new cabinet four days after the decree, but, admitting that all was not apolitical, he said that the cabinet represented the maximum that could be achieved at the time.[105]

This was the inescapable limitation which bound Soekarno: in his new position of responsibility under the revolutionary constitution he faced political forces no less powerful and persistent than those which had plagued every government in the past. To deal with these forces, Soekarno

---

103 The text of the decree can be found in *B.K.S.-P.M. Menjongsong Kembali ke U.U.D. '45*, p. 185, and numerous other publications.
104 See Ministry of Information, *Keterangan Pemerintah tentang Penjelesaian Andjuran Presiden/ Pemerintah*.
105 *Bintang Timur*, July 13, 1959.

had his own considerable stature and political skill and was aided by the natural balance of competing groups; but this did not permit him a great deal of leeway. The possibility of political innovation was defined by the groups then existing. No new organization suddenly appeared with the new constitution to embody and drive forward the program of Guided Democracy. Compelled to work with what there was, Soekarno could not avoid a perpetual struggle for positional advantage.

His foremost concern was the army. It was not that Nasution was ambitious to succeed to the presidency; rather, Soekarno seems to have feared that the Chief-of-Staff was designing to become the power behind the presidency. Soekarno's personal influence over Nasution was quite limited, in a social-political structure that depended to an important extent upon personal relationships. The army had been forcing the situation since 1957. It was largely responsible for bringing about the transformation of the political system, and now maintained a degree of control over the country that seriously restricted Soekarno's freedom of political leadership. The resulting tension was compounded by frequent differences of view between Soekarno and army leaders, particularly with respect to the PKI. Following the establishment of the new government in mid-1959, Soekarno concentrated on breaking out of the confining net held by the army. He set out to restore the balance between it and other groups, to divide the officer corps, and to weaken Nasution. Within a few years he was to achieve remarkable success in these efforts, but it was always limited and the army remained the chief political force with which he had to contend. If Nasution's ambitions were limited, he was not prepared to relinquish them such as they were, and particularly during the next two years he wielded great power. The net result was a pattern of negotiation between the General Staff and Soekarno in which a mutually unsatisfactory outcome had almost always to be expected.

In the negotiations to form a new cabinet, Soekarno tried directly to weaken Nasution and, perhaps, to set him up for a hard fall later. He proposed that Nasution enter the cabinet and resign his post as Chief-of-Staff of the army, possibly in the hope of having a hand in choosing a new Chief-of-Staff. This Nasution declined to do, stating publicly that he would obey the Commander-in-Chief but that he wanted to remain in the army.[106] The General Staff and regional commanders supported him. Soekarno backed down, but Nasution agreed to become Minister of Defense and Security while retaining his command. This was the point of greatest tension in the cabinet negotiations, and Nasution's strength vis-a-vis Soekarno was evident. The officer corps also made it clear at this time that they would brook no civilian interference in the selection of army leaders.

Nasution's role in selecting the new cabinet was considerable, this being the first major opportunity to tread the "middle-way" at a high level. Several other military officers were appointed to cabinet positions. In addition Nasution's judgment influenced the choice of other members whom army leaders trusted; thus IPKI won a larger role. Although Soekarno had his way in appointing a number of left-wing ministers, Nasution successfully opposed the appointment of Communists to the cabinet.

Soekarno was to head the new presidential cabinet.[107] Following the cabinet decision of February, this had been a matter of concern to some, for government leaders (including Soekarno) felt that the burden might be too onerous for the President, who abhorred administrative detail. Consequently it was decided to appoint a First Minister who would handle the daily tasks of cabinet direction. The natural choice for this position was Djuanda, who retained the respect of Soekarno and Nasution and was less objectionable to others in the Government than anyone else equally capable. Actually his functions did not differ greatly from what they had been in the Kabinet Karya, for he continued to represent the Government before Parliament and to bear responsibility for putting its program in order. Politically he also continued to serve as a buffer between Soekarno, Nasution, and the various parties and groups pressing upon the Government.

The rest of the cabinet was organized in a new style approximating staff and line terms; presumably Nasution's influence was felt in this innovation too. The cabinet consisted of nine core ministers (*menteri inti*) each responsible for coordinating several junior ministers (*menteri*

---

106 *Pedoman*, July 4, 1959.
107 The terminological confusion surrounding the rapid change to a presidential system was partly responsible for the awkward title "President/Commander-in-Chief/Prime Minister."

muda). In addition, there were seven ex-officio ministers. On July 9th the core ministers were announced. A few more days were needed to fill the other positions.[108] The cabinet was as follows:

Prime Minister	Soekarno
First Minister	Ir. H. Djuanda

Core Ministers

1.	Security and Defense	Lt. Gen. A. H. Nasution
2.	Finance	Ir. H. Djuanda
3.	Production	Col. Suprajogi
4.	Distribution	Dr. J. Leimena
5.	Development	Chaerul Saleh
6.	Foreign Affairs	Dr. Subandrio
7.	Internal Affairs/Regional Autonomy	Ipik Gandamana
8.	People's Welfare	Muljadi Djojomartono
9.	Special Affairs	Mr. Muh. Yamin[109]

---

108 See Notosoetardjo, *Kembali kepada Djiwa Proklamasi 1945*, pp. 11-12; *Pos Indonesia*, July 10; *Suluh Indonesia*, July 11; *Pos Indonesia*, July 12, 1959.

109 Originally Yamin was appointed as Core Minister of Social and Cultural Affairs, in charge of the Ministry of Education and Culture. Minister Prijono protested against this, however — there was some personal animosity between the two men, and the Junior Minister's pride was at stake — and Yamin's Ministry was changed to one without portfolio status.

The junior ministries were arranged as follows under the coordinative and supervisory responsibilities of the core ministries:

First Minister	Security/Defense	Finance	Production
1. Information	1. Defense	1. Finance	1. Agriculture
	2. Justice		2. Public Works & Power
	3. Police		3. Labor
	4. Veterans		

Development	Distribution	People's Welfare
1. Basic Industries	1. Land Communications	1. Health
2. People's Industries	2. Sea Communications	2. Social Affairs
3. Agrarian Affairs	3. Air Communications	3. Religion
4. Transmigration, etc.	4. Trade	

The remaining junior ministers were directly responsible to the Prime Minister.

Junior Ministers

1. Information	Maladi
2. Defense	Maj. Gen. Hidajat
3. Justice	Mr. Sahardjo
4. Police	Sukanto Tjokrodijatmodjo (Chief of State Police)
5. Veterans	Col. Sambas
6. Finance	M. Notohamiprodjo
7. Agriculture	Col. Dr. Aziz Saleh
8. Public Works and Power	Ir. S. Dipokusumo
9. Labor	Ahem Erningpradja
10. Basic Industries/Mines	Chaerul Saleh
11. People's Industries	Dr. Suharto
12. Agrarian Affairs	Mr. Sadjarwo
13. Transmigration, Cooperatives, and Village Development	Lt. Col. (titular) Achmadi
14. Sea Communications	Abdul Mutalib
15. Land Communications (Post and Telecommunications)	Maj. Gen. Djatikusumo
16. Air Communications	Air Col. Iskandar
17. Trade	Arifin Harahap
18. Health	Col. Dr. Satrio
19. Social Affairs	Muljadi Djojomartono
20. Religion	K. H. Wahib Wahab
21. Education and Culture	Prof. Dr. Prijono
22. Mobilization of People's Energies	Sudibjo and Sudjono (co-ministers)
23. Cabinet Liaison with Parliament and the People's Consultative Assembly	W. J. Rumambi
24. Cabinet Liaison with Alim Ulama	K. H. Fatah Jasin

Ministers Ex-Officio

1. Army Chief-of-Staff (Nasution)
2. Navy Chief-of-Staff (Martadinata, late July)
3. Air Force Chief-of-Staff (Suryadarma)
4. Chief of State Police (Sukanto)
5. Chief Prosecutor (Gatot Tarunamihardja)
6. Vice-chairman, High Advisory Council (Roeslan Abdulgani)
7. Chairman, National Planning Council (Yamin)

The cabinet was explicitly non-party, and several ministers resigned from their parties. These included Leimena (Parkindo), Subandrio and Sadjarwo, both of whom had joined the PNI before the cabinet reshuffle of 1958 and had been appointed to the party council, and Ipik Gandamana (IPKI), the former governor of West Java.[110] Of all the ex-party men in the cabinet, however, only Fatah Jasin and Wahib Wahab had been firm party members, and if they resigned from the NU, they nevertheless continued to consider themselves in the party leadership. Clearly the role of the parties in the new cabinet was quite small. The PNI was particularly disappointed in its poor representation; indeed, it was all but ignored, no inner circle PNI leader receiving a post. Ironically, the NU was better treated, because of the necessity to represent Islam. In one sense the new cabinet marked the rise of NU as the chief Islamic party, Masjumi fading into a permanent and weak opposition.

The name of the new cabinet was changed from Kabinet Karya to *Kabinet Kerdja* (work), both qualifiers meaning the same thing; Soekarno said the change was only for the sake of a distinction.[111] He himself determined the Government program, which was a simple and straightforward one of three basic goals: (1) adequate food and clothing for the people,[112] (2) restoration of security, and (3) anti-imperialism —

---

110 *Pos Indonesia*, July 10 and 12, 1959.
111 Notosoetardjo, *Kembali kepada Djiwa Proklamasi 1945*, pp. 621-622.
112 Soekarno used the Javanese term *sandang-pangan* (clothing and food) to describe this item of the program. It bears the broader connotation of all the necessities of life, cheap and in abundance. When he announced the program, Soekarno apologized for using a "regional term." The interesting thing about this is that it illustrates a rather modest attitude on his part during the period of cabinet negotiations and for a few weeks thereafter. He seems to have been quite

including, most importantly, the acquisition of West Irian. Soekarno assumed responsibility for this program, though he hedged somewhat in saying that if it were not fulfilled within two or three years he would consider himself one-half a failure.[113]

The new cabinet was received with a mixture of hope and skepticism. Some regarded its organization optimistically, and the hyperpositive attitudes of several ministers seemed encouraging.[114] In one or two Ministries to which men of well known ability were appointed — Justice, for example — morale definitely picked up with the belief that authority would now at last be given to the technically meritorious. Many were also encouraged by the Government's apparent determination to change work habits, to weed out corruption, and to give efficiency priority. But the inclination of most groups, as so often in the past, was towards a "wait and see" reservation of judgment until results could be observed. Among the politically aware there was no hiding the disappointment aroused by the Kabinet Kerdja. It was obvious that political dickering had played no small role in constructing the cabinet. And there were few new faces; a majority of the key ministers were regarded as political hacks who had been around too long already, and from them little that was novel and imaginative could be expected. A right-wing comment on the cabinet was that it was nondescript. To those on the left it seemed that the make-up of the cabinet was out of character with the return to the spirit of 1945.[115]

Under the 1945 Constitution, Soekarno appointed the new Supreme Advisory Council (Dewan Pertimbangan Agung, DPA) in late July. It was in fact the direct successor to the National Council, whose functions and procedures it inherited. Soekarno remained its chairman, Roeslan its vice-chairman. But there was a vital difference in membership between

---

consciously solicitous of regional, religions, political and other sensitivities. Possibly he was deeply concerned over the great burden of responsibility which he now had to bear, and he was clearly aware of how difficult it would be to lead a Government in the face of so many forces which were beyond his control.

113 *Pos Indonesia*, July 10, 1959.

114 Chaerul Saleh, Leimena, Suprajogi, and Djuanda, for example, won kudos for appearing in their offices hard at work by eight o'clock, and Maladi told journalists that they could call on him at any time before three a.m. at his office. *Suluh Indonesia*, July 23, 1959.

115 See *Bintang Timur*, July 13, 1959. The editorial, noting that both the United States and Britain were pleased with the new cabinet, declared that this was ample indication that the ministers were not sufficiently revolutionary.

the National Council and the DPA. There were ten holdovers from the former (besides Soekarno and Roeslan) in the 46 member DPA.[116] These and a majority of the new members whom Soekarno appointed were on the radical nationalist left. But in addition, unlike the National Council, the top leaders of several parties were chosen by Soekarno to sit in the DPA as representatives of political groups.[117] Soekarno thus had the major party leaders of the nation (except Masjumi) before him, and they for their part were given something of a forum in which to defend their parties' interests. A year later, when the party system was "simplified," only the parties represented in the DPA — the PNI, the PKI, NU, the PSII, Perti, Murba, Partindo, Parkindo, and the Partai Katholik — plus IPKI escaped abolition. The organization of the DPA consisted of three categories of representatives: political groups, regions, and functional groups. Several years later these were to become the basic categories of a new election law.[118]

The National Planning Council was also announced towards the end of July. Yamin was appointed chairman of the 77-member body, which was constituted of regional and functional representatives, with an implicit political representation distributed among them.[119] The Council

---

116 Sukarni, Iwa Kusumasumantri, Tjilik Riwut, Rumage-sang, Moh. Padang, Munir, Sujono Atmo, Rasuna Said, Henk Ngantung, Armunanto.

117 Party representatives were Suwirjo and Manuaba (PNI); Idham Chalid and Saifuddin Zuhri (NU); Aidit and Njoto (PKI); Arudji Kartawinata (PSII); K. H. Rusli Abdulwahid (Perti); Sukarno (Murba); Asmara Hadi (Partindo); Tambunan (Parkindo); Kasimo (Catholics).

118 Regional representatives were: Iwa Kusumasumantri and Dul Arnowo (Java); Tjilik Riwut (Kalimantan); Rumagesang (West Irian); Moh. Padang (Moluccas); Sutetje (Lesser Sundas); Andi Pangerang (Sulawesi); Col. Sjamaun Gaharu (Sumatra). Functional group representatives: Asmu and Bambang Murtioso (Peasants); Munir and Datuk (Labor); Dasaad (National Entrepreneurs); Adam Malik (Generation of '45); Maj. Gen. Gatot Soebroto (Army); Air Commodore Abdurachman (Air Force); Naval Commodore Nazir (Navy); Police Commissioner Jasin (Police); Farid Ma'ruf and Wahab Chasbullah (Alim Ulama); Msgr. Sugiopranoto or Msgr. Patmoseputro (one or the other, Catholics); Wenas (Protestants); Sugriwe (Hindu Bali); Sujono Atmo (Youth); Rasuna Said and Emma Puradiredja (Women); Henk Ngantung (Artists); Armunanto (Journalists); Prof. Djokosoetono and Tumakaka (Intellectuals); Siauw Giok Tjhan (Chinese minority); Prof. Utrecht (Indo-European minority). Several of these members were also associated with political parties. For example, Utrecht belonged to the PNI, Siauw Giok Tjhan was the chairman of Baperki, Sujono Atmo was close to PKI circles; Wahab Chasbullah was an NU leader. Functional groups were never to become completely free of party influence, and to that extent the parties were quite right in questioning whether there was any basis for creating wholly new organizations to represent "functional interests."

119 See Notosoetardjo, Kembali kepada Djiwa Proklamasi 1945, pp. 14-15, for the membership of the National Planning Council. Several former members of the National Council were appointed to the Planning Council. There was also a strong delegation from various universities. The army

encouraged considerable optimism, for it brought together a number of men respected for their technical abilities. It quickly set to work devising a national overall development plan which was to be completed within one year; the speed boded ill for the quality of the plan.

Under the 1945 Constitution, Soekarno was responsible only to the People's Consultative Assembly. He appointed this body on a provisional basis in mid-1960, pending the time, far in the future, when elections would be held. Following the inauguration of the Kabinet Kerdja in July 1959, Soekarno requested the existing Parliament to continue to function under the 1945 Constitution, making such procedural changes as were necessary. Speaker Sartono and party leaders made it clear that they still regarded their Parliament as an important part of the political system. Masjumi particularly emphasized the point that Parliament, with or without elections, remained a legitimate institution; it was the only national governing body in which Masjumi still had a voice.[120] Despite Masjumi's views and the pride of many MP's, however, Parliament — especially without elections — was at the mercy of the executive. For henceforth it was essentially Soekarno who determined which governing institutions would enjoy legitimacy.

Such optimism as the new Government encouraged began to disintegrate in the second half of 1959 as tensions exploded into incidents here and there. The most important conflict centered around efforts to drive the army back and reduce its authority.[121] Against renewed attacks on martial law and the prohibition of political activities, Nasution argued that both were essential to defend the integrity of the Decree of July 5; but the prohibition was partially relaxed on Soekarno's insistence. At the same time, Air Force Chief-of-Staff Suryadarma demanded that Soekarno take direct charge of all the services, making it clear that the air force did not want to be under Minister Nasution. Nasution refused to hear of

---

was well represented, more so from the regions than from functional groups.

120 Within eight months Masjumi was to be outside of Parliament also. The PKI, on the other hand, was now in every major institution of the government except the cabinet.

121 In late July the Chief-of-Staff of the Navy was dismissed, causing some tension in that service also. Admiral Subijakto was relieved of his command partly in connection with the protests of a group of naval fliers based in Surabaja who felt that he had discriminated against them in selection for training abroad. There were other dissatisfactions with the Admiral, who had commanded the navy for a decade. Subijakto was later appointed ambassador to Turkey. His replacement was a younger officer, Martadinata.

this, however, and the matter was soon settled in favor of the status quo; but Soekarno got in a blow by calling the air force the apple of his eye and promising it new equipment. Over Nasution's objections, Soekarno not only made it possible for the PKI to hold its national congress in September 1959 but also personally addressed the meeting. On another score Nasution won: when Chief Prosecutor Gatot Tarunamihardja attempted to prosecute Col. Ibnu Sutowo and Lt. Col. Soekendro, army intelligence chief, for their part in the Tandjung Priok barter of late 1958, the General Staff promptly had Gatot arrested. Gatot was later replaced by a new Chief Prosecutor whom army leaders were instrumental in choosing.

Government policy after July contributed to the decline of public morale. The cabinet had quickly set about devising a program to deal with economic problems, but it was not to achieve significant success. With poor timing so soon after the formation of the new Government, in mid-August an anti-inflationary money-cutting measure was put into effect. Large denomination bills were reduced in value by 90 per cent, and bank holdings were frozen. Ultimately the measure was ineffective, for the volume of money in circulation, which had been reduced by 50 percent, grew rapidly again, partly because of government expenditures. Moreover, those with little money were hurt nearly as much as those with a great deal. Thereafter matters got worse, not better.

The 1945 Constitution institutionalized the power structure which had evolved since 1957, Soekarno and the army having overturned the unsympathetic constitution of 1950. From one point of view, the new political system was only a permanent form of the martial law system, many of whose essential lines had been worked out during the previous two years. But there was still a lengthy period of evolution to come.

The striking aspect of Guided Democracy as it developed after the restoration of the 1945 Constitution was that it contained many political but few institutional controls. For institutions were pulled apart and broken down but poorly reassembled. Increasingly, the political institutions of the state came in formal terms to depend upon Soekarno as keystone. He appointed the members of Parliament, the People's Consultative Assembly, the cabinet, and the DPA, and the higher officials of regional government; and those whom he appointed were naturally obliged to him. Equally important, the changing economic structure of

Indonesia, with a progressive concentration of economic power in the ministries of the state, deprived potentially powerful groups of a base of wealth from which to oppose and control the government. Yet Soekarno himself never acquired an organization capable of executing policy over the obstructions of vested political interests. Consequently only those programs that did not threaten the elite could be attempted seriously, and these frequently were in the realm of foreign affairs. Soekarno moved rapidly into a prime role of ideological articulation and legitimation, and the more he served this role and that of political keystone the more he was depended upon to perform it.

The essential reward of the army within the 1945 Constitution system was the institutionalization of its political role. It no longer depended upon temporary martial law for the right to participate, for as a functional group it belonged permanently in the political order. The threat to the political, social, and economic interests of the army elite therefore receded, though the officer corps remained unwilling to give up the special authority offered by martial law. The gradual absorption of the army elite into the already existing broader national elite rendered it politically somewhat more divisive and vulnerable yet also more moderate. Within the political system, the officer corps tended to become simply another political group competing for the perquisites of governmental authority. Despite its overwhelming physical power, the army lacked a political program and ideology of its own; it therefore sought these within the government, becoming the chief actor in the intense ideological activity which characterized Indonesian politics after 1959.

The party system was a deflated appendage of the new political system. In the conflict of Guided Democracy the parties lost out. The PNI and NU, the two center parties, chose almost from the beginning to collaborate with the evolving order and ended up as weak hangers-on. They obtained quite a lot in the way of honors, prestige, and material rewards but gradually lost their bases of power and had little to contribute to policy innovation. Elections were postponed time and again, but only the PKI and a few leaders of the other parties felt this to be any real loss. The non-Communist parties continued to make organizing motions among the peasantry, labor, and various other groups; in May 1959 the PNI established a new cultural organization (Lembaga Kebudajaan Nasional, National Cultural Institution) to compete — quite unsuccessfully — with the PKI's Lekra. But by and large the leaders of the PNI and NU were, if not completely satisfied, at least willing to live with their positions.

It is an irony of some significance that Guided Democracy petrified most of the parties into precisely the kind of organizations they had been condemned for being earlier. In 1956-1957 the parties were justly accused of being top heavy, their leadership feeling little bound by or concerned with the lower party echelons or the people whom they were supposed to represent. There is some doubt whether the election process would eventually have developed a closer bond between leaders and rank and file, for this would depend also upon a different view of authority emerging among the electorate. But despite the experience of 1955 — which did little to alter the character of the parties — parliamentary elections did threaten the parties with a sanction that might have forced them in time to serve a more representative function. The electoral success of the PKI may be attributable in large part to the fact that it heeded popular interests. In any event, the emergence of Guided Democracy, along with the disappearance of elections as a formal source of political legitimacy, finally turned the parties into bodyless heads, existing largely on the pleasure of an authority over which they had little control. The proof of this point is that the leadership of no party changed appreciably after 1959; no new cadres moved up from the dwindling ranks. The average age of the parties' elites has increased by one year every year.

The same is generally true of the Government. Soekarno, inclined to choose men on the basis of loyalty rather than merit, had more confidence in his ability to control older generation leaders. To some extent, this malady spread even to the army, though the functional hierarchy of military organization kept rather more men moving up than in the civilian polity. The result has been the paradox of a revolutionary ideology being wielded authoritatively by a group of leaders many of whom are approaching 50 and 60 years of age. What is significant in this — for there is no reason why a 50-year-old cannot be a revolutionary — is that the ideology of this generation of Indonesian leaders derives largely from the struggle against colonialism and very often from much older traditional concepts of political authority and responsibility. Under Guided Democracy there was a shift in emphasis from a vaguely defined goal of economic development to one of nation-building, partly because of the difficulty of achieving rapid economic growth. At the same time, this was accompanied by an almost uncontrollable turning back to traditional (and natural) political habits, justified in one way or another by ideology.

This is not to say, however, that the ideology is un-moving in its context or that it does not satisfy felt needs. It does, but primarily in terms of such standards as the glory of the state and the search for an explicit national identity. These standards have been declining in importance for younger leaders — many of whom are as yet politically uninitiated — in part because they are more confident of their own vocational skills than older men who have had little opportunity to become practitioners in anything but politics. The concerns of older generation leaders have been almost entirely political, which helps to explain both their penchant for ideological activity and also the higher political, rather than economic, content of ideology under Guided Democracy.

From much of what has been said above about the decline of the party system the PKI is exempt, for in a sense it kept its feet firmly planted in both systems — the parliamentary and the Guided Democratic. It continued to work feverishly to keep its popular support while adjusting to the requirements of membership in the new structure. Peaceful transition remained the foundation of PKI policy, and in part by retaining Soekarno's favor it stayed alive and powerful. But this also meant giving in to the demands of the new system. The PKI had to accept Soekarno's terms, putting a brake for a while on its own revolutionary drive — which however remained much greater than that of any other group. This was to some extent a debilitating policy for the PKI and caused noticeable internal stress, for by going along with Guided Democracy the party suffered both frustration and, among some followers, a too ready willingness to enjoy the benefits of partial membership in the regime. Nevertheless, the power of the PKI grew steadily.

1959 through 1961 were years of further consolidation for the Government and the forces of Guided Democracy. The peak period of opposition and strain under the new system came in 1960, when the constant threat of the army was temporarily reduced to acceptable proportions. In the following years internal conflict remained insoluble but essentially stable as Indonesia moved into a period whose dominant theme was an intensely active foreign policy.

APPENDIX
THE CONSTITUTION OF 1945*

Preamble

Whereas independence is the right of every nation, therefore colonialism must be abolished from the face of the earth as it is contrary to the dictates of human nature and justice.

And the struggle for Indonesian independence has now reached that glorious moment, having led the Indonesian people safely to the threshold of independence for an Indonesian State which is free, united, sovereign, just, and prosperous.

With the blessing of God Almighty and impelled by the noble ideal of a free national life, the Indonesian people do hereby declare their independence.

Further, in order to establish a government of the State of Indonesia which shall protect the entire Indonesian people and the whole of the land of Indonesia, and in order to promote the general welfare, to improve the standard of living, and to participate in establishing a world order founded upon freedom, eternal peace, and social justice; therefore the Independence of the Indonesian People is embodied in a Constitution of the State of Indonesia, which Constitution shall establish a Republic of the State of Indonesia in which the people are sovereign and which is based upon: Belief in the One Supreme God, a just and civilized humanitarianism, the unity of Indonesia, and a democracy guided by the wisdom arising from consultation and representation, which democracy

---

* In translating the constitution, I have relied also on several other translations which have appeared since 1945, including two published by the Ministry of Information in Djakarta.

shall ensure social justice for the whole Indonesian people.

CHAPTER I

Form and Sovereignty

Article 1

1. The State of Indonesia is a unitary state and in form a Republic.
2. Sovereignty is vested in the people and exercised fully by the People's Consultative Assembly (Madjelis Permusjawaratan Rakjat).

CHAPTER II

The People's Consultative Assembly
(Madjelis Permusjawaratan Rakjat)

Article 2

1. The People's Consultative Assembly consists of the members of the Council of Representatives (Dewan Perwakilan Rakjat, Parliament) and delegates of the regions and other groups in accordance with rules prescribed by law.
2. The People's Consultative Assembly shall assemble in the capital at least once every five years.
3. All decisions of the People's Consultative Assembly shall be taken by majority vote.

Article 3

The People's Consultative Assembly shall decide upon the Constitution and determine the basic outlines of state policy.

CHAPTER III

The Executive

Article 4

1. The President of the Republic of Indonesia is vested with the power of Government in accordance with the Constitution.
2. In exercising his responsibilities, the President is assisted by a Vice-President.

Article 5

1. The President, acting with the consent of the Council of Representatives, exercises legislative powers.
2. The President shall enact such government regulations (peraturan pemerintah) as are necessary for the proper execution of the laws.

Article 6

1. The President shall be a native-born Indonesian.
2. The President and the Vice-President shall be elected by the People's Consultative Assembly by majority vote.

Article 7

The President and Vice-President hold office for a term of five years, and thereafter are eligible for re-election.

Article 8

In the event of the President's death, resignation, removal from office, or inability to exercise his duties during the term of his office, he is succeeded by the Vice-President until that term is expired.

Article 9

Before assuming their offices, the President and Vice-President shall, by religious oath or affirmation, solemnly declare before the People's Consultative Assembly or the Council of Representatives as follows:

Oath of the President (Vice-President): "I swear before God, that to the best of my ability I shall faithfully and conscientiously fulfill the duties of the President of the Republic of Indonesia, maintain the Constitution and faithfully execute all laws and regulations, and dedicate myself to the service of State and Nation."

Affirmation of the President (Vice-President): "I do solemnly affirm, that to the best of my ability I shall faithfully and conscientiously fulfill the duties of the President of the Republic of Indonesia, maintain the Constitution and faithfully execute all laws and regulations, and dedicate myself to the service of State and Nation."

Article 10

The President holds the highest authority over the Army, Navy, and Air Force.

Article 11

The President, with the consent of the Council of Representatives, declares war, makes peace, and concludes treaties with other states.

Article 12

The President is empowered to proclaim martial law. The conditions governing a proclamation of martial law, and the consequences thereof, shall be prescribed by law.

Article 13

1. The President appoints diplomatic representatives and Consuls.
2. The President receives the diplomatic representatives of foreign states.

Article 14

The President has authority to grant pardon, amnesty, abolition, and rehabilitation.

Article 15

The President has authority to bestow titles, decorations for merit, and other marks of honor.

CHAPTER IV

The Supreme Advisory Council
(Dewan Pertimbangan Agung)

Article 16

1. The composition of the Supreme Advisory Council shall be determined by law.
2. The Supreme Advisory Council is responsible for giving advice on matters submitted to it by the President, and has the right to submit proposals to the Government.

CHAPTER V

The Ministries

Article 17

1. The President is assisted by Ministers of the State.
2. Ministers are appointed and discharged by the President.
3. The Ministers direct Departments of the Government.

CHAPTER VI

Local Government

Article 18

The division of the territory of Indonesia into large and small units and the composition of their government shall be prescribed by law, with due regard for and observance of the principle of consultation and the traditional rights of areas with extraordinary status.

CHAPTER VII

The Council of Representatives

Article 19

1. The composition of the Council of Representatives shall be prescribed by law.
2. The Council of Representatives shall assemble at least once every year.

Article 20

1. Every statute requires the consent of the Council of Representatives.
2. In the event that a bill is rejected by the Council of Representatives, that bill may not be submitted for a second time during the same session of the Council of Representatives.

Article 21

1. Members of the Council of Representatives have the right to initiate bills.
2. In the event that such a bill is approved by the Council of Representatives but rejected by the President, that bill may not be submitted for a second time during the same session of the Council of Representatives.

Article 22

1. In cases of emergency, the President has the authority to enact government regulations in place of statutes.
2. Government regulations thus enacted shall be submitted to the next session of the Council of Representatives for ratification.
3. In the event that such government regulations are not ratified, they are revoked.

CHAPTER VIII

Finance

Article 23

1. A budget of receipts and expenditures shall be determined each year by the Council of Representatives. In the event that the Council of Representatives does not approve the budget proposed by the Government, then the budget for the preceding year remains in force.
2. Every tax imposed for the purpose of government revenues shall be based upon a statute.
3. The form and denominations of currency shall be determined by law.
4. Other matters concerning public finance shall be prescribed by law.
5. To examine all matters pertaining to public finance, a Financial Auditing Office (Badan Pemeriksa Keuangan) shall be established by law. The results of its audits shall be presented to the Council of Representatives.

CHAPTER IX

The Judiciary

Article 24

1. Judicial authority is vested in a Supreme Court and such other judicial

bodies as are established by law.

2. The organization and competence of the courts shall be determined by law.

Article 25

The conditions of appointment and removal from office of judges shall be prescribed by law.

CHAPTER X

Citizenship

Article 26

1. Native born Indonesians and others naturalized according to law are citizens.
2. The conditions affecting citizenship shall be prescribed by law.

Article 27

1. All citizens have the same status in law and in government and shall, without exception, respect the law and the government.
2. Every citizen has the right to work and to a reasonable standard of living.

Article 28

The freedom of assembly and association, of expression of spoken and written opinion, and similar freedoms shall be provided for by law.

CHAPTER XI

Religion

Article 29

1. The state is based upon Belief in the One Supreme God.
2. The state guarantees the freedom of every inhabitant to embrace his own religion and to worship according to his religion and his beliefs.

CHAPTER XII

National Defense

Article 30

1. Every citizen has the right and the responsibility to participate in the defense of the state.
2. Matters concerning defense shall be provided for by law.

CHAPTER XIII

Education

Article 31

1. Every citizen has the right to an education.
2. The Government shall provide and manage a system of education, which shall be provided for by law.

Article 32

The Government shall promote and develop the national culture of Indonesia.

CHAPTER XIV

Social Welfare

Article 33

1. The economy shall be organized as a cooperative endeavor based on the principle of family life.
2. The State shall control those means of production which are important for the state and which dominate the economic life of the people.
3. The land, the water, and the natural resources contained therein shall be controlled by the state and exploited for the greatest prosperity of the people.

Article 34

The poor and the orphaned shall be cared for by the State.

CHAPTER XV

The National Flag and Language

Article 35

The Indonesian National Flag is the Honored Red and White.

Article 36

The national language of Indonesia is Indonesian.

CHAPTER XVI

Amendment of the Constitution

Article 37

1. In order to amend the Constitution, a quorum of two-thirds the

membership of the People's Consultative Assembly is required.

2. Decisions shall be taken by a two-thirds majority of those attending.

Transitional Provisions

Article I

The Preparatory Committee for Indonesian Independence shall prepare and arrange the transfer of administration to the Government of Indonesia.

Article II

All existing state institutions and laws shall remain in force so long as new ones have not been created in accordance with this Constitution.

Article III

The President and Vice-President shall be elected initially by the Preparatory Committee for Indonesian Independence.

Article IV

Before the formation according to this Constitution of the People's Consultative Assembly, the Council of Representatives, and the Supreme Advisory Council, their authority shall be exercised by the President with the assistance of the National Committee.

Additional Provisions

www.ingramcontent.com/pod-product-compliance
Lightning Source LLC
Chambersburg PA
CBHW022348280326
41935CB00007B/123